Music and Cinema

MUSIC / CULTURE

A series from Wesleyan University Press

Edited by George Lipsitz, Susan McClary, and Robert Walser

✳

Music and Cinema

EDITED BY JAMES BUHLER,
CARYL FLINN, AND DAVID NEUMEYER

✳

WESLEYAN UNIVERSITY PRESS

Published by University Press of New England

Hanover & London

Wesleyan University Press

Published by University Press of New England, Hanover, NH 03755

© 2000 by Wesleyan University Press

Printed in United States of America

5 4 3 2 1

Library of Congress Cataloging-in-Publication Data

Music and cinema / edited by James Buhler, Caryl Flinn, and David Neumeyer.
    p.   cm. — (Music/culture)
    Includes index.
    Contents: Leitmotif: new debates and questions — Beyond classical film music —
Style and practice in classical film music — Gender, ethnicity, identity —
Methodological possibilities.
    ISBN 0–8195–6410–9 (cl : alk. paper) — ISBN 0–8195–6411–7 (pa : alk. paper)
    1. Motion picture music — History and criticism. 2. Musical films — History
and criticism. I. Buhler, James, 1964–   II. Flinn, Caryl. III. Neumeyer, David.
IV. Series.
ML 2075.M875   2000
781.5'42 — dc21   00–023696

Contents

✴

Music and Cinema

DAVID NEUMEYER
WITH CARYL FLINN AND JAMES BUHLER[1]

Introduction

✱

Writing of the current situation in cinema studies, an imputably chaotic field of psychoanalytic theory, cultural studies, lingering semiotics, a resurgent historical positivism, and philosophical formalism, Peter Lehman reminds us that "no theories exist outside . . . a context of use value to someone"; therefore, "no theory can be all-inclusive and simply right: . . . there will never be an end to film theory as long as people care about the subject."[2] The same might have been said of musicology, except that what "lingers" there is positivism and a couple of brands of formalism (the latter especially among the music scholars who call themselves, for the most part misleadingly, theorists), and what is resurgent is the subjectivity and critical polemic of an era before it was assumed that the canon of high-art music is fixed and eternal (and therefore the priorities of music education equally fixed and immutable).

Film music has played almost no role in heating the seas to boiling in either film studies or musicology, despite the fact that music has been a part of film presentation and production since the very beginning. Indeed, the two persistent tropes that have structured the critical and scholarly literature on the subject are "neglected art" and "unheard melody." To Roy Prendergast, music's place in film as a commodity has masked the aesthetic dimension of (mainly) Hollywood composers' work and, implicitly, has prevented both proper understanding and due placement in the musical canon. More recently, Claudia Gorbman has reminded us that narratological study of film music inevitably leads to the conclusion that, in classical sound film at least, music is subordinate to narrative. Music is "unheard" because its narrative functions are folded into, or readily overcome by, others: on the soundtrack, dialogue routinely takes precedence over music.[3] Curiously, then, the literature on film music has long reflected a presumed equivalence between the status of film music and its study: the relatively unattended subject was every bit as sequestered, unregistered, "silenced," as the role conventionally bestowed upon film music in classical Hollywood filmmaking.

Today, when music roars from theater speakers with the hyperclarity of digital sound, it is increasingly difficult to think of film music as unheard—one can hardly ignore its presence, much less neglect it. Therefore, film music should by now have reached a status of fashionable significance in the disciplines of both cinema studies and musicology; accordingly, it should have come under close scrutiny from historical, theoretical, and analytical points of view. To be sure, over the past decade, or roughly since the publication of Gorbman's groundbreaking study, film-music scholarship has turned into something of a growth field, with monographs, dissertations, and anthologies appearing at an increasing pace. Yet, despite the expanding activity, film music remains at the periphery of its parent disciplines. The very challenges that make the study of film music intellectually exciting also inhibit its move to the center of either cinema or music scholarship. A pessimistic—yet pragmatic—conclusion is that the study of film music is likely to remain always marginal because its irreducible interdisciplinarity alienates it from the one discipline or the other.

Institutional structure is heavily implicated in this marginalization: ties to home disciplines have tended to unravel any interdisciplinary consensus as it emerges. If a musicologist deplores the interpretive gaffes of those scholars lacking formal music training, the film scholar bemoans excruciatingly tight-lensed score analyses that pay only passing regard to cinematic concerns. Given the strong historical tradition in cinema studies that considers music as subordinate to the image and narrative, film scholars (who frequently come to cinema from literary studies) have had little incentive to learn the highly specialized vocabulary of what is understood, for better or worse, as a "secondary" element of production and representation. There seems to be an equally modest impetus for musicologists to learn strategies for reading films or to study the circumstances of their production or reception, as cinema music occupies no place to speak of in the "official" canon of twentieth-century music.

It is not surprising, therefore, that both Gorbman and Martin Marks have recently written about the daunting task of the film-music scholar; both argue that to take fullest advantage of the intellectual resources available, one should be familiar with the literatures and methods of the two separate fields.[4] As we have already suggested, such a recommendation is easier said than done because of the institutional obstacles to training in both disciplines. Still, in the past decade or so, the fields of musicology and film studies have—against the odds—moved a bit closer together. Exemplifying the interdisciplinarity that has marked the cinema from its inception, film scholars are vigorously pursuing aesthetic and historical concerns from new angles, including rigorously formalist and historicist ones. At the same time, musicologists are rushing to integrate insights gleaned from fields such as hermeneutics, critical theory, and sociology into their traditionally positivist historiography, as they seek to overcome (among other things) the limitations of a Beethoven-centered canon.

Music and Cinema presents the field of film-music studies as it exists now, and so, following the situation of the parent disciplines, we juxtapose a panoply of theoretical approaches and methodologies. Some of our contributors, such as Jeff Smith, offer new appreciations of undertheorized composers and sedulously consider industrial and commercial pressures on a composer's style (in Smith's case, Henry Mancini). Others, such as James Buhler, Caryl Flinn, and Kathryn Kalinak, use film music as a means to engage a wide spectrum of theoretical issues. Some pieces offer close formal analyses (Murray Pomerance, Ronald Rodman), while others draw from cultural issues such as gender for the primary material of argument (Lucy Fischer, Michelle Lekas). And Rick Altman's groundbreaking piece offers a new model of analysis that is as historically sensitive as it is analytically savvy.

Film music's interdisciplinarity, like that of the cinema itself, produces and is produced by a wide array of methodologies that can sometimes operate in direct conflict with one another. (The irony, of course, is that this tension is at odds with what many of us have at one time or another argued is the aim of Hollywood film music: to achieve seamless unity and cohesion—a passive accord vis-à-vis other cinematic elements.) Certainly, acquiescence, passivity, and unity fail to characterize the work of film-music scholars, and so internal conflicts here are inevitable: we have made no attempt to suppress implied or even overt disagreements among our authors. Many of the differences are methodological. For instance, Annabel Cohen's overview of cognitive psychology's potential contribution to film-music studies stands apart from the psychoanalytical assumptions that undergird Wendy Everett's and Krin Gabbard's explorations of human memory and ego formation. Likewise, the manner in which Fischer places film music within a larger frame of Art Deco aesthetics seems at first glance very different from Marks's musical-stylistic comparison of two soundtracks from the early 1940s. Yet, as is often the case with methodological disputes, what appears to be contradictory at one level of analysis turns out to be shared interest at another. Both Marks and Fischer skillfully deploy close reading of films, and both situate their readings of film texts within carefully delimited historical frameworks. In fact, productive connections can be found between nearly any two articles, connections that transcend the boundaries of our five section headings (attention to gender issues is not restricted to "Gender, Ethnicity, Identity," for example). Likewise, contemporary critical theory informs nearly all of the pieces, just as film music *itself* is at some level a concern of every piece in the collection.

Our interest is eclectic: we do not seek to prioritize one methodology or group of methodologies over another. Indeed, the polemical motivation behind this anthology is simply to present rigorous critical approaches that show the range of current film-music scholarship based within musicology *and* within cinema studies. To this we should add that both of these "bases," however institutionally separate they may be, are today marked by various historiographic concerns and interventions, by studies in psychology, contemporary critical theory (including feminism, race and postcolonial theory), aesthetics, popular culture, and cultural studies. In other words, although this anthology suggests what musicologists and film scholars together might contribute to the field of film music, what both sets of scholars bring to the field often comes from the productive spaces beyond these two disciplines, strictly defined.

The first group of essays shows the extent to which certain *idées réçues* are undergoing critical reassessment. In "*Star Wars,* Music and Myth," James Buhler interrogates the common remark that the music in this trilogy is Wagnerian in both form and function. Acknowledging that, for Wagner, the primary function of the leitmotif was the production of myth, however self-consciously constructed, Buhler argues that film music has typically assigned the leitmotif a more mundane, "secularized" function: signification. In *Star Wars,* a series seemingly saturated in myth from its opening moment, music resurrects its Wagnerian, mythologizing function. By highlighting inconsistencies in leitmotivic deployment, Buhler reveals the instability, indeed, the fictive nature, of the prelapsarian grandeur to which the films seem to aspire.

Scott Paulin approaches the issue from a different direction, as he insists on crucial and often overlooked disjunctions between Wagner's notion of the leitmotif and its deployment in classical Hollywood film. Acknowledging the privileged—indeed, fetishized—place Wagner holds in American film-music criticism and scholarship, "Richard Wagner and the Fantasy of Cinematic Unity" asserts that writers on film music have broadly misapplied Wagnerian concepts of the leitmotif, the unending melody, and the *Gesamtkunstwerk*. Whatever cultural value these terms may have had (to legitimate and to "sell" early film to its audience), they have few consequences in the functions that music actually served in the cinema.

Leitmotif-as-name is Justin London's subject. Exploring implications of the question "What exactly goes on, referentially speaking, in the case of a musical leitmotif?" London draws on Saul Kripke and other analytic philosophers of language to propose that musical leitmotifs may obtain some capacity for reference if they are understood to function as proper names. Attending to the particulars of leitmotivic technique in film permits perhaps the clearest picture of the extent and limits of music's capacity for extramusical reference. By way of example, London revisits Claudia Gorbman's well-known analysis of Max Steiner's score for *Mildred Pierce* (1945).

Critics have rightly observed the tendency of film-music criticism and scholarship to privilege Hollywood practices—especially those of its so-called golden age. Accordingly, the second group of essays examines music in contemporary, non-Hollywood narrative films and explores a variety of social, historical, and aesthetic issues in the process. In "Songlines," Wendy Everett argues that popular songs in recent European autobiographical films are used in ways that interrogate identity and personal memory, issues that have been prevalent in contemporary continental filmmaking. Using texts such as Dennis Potter's *Lipstick on Your Collar* (1993) and Terence Davies's *The Long Day Closes* (1992), Everett demonstrates that, even in what could easily be highly nostalgic artifacts, popular songs self-consciously, and even ironically, undercut the passive anteriority with which film music is often associated. "Song," she writes, "provides the moment in the narrative when history and fiction, personal and public, present and past, intersect." Caryl Flinn's essay focuses on the New German Cinema, a film movement well known for the questions it raised about national identity, history, loss, and fragmentation. Flinn illuminates ways that musical strategies in films by R. W. Fassbinder, Alexander Kluge, and others participate within the movement's larger attempt to problematize a national history that would pass itself off as seamless, teleological, or untroubled. Some of these choices, such as composite soundtracks, fragmenting and "damaging" recognizable canonical works like Beethoven's Ninth Symphony, suggest a suspicion of unity or origins; for Flinn they also suggest different kinds of relationships to the past and alternatives to the model of "mourning" that has dominated discussions of postwar German film. In the final essay of the section, Krin Gabbard considers the implications and contradictions in director Robert Altman's claim that his jazz-infused *Kansas City* (1996) was constructed *like* jazz. Careful background research reveals the historical precision Altman lavished on it; Gabbard then suggests that Altman unconsciously returned to an idealized youth in which a fantasmatic identification is forged between the white director and the young Charlie Parker. In the course of this discussion, Gabbard not only touches on the issues Altman's score raises in terms of black and white male (American) identity but intimates that film music can offer an identifactory conduit through which idealization can occur.

The next four essays converge on particular instances of compositional style and practice, each offering close readings of films to make different points. Martin Marks analyzes music's dramatic functions in two classical Hollywood films produced by Warner Brothers: *The Maltese Falcon* (1941) and *Casablanca* (1942). Emerging from the same studio at almost the same time, these two films illustrate the diversity possible within classical Hollywood film-scoring practice. Marks notes that the music in *Casablanca* is widely remembered and that its diegetic music possesses clear-cut narrative functions, as in the famous musical duel between "Wacht am Rhein" and "La Marseilles." In the underscoring, Max Steiner made use of contrasting musical sources to "move us completely [and clearly] into the film world." By contrast, Adolf Deutsch's score for Huston's film noir is harder to identify, to "notice," because it is largely music of nuance and transitions, appearing in fragmented, incomplete forms.

The focus of Ronald Rodman's study is Herbert Stothart's ingenious, intricate score for the Nelson Eddy–Jeannette MacDonald vehicle *Maytime* (1937), a notable exemplar of 1930s film operetta practices. Using less and less of a composer's original music over his tenure at MGM, Stothart replaced the operetta music with pastiches of opera excerpts and popular song. The pastiche was anything but haphazard, however: Rodman details the composer's careful attentiveness to both the narrative and musical structure of the pastiche. Developing Rick Altman's classic notion of the musical's "dual-focus narrative," Rodman explores the extent to which song pairings, distinct singing styles, and key areas helped delineate and separate traits of the two central characters.

In "Finding Release," Murray Pomerance offers an extended close reading of the famous Albert Hall cantata sequence from Hitchcock's *The Man Who Knew Too Much* (1956). The film foregrounds music in this sequence: the scene—whose emblem is a musical score—is carefully "composed" to the music and thus cannot be construed as a visual form merely decorated by music. Instead, this moment in the film is itself transformed into what might be termed visual music.

Finally, in "That Money-Making 'Moon River' Sound," Jeff Smith explains how Henry Mancini was able to develop his own style while not losing sight of the commercial imperatives of his time; indeed, Smith argues, Mancini showed how the two could be successfully interwoven, in particular through thematic organization and orchestration. As a composer participating in a broader shift toward the use of pop music in film, Mancini represents a particular historical configuration that required film music to be both dramatically effective and commercially astute, a lesson not lost on composers since.

The next three papers elaborate the diversity with which music participates in gender construction and identity. With a broad lens focused on cinema as an institution, Michelle Lekas argues that film relies on noncinematic associations—her concern is with the operatic—to function as locus points of emotional intensity and spectacular excess. As she puts it, film's narrative and verisimilitudinous pretensions are "punched up" and sidelined through intense, operatic moments. Using a variety of examples—from *The Lost Weekend* (1945) to the "false" opera "Salaambo" from *Citizen Kane* (1941)—Lekas shows how these moments of spectacle and excess are as feminized as they are fetishized, rendered both seductive and dangerous. Her theoretical discussion contributes considerably to the ongoing debates on cinematic excess, spectacle, and gender.

Taking a historically specific moment, Lucy Fischer's "Designing Women" illuminates the influences of ballet, fashion, decorative sculpture, and black performers in Paris on the film musical of the 1930s. Extending her well-known work on Busby Berkeley, Fischer argues that the musical's generic capacity to absorb considerable amounts of abstraction and spectacle enabled it to borrow easily from modernist styles of the period. Here her historical and aesthetic focus falls on Art Deco, a movement that constructed woman (especially privileging the dancing female body) in ways that, as Lekas also observes, still placed the female form on the side of decorative spectacle, exoticism, seemingly "isolated and complete in itself" and potentially at odds with productive narrative and textual boundaries.

In "Disciplining Josephine Baker," Kathryn Kalinak picks up on femininity's purported disruption of boundaries as she examines Josephine Baker in the French musical *Princess Tam Tam* (1935), a film that is literally a colonialist's dream, a "color-blind utopia." As Kalinak shows, Baker's exaggerated ethnicity exemplifies North Atlantic cinema's compulsion to exoticize and render "other" its spectacular allure. Baker, for instance, is insistently associated with primitivism, animality, as well as spontaneous expression and movement—in stark contrast to Euronovelist Max de Miracourt's "writer's block." Further, Kalinak asserts that the construction of Josephine Baker demonstrates the necessity for openness to boundary-crossing, for methodological interdisciplinarity (or even "nondisciplinarity") in contemporary scholarly circles.

The last section in the volume brings methodological concerns to the fore, particularly in the area of analysis. Rick Altman (with McGraw Jones and Sonia Tatroe) tackles the problem of transcription in analyzing film soundtracks. How does one discuss the specific relationships of music to sound effects or dialogue at a given point in a film? How can loudness, sound quality, points of emphasis, audibility and pitch—and their complex, simultaneous interactions—be more carefully identified? Challenging Michel Chion's somewhat notorious claim that "there is no soundtrack," Altman and his researchers propose instead an analytical model of the mise-en-bande, the acoustic equivalent to the multifaceted (and much more attended) mise-en-scène. At once historical and theoretical, "Inventing the Cinema Soundtrack" examines several films from the early sound period with this new method to observe how acoustic conventions and interrelationships were gradually established for film's mise-en-bande.

In the closing essay, Annabel Cohen brings to the volume the viewpoint of cognitive psychology. She argues that this methodology challenges prevailing humanist approaches to film-music studies, and she presents two theoretical perspectives: a bottom-up approach that emphasizes innate aspects of perceptual experience, and a top-down approach that emphasizes the role of learning and the accumulation of knowledge that abets the acquisition of new information within human memory. After reviewing several experiments for data to verify statements about film-music effects, Cohen proposes a cognitive model of music's role in the interpretation, memory, and sense of reality generated by cinema.

It may well be that film-music studies will eventually need to adopt a team approach, like film production itself, in order to overcome some of the more intractable research and critical issues in the field; in so doing, of course, it would depart from the traditional humanities model of solitary scholarship. As editors, we have certainly felt the benefits of interaction within our own working relationship (two of us come to film music from musicology; one from cinema studies), and this has been one of the more stimulating aspects of working together on this anthology. For us, the value of an interdisciplinary forum goes without saying.

It has also been gratifying to see the extent to which new directions are being charted in the field, but equally so to find that scholars from both disciplines are now revisiting, revising, and challenging earlier work. That is to say, film-music scholarship is now a discipline with a past; none of us exploring the subject confronts a blank page. And, as one would expect, the central questions persist, defined and redefined over decades now: the problem of music's presence in cinema (do movies *need* music?), cinematic and musical discontinuity (film music isn't concert music—or opera, either), music's relation to narrative (especially the diegetic/nondiegetic polarity and its relation to source and background music), and cultural and institutional matters such as historiography, culture, and canon formation (how do musicology and cinema studies "share" the same object of study? how have they themselves been situated in the twentieth-century's culture(s) of technology?).

Intertwined with these are issues such as stylistic originality as a value in film music, the appropriation of historical musical styles, aesthetic valuation in general and how to determine that value (what is *good* movie music?), music as transcendent (utopian or mythic), the historical patterns of music in theater and their relation to the practices of film, the politics of academization, ownership of the musical canon and the consequences of its appropriation for other discourses, production/performance (what is the status of the composer?), film music's definition from a philological point of view (what *is* the text for film music?), the place of music—and the implications of that place—within the soundtrack (sound design), the sheer mechanics of any poetics of film music (including modes of analysis for music, sound, and image), the psychology and cognition of listener/spectators, the devaluation of pitch design in favor of timbre, the nature of "music/film" temporality (and its relation to other temporalities in film), and a critical practice caught between disciplinary interests and the promotion of copyrighted properties.

Our authors address many of these questions. Herewith, a few additional comments on music's place in cinema, music and narrative, source and background music, and scholarship, commerce, and canon formation.

Do films really *need* music? In their classic 1927 text on music in the silent film, Hans Erdmann and Giuseppe Becce, both experienced composers, approach the question directly.[5] First they observe that music is not generally considered a part of the production process of a film but belongs strictly and specifically to theater performance; they also draw a parallel between the evolution of film toward the status of art (*Kunstfilm*) and a simultaneous movement away from an indiscriminate, unfocused musical accompaniment (which they associate with coffeehouse entertainment) toward a music well synchronized in affect and connotation (their term for this is *musikalische Filmillustration*) (3–4). They then note that the question of film viewing and music audition in combination has been debated for some time already; in particular it was proposed that films need music because humans are conditioned to expect movements and action to be associated with sound. Rejecting this as inadequate to justify *music*, Erdmann and Becce offer a variation on that argument. They say that the inevitable rhythmic patterns of films unfolding in time are best endowed with signifying depth through music:[6]

exactly at the moment in which film events approach the artistic, they must—as a time-art—dispose themselves according to some type of rhythmic design (*Rhythmik*). We know that all rhythms strive to express themselves acoustically . . . [and] therefore, film practice has acted as if—indeed, has decided that—films cannot be without music; . . . film musicians concern themselves with giving this existing practice appropriate meaning. (5)

In the early 1930s, Virgil Thomson—still using silent film as his frame of reference—offered a very similar answer to the question of whether films need music. Music provides temporal rhythms or continuity that film does not possess on its own: "The cinema is naturally a discontinuous medium. Narrative or dramatic continuity is achieved therein only by effort and much care, against the grain, as it were, like playing legato on the trombone."[7] Thomson wrote these words several years before he composed his own film scores for two Pare Lorentz documentaries, *The Plow that Broke the Plains* and *The River* (both 1936).[8] In the intervening time, silent film gave way permanently to sound, and music's place in the cinema artifact changed radically. In his later writings on the subject, however, Thomson saw no reason to rescind his claim that the difficult task of achieving "dramatic continuity . . . against the grain" constitutes the pragmatic first problem of both film editing and music composition. As late as 1945, he argued that the feature film still poses problems, and now he identifies dialogue as the culprit: "It is speech that has brought back the film's essential jerkiness, by interrupting the musical continuity."[9] A few years later still, Aaron Copland repeated Thomson's argument, under the heading "Building a sense of continuity": "The picture editor knows better than anyone how serviceable music can be in tying together a visual medium which is, by its very nature, continually in danger of falling apart. One sees this most obviously in montage scenes where the use of a unifying musical idea may save the quick flashes of disconnected scenes from seeming merely chaotic."[10] One can acknowledge and appreciate the musician's point of view while observing that Thomson and Copland do an injustice to the techniques and practices of continuity editing, already mature by the mid-1920s.

Claudia Gorbman recounts a range of early justifications for music in the silent cinema—from historical arguments (music's importance in melodrama; the value to narrative of the catalogue of codings for affect, time and place, character identification, and so forth), to practical ones (drowning projector noise), aesthetic ones (imparting a sense of spatial realism through sound; supplying the missing inflections of speech-sound; and the rhythmic parallelism cited by Erdmann and Becce), and psychological ones (revivifying the mechanically reproduced image; imparting a sense of collective experience).[11] The transfer of music into the sound film is another matter. Here Gorbman rejects the few arguments available in the literature; instead, she says that music's semiotic functions do persist from silent film, but its temporal-rhythmic role shifts to overcoming the "relentless linearity" forced on film by sound realism, and its psychological role shifts to drawing in and holding the viewer: "Music removes barriers to belief; it bonds spectator to spectacle, it envelops spectator and spectacle in a harmonious space. Like hypnosis, it silences the spectator's censor." Finally, then, Gorbman argues for a combination of the pragmatic and the aesthetic: "music has persisted as an integral part of the sound film because it accomplishes so many things at once."[12]

George Burt, on the contrary, is a true believer: writing with a composer's experience, he never questions music's presence in film but, taking its power to transform as a given, justifies it aesthetically through evidence of the special artistic insights that film composers bring to bear on cinema (such insights being defined primarily as those of Hollywood's "second generation," composers whose careers, by and large, began in the 1950s; prominent among them are Alex North, Elmer Bernstein, Jerry Goldsmith, and Leonard Rosenman).[13] Apropos of Erdmann and Becce's comments on the central role of film temporality, Burt expends considerable effort and great care in discussing questions of pacing and timing in film scores (79–142); from the composer's point of view, discontinuity is an issue of the organization of time. He does not, however, notice the danger to the status of a composer's "insight" (not to mention professional status) inherent in a story Burt himself relates: One day in a hotel room, writer Ivor Montague unwittingly turned on the radio instead of the television volume control but nevertheless found that the "Viennese waltzes [playing on the radio] apparently said something curiously revealing about each of [several unrelated] sequences, [which] seemed to be bound together, sharing a common point of view" (33). Burt takes this, not as evidence that music's functions are secure even if the standing of original film music is fragile, but as proof that music, especially if it is in a unified style, can overcome filmic discontinuity.[14]

Unlike Burt, the philosopher Noël Carroll adopts a notably skeptical posture on the question of music's presence in film: he decries a lack of experimental evidence for music's effects in film and supposes "that spectators will not be bothered by talking films without music, if the dialogue is sufficiently interesting to them."[15] Significant pockets of the film repertoire would seem to bear out that supposition, especially filmed stageplays and comedies that rely heavily on dialogue. A film such as *His Girl Friday* (1940), for instance, has very little music but, even so, does not eliminate it altogether: a bright, if somewhat convoluted, fox-trot accompanies the main titles, a more subdued passage covers the prologue (a single title-card insert), and—roughly ninety minutes later—music comes in again under dialogue shortly before the fox-trot returns for the end credits. It was (and still is) difficult to do without music for opening and ending credits and the occasional source-music tune played on a radio or in a club or even hummed by one of the actors. Although it might be, as Gorbman argues, that music was useful in the early cinema simply to cover up projector noise, that it was needed by theatrical convention, and that it filled what would otherwise have been the vast silences of the feature films of the 1920s,[16] it is important to keep in mind that practices in the sound era have varied greatly. It remains an open question, for example, whether the "wall-to-wall" scoring encouraged (or required) by David O. Selznick (in *Gone With the Wind* [1939] or *Rebecca* [1940]) was somehow more effective than minimally scored gangster films (such as *Public Enemy* [1931]) or filmed stageplays (such as *The Philadelphia Story* [1940]).[17] To be sure, one might speak of the semantic richness of added music, but that is not the same thing as necessity. Whether music has the same status as actors, scenery, dialogue, or even continuity editing as an indispensable element of film remains an unsettled issue.

Whatever the shakiness of the historical or aesthetic grounds for the relationship of movies and their music, nearly everyone agrees that film has substantial aesthetic (or, at least, cognitive) constraint; therefore, music supplements something missing from mechanically reproduced image and sound. For Mary Ann Doane, "music marks a deficiency in the axis of vision"; it fills a lack.[18] In 1940s-era women's films, she says this lack is emotion, and that filling it is "necessary." But Doane equalizes the burden: in melodrama at least, "it is as though music continually announces its own deficiency in relation to meaning" (97). Carroll, coming from a very different (indeed, antagonistic) ideological position, says much the same: a "movie" (consisting of imagetrack, dialogue, and sound effects) and music—even if not "necessary"—complement one another in that each "supplies something that the other system standardly lacks, or, at least, does not possess with the same degree of effectiveness."[19] Although Doane and Carroll differ markedly on whether music should be construed as a supplement or complement to the image, they agree that what music adds to the image is a specificity of emotion.

Caryl Flinn summarizes the issues more broadly in terms of a "restoration of plenitude."[20] If some lamented that the advent of sound meant a loss of film's ontological status as an art of images, others hailed the ability of sound to enhance immediacy, to reduce the distance between viewer and screen. Music's special role in this was not so much to enhance realism (by papering over silences in the soundtrack) as it was to (appear to) restore unity of sound and image by "bestow[ing] 'a human touch' upon the cinematic apparatus, something that the apparatus intrinsically lacks due to its technological basis" (42). In a similar way, music was "needed" to correct problems in film texts themselves, a notion familiar from the oft-cited sentiment among production professionals that music can "save a picture" (this notion was behind Copland's comment about film editors' appreciation of music).[21] Flinn connects the idea productively with Doane's theory of film as a "fantasmatic" body held together by "the illusion of organic unity and a perceptual cohesion within the film text which in turn is enjoyed by the listening and viewing subject" (45): music can foster and further the construction of this unity so critical to film—it can, in short, save a picture in much the same way a doctor can save an ailing patient.[22]

"Through text, music becomes visual." So writes Ellen Rosand of George Friedrich Handel's accomplishments at vivid text-painting and portrayal of emotions (the Baroque *Affect*) in his early oratorio *La Resurrezione*.[23] Music's relations with language, with text and story, are ancient and complex. With respect to the young art of cinema, most authors dwell not on the question discussed above—*why* music should be present in film—but, assuming it should, on *how* it functions in relation to film narrative.[24] Music can be understood as one part of a whole that is a film's narrative system. Given that the imagetrack and dialogue carry the burden of information, music would seem clearly to be subordinate in this realm. Thus—consistent with viewpoints of Doane, Carroll, and others mentioned above—music can relax or intensify the pacing of a scene, it can reflect emotion or create atmosphere, it can evoke social or ethnic stereotypes or localize time or place (military fanfare or march, church music, a minuet, can-can, or tango), and it can closely imitate screen action (for obvious reasons, this is often labeled "mickey-mousing"). However, it can also participate in the primary semantic level of the film by adding referential or narrative dimensions missing from the imagetrack (by quoting military music, though no soldiers are present, for example, or by recalling a theme associated with an earlier event in the film).

The essay by Copland cited earlier originated as a newspaper article offering a composer's hints for moviegoers; in it, Copland constructs a list of functions that amounts to an informal analytic heuristic. Thus, "music serves the screen [by] creating a more convincing atmosphere of time and place, . . . underlining psychological refinements—the unspoken thoughts of a character or the unseen implications of a situation, . . . serving as a kind of neutral background filler, . . . building a sense of continuity, . . . [or] underpinning the theatrical build-up of a scene, and rounding it off with a sense of finality."[25] Each element of Copland's list reappears in Gorbman's seven rules for classical film-music practice, which collectively form a set of principles or conventions that she proposes as the musical parallel to continuity editing of the imagetrack. For Gorbman, continuity editing overcomes and hides the inevitable disjunctures that result from splicing between lengths of film; it removes attention from the technical problem and turns the cutting process into an agent of narrative.[26] Music also becomes an agent of narrative by subordinating its performance qualities to the imagetrack. Music is "inaudible" for Gorbman in the same way that continuity editing is "invisible." In Caryl Flinn's wonderfully trenchant phrasing of an Adorno and Eisler insight, "music's current ideological function is . . . to generate the illusion of having none."[27]

Coming from quite a different direction, Lawrence Kramer folds Gorbman's views into his schema for a musical narratology.[28] Despite its deep history, few questions in musicology—or in music-analytic method—are so vexed as the relation of music and narrative. Although the locus of the problem has traditionally been in program music (pure instrumental music with an illustrative title or prescribed program; for example, Beethoven's Symphony no. 6 [*Pastoral*] or Richard Strauss's tone poem *Ein Heldenleben*), scholars have more recently imposed concepts of narrative derived from literary theory on traditional reading strategies for musical design ("form").[29] In reaction, others—notably Jean-Jacques Nattiez and Carolyn Abbate—have rejected this sort of narrativity as a chimera because it confuses issues of narrative and narration, or what is told with the telling. In their view it is not music that typically narrates; rather, people narrate their experience of music and confuse that narrative with the music itself. Still, there is a real sense in which Abbate's and Nattiez's skepticism toward musical narratology derives from formalist presuppositions. They simply reinscribe music's cognitive/aesthetic isolation as "absolute": sui generis, music can at best "imitat[e] narrative modes."[30]

But Kramer sees exactly this claim as an opening for a musical narratology: "if such imitation is really a semiological capacity, then the protean, inveterately ramifying character of signification all but guarantees that other capacities are also in play" (100). He develops the idea of (musical) narrative as performance rather than design (form), and he upends traditional biases toward continuity and closure by emphasizing distinctions between narratography (essentially, disruptive effects created within an individual work), narrativity (social construction of narratives), and narrative (story). In relation to the last of these, music can act only as a supplement (after Derrida); that is, music is added to the apparent whole of a story and thereby reveals the latter's lack, the gaps and fissures in its illusion of unity (111). Here, Kramer meets Gorbman, Doane, and other suture theorists of film. The "sheer flatness" of the screen works against drawing the viewer into the filmic spectacle; recorded speech overcomes this deficit, except in certain circumstances: "Where speech must be minimized or lost, in lyrical montage or narrative situations of action, suspense, or passion, music is conscripted as a further supplement" (112). Music's power is transitory, however: "film does not promote the kind of full displacement of narrative by music so common at the opera. . . . Once our distance from the screen collapses, the rhetoric of the camera is altogether compelling" (113).[31]

If the attention given by Kramer to disruptive elements in narrative is relatively new to musicology-based criticism, it is a familiar part of the terrain in film studies. In academic film-music criticism, specifically, the issue has traditionally been framed in terms of a dispute over synchronization and counterpoint. This was the debate engaged most vigorously—and then kept alive partly because of their influence—by Adorno and Eisler in *Composing for Films*, who simply took over an issue already simmering in the profession.[32] At its most innocent, the latter was simply a disagreement over scoring-style preferences. As Max Steiner put it in 1940:

The two different schools [of film composition] are . . . the difference between "Mickey Mouse" and "over-all" scoring. The "Mickey Mouse" scoring (my way of scoring) is a method which I consider the best for the screen, as it fits a picture like a glove. In other words, if I were to underline a love scene in a parlor and we were to cut away to a boat on the water, I would try and write my music so that the love theme would modulate into some kind of water music or what have you, as naturally the love theme would have nothing to do with the boat as the locale would be changed and probably would indicate time elapse. The "over-all" school does not believe in this and would keep right on playing regardless what happens—or maybe they consider it too much trouble to write so intricately.[33]

Steiner favored the close synchronization he describes here as "fit[ting] a picture like a glove"; not surprisingly he exaggerates the level of indifference in the "over-all" scores of his competitors, which were often congruous with the general mood or character of a scene but did not attempt to mimic details of action or dialogue references.[34] Adorno and Eisler harden the distinction Steiner refers to into a firm opposition of music that aided and abetted screen action through synchronization (a term that absorbed both of Steiner's types) and one that had an independent character (in "counterpoint" with the screen action), a notion consistent with calls for equal status for image and sound (and autonomy for the latter) by powerful figures of the previous decade such as René Clair, Sergei Eisenstein, and

Rudolf Arnheim. As Flinn reminds us, discussants in all these texts tend to conflate imagetrack with narrative; it is the latter, and not the imagetrack per se, that is normally meant to parallel or to "counterpoint" music.[35] Furthermore, music is not film sound, and the claim for music to be in a contrapuntal relationship to image or narrative is somewhat different than the same claim for sound in general.

Today it might not be difficult to see the issue of synchronization and counterpoint as historical,[36] had it not been transformed and insinuated into the debate over critical/analytic modes that emphasize cultural and ideological discourses and their work to disrupt apparently closed texts, as opposed to modes that emphasize aestheticism and close readings of texts (which "inevitably" stress continuity and unity—or "synchronization" broadly construed).[37] Much of this has followed fault lines between culture critics, on the one hand, and traditional historians and (neo)formalists, on the other. Study of the question of synchronization and counterpoint has essentially stalled, then, draped too easily, as it is, on very similar professional debates within musicology and film studies.

To turn the last statement around, we may draw on observations made earlier to say that the one thing musicology, film-music scholarship, and film studies may reasonably be said to have in common is the variety of ideologically distinct modes of study readily available, supported by historical or interdisciplinary grounding, and accepted by some significant subset of each community. Young though it is as a distinct discipline, film-music scholarship and academic criticism represents this variety surprisingly well. Lawrence Kramer drafts film music, if only briefly, into his agenda for a postmodern musicology, while Kathryn Kalinak defends synchronization on cognitive grounds: if we expect a certain musical style for a film scene and "these expectations are thwarted, most spectators would feel manipulated, even cheated. . . . The farther music and image drift from a kind of mutual dependency, the more potential there is for the disruption or even destruction of the cinematic illusion."[38] Mostly ignoring the film literature, Nicholas Cook constructs a narrowly musicological theory and analytic heuristic for what he calls "musical multimedia," while Michel Chion draws music ineluctably and irretrievably into cinematic sound design.[39] Martin Marks continues his project of an extraordinarily thorough music-historical study (based on traditionalist models) combined with sympathetic affective-functional readings of music in films, a project in which gaps or ruptures in texts are seen as moments in a historical evolution, not as inevitable properties of all attempts to create texts. Anthony Newcomb shows that Carl Maria von Weber's famous (and influential) Wolf's Glen scene from *Der Freischütz* is probably based on a phantasmagoria, an urban middle-class entertainment centered on an early projector of the same name (and a successor to the magic lantern).[40]

David Bordwell and his co-authors use vaguely Marxist economic categories to write a monumental history of production, technique, and style, using a strategy of careful analysis of the production techniques in a number of American films released between 1915 and 1960 in order to demonstrate how "the concept of a mode of film practice can historicize textual analysis and connect the history of film style to the history of the motion picture industry."[41] Susan McClary celebrates the influence of Bizet's opera *Carmen* on popular culture by pulling from its many film versions four that especially highlight the contradictions in the original's cultural and sexual politics.[42] In *Cinema Journal,* Ken Darby augments thematic/motivic readings of three John Ford westerns with specific historical information about cues, composers, and sources; while Anahid Kassabian, in an anthology devoted to rethinking musicology, uses three recent action films (as well as *Dirty Dancing*) to interrogate constructions of nationalism and gender identity and also to criticize "both art music and popular music studies [for] ignoring the immense fabric of ideological work performed by musical discourses that, like film music, have been ignored in the constitution of both fields."[43]

One element in film narrative cuts across the cultural practices of film and film-music theory uniquely, forming one of the more durable polarities in film-music theory and practice: source/background, or diegetic/nondiegetic. If music serves a film's narrative system, then the primary axis along which film music moves is determined by the implied physical space of the narrative world. Thus, music's "spatial anchoring" is either secure or undefined.[44] In the former case music emanates (or appears to emanate) from a "source" within the depicted world, that is, the diegesis; it is "source" music. In the latter case, the music is not grounded in the physical world; it is "background" music or underscoring. Something of a consensus has emerged on theoretical questions raised by the polarity of source and background music: typically, the relationship of these two is highly complex; the simplest situation, in which the types are strictly isolated in their respective diegetic or extradiegetic spheres, is an extreme case; in practice, music can and does routinely cross the membrane that separates them and the resulting play of functions is often crucial to music's "scripting" into a film by director, screenwriter, or composer.

Most authors on the subject address the issue in one way or another, but Royal S. Brown, especially, offers a series of astute close readings that exemplify the narrative power obtained by blurring distinctions between diegetic and nondiegetic music.[45] His examples, mainly drawn from Hitchcock films, also serve to highlight the director's "alignment of a villain with a work or works of diegetic music [in a way that] gives him/her the metaphorical control of the narrative—paralleling that of the filmmaker—needed to bring about the evil deed(s)" (84). And, drawing on Mulvey, Brown demonstrates how films such as *Rear Window* and *Laura* (but also three early films by Marlene Dietrich) effectively fetishize women as much through the soundtrack, especially music, as through the image (85–89).

Regardless of disciplinary or ideological alignments, in nearly every case writers on film music have to date given precedence to nondiegetic orchestral music and to the dramatic feature film. Kalinak, for example, goes so far as to assert that, because a substantial percentage of the earliest sound films were "restricted" to source music, "this meant that, in many films, there was no musical accompaniment at all."[46] And Brown asserts matter of factly that the symphonic background score "has become a permanent fixture of commercial cinema," and, therefore, "song scores for film musicals . . . fall outside the scope of this study."[47] Even when musicals are given attention, there is cause for complaint, as when Gillian Anderson criticizes Rick Altman's classic *American Film Musical* for barely ever mentioning music.[48] And film-music soundtrack collectors, who as a group have a strong bias toward orchestral music, often complain to online discussion groups such as FILMUS-L about recordings that include songs along with the orchestral background music from a film.[49]

Although one of the reasons for the bias must certainly go back to industry efforts in the mid-1930s and again in the 1950s to upgrade the perceived status of their products from "entertainment" to "art," a hard-and-fast distinction between diegetic and nondiegetic functions for music was not created by the industry. The terms "background" (or "underscoring") and "source" may be routinely used—and their definitions well understood—in film-music composition and criticism today, but they are *not* coextensive with the categories used in many Hollywood studio cue sheets of the 1930s and 1940s: "visual vocal" or "visual instrumental" and "background vocal" or "background instrumental."[50] The first pair of terms, "visual vocal" and "visual instrumental," refers to *onscreen* source music only, while "background vocal" and "background instrumental" may refer to offscreen source music or to underscoring. The reasons for these distinctions were related to production economics: onscreen performances generally commanded higher copyright permissions fees than did background uses. For example, when Warners' music director, Leo Forbstein, negotiated for the use of "Old Man Mose" in *Casablanca* (1942), the rates he was quoted by the New York office were $350 for background instrumental use, $500 for background vocal, $750 for visual instrumental, and $1000 for visual vocal.[51]

On the other hand, the studio structure of classical Hollywood tended to insulate work on diegetic and nondiegetic musics from one another, if only because diegetic musics were often dance-band arrangements. Typically, the background-score composer did not do dance-band or song arrangements: for example, in *Casablanca,* Max Steiner wrote the background score but Frank Perkins did the song arrangements. Of course, the career path followed by Steiner himself—from "arranger" to "orchestrator" to "composer"—did remain available, an industry structure still in place today, decades after the dissolution of the old studio music departments. The "composer," in other words, held a somewhat privileged status in the Hollywood studio music department. The most successful composers received an intertitle to themselves in the film's main-title sequence, usually just before the director and producer (this solo billing was part of Steiner's contract when he moved from RKO to Warners in 1936).[52]

Nevertheless, despite a long history of attempts to merge high art and the cinema—starting with Saint-Saëns's score for *L'Assassinat du Duc de Guise* (1908)[53] and the Pathé and Edison Companies' filming of opera scenes after 1910,[54] through similar efforts by Warners with Vitaphone shorts in the mid-1920s, to Warners' importation of Erich Wolfgang Korngold in 1935, Stravinsky and Schoenberg's abortive negotiations with MGM about the same time,[55] several "opera-musicals" (such as *Maytime* [1937]; see Rodman's essay, this volume) in the mid-to-late 1930s, and finally Disney's *Fantasia* (1940)—film composers in the United States never achieved the same status as their colleagues who wrote for the concert stage or opera.[56] Despite professional education that was the same in most instances, concert composers were able to command respect that film composers who ventured into writing concert works never could (especially after 1950), the most notable among the latter being Franz Waxman and Bernard Herrmann. Others who had been accepted as concert composers, especially Korngold and Miklós Rózsa, but others such as Ernst Toch and George Antheil as well, sullied their reputations by subsequently working for the film industry.[57] Ironically, Stravinsky and Schoenberg preserved theirs precisely because, despite sporadic efforts, they never were able to land a contract.[58]

Still, it would be incorrect to suggest that film composers never succeed in the concert hall, especially today, when the economics of changing audiences and the continuing series of cracks in the critical monolith that supports the professional orchestra organizations have combined to give film composers their best opportunity ever for general acceptance—even if in some quarters that acceptance remains grudging at best.[59] Journals that primarily serve soundtrack collectors—the best being *Film Score Monthly* and *Soundtrack! The Collector's Newsletter*—and groups such as the Society for Film Music (formerly the Society for the Preservation of Film Music) play a significant role in this pattern of change, as well,[60] as they do in the process of canonization that has been under way since the first burst of soundtrack recordings in the early 1970s. Indeed, it is the compact disc market and its ancillary cultures (such as the periodicals, organizations, and e-mail lists mentioned above) that are the primary agents in creating this canon and are therefore acting much as anthologies of poetry and collections of fortepiano music did in establishing the canons of European literature and music at the beginning of the nineteenth century.[61] Diegetic historical musics (Vivaldi, Beethoven, Chopin, and so forth)—and even some contemporary orchestral music—can be absorbed into the soundtrack CD market easily; witness such marketing devices as "Rachmaninov at the Movies."

But diegetic music has always consisted primarily of popular music styles and genres—song or dance performances—and belongs to entirely different markets than orchestral soundtracks, markets where a source in film is no more than an occasional factor, sporadically producing a hit tune (a tradition at least as old as Erno Rapee's "Charmaine" and *What Price Glory?* [1927] and as young as Celine Dion and *Titanic* [1997]). The most strikingly imaginative path now is being charted by a number of younger classical artists; sweeping aside prejudices of their elders, they draw together a wide range of musics with enthusiasm and a stunning stylistic egalitarianism: Nadia Salerno-Sonnenberg's recent CD *Humoresque,* for example, moves effortlessly from one of Franz Waxman's background cues to his *Carmen Fantasy* to a Gershwin song to a Bach solo sonata.[62]

The distinction between source and background or diegetic and nondiegetic, thus, is entangled not only with the question of genre but also with the construction and defense of film-music canons. And it assumes a culturewide system of genre distinctions that has motivated arts commerce throughout this century: for music, the genres were once the categories defined by sheet-music publishers (and recognized in affect topics for silent-film performance); now they are the categories of Tower Records and the Schwann catalogue, and the crossover artists are those who blur the boundaries and redefine genres in a process that is a musical replication of the one defined for cinema by Rick Altman.[63] Film music was vigorously "crossover" in character during the silent era; the distinction between diegetic and nondiegetic music enforced by the aesthetic of the real hardened the categories during the 1930s and 1940s, although instrumentation and harmonic styles remained close enough that operetta musicals (see Rodman's essay, this volume) and strikingly integrated scores were possible (such as Steiner's *Casablanca,* Waxman's *Sunset Boulevard,* or the multicomposer *Meet Me in St. Louis,* whose impression of unity probably comes from Conrad Salinger, who wrote arrangements for production numbers and composed some of the background cues).

The distance between genres increased sharply as popular music turned to rock and roll, but this eventually led—in the 1980s—to the point where crossover abilities were again prized (the ability to write in orchestral, jazz, and rock styles, and blend them when needed); now commonplace, this skill was particularly associated first with Michael Kamen. The juxtaposition of musical styles in some films over the last two decades has also become, perhaps not more varied than in the past, but—like Salerno-Sonnenberg's *Humoresque*—freerer and more convincing, as witness the complex scores in some films of the New German Cinema (see Flinn's essay, this volume), or the traditional underscoring, Bach concertos and solo cello suites, and pop songs from the 1960s and 1970s used in *Truly, Madly, Deeply* (1991).[64]

One of the curiosities of this cultural process is the tenuous link between film and film music; that is to say, the processes forming these canons have very distinct patterns and trajectories. Both share an aversion to commercialism if not to commerce per se, and items of the film-music canon acquire an extra edge of legitimacy if the music is associated with a film or director that enjoys respect (such as Welles's *Citizen Kane* or Hitchcock's *Psycho*), but film music is much more likely to be canonized solely through the imprint of the composer-auteur with little thought being given even to the intrinsic aesthetic quality of the interaction of the music with the other components of the film. To judge from some classics of the film literature, from the appearance of Steven Smith's book (the first comprehensive modern biography of a film composer), and from the fan literature, the favored candidate for the job of film music's "Beethoven" is Bernard Herrmann.[65]

Film scholars do need to confront their reliance on dramatic feature films as the core repertoire of the cinema, but they have, until recently at least, not had to fight an overactive allegiance to contemporary Hollywood because the commercial and "academic" canons were quite different, the latter focusing on French, Russian, Japanese, Italian, Swedish, and early Hollywood film repertoires. A distinction between "popular" and "academic" canons is certainly present in music as well, but the situation is considerably more complex due to institutional factors, especially the oppressive presence of the Beethoven-centered canon, oriented toward instrumental rather than vocal or dramatic music. Harold Powers (among others) has cleanly formulated the point that musical canons are cultural, based not on inherent value but on status.[66] The German canon, with its roots in nineteenth-century

German national identity,[67] persists for a confluence of historical reasons, but especially due to the predominance in the United States of musicians with German (and German-Jewish) ancestry and/or training around the turn of the century, later reinforced by the influx of exiled German musicologists during the 1930s,[68] most of whom resisted any challenges to the established canon. These trends remain strong in the United States, so much so that even now, at the end of the century, it has proved impossible to rewrite textbooks to acknowledge the overwhelming influence of Debussy and Stravinsky on nearly every significant composer of the twentieth century. The "tenacious narrowness of [the] canon," as Christopher Williams puts it, and a "self-perpetuating historiographic framework" bring into question whether even the new musicologists (those who have taken up nontraditional paradigms) really have their heart in changing the canon much at all.[69]

The rather dismal results of a recent panel on classical music and musicology in film would seem to bear out this pessimism, as the participants, although nominally well-disposed toward their subject, in fact seemed more concerned with establishing yet again that popular culture formations are based on ignorance of historical facts, not with actually engaging the medium or its cultural challenges to musicology in any consequential way.[70] Given that attention lay primarily with historical costume films, it seems strange indeed that no one drew on Robert Rosenstone's defining theoretical work in this area or on essays in the issue of *Film History* devoted to historiographical questions.[71] External sources aside, however, one might reasonably have hoped for some effect from Gary Tomlinson's call for a historiography whose goal is no longer the traditional close reading of texts but narratives of dense historical contexts, the rich traces of signification that pass through the culturally constructed artifacts we call artworks.[72]

Thus, the process of canon formation—which is inevitably tied to the construction of historical narratives and so to questions of historiography as well as politics—will undoubtedly continue for film music; but its effects are not easy to predict because the constituencies involved differ substantially in their priorities. So long as diegetic music is hostage to that process, however, Kassabian's critique of the discipline(s) will stand, and it is difficult to imagine how a comprehensive history of twentieth-century music can ever be written.

Even larger issues loom: the process of canon formation is greatly complicated by the increasing instability of the genre "film." The definition of this term is hardly a new problem, but it takes on particular urgency when related to the internet.[73] Technologically driven options from easily affordable digital movie production to MP3 files for music distribution are provoking questions far more disruptive to established wisdom than old dilemmas about the status of 8 mm home movies or 16 mm student films. Nor are predictions chary of the grandiose: consider Siegfried Zielinski's claim that "the classic institutions for the mediation of film—cinema and television—are . . . no more than interludes in the broader history of the audiovisual media." To Zielinski, founding director of the Academy of Media Arts in Cologne, these changes are "not simply a cultural loss but also . . . a challenge: the new audiovisions have to be confronted squarely to make strategic intervention possible."[74]

Such claims aside, and acknowledging the obvious weaknesses of future scenarios (especially where technology is concerned) we may observe that it is hardly short of remarkable to find music owning such a secure place in this "broader history of the audiovisual media." Thus, we might edit Peter Lehman's remark, cited at the beginning of this introduction, to read "there will never be an end to histories and theories of music in media as long as people care about the subject." In what follows, find that subject very much alive.

Notes

1. The principal author of this introduction is David Neumeyer, who thanks his co-editors for their generous contributions: Caryl Flinn composed the original draft of the opening sections (since rewritten twice), edited a draft of the article summaries, and prepared a thorough and perceptive critique that has greatly improved the final sections; James Buhler edited the entire text and in the process contributed several original sentences, scattered throughout.

2. Peter Lehman, introduction to *Defining Cinema,* ed. Peter Lehman (New Brunswick: Rutgers University Press, 1997), 11.

3. Roy Prendergast, *Film Music: A Neglected Art,* 2d ed. (New York: Norton, 1992). The original edition appeared in 1977. Claudia Gorbman, *Unheard Melodies: Narrative Film Music* (Bloomington: Indiana University Press, 1987). Apart from the technological challenges of recording and rerecording, music's relation to the image (and so to narrative) was a central issue in the 1930s. See, among others, Fred Steiner, "What Were Musicians Saying About Movie Music During the First Decade of Sound? A Symposium of Selected Writings," in *Film Music I* ed. Clifford McCarty(New York: Garland, 1989), 81–107; and David Bordwell and Kristin Thompson, "Technological Change and Classical Film Style," in *Grand Design: Hollywood as a Modern Business Enterprise, 1930–1939,* ed. Tino Balio, vol. 5 in the *History of the American Cinema* series (New York: Scribner, 1993), 109–41.

4. Claudia Gorbman, "Film Music," in *The Oxford Guide to Film Studies.* ed. John Hill and Pamela Church Gibson (London: Oxford University Press, 1998), 43; Martin M. Marks, *Music and the Silent Film: Contexts and Case Studies, 1895–1924* (New York: Oxford University Press, 1997), 3–4. For film scholars, the benefits of such cross-disciplinary work include a richer view of film as a historical, cultural, and aesthetic artifact and a greater access to tools with which to read a formal element that has remained a relatively closed book to them. For musicologists, the benefits include a richer view of the traditional genres of concert music, musical

theater, and opera in the light refracted through the prism of film music, and the enabling of some meaningful steps toward a more comprehensive history of music(s) in the twentieth century.

5. Hans Erdmann and Giuseppe Becce, with Ludwig Brav, *Allgemeines Handbuch der Film-Musik*, vol. 1 (Berlin–Lichterfelde/Leipzig: Schlesinger, 1927).

6. Claudia Widgery has investigated this film/music rhythmic parallelism at length in three documentary films: *The River* (1937), *The City* (1939), and *Valley Town* (1940); see "The Kinetic and Temporal Interaction of Music and Film: Three Documentaries of 1930's America" (Ph.D. diss., University of Maryland, 1990).

7. Virgil Thomson, "A Little About Movie Music," *Modern Music* 10, no. 4 (1933): 188. Most of this quote is also given by Fred Steiner, who discusses the context of quotes from several writers contemporary with Thomson: Steiner, "What Were Musicians Saying," 88.

8. Thomson's best-known film score, for Robert Flaherty's *Louisiana Story*, was written more than a decade later.

9. "How to Write A Piece of Music," in *The Virgil Thomson Reader* (Boston: Houghton Mifflin, 1981), 150–51.

10. Aaron Copland, *What to Listen For in Music*, 2d ed. (New York: McGraw-Hill, 1957), 257–58.

11. Gorbman, *Unheard Melodies*, 33–40.

12. Gorbman, *Unheard Melodies*, 53 ff.; direct citations are from p. 55. Gorbman's claim about music and film spectatorship, which is derived from the psychoanalytically based suture theory, has been challenged recently; see Jeff Smith, "Unheard Melodies? A Critique of Psychoanalytic Theories of Film Music," in *Post-Theory: Reconstructing Film Studies*, ed. David Bordwell and Noël Carroll (Madison: University of Wisconsin Press, 1996), 230–47. Gorbman, "Film Music," contains a response to Smith (47); see also comments by Wendy Everett in her essay included here.

13. George Burt, *The Art of Film Music* (Boston: Northeastern University Press, 1994).

14. Partly in defense of Burt's presuppositions, we might point out one aspect of the film composer's status that has been very little examined to date: the notion that the composer (usually) stands in a privileged position because she or he is one of the last to see the product and so, being situated between the film's production and audition, is therefore in a position to imprint his or her interpretation or reading permanently on the film itself. To this, see Robynn Stilwell, "'I just put a drone under him . . .': Collage and Subversion in the Score of 'Die Hard,'" *Music and Letters* 78, no. 4 (1997): 551–80, esp. 552.

15. Noël Carroll, *Mystifying Movies: Fads and Fallacies in Contemporary Film Theory* (New York: Columbia University Press, 1988), 216.

16. Gorbman, *Unheard Melodies*, 36–37. For work challenging these claims, see articles by Rick Altman cited in his essay included here and also his "The Silence of the Silents," *Musical Quarterly* 80, no. 4(1996): 648–718. See also Paulin's essay included here.

17. To be sure, some films *must* have music because it is part of the subject matter or a core element of the film's genre: in their essays included here, Fischer, Kalinak, and Rodman discuss film musicals, and Gabbard explores a Robert Altman film that succeeds "more than almost any other Hollywood film in folding jazz performance into a cinematic narrative."

18. Mary Anne Doane, *The Desire to Desire: The Woman's Film of the 1940s* (Bloomington: Indiana University Press, 1987), 85.

19. Carroll, *Mystifying Movies*, 219.

20. Caryl Flinn, *Strains of Utopia: Gender, Nostalgia, and Hollywood Film Music.* (Princeton: Princeton University Press, 1992), 40–46.

21. In his essay included here Buhler explores an interesting twist on this familiar idea, as he argues that John Williams endows his score for *Star Wars* with only a superficial nod to Wagnerian melodic and motivic development, thereby exposing (consciously or not) a critique of the film's basic narrative argument.

22. Doane's arguments are worked out in "The Voice in the Cinema: The Articulation of Body and Space," *Yale French Studies* 60 (1980): 33–50; and "Ideology and the Practice of Sound Editing and Mixing," in *Film Sound: Theory and Practice,* ed. Elisabeth Weis and John Belton (New York: Columbia University Press, 1985), 54–62. Paulin's essay (included here) situates this theoretical position in relation to Wagnerian music drama.

23. Ellen Rosand, "Handel Paints the Resurrection," in *Festa musicologica: Essays in Honor of George J. Buelow,* ed. Thomas J. Mathiesen and Benito V. Rivera (New York: Pendragon, 1995), 52.

24. Cohen's essay (included here) summarizes the research literature relevant to this question, relates it to the film-music literature, and proposes a cognitive model for the way in which "musically-generated affective associations and film meanings account for a sense of reality or suspension of disbelief created by films."

25. Copland, *What to Listen For in Music,* 256–58.

26. Gorbman, *Unheard Melodies,* 72.

27. Flinn, *Strains of Utopia,* 5.

28. Lawrence Kramer, *Classical Music and Postmodern Knowledge* (Berkeley and Los Angeles: University of California Press, 1995).

29. See, for instance, Anthony Newcomb, "Schumann and Late Eighteenth-Century Narrative Strategies," *19th Century Music* 11 (1987): 164–74.

30. Kramer, *Classical Music,* 100. On the other hand, see London's essay (included here) for a description of the cognitive mechanics of "naming" that underlie the musical leitmotif in film.

31. Kramer has written about film elsewhere: "The Singing Salami: Unsystematic Reflections on the Marx Brothers' *A Night at the Opera,*" in Jeremy Tambling's *A Night in at the Opera: Media Representations of Opera* (London: Libbey, 1994), 253–65). In that essay, he calls the Marx Brothers' *A Night at the Opera* "a love death" in relation to Verdi's *Il trovatore,* which the film parodies; he argues that "the power of the film turns out to depend on the power of opera, even to embody an aspiration to the condition of opera. The film's conclusion is 'triumphant' only insofar as it is—absurdly—operatic" (257–58). For an overview of the ideological and analytical problems of filmed opera, see Tambling's introduction to the same volume, "Opera in the Distraction Culture," 1–23.

32. Theodor W. Adorno and Hanns Eisler, *Composing for the Films* (London: Athlone, 1994); reprint of the 1947 edition, which appeared under Eisler's name alone.

33. Max Steiner, interoffice memo to Carlyle Jones, Warner Bros. Pictures, 11 March 1940.

34. Steiner further exaggerated by seeming to suggest that he did not use "overall" scoring himself for some cues in many of his films and that the "mickey-mousing" method was unique to him (it was not: for example, Alfred Newman's score for *Foreign Correspondent* [1940] is a strongly leitmotivic score whose motifs constantly move in and out of the orchestra in response to visual cues; they are simply less intrusive than the figures in a Steiner score often are). Fred Steiner quotes several authors from the period on the question of continuity ("What Were Musicians Saying," 92–100).

35. Flinn, *Strains of Utopia,* 35. See also her somewhat different interpretation of

the counterpoint theorists, including Eisenstein; and Adorno and Eisler: *Strains of Utopia*, 46–47.

36. Kathryn Kalinak, *Settling the Score: Music and the Classical Hollywood Film* (Madison: University of Wisconsin Press, 1992), 29.

37. James Buhler and David Neumeyer, Review of Flinn, *Strains of Utopia*, and Kalinak, *Settling the Score*, *Journal of the American Musicological Society* 47, no. 2 (1994): 372–77.

38. Kathryn Kalinak, *Settling the Score*, 15. For a detailed demonstration of extraordinarily close synchronization between music and image in an extended scene from a Hitchcock film, see Pomerance's essay (included here).

Music does not play much of a role in film-studies' narrative models, but it is not difficult to see how music could be integrated. For some preliminary steps in that direction, see Neumeyer, "Source Music, Background Music, Fantasy and Reality in Early Sound Film," *College Music Symposium* 37 (1997): 13–20; and "Performances in Early Hollywood Sound Films: Source Music, Background Music, and the Integrated Sound Track," *Contemporary Music Review* (forthcoming). Also see *Psychomusicology* 13 (special issue on film music, edited by Annabel Cohen) and Cohen's essay (included here) for reports on some recent research on cognitivist models and film music.

39. Nicholas Cook, *Analysing Musical Multimedia* (London: Oxford University Press, 1998); Michel Chion, *Audio-Vision: Sound on Screen*, trans. Claudia Gorbman (New York: Columbia University Press, 1990).

40. Martin M. Marks, *Music and the Silent Film: Contexts and Case Studies, 1895–1924* (New York: Oxford University Press, 1997); Anthony Newcomb, "New Light(s) on Weber's Wolf's Glen Scene," in *Opera and the Enlightenment*, ed. Thomas Bauman and Marita Petzoldt McClymonds (Cambridge: Cambridge University Press, 1995), 61–88. See Marks's essay (included here) for an excellent instantiation of his approach.

Angela Miller offers a parallel in the panorama paintings of the same period and their several photographic successors; in showing that vestiges of this mode of entertainment survived in the movies, she demonstrates "continuity of the visual culture, and in some cases, of technology, connecting the panorama and the cinema"; "The Panorama, the Cinema, and the Emergence of the Spectacular," *Wide Angle* 18, no. 2 (1996): 34–69; citation from p. 58.

41. David Bordwell, Janet Staiger, and Kristin Thompson, *The Classical Hollywood Cinema: Film Style and Mode of Production to 1960* (New York: Columbia University Press, 1985), xiv. Musicians may be surprised that the familiar method of style analysis promulgated by the authors of *Classical Hollywood Cinema* could be considered in any way novel or controversial. Aside perhaps from the overt neo-Marxist bent to the economic history in the sections contributed by Staiger, *Classical Hollywood Cinema* differs little from historical and stylistic studies based on the German models traditional in musicology, or indeed from the dominant project of music theory—or, to be precise, what the dominant project of music theory might be if music analysts, especially Schenkerians, and music-cognitivists actually communicated seriously with one another. For a good discussion of this latter problem, see Ian Cross, "*Music Analysis* and Music Perception," *Music Analysis* 17, no. 1 (1998): 3–20. On the internal contradictions in the American Schenkerian agenda, see Robert Snarrenberg, "Competing Myths: The American Abandonment of Schenker's Organicism," in *Theory, Analysis, and Meaning in Music*, by Anthony Pople (Cambridge: Cambridge University Press, 1994), 29–56. For critique of a partly "Schenker-inspired" cognitive analytic system, see reviews of Fred Lerdahl and Ray Jackendoff, *A Generative Theory of Tonal Music* (Cambridge, Mass.: MIT Press, 1983); Edwin Hantz, *Music Theory Spectrum* 7 (1985): 190–202; John Peel

and Wayne Slawson, *Journal of Music Theory* 28, no. 2 (1984): 271–93; and replies: Lerdahl and Jackendoff, "Reply to Peel and Slawson," *Journal of Music Theory* 29, no. 1 (1985): 145–60; Peel and Slawson, "Reply to Lerdahl and Jackendoff," *Journal of Music Theory* 29, no. 1 (1985): 161–67.

In this regard, it is telling that the late Naomi Cumming's critique of Eugene Narmour's cognitivist music theory is couched in exactly the same terms as Seymour Chatman's complaint about Bordwell's (neo)formalist theory of film narrative: depersonalizing the active analytic process goes too far, denying the narrator, denying subjectivity in analysis: Naomi Cumming, "Eugene Narmour's Theory of Melody," *Music Analysis* 11, nos. 2–3 (1992): 354–74, as cited in Cross, "Music Analysis and Music Perception," 14; Seymour Chatman, *Coming to Terms: The Rhetoric of Narrative in Fiction and Film* (Ithaca: Cornell University Press, 1990), 124–30. Cumming elaborates her concept of music's expressive meanings in a groundbreaking essay, "The Subjectivities of 'Erbarme Dich,'" *Music Analysis* 16, no. 1 (1997): 5–44.

For musicologists searching the recent film literature for a centrist position that combines a traditional "fact-finding" style of historical research and a progressive intellectual agenda, the best examples to date are Virginia Wright Wexman, *Creating the Couple: Love, Marriage, and Hollywood Performance* (Princeton: Princeton University Press, 1993); Jackie Stacey, *Star Gazing: Hollywood Cinema and Female Spectatorship* (London: Routledge, 1994); Gaylyn Studlar, *This Mad Masquerade: Stardom and Masculinity in the Jazz Age* (New York: Columbia University Press, 1996). For a good review of the issues as they pertain specifically to reception studies, see Barbara Klinger, "Film History Terminable and Interminable: Recovering the Past in Reception Studies," *Screen* 38, no. 2 (1997): 107–28.

42. Susan McClary, *Georges Bizet, Carmen* (Cambridge: Cambridge University Press, 1992). For a striking twist on this trope, see Lekas's essay (included here) which explores some of the same issues through the operatic scene from *Citizen Kane.*

43. Ken Darby, "Musical Links in *Young Mr. Lincoln, My Darling Clementine,* and *The Man Who Shot Liberty Valance*," *Cinema Journal* 31, no. 1 (1991): 22–36; Anahid Kassabian, "At the Twilight's Last Scoring," in *Keeping Score: Music, Disciplinarity, and Culture,* ed. David Schwarz, Anahid Kassabian, and Lawrence Siegel (Charlottesville: University Press of Virginia, 1997), 258–74; the quotation is from p. 272.

44. Christian Metz, "Aural Objects," in *Film Sound: Theory and Practice,* ed. Elisabeth Weis and John Belton (New York: Columbia University Press, 1985), 154. The French-language original of Metz's essay was published in 1975.

45. Royal S. Brown, *Overtones and Undertones* (Berkeley and Los Angeles: University of California Press, 1994), 67–91. Others who have discussed the source/background distinction include Gorbman, *Unheard Melodies,* and "Film Music"; Kalinak, *Settling the Score;* Buhler and Neumeyer, Review of Flinn and Kalinak; Neumeyer, "Source Music, Background Music" and "Performances in Early Hollywood Sound Films"; and Jeff Smith, in his essay included here. Flinn explicitly rejects the distinction as a guiding element in her readings (*Strains of Utopia,* 11–12).

46. Kalinak, *Settling the Score,* 67.

47. Brown, *Overtones and Undertones,* 22.

48. Gillian B. Anderson, review of Rick Altman, *The American Film Musical,* in *American Music* 12, no. 1 (1994): 88–89.

49. FILMUS-L@LISTSERV.INDIANA.EDU. The list moderator is Stephen H. Wright.

50. This information comes primarily from cue sheets for productions by United Artists and Selznick Productions, plus a few each from Republic Pictures, MGM, Universal, and Warner Bros.

51. This information comes from business records housed in the Warner Bros. Collection, University of Southern California. The prices involved are rather high (which probably influenced Forbstein's decision not to use the song); Warner's paid only $500 for visual vocal use of "Shine," that took the spot intended for "Old Man Mose," and $1000 for unlimited use of "As Time Goes By" (a sum which was paid to Harms, Inc., a music publishing company owned by Warners).

52. The same treatment was generally extended to composers (and lyricists) of musicals, especially those who had a marketable name through success on Broadway.

53. Marks offers an excellent introduction to this score (*Music and the Silent Film,* 50–61).

54. Rick Altman, "Introduction: Sound/History," in his *Sound Theory/Sound Practice* (New York: Routledge, 1992), 116.

55. William H. Rosar, "Stravinsky and MGM," in *Film Music I,* ed. McCarty, 109–22.

56. Christopher Palmer, *The Composer in Hollywood* (London: Marion Boyars, 1990), 9.

57. Tony Thomas, *The Art and Craft of Movie Music* (Burbank, Calif.: Riverwood, 1991), 82–83.

58. Copland and Virgil Thomson, as it happens, are special cases: they were composers, with mainly New York roots, who worked in documentaries; therefore they rarely suffered from the stigma of Hollywood. In Copland's case, too, his work in Hollywood was always "moonlighting": even *The Heiress*—whose (slightly mangled) score won him an Academy Award—didn't interfere with the continuing advancement of his compositional oeuvre and concert career. A cultural-studies–oriented body of work is badly needed on the New York/Los Angeles, East/West polarity established to protect the hegemony of New York in classical music-making: serious/commercial; advanced styles/conservative or epigonal; moral/questionable or debauched; high-quality performance/second-rate performance. In the meantime, for a delightful anecdotal history that undercuts these critical distinctions by demonstrating in a very personal way both the quality and the complexity of musical life in Los Angeles in the 1940s and 1950s, see Don Christlieb, *Recollections of a First-Chair Bassoonist: 52 Years in the Hollywood Studio Orchestras* (Sherman Oaks, Calif.: Christlieb Products, 1996).

59. See for example Jerry Goldsmith's comments in Vincent J. Francillon, "Jerry Goldsmith: An Interview," *Cue Sheet* 10, nos. 3–4 (1993–94): 25–26.

60. Gorbman comments on these constituencies in similar terms ("Film Music," 44).

61. James Parakilas, "The Power of Domestication in the Lives of Musical Canons," *Repercussions* 4, no. 1 (1995): 17; Friedrich Kittler, *Discourse Networks 1800/1900.* (Stanford: Stanford University Press, 1990), 146–47. This is, of course, not to say that traditional magazine reviewers and scholarly writers have failed to pay attention to this issue or lack any influence, only that their influence is small compared with others. For a frank bit of criticism aimed at sorting out some evaluative criteria, see Royal S. Brown, "Film Music: The Good, the Bad, and the Ugly," *Cineaste* 21, nos. 1–2 (1995): 62–67; the same voice breaks through sporadically in *Overtones and Undertones.* For a particularly well executed example of canonical history-writing, see Stephen Handzo, "The Golden Age of Film Music," *Cineaste* 21, nos. 1–2 (1995): 46–55. Broadly speaking, composer biographies and style studies, tradebook surveys, and textbooks serve the same purpose, although they sometimes pass over into reports on research, as well: Steven C. Smith, *A Heart at Fire's Center: The Life and Music of Bernard Herrmann* (Berkeley and Los Angeles: University of California Press, 1991); Fred Steiner, "The Making of an American Film

Composer: A Study of Alfred Newman's Music in the First Decade of the Sound Era" (Ph.D. diss. University of Southern California, 1981): Tony Thomas, *The Art and Craft of Movie Music;* Palmer, *The Composer in Hollywood;* Jon Burlingame, *TV's Biggest Hits: The Story of Television Themes from "Dragnet" to "Friends"* (New York: Schirmer Books, 1996); Fred Karlin, *Listening to Movies: The Film Lover's Guide to Film Music* (New York: Schirmer Books, 1994); Laurence E. MacDonald, *The Invisible Art of Film Music: A Comprehensive History* (New York: Ardsley House, 1998).

62. Nadia Salerno-Sonnenberg, *Humoresque* (New York: Nonesuch Records, 1998), album number 79464–2.

63. Rick Altman, "Reusable Packaging: Generic Products and the Recycling Process," in *Refiguring American Film Genres: History and Theory,* ed. Nick Browne (Berkeley and Los Angeles: University of California Press, 1998), 1–41.

64. Robynn Stilwell, "Symbol, Narrative and the Musics of *Truly, Madly, Deeply,*" *Screen* 38, no. 1 (1997): 60–75.

65. Smith, *A Heart at Fire's Center.*

66. Harold Powers, "A Canonical Museum of Imaginary Music," *Current Musicology* 60 and 61 (1996): 6.

67. Sanna Pederson, "The Symphony After Beethoven," *Repercussions* 2, no. 2 (1993): 5–30; Gary Tomlinson, "Musical Pasts and Postmodern Musicologies: A Response to Lawrence Kramer," *Current Musicology* 53 (1993): 18–24.

68. Pamela Potter, "Musicology under Hitler: New Sources in Context," *Journal of the American Musicological Society* 49, no. 1 (1996): 108.

69. Christopher A. Williams, "Of Canons and Context: Toward a Historiography of Twentieth-Century Music," *Repercussions* 2, no. 1 (1993): 31–32, esp. 37.

70. The panel texts were subsequently published in *Musical Quarterly* 81, no. 2 (1997): Robert. L. Marshall, "Film as Musicology: *Amadeus*" (173–79); Ellen T. Harris, "Twentieth-Century Farinelli" (180–89); Lewis Lockwood, "Film Biography as Travesty: Immortal Beloved and Beethoven" (190–99); Jeffrey Kallberg, "Nocturnal Thoughts on *Impromptu*" (199–203); Kay Kaufman Shelemay, "'What's Up, Doc?' A View of 'Reel' Musicologists" (204–9). Only Kallberg shows any real sense of engagement with film qua film, with his premise that *Impromptu* "offers one of the most plausible accounts that I have seen (and in this assessment I am including all the standard biographies) of how the seemingly unlikely pairing of Chopin and Sand could ever have happened" (199).

71. Robert Rosenstone, *Visions of the Past: The Challenge of Film to Our Idea of History* (Cambridge, Mass.: Harvard University Press, 1995); Rosenstone, ed., *Revisioning History: Film and the Construction of a New Past* (Princeton: Princeton University Press, 1995); Richard Koszarski, ed., special issue: "Philosophy of Film History," *Film History* 6, no. 1 (1994). For an especially perceptive review of both Rosenstone books, see Guy Westwell, review of Robert Rosenstone, *Visions of the Past* and *Revisioning History,* in *Screen* 38, no. 1 (1997): 99–105.

72. See, for example, Tomlinson, "Musical Pasts and Postmodern Musicologies," and "Tomlinson Responds," *Current Musicology* 53 (1993): 36–40.

73. For a concise and particularly perceptive essay on "film" in relation to historical practices, see Raymond Williams, "Film History," in his *What I Came to Say* (London: Hutchinson Radius, 1989), 132–46.

74. Siegfried Zielinski, *Audiovisions: Cinema and Television as Entr'actes in History* (Amsterdam: Amsterdam University Press, 1998). The quotations were taken from the press's web site: http://www.uva.nl/aup/aup.html.

PART ONE

�֍

LEITMOTIF: NEW DEBATES AND QUESTIONS

✖

JAMES BUHLER

Star Wars, *Music, and Myth*

✳

"Origin is the ideology of regression."
—Theodor W. Adorno

Frames and Fanfares: The Lost Plenitude of Origin

"A long time ago in a galaxy far, far away . . ."

Each film of the *Star Wars* series begins ostensibly with this text. The graphic design and layout establish the spatial and temporal distance that the text proclaims. The small blue lettering and the ragged, informal layout on the plain black backdrop make the text seem almost intimate, despite the mythic intention of the enigmatic utterance. This image is the most proximate to us in the whole film. The intimacy of this moment is established at least in part by the silence on the soundtrack. This silence is marked by the end of Alfred Newman's Twentieth Century–Fox fanfare, whose presence not only recalls an earlier "heroic" era of filmmaking, thus anticipating the restorative gesture of the trilogy as a whole; it also establishes an oscillation between presence and absence on the soundtrack, an oscillation that puts the soundtrack into play from that moment of silence. The Fox fanfare is therefore not incidental to the sonic structure of the film but crucial to the perception of this silence as absence.

All of this works to put the crucial next shot on display as a moment of origin and pure presence: music erupts out of the silence with a radiant but transparent B♭ chord, which restores the tonality of Newman's fanfare, just as the luminous title (figure 1) suddenly appears in giant black letters rimmed with gold, monumentality replacing the impersonal intimacy of the blue lettering. Image and music for the first time coincide. We witness the creation of a world, and this is the nodal point—the original image of plenitude—from which everything else in the series flows: the mythic aura of *Star Wars* is born of this synchronization of music and image.[1] While

Figure 1. *A New Hope* (1977). Primal Origin: This image, the first frame of the title sequence, is cropped so that its boundaries extend beyond the frame of the screen. The letters are also opaque rather than transparent: the field of stars is not visible through the letters.

grasping to understand what makes the synchronization of the opening B♭ chord of his score with the title so effective, John Williams invokes the notion of a mythic archetype, suggesting that "the combination . . . must speak to some collective memory . . . that we don't quite understand. Some memory of Buck Rogers or King Arthur or something earlier in the cultural salts of our brains, memories of lives lived in the past, I don't know. But it has that kind of resonance—it resonates within us in some past hero's life that we've all lived."[2] Yet the synchronization that is implied here never quite occurs: its image of plenitude is rent with absences. The dark interior of the lettering, which at first seems transparent, is in fact void and inscrutable. The enigmatic graphic image of the title finds a correlate in mythic discourse, of which Roland Barthes writes "its form is empty but present, its meaning absent but full."[3]

The aura of this opening derives from this paradox. The title is at first framed so that it exceeds the boundaries of the screen, suggesting that the content of this image defies representation. The originary moment of plenitude is lost before it can really be absorbed as the title immediately begins to recede into the distance, uncovering a tapestry of stars. The process enacts a regression from origin, a slipping of presence into absence as the title vanishes into the void; it also reveals, however, the moment of pure presence, the moment of origin, as obscuring and curiously two-dimensional. At first too close to the camera, it rapidly becomes too distant. This first shot thus articulates, somewhat enigmatically to be sure, a dialectic of presence and absence that is perhaps less naive than it might at first seem: with distance comes regression from origin and loss of plenitude but also a feeling of depth.

The opening measure of Williams's score (example 1) resembles the title it accompanies: radiant but indefinite; world-defining and timeless. More and less than the B♭ chord it seems to be, this sound is a cipher in need of decoding. The music proclaims itself present even as it seems ethereal if not ghostly. This quality of the sound is a function of the un-balanced orchestration, which emphasizes the root of the B♭ chord throughout the entire orchestra at the expense of the third and fifth. The well-balanced brass chord—the trumpets, in the bright upper register, and the horns, also in the upper register, are in close position while the

Example 1. *Star Wars,* Main Title, opening chord.

trombones and tuba take the root below—compensates somewhat, but not entirely, for the predominance of B♭ in the rest of the orchestra. The orchestration endows the basic B♭ with the sense of major without making it hyperexplicit. The B♭ acquires an aura, as it were, of major rather than the substance. The compositional intention of this opening chord is made apparent as the full orchestra drops out and the remaining brass instruments quickly collapse back to fanfare bursts on B♭.[4] Where the opening B♭ establishes a musical space, the fanfare that follows initiates the melodic impulse, first rhythmically, then in terms of pitch. The trombones and trumpets dance in a close canon, fragmenting the impenetrable unity of the opening B♭ chord and marking the thematic profile of the theme to come. The counterpoint, which unfolds in quartal rather than triadic harmony, endows the musical space with volume, much as the receding "Star Wars" transforms the flat, two-dimensional screen into three dimensions with the addition of perspective. In this instance, the melodic content of the fanfare gives the music a feeling of depth and volume as well as a sense of motion. But the quartal harmony makes this motion seem indefinite: like the title, the fanfare moves toward a vanishing point that lies at infinite regress.

It is only with the addition of the F dominant as an anacrusis to the main theme itself that the music begins to impose an order on this so far timeless and undifferentiated sonic space. The tonal motion from dominant to tonic endows the music with a temporal dimension. Music precedes the narrative and calls it into being. Music imposes its tonal order before the text outlining the saga—the first instance of a syntactically complete ordering of text—appears onscreen. The lack of synchronization between the music and the text here is itself significant inasmuch as it underscores the rift within the primal unity of music and image that obtained at the original instant. The presentation of the text here is itself novel, one of the most striking images in a film filled with striking images: the text rolls out in linear perspective so that the text plane seems to drift in space like a message in a bottle. The equation the film posits between linear perspective and tonal motion here is also quite perceptive, if ideologically loaded in ways the film perhaps does not fully anticipate. Just as perspective positions viewers (here the tilt tells us that we are not the addressee of this text) and relates figures to the background, so too tonality positions listeners, providing a musical context by which to evaluate the salience of musical figures. Moreover, both perspective and tonality naturalize the viewing and listening experience respectively.

Each phrase of the main title ends solidly, but none of them cadences on the tonic. This lack of a tonic cadence has the effect of leaving the music open, just as the text of the synopsis initiates the action, leaving much unexplained. The music departs from the thematic material of the Main Title as the text drifts off into space. As the text dissolves in the distance, the music loses tonal coherence and becomes ambiguous if not quite atonal. An amorphous piccolo melody drifts over the murky and rather static harmony just before the camera tilts down, a highly subjective camera motion that initially seems to position the audience above the action. The motion of the camera here is significant in that throughout the entire title sequence the camera has remained stationary, its absolute stability acting as a sure foundation of the world being built through text, graphics, and music. We have no reason to doubt the objectivity of the text, indeed, the truth of all we hear and see so long as the camera remains fixed and the tonality clear. Stable tonality is to the ear what the stable camera placement is to the eye: once the camera moves and the tonality dissolves, everything becomes subject to interpretation. The movement of the camera initiates the action before the action itself, implicating the audience in what it sees: it is the desire of the audience to move the camera, to get the action going so that it may return to that opening moment of plenitude that never was; but the action itself therefore represents a fall from grace, a theater in which the stability of truth no longer obtains.

Sound Design: Music contra Effects

Your eyes can deceive you. Don't trust them.   —Obiwan, *A New Hope*

If, from its very first appearance, music is thus linked with the production of myth in *Star Wars*, sound effects are linked with technology. The soundtrack in fact is an arena of contention between myth and technology, between past and future, between the Force and the Darkside. This is made evident in the way that sound effects initiate the diegetic soundtrack in each film, at first melding with the music-track and then displacing it. In each film, an indefinite low rumble emerges out of the music as the camera tilts down. The very first sound effect precedes the image, positing a continuity between music and noise. In *A New Hope*, a violent explosion of light and sound after the camera tilt brings the rebel ship into being, revealing a link between synchronization and violence that had been sublimated in the opening. Immediately after this explosion, the triangular nose of an Imperial cruiser appears at the top of the screen and ominously begins to fill it, much as the text scrolling out in perspective had filled space following the initial moment of synchronization (see figures 2 and 3). Comparing this sequence with the opening suggests an association of the Empire with an inverted worldview: where the text had rolled out in a naturalized perspective, here perspective is denaturalized and momentarily obliterated. Sound effects, too, are linked with this denaturalized vision of technology just as music, but especially tonality, had been linked with the natural unfolding of the text.

In *The Empire Strikes Back* and *Return of the Jedi* the initial displacement of music by sound effects is, by contrast, quite gradual. The opposition between the effects and music is not dramatized with the spectacle of violence as it is in the first film: the tilt down in *The Empire Strikes Back* simply identifies the low rumble as belonging to an Imperial starship just as the camera motion in *Return of the Jedi* reveals the ghostly skeleton of a Death Star under construction before one of the Imperial star cruisers comes floating in over the top of the screen, replicating the memorable shot from the first film discussed above. In all three cases, however, a basic succession holds: we hear before we see, which grants an initial precedence to the aural over the visual.

The introduction of sound effects differs in one crucial respect from the music: whereas the opening B♭ chord of the score had been synchronized to the title card, diegetic sound is initially characterized by a *lack* of synchronization with the image and its source. These paired associations— music with an initial moment of synchronization that dissolves in order to move beyond the bonds of the image, and sound effects with an initial moment of nonsynchronization that becomes bound to an image—create a

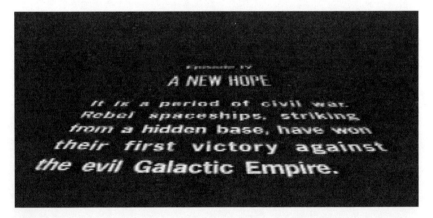

Figure 2. *A New Hope.* "Natural" Perspective: In this sequence, the text enters from the bottom of the screen and scrolls out in linear perspective, since the Renaissance associated with naturalistic representation. The vanishing point creates the impression of a triangle with its point up.

Figure 3. *A New Hope.* Inverted Worldview: Exactly reversing figure 2, the Imperial cruiser enters from the top of the screen and its triangular shape is oriented point down. The image is almost frightening, not simply because the ship is so immense, but also because its entrance at the top of the screen frustrates the attempt to decode it according to the "natural" conventions of linear perspective.

conflict of more than passing interest on the soundtrack. From the camera tilt that initiates the action in each of the films, sound effects are associated with images of technology, radical human interventions in the material world, whereas, after its initial moment of synchronization, music dissolves its bond to the image, allowing it to point to what extends beyond the material reality of cultural mediation, namely the Force. Indeed, the filmic representation of the Force depends crucially on music, which is why it is appropriate to speak of a conflict, perhaps even a dialectic between music and effects on the soundtrack. Sound design is more than a simple question of taste in these films; it is the very means by which the mythical world is constituted as agonistic. It is therefore imperative to decipher the meaning of the mise-en-bande,[5] especially the fact that effects nearly always take precedence over the music in the soundtrack.

Once effects appear on the soundtrack, the music does not yield its place willingly. This is music that is composed and recorded in such a way that it can compete with sound effects. Even where the mixing of the music is so low that it hardly sounds above a low murmur, its presence is important because this mixing leaves the impression that the music has been suppressed. In other words, the specificity of the music under the sound effects gives the mise-en-bande its distinctive quality of conflict: the music does not make room for sound effects in general any more than the sound effects take account of the music. Music can be supplanted from the soundtrack only by means of external force: the intervention of the mixing board. Thus, sound effects must generally impose themselves on the music, ripping the tapestry the music weaves to pieces.

At the first appearance of the ships in *A New Hope,* music is generally mixed at a markedly lower sound level than effects. At points, the music is almost inaudible. The pounding ostinato figures in the strings and the brass bursts of the Rebel Fanfare,[6] both consisting of compact motives with strong, distinctive rhythmic profiles, are two of the musical gestures that nevertheless manage to be heard clearly over the sound effects. But they obtain this audibility by radically simplifying the musical means so that they almost seem to mimic sound effects: the string figure simply hammers away at the same pitch over which the fanfare figure is stated baldly at harmonically distant levels. Strikingly, one of the first lulls in the sound effects during this opening sequence follows Darth Vader's entrance on the rebel ship, which allows his presence to be marked by an aggressive and highly dissonant musical stinger that assaults the tonal universe much as weapons fire assaults the soundtrack. This dissonant musical gesture sets Vader apart from the rest of the Imperial troops precisely because the music suddenly comes forward and takes note of him. Yet even for Vader, sound effects are inescapable, as his labored mechanical breathing, which is as responsible for defining his character as are his black cape and mask, dominates the pauses in the dialogue.[7]

The unsettling sonic effect of Vader's entrance is reinforced by the immediate cross-cut to Leia placing the message to Obiwan inside Artoo. The sound design here grants a sense of momentary sanctuary to this brief subsequence: the music levels are elevated as the Force theme appears, the first moment of tonal and thematic stability in the music since the opening credits. Indeed the way the mise-en-bande works here to create this feeling of sanctuary is partly responsible for establishing an association of the Force theme with hope. The laser blasts, though now mixed at a significantly lower level, as though in a distance, threaten the sonic space without actually interfering with our perception of the music. Likewise, the droid noises, parallel to Vader's breathing, do not arrest our attention on the soundtrack in the same way as does Vader's breathing. It is instructive to think about why this might be so. All of the noises associated with Vader and the droids are pseudo-organic, the products of autonomous, individual locomotion, dialogue, and breathing, and so distinct on that account from weapons fire and engine noises. Artoo's beeps are perceived as dialogue, and the sounds of C3PO moving about are clearly synchronized to his movements. In both cases, the sound source is quite evident.

Vader's breathing, however, is different. Here we have a pseudo-organic sound—indeed perhaps the organic sound par excellence—where the source is unseen. We do not really see his breathing. We can, to be sure, attribute the sound to Vader, but unlike C3PO, where the mechanism of his joints is quite apparent, Vader's breathing apparatus is concealed by his attire. What is frightening about Vader is the way everything that is organic and human about him is masked by technology without completely destroying the sense that something is alive in there. In *A New Hope*, the music takes note of Vader, marking his presence much more so than the droids, toward whom the music is surprisingly indifferent, but without assigning a distinctive theme to him. In the later two films, Vader's musical character congeals in the ponderous leitmotif of the Imperial March, which, as we will see, not only sets up a thematic conflict within the score, but even more important, creates the potential for a dialectical engagement within the leitmotif between semiotic and mythical uses of the device.

Excursus on the Leitmotif: The Entwinement of Myth and Signification

Luke, help me take this mask off. —Darth Vader, *Return of the Jedi*

While film music borrowed the basic idea of the leitmotif from Wagner, his deployment of it differs from most filmic uses of the device in one fundamental sense: its self-conscious relation to myth. Where film simply takes the signifying function of the leitmotif at face value, severing its link to myth as it were, Wagner uses the leitmotif to put signification, the language-like character of music, into play. In other words, Wagner's leitmotifs both signify and resist signifying. As Carl Dahlhaus puts it, a leitmotif seems to require naming yet always extends beyond any meaning captured by that name.[8] In other words, the "primal baptism" linking the leitmotif as signifier with a signified often fails in Wagner's dramas as the motif reverts to music again, absorbed into the musical unfolding.[9] Sometimes a motif appears that cannot be directly related to the drama; sometimes it cannot be fixed securely to a signified at all. Often it is the linguistically constructed drama that yields to the music, as the action is suspended momentarily to allow the presentation of a summarizing musical statement that bears only tangentially on the scene. This reversion to music in Wagner's music dramas is made possible by musical logic, which can justify the recurrence of a motif musically that might seem wholly enigmatic from the perspective of linguistic signification. Moments of musical summary arrest the flow of language in the dramas, dissolving the bond that otherwise obtains between the leitmotif as signifier and its signified and giving this music a mythic substrate, a fluid semiosis that itself points to an intelligible realm beyond signification. In this way, myth and music become directly allied against linguistic signification, that is, communication.[10] The musical quality of the leitmotif prevents it from devolving wholly into a linguistic entity; it becomes the structural analogue to myth. What is beguiling about Wagner is that he makes music's resistance to signification, the sine non qua of music vis-à-vis language, into the very mythic substrate of his music drama: music free of language in Wagner does not resist myth; it produces it.[11]

Film music, on the contrary, divests the leitmotif of this mythic element only to surrender the most musical aspect of the leitmotif: this is the meaning of the oft-misunderstood attack on the leitmotif in *Composing for the Films*. One of the objections Adorno and Eisler raise against the leitmotif in film is that film composers do not take account of its formal requirements. Wagner's leitmotifs, which tend to be brief and salient in themselves, require "a large musical canvas if [they are] to take on the structural meaning beyond that of a signpost."[12] In particular, the relatively short sequences and the extensive cross-cutting common to film emphasizes discontinuity rather than the continuity needed to allow a motif time to be presented sequentially as Wagner's are. Film composers simply appropriate the idea of the motif without understanding the crucial structural importance of musical sequence. In his book on Wagner, Adorno suggests that Wagner's technique of sequential exposition embeds the motif within a coherent musical form while also retaining the quality of musical mobility that Wagner so cherished.[13] Because the motif in Wagner is governed by the musical process of the sequence, it is impossible for its meaning to be completely severed from that musical process, which is why for Adorno the leitmotif is more than a signpost in Wagner. Consequently, leitmotifs do not so much attach themselves to concrete referents as they endow "the dramatic events with metaphysical significance."[14] The primary purpose of Wagner's leitmotif is the production of myth not signification.

Film music, by contrast, has secularized the leitmotif, demythologizing it precisely by emphasizing its linguistic quality, the process of signification. Film typically deploys leitmotifs in a much more consistent manner than does Wagner; the motifs are much more rigidly bound to the action in film, and they are consequently rarely granted the independence motifs have in Wagner's dramas, which is one reason the music in cinema rarely obtains the level of independence of music in Wagner's dramas. A leitmotif in film is seldom allowed to arrest the cinematic flow for a summarizing statement of a motif as Wagner halts the dramatic flow to make way for a statement of his motif. While the filmic deployment of leitmotifs thus serves as a critique of Wagner's mythical impulses, it also serves as the utmost development of the least musical (because most linguistic) aspect of Wagner's compositional thought.

Demythification does not save the leitmotif, but simply reveals its poverty. As Adorno notes, leitmotifs rarely serve as anything more than musical calling cards in film: "Via the ingenious illustrative technique of Richard Strauss, [the degeneration of the leitmotif] leads directly to cinema music where the sole function of the leitmotif is to announce heroes and situations so as to help the audience to orient itself more easily."[15] Adorno condemns the devolution of the leitmotif toward language here, because it transforms music into a means, a technology even, rather than the thing itself, the expression; Adorno had already found this aspect of the leitmotif troubling in Wagner. From the perspective of the philosophy of language, Wagner's leitmotifs, Adorno argues, are essentially as arbitrary as words, and it is this element of arbitrariness that the expressive dimension of music has difficulty bearing. "Wagner's leitmotifs stand revealed as allegories that come into being when something purely external, something that has fallen out of a spiritual totality, is appropriated by meaning and made to represent them, *a process in which signifiers and signifieds are interchangeable*."[16] Myth does not banish this linguistic element in Wagner; it merely disguises it, a disguise that serves the purpose of Wagner's phantasmagoria.

Just as Wagner's mythic impulse does not free the leitmotif of its linguistic element but actually leads back to it, so too the demythifying impulse of film music leads not away from myth but back toward it. This is the riddle of the leitmotif, which entwines myth and signification in a knot almost impossible to solve. The leitmotif draws attention to itself; it must be heard to perform the semiotic function attributed to it. The leitmotif says: listen to me, for I am telling you something significant. So long as it remains music, however, its meaning remains veiled. The clarity promised by the linguistic function dissolves but leaves us believing that this would all make sense if we gave ourselves over to the music. Even in its wholly demythologized state, the function of the leitmotif remains mythic, the unification of what is actually disparate. "False clarity is only another name for myth; and myth has always been obscure and enlightening at one and the same time: always using the devices of familiarity and straightforward dismissal to avoid the labor of conceptualization."[17]

As Caryl Flinn points out, the signifying capabilities of music help mystify the diegetic world of the film by rendering its inner properties apparent to us, whereas in our world such properties are always necessarily hidden.[18] This is true especially of the leitmotif, which is responsible, to a very large extent, for the sense of false clarity that characterizes much classic Hollywood cinema. Through the leitmotif, film becomes a mythic discourse, in which its mythic impulse hides behind an apparent demythologization. Demythologization in film music thus comes to serve the function of a more insidious mystification, because that mystification sublates its myth into entertainment, which seeks the status of art while absolving itself of the responsibility that art demands.

The Nature of the Force

With our combined strength, we can end this destructive conflict and
bring order to the galaxy. —Darth Vader, *The Empire Strikes Back*

If the overt mythic quality is what distinguishes Wagner's leitmotifs from general film practice, then Williams's music to *Star Wars,* especially *A New Hope,* comes as close as any film music to the tone of Wagner. *Star Wars* is likewise self-consciously mythic: it unfolds in mythic time that grants the recurrence of leitmotifs, especially orchestral climaxes, a kind of summarizing power that is more than simply the recurrence of linguistic tokens.[19] A certain inconsistency of leitmotivic deployment serves as a trace of self-conscious mythologization because such moments belie another logic at work besides the obvious signifying one—a musicomythic logic. The mythic quality of the music lies in the perception of a semiosis in flux, the way the leitmotifs resist all signifieds as in the world of myth. The "Binary Suns" cue in *A New Hope* is the prototype of such mythic usage. When Luke steps outside with the two suns hanging in the sky as background, a full statement of the Force theme accompanies him despite the fact that at this point in the film nothing about the Force has been revealed. The "primal baptism" that will link signifier and signified does not occur until Ben explains the Force to Luke later in the film. Moments like this one when the music seems not entirely bound up with its semiotic function are what gives this music its mythical character. The music seems to intuit connections that are beyond immediate rational comprehension.[20]

This semiotic failure is the mark of the mythic, pointing to a realm beyond reason, beyond language—a realm that in *Star Wars* functions as the domain of the Force, which, as with Wagner's mythic substrate, cannot be represented other than through this failed link between signifier and signified in music. Music is therefore fundamental to the representation of the Force. If the antagonism between music and effects inscribes on the soundtrack an opposition between the Force and technology, between sacred and secular worldviews, then the opposition of the Force and the Darkside manifests itself musically both in terms of leitmotivic deployment and the actual thematic structure. In terms of leitmotifs, those associated with the Force (the Force itself, but also Luke's theme, Princess Leia's, Yoda's, etc.) participate in a fluid semiosis where the bond between the leitmotif and what it signifies frequently dissolves, as the leitmotif sheds its signlike property and reverts to music.

By contrast, the leitmotifs of the Darkside, in particular the Imperial March, strictly adhere to a signified. The Darkside is associated only with the leitmotif as a means, with its instrumental, technological deployment—that is, music as mere signification. With the Darkside, music no longer signifies in a mythic manner; it no longer signifies what lies beyond signification. Especially after *A New Hope*, no leitmotif functions more consistently as a sign than the Imperial March. Indeed, the semiotic property of this theme is so emphasized in *The Empire Strikes Back* that it does actual damage to the compositional integrity of the score, which often mechanistically matches each cut to the Imperial fleet or Vader with a blast of the ponderous theme. It is difficult to gauge the exact contribution of Williams to this mechanistic layout, as the film was recut so substantially after it was supposedly "set" that much of the score, especially in the early part of the film, proved unusable in the form Williams wrote it.[21] Many shots that use the bombastic concert version of the Imperial March in the film are much more subtly rendered in Williams's score, though his score, too, is dominated by this theme. The constant recycling of the ponderously scored concert version of the march in the final cut of the film, however, has the effect of emphasizing the identity of the music, the music as a sign; in that respect, the opposition between the Force and the Darkside within the music is intensified.

This opposition between the Force and the Darkside extends to the structure of the themes themselves. As the opening of the Imperial March illustrates (example 2), the Darkside is represented musically not primarily through dissonance, not really even through chromaticism, but rather through the abrogation of the dominant.[22] Most typically, the march is introduced with a vamp: pounding rhythms on the tonic move to minor ♭VI on the fourth beat of each measure. The concert version, for instance, opens with two measures of oscillation between octave Gs and an E♭ minor chord in root position, an oscillation that establishes an important juxtaposition between G and E♭. In measure 3, the harmony of the vamp grows ambiguous: the octave Gs remain prominent, but the chord on beat 4 is no longer simply minor ♭VI. Rather, elements of the dominant—actually a diminished chord with dominant tendencies (F♯[= G♭]–A–E♭)—collide with the E♭ minor chord, and the whole complex sounds over a pedal G. Yet, because the first two measures "prime" our ears to hear an oscillation between minor I and minor ♭VI, the resulting sonority sounds more like an altered minor ♭VI over a tonic pedal than a dominant-substitute diminished chord.

Example 2. *Star Wars,* "Imperial March" (concert version), mm. 1–8.

It is almost as though the region of ♭VI has swallowed up the dominant implications of the diminished chord here. The lowered third of minor ♭VI is the flatted tonic (G♭), that is, the enharmonic equivalent of the leading tone (F♯), the characteristic dominant tendency tone. The flatted tonic absorbs, as it were, all traces of the strong dominant function of the leading tone into the region of ♭VI, a region that in tonal terms should be major but here is inflected toward minor. The tune itself (mm. 5ff.) replays something of the same opposition that characterizes the harmony: it circles around G but feigns major, melodically outlining an E♭-major triad while sardonically harmonizing it with the oscillating vamp from the introduction.[23] In measures 7 and 8, the melody, like the harmony throughout, attacks the dominant function of the leading tone, enfolding G♭ in a descending arpeggiation of minor ♭VI that leads back to the tonic but in a way that the note is emphatically not allowed to show its enharmonic tonal face as the leading tone F♯; indeed, that an unaltered E♭-minor chord underpins the melodic G♭ here drives the point home. Likewise, even at the end of the tune (mm. 15–16), any dominant function that remains to the leading tone is highly attenuated as an altered subdominant (C–E♭–G♭–B♭) leads plagally to G. Here, too, the strong tonal tendency of the leading tone is mitigated, even neutralized.

Similar tonal procedures govern the Emperor's theme, which unfolds in a series of tonally unrelated triads, once again primarily minor, often a minor third or tritone apart (example 3). The untexted male chorus swinging between G minor and B♭ minor only to veer suddenly to C♯ minor is highly effective, well scored, and the whole thing has an elemental, otherworldly quality. It is as if these triads were being moved in sonorous blocks against their tonal will. The music gives the impression that only a very powerful sorcerer, perhaps only a god, could animate these chords thus, could make them progress so against their tonal nature.[24]

What is interesting about these two musical representations of the Darkside is that they both avoid an association with atonality and hence musical Modernism. While the music of *Star Wars* never embraces Modernism, the score, unlike the film, is not antimodern. As the tonal procedures of these two themes demonstrates, Williams does not associate atonal dissonance with the Empire, though this would have been the obvious choice given the trilogy's antimodern bent. Atonality, where it appears at all in these films, is generally restricted to appearances of the exotic, the primitive, and the unintelligible (the sand people for instance) or moments of great anxiety and excitement (battle sequences and the like). The tonal transgressions of Empire themes, by contrast, lie on the pretonal side: the material is often consonant, even triadic; it is just not deployed tonally.

Williams's reluctance to align modern music with the Empire is what saves the score and ultimately the film itself from turning into an antimodernist screed. Instead of sharpening the trilogy's antimodernist polemic, the music clarifies what is ambiguous in the story: the confrontation between ideals of social harmony. This becomes especially evident by comparing the

Example 3. *Star Wars*, The Emperor.

Imperial March to the Main Title theme, which is likewise a march but with a clear harmonic thrust: where the Imperial March seems ruthlessly ordered but stuck in place almost by the force of will, defying proper tonal motion, the Main Title soars, freely resting on the dominant.[25] "When I thought of a theme for Luke and his adventures," Williams states, "I composed a melody that reflected the brassy, bold, masculine, and noble qualities I saw in his character."[26] In general, the music of the Rebels is banal albeit thrilling, full of pathos at times but constructed so that it always *seems* natural. Yet in its very first appearance, the Main Title theme is already wearing a mask. The cross-rhythms, which are musically more interesting than the tune itself, divert our attention from the melodic content, disguising the general banality of the musical construction.

Here then is the opposition inscribed in the musical representations of the Rebels and the Empire: imposed order versus naturalized order. Where the social order of the Rebels appears natural, its technology just outdated enough to seem charming rather than threatening, the social order of the Empire appears a distortion, its technology ruthless and grotesque. These conceptions are brought over into the music, where all compositional force is brought to bear on making the themes associated with the Rebels seem natural or at worst fantastic, while those of the Empire sound rigid, ponderous, and above all unnatural. The music, in other words, works to naturalize the order of the Force while it denaturalizes the order of the Darkside, revealing it as arbitrary and artificial, a kind of technology. In musical terms, this means that the music for the Rebels and the Empire do not differ fundamentally in terms of the necessity of ordering dissonance; rather, their differences lie in how that dissonance is to be ordered. Within the score, the image of naturalized harmony associated with the Force is tonality, especially the dominant. This association with the dominant gives insight into the Force: the Darkside is an arbitrary power, a force that is wholly willed without respect to the inner nature of the thing, whereas the good side of the Force, like the dominant, is an unforced force, a force that takes account of the natural state of things; that is, where they want to go. The good side channels, as it were, rather than forces. In this way the music of the Rebels recalls an irrevocable time when technology still worked and was charged with the utopian spirit of the future, when order was happy, when harmony was possible.

The stages that Luke passes through in coming to master the Force, though not so straightforward as the musical conception, confirm that the Darkside is in essence a technological use of the Force. In both *A New Hope* and *The Empire Strikes Back,* for instance, Luke's understanding of the Force remains rudimentary, and he is susceptible to being turned toward the Darkside in these films (especially *The Empire Strikes Back* where the seduction is an important theme of the film) precisely because his understanding of the Force at this point coincides with the Darkside. What Luke wants to learn about the Force is how to use it instrumentally; that is, how to use it to dominate nature and utterly defeat Vader. This is his only aim. Luke's instrumental conception of the Force—the Force as a technological control of nature—makes him little different than Vader in that respect. Vader's protestations against trusting in "technological terrors" notwithstanding, the Darkside fetishizes technology, much as the Imperial March fetishizes not only the tonic note, but especially the unnatural, almost mechanical harmonic oscillation between minor I and minor ♭VI. With respect to the fetishization of technology, we need think not only of Vader ("he's more machine than man," Obiwan says of him) but even more so of the two Death Stars, whose spherical, worldlike shapes bear, in negative form, the unmistakable imprint of a utopia realized through technology. Yet in both *A New Hope* and in *The Empire Strikes Back*, Luke's light saber is perhaps the most fetishized piece of technology of all, although this fetishization is naturalized by casting the saber as a phallus, relic of the Father.[27] In these two films Luke sees the Force only as an exotic, advanced technology, a particularly efficient way of manipulating things. It is this conception of the Force as a technology that leads to the failure in the cave.[28] Only through the symbolic castration of his hand (and the light saber contained within it) does Luke overcome the technological conception of the Force and finally comprehend the teaching of Yoda.

Specters of Revolution

Wotan is the phantasmagoria of the buried revolution. He and his like roam around like spirits haunting the places where their deeds went awry, and their costume compulsively and guiltily reminds us of that missed opportunity of bourgeois society for whose benefit they, as the curse of an abortive future, re-enact the dim and distant past.
—Theodor W. Adorno, *In Search of Wagner*

In an insightful albeit politically intemperate tract on the *Star Wars* films, Hal Colebatch uncovers how an appeal to nature underlies the legitimacy of the Rebels vis-à-vis the Empire. The Rebels, he says, are actually defenders of natural law. The value of *Star Wars*, he admits, is "reactionary," since it seeks to "[restore] a better past that has been usurped." These films "are about rebellion and counter-rebellion and, either directly or by implication, about natural order and natural law. In [them] the good side is seen and named by the Enemies as 'rebels,' and indeed they are in rebellion against the domination of evil empires. They are, however, counter-revolutionaries, fighting to preserve the natural order against the usurpers."[29] The Empire, by contrast, does not offer a "natural order," "but an 'order' artificially imposed for Utopian ends."[30] In fact, Colebatch goes so far as to claim that *Star Wars* is "anti-utopian," because it is "about the rejection of grandiose, totalitarian schemes of empire-building."[31] Although Colebatch uncritically follows the series in naturalizing the order of the Rebellion, and so does not see the utopian dimension in every restoration project, he does point to something crucial: the sense in which the Empire represents symbolically the miscarriage of a technological utopia. The turn from technology to the Force is a result of despair over the lost utopian hope for a better world that technology once promised. In this sense, Colebatch is perfectly correct to read an anti-utopian theme in *Star Wars*. What he ignores is that the resonance of this theme has to do with the unmet hopes of a failed revolution rather than any anti-utopianism per se. The ideological power of the Force resides precisely in its relation to Utopia, in the way that it becomes the repository for utopian energies. This, no doubt, is the purpose of religion in conservative thought: to redirect those utopian impulses that capitalism collects but cannot safely discharge on its own. While Colebatch believes that the appeal of *Star Wars* is a result of increasing secularization,[32] a better interpretation might be reading this appeal as a loss of faith in the utopian promise of secularization, the project of Modernism.

The Death Star is the negative image of this new secularized world, the one the technological revolution would have wrought. It is a wholly technological world, a world constructed with all means of technology possible. But this technological marvel is portrayed as hostile to organic life. This is surely the point of showing the Death Star destroy the "peaceful" planet Alderaan in *A New Hope:* it shows how the technological world threatens to reduce the organic world to rubble. Yet the Death Star contains the strongest imprint of Utopia in the trilogy as it is really the only image of a future the films allow. The Death Star, like Valhalla in Wagner's *Ring*, thus becomes an emblem of a failed revolution, and it has to bear the symbolic consequences for the failure: we demand the obliteration of the Death Star, which we consume as spectacle, as payment for the failure of our dreams. For *Star Wars* as for Wagner's *Ring*, myth is reaction to failed revolution, to the inability to change the world. Myth serves to justify the failure, attributes that failure to the way of the world—fate—rather than a failure of human imagination and fortitude. We accept Yoda's statement of fate, "that is the way of things, the way of the Force," and thus receive absolution from the guilt of our failure.

The *Star Wars* series looks to the past—to the return of the Jedi—rather than to the future. The new hope is bound not to the technological promise of the future, a revolution that would change existing social relations, but to the restoration of a past that never was. This has the effect of naturalizing the social relations of the Old Republic as timeless and casting technology (really, history itself) in an adversarial position with respect to the Republic. *Star Wars* despises time, preferring even death to any meaningful change. While everything associated with the Jedis appears eternal and their absence is portrayed as an aberration, the Emperor looks ancient, like someone who has lived beyond his allotted time, much more so than Yoda does even at his death. Ben, on the contrary, always seems ghostly, a visitor from the spirit world—first metaphorically in that he is portrayed as someone who has outlived his life span, and then literally when he dies and returns as a ghost. Adorno makes the following point about Wotan, who in his guise as the Wanderer, is a mythic forerunner of Ben: "As the spirit of the ancient, now dispossessed god, the Wanderer is also the embodiment of the dispossessed but new revolution. Since the Wanderer only speaks, he necessarily drops out of the action; his aura arises from his position outside society."[33] Like Wotan, Ben's power and aura derive from his extraterritoriality, his position outside society: "If you strike me down, I shall become more powerful than you can imagine."

Rebellion and Restoration

I've got a really bad feeling about this.   —Han Solo, *A New Hope* (and elsewhere)

It is faith in restoration that fundamentally differentiates *Star Wars* from Wagner's *Ring* cycle, which likewise, according to Adorno, posits a false revolution. Wagner, however, opts for annihilation rather than a leap into the past. His art remains steadfastly committed to the music of the future, even if that future is tinged with pessimism and is ultimately without hope for a better world. What *Star Wars* lacks from Wagner's universe is this pessimism, which is Wagner's critical force, his dissatisfaction with existing relations. As Adorno notes, it is "paradoxically . . . the pessimism of the *Ring* that contains an incipient admission that the rebellion of Natural Man ends up in a reaffirmation of a social system that is seen as natural."[34] *Star Wars* retains hope, blunting the edge of pessimism by projecting its Utopia into the past as the "natural" state of the Old Republic.

The music of *Star Wars* is heavily implicated in the task of elevating restoration and recurrence over substantive change. Thus, all musical development in the trilogy is without consequence, as time and again the music merely celebrates a return to what has already occurred. The music for the Throne Room sequence that concludes *A New Hope*, for instance, functions formally as a recapitulation that is satisfied with thematic identity—a return to a prior state rather than something new. The cross-rhythms in the accompaniment, while highly effective at rendering the theme climactic, give the music a martial character (Williams without irony refers to it as "a kind of imperial procession")[35]—and this martial character makes it seem as if the order the music enacts is violently imposed rather than internally motivated. This is not music that seeks legitimacy on its own merits.[36] The absence of substantive thematic work means that the music lacks a dialectic that could justify the triumphant tone.[37] Instead of seeming heroic, the triumph here is empty and bombastic, celebrating a victory over what posed no compositional threat. The triumph becomes empty ritual, a mere sonic spectacle that transforms the defeated into a victim of the collective.

This feeling of an overbearing order is furthered by the cinematography, which recalls act 3 of Wagner's *Parsifal,* perhaps a visual inspiration for the Nuremberg rallies recorded in Reifenstahl's *Triumph of the Will.* In the Throne Room, soldiers stand in military formation with the tall lines of the Mayan monuments symmetrically framing the background. The grandiose formality of this self-consciously "beautiful" shot is contrasted with the rather more intimate informality of the shot on the platform. The marked contrast between these two shots serves to humanize the "leaders"—Leia especially. Leia's laughs, which are calculated to seem spontaneous, are especially effective in this respect. The musical analog to the humanizing shot is the processional music in D♭ (Williams calls it "Hope and Glory" music), which offers the possibility of a variant rather than a mere thematic iteration. Unlike variation, a thematic variant, Mahler's crucial compositional innovation, never posits a particular thematic statement as the primary, structural one.[38] Instead, through a chain of variants, the theme seems to evolve and expose different facets of its character as the work unfolds, giving the music the feel of a narrative sequence. The tone of the "Hope and Glory" music is in fact very Mahlerian: the ever widening intervals give a better sense of ecstasy and release than the ponderously scored Force theme ever did. Yet even this music ultimately carries no structural weight. Nothing remains of it to alter the thematic process, to give the theme a meaningful history. The "Hope and Glory" music, too, turns out to be inconsequential, as it leads only to a return of the Main Title theme for the end credits, another gesture of recapitulation, a return of what has already occurred. The contrasting middle section of the main theme, which had appeared already in the "Hope and Glory" theme, is treated quite freely in the end credits, giving the whole restatement a quality of openness elsewhere lacking. Yet here again this openness yields not something new but only a return of the title theme, now with the extra measures at the end of the contrasting strain (cf. mm. 35–37 of the Main Title) removed rather than expanded as it might have been. Williams normalizes what is deviant rather than preserving it; he excises the deviation so as to restore the theme to its presumably primal shape.

Hence, nothing actually happens musically in any of these scores. The themes simply remain the same; none of them are really born of a thematic process, despite the obvious motivic relations among the themes.[39] The musical logic throughout Star Wars remains that of an original and its derivatives. Each theme has a characteristic shape and orchestration, and deviations serve not to carve out the possibility of a thematic variant but to communicate semantic content, although that runs counter to the mythic intention. When we hear a polytonal version of, say, the Rebel Fanfare, we know this represents not so much a thematic variant as something gone thematically awry. The polytonal deviation here carries only semantic information. Musically it is an inconsequential variant without import for the original, which we still hear along with the variant as deviation from pure origin.

The lack of substantive thematic work therefore relates back to both origin and the signifying aspect of the leitmotif. Adorno suggests that Wagner's leitmotifs "founder" because the sequential procedure does not permit substantive transformation of the material.[40] The sequence fails as an expositional device because it marks time without pushing the gesture toward something new, toward something other than it is. The music of Star Wars, on the contrary, tends more toward developmental procedures, such as motivic fragmentation, than to sequence. Yet the purpose of the developmental passages in Star Wars is not Durchführung, a leading through to a dialectical synthesis as in sonata form; like Wagner's sequences, if more incoherently, they are a means of marking time.

The development is only apparent. Rather than pushing music forward to something new, development simply agitates, which affects, among other things, the function of modulation in the score. Where the thematic construction of the films is largely diatonic, especially for the themes associated with the Rebellion, and often harmonically rounded as well, the large-scale construction is amorphous: the music nervously flits from one key to another with little sense to the overall progression other than that the theme constantly sound fresh. In other words, Williams does not deploy modulation so much structurally as coloristically: a change of key brightens or darkens the sound, makes the old sound new, or perhaps increases the tension. Harmonically, modulation makes the music sound frenetic; it is constantly on the move, impatient with staying in place. Thus even in his concert suite, Williams shows little concern with large-scale harmonic rounding, and the movements often end in a key other than that in which they began.[41] Lacking a structural function, modulation comes to serve the purpose of pseudo-development, which circles about and agitates without leading anywhere in particular,[42] and it is this frenetic churning in place that substitutes for consequential thematic work in the score.

Both Williams's clear thematic profiles and pseudo-developmental elaborations and Wagner's gestural motifs and sequential expositions thus prove inadequate to enacting a musical process beyond marking musical time as mere duration. Perhaps the fundamental problem lies less in the sequential exposition and concomitant lack of thematic working out (as Adorno suggests); perhaps the problem lies more within the semiotic structure of the leitmotif itself, which requires the recurrence of thematic identity as a condition of semiosis, even when that semiosis is in a state of constant flux, and which can interpret nonidentity only as a deviation for semantic effect. The leitmotif projects the primacy of the original state as an ideal even where it participates in the fluid semiosis of myth: we long for the return of the thematic model, just as Obiwan longs for the return of the natural order of the Old Republic. (That we also long for the return of the strong tonal orientation of the Rebel themes likewise demonstrates the strong naturalizing power of tonality; tonality in this respect is the musical analog to the Old Republic.) Everything seeks to escape the eternal flux of myth and to return home to the semiotic (and tonal) stability of origin. Yet, throughout *Star Wars*, Williams's score associates such semiotic clarity with the Darkside because the linguistic function implies an instrumental rather than mythic invocation of music.

Herein lies the ultimate irony of both the series and its music: restoration of origin entails regression to the Darkside, which is nothing but the recurrence of primal violence: the split between dark and light, sound and music, is the condition of possibility of origin. This split finds exquisite expression in the very opening of the score, as the unpitched triangle—a noise—and the high B♭ tremolo of the violin join to paint the shimmering afterimage of the originary primal moment, which itself combines music (the B♭ chord in the orchestra) with noise (the sound of a cymbal crash). The aura of the opening chord lasts only as long as the union of the tremolo and the triangle: when the violin reattacks its high B♭ at the beginning of the Main Theme (m. 4), the aura has vanished. The music fills this absence with violence, delivering sharp blows through the cross-rhythms. Musically, too, regression to origin can never vanquish the Darkside because the Darkside is always already there at the primal moment that never was.

Notes

1. See Kathryn Kalinak, *Settling the Score: Music and the Classical Hollywood Film* (Madison: University of Wisconsin Press, 1992), 193.

2. Craig L. Byrd, "Interview with John Williams," *Film Score Monthly* 2, no. 1 (January–February 1997), http://www.filmscoremonthly.com/features/williams. html. Accessed 14 January 1999.

3. Roland Barthes, *Mythologies,* trans. and ed. Annette Levers (New York: Hill and Wang, 1972), 124.

4. The five takes of the Main Title available as a supplement on the recent release of the Special Edition CD demonstrates that the opening of the score gave Williams considerable trouble. The first three takes mediate between silence and sound by means of a pickup, each apparently rendered in slightly different fashion. This pickup has the disadvantage of introducing the dominant right at the beginning, which produces the effect of the music coming forth out of the tension of the dominant rather than being created out of nothing as it occurs in the final version. Moreover, the pickup places more emphasis on the tonic, sets it in place, as it were. The effect produced is very unlike the graphic of the title itself, which is on the move from the moment we see it. The fifth take of the theme is interesting, too, for its insubstantiality. Rather than the B♭ chord, we hear only octave B♭s and then the fanfare. The effect is much more creation ex nihilo than the demarcation of timeless space followed by a creation ex nihilo, as in the version opted for in the film. If the pickup in first three takes had made the B♭ chord too specific, the last one lacks any sense of being there at all. Yet the very existence of the fifth take shows that someone was still uncertain that the fourth take had captured the moment musically in the right way.

5. For a theoretical explication of the *mise-en-bande,* see Rick Altman (with McGraw Jones and Sonia Tatroe), "Inventing the Cinema Soundtrack: Hollywood's Multiplane Sound System" in this volume.

6. Rebel Fanfare is the term Michael Matessino uses for the leitmotif that first occurs as the Rebels prepare to be boarded at the opening of *A New Hope* ("A New Hope for Film Music," liner notes to *The Star Wars Trilogy: A New Hope* [Lucasfilm, Ltd. CD 09026–68746–2, 1997], 11). Its distinctive sound, the juxtaposition of major triads a minor third apart, is derived from a cadential figure of the title theme.

7. Kalinak, *Settling the Score,* 193.

8. Carl Dahlhaus, *Nineteenth-Century Music,* trans. J. Bradford Robinson (Berkeley and Los Angeles: University of California Press, 1989).

9. Cf. Justin London, "Leitmotifs and Musical Reference in the Classical Film Score," in this volume.

10. Indeed, Lévi-Strauss has gone so far as to suggest that myth and music share the characteristic "of both being languages"—"forms of expression" might be a better term—"that, in their different ways, transcend articulate expression," that is, language. *The Raw and the Cooked,* trans. John and Doreen Weightman (Chicago: University of Chicago Press, 1983), 15.

11. Theodor W. Adorno, *In Search of Wagner,* trans. Rodney Livingstone (London: Verso, 1989), 125.

12. Theodor W. Adorno and Hanns Eisler, *Composing For the Films* (London, Athlone, 1994), 5.

13. Adorno, *In Search of Wagner,* 36.

14. Adorno and Eisler, *Composing for the Films,* 5.

15. Adorno, *In Search of Wagner,* 46.

16. Ibid., 45; my emphasis.

17. Max Horkheimer and Theodor W. Adorno, *Dialectic of Enlightenment,* trans. John Cumming (New York: Continuum, 1989), iv.

18. Caryl Flinn, *Strains of Utopia: Gender, Nostalgia, and Hollywood Film Music* (Princeton: Princeton University Press, 1992), 108–9.

19. The self-conscious mythic tone of *Star Wars* connects it to the phantasmagoria of Wagner: at the root of its effectiveness is that *Star Wars* makes us believe in "the absolute reality of the unreal" as Paul Bekker once remarked about Wagner's

music dramas. As Adorno so astutely notes, Bekker's remark relates the mythic component of Wagner's music dramas to the commodity form, which wants us to forget the labor invested in producing the commodity. *Star Wars* partakes of this same economy: it wants us to believe, if not in its universe per se, then in the reality of its illusion qua illusion, its myth of entertainment. "Phantasmagoria," Adorno writes, is "the point at which aesthetic appearance becomes a function of the character of the commodity. The absolute reality of the unreal is nothing but the reality of a phenomenon that not only strives unceasingly to spirit away its own origins in human labor, but also, inseparably from this process and in thrall to exchange value, assiduously emphasizes its use value, stressing that this is its authentic reality, that it is 'no imitation'—and all this in order to further the cause of exchange value" (*In Search of Wagner*, 90). The spectacle of sound and images in *Star Wars* is not simply empty and "unreal"; rather, this spectacle receives a kind of false import from the mythic substrate, which suggests that the spectacle is significant, that it contains something authentic, universal, and true beyond its status as a commodity, when in fact this pseudo-authenticity itself is the very thing that furthers its exchange value as a commodity among other commodities.

20. Significantly, the use of the Force theme in the Binary Suns cue was not Williams's idea but Lucas's. Williams had written a different cue, amorphous and moody, darker and more troubled than the one used in the film; this cue utilized neither the Force theme nor any of the leitmotifs of the film, probably because the scene itself lacked a clear motivation for a connection. The music here draws a connection that cuts across the film, revealing a latent connection that could not otherwise be known. Here, Lucas shows himself to be quite sensitive to the mythographical possibilities of music, which in turn suggests that the conflict between effects and music on the soundtrack is probably not accidental. Lucas is someone attuned, not indifferent, to music.

21. Michael Matessino, "John Williams Strikes Back," liner notes to *The Star Wars Trilogy: The Empire Strikes Back* (Lucasfilm, Ltd., CD 09026–68747–2, 1997), 9 and 12.

22. Williams himself is less than forthcoming about revealing the musical procedures that make the march so effective. Speaking about how the march represents Darth Vader, he says, "brass suggests itself because of his military bearing and his authority and his ominous look. That would translate into a strong melody that's military, that grabs you right away, that is, probably simplistically, in a minor mode because he's threatening. You combine these thoughts into this kind of a military, ceremonial march, and we've got something that perhaps will answer the requirement here" (Byrd, "Interview with John Williams"). As the analysis below suggests, Williams's invocation of the minor mode here is something of an interpretive red herring—the Force theme, after all, is also set in the minor. Rather, an interpretive cue needs to be taken from the almost inconspicuous clause that ends the sentence: "because he's threatening." In musical terms, we might ask: How does the march stage a threat to tonal order? It is this that the march captures so uncannily well.

23. Cf. Kalinak, *Settling the Score*, whose analysis of the theme is quite muddled.

24. In this respect, music symbolically links the Darkside to technology, though the Empire fears technology even as it fetishizes it.

25. Kalinak's analysis of the Main Title is like her analysis of the Imperial March, less than adequate. Her claim that the Main Title is a "modified sonata allegro form," for instance, makes little sense (*Settling the Score*, 193).

26. Michael Matessino, "A New Hope for Film Music," 11.

27. This fetishization extends to the music: the Main Title theme overemphasizes the leap to the high B♭, repeating the gesture far too many times so that it comes to seem almost ritualistic.

28. It is perhaps worth pointing out here the way the music strengthens the connection between the snow creature's lair and the cave on Degabah: both scenes share not only a subterranean locale, but both also make use of that technological musical marvel, the synthesizer. The musical effect of the synthesizer in these two scenes is without doubt quite different, but the instrumental connection nevertheless suggests an affinity: both scenes emphasize the way Luke associates the Force directly with the light saber. The use of the synthesizer, a kind of intrusion of the sound effects into the musical portion of the mise-en-bande, serves perhaps to indicate Luke's misappropriation — or at least misapprehension — of the Force.

29. Hal Colebatch, *Return of the Heroes: The Lord of the Rings, Star Wars and Contemporary Culture* (Australian Institute for Public Policy, 1990), 37.

30. Ibid., 11.

31. Ibid., 16.

32. Ibid., 95.

33. Adorno, *In Search of Wagner*, 135.

34. Ibid., 139.

35. Byrd, "Interview with John Williams."

36. The music of the *Star Wars* trilogy is at its most problematic when it turns celebratory, especially at the end of *A New Hope* and *Return of the Jedi*. The changes in the recent rerelease confirm that even the filmmakers found the ending of *Return of the Jedi* flawed. Not that the new ending improves matters much; indeed, in some ways it makes things worse. The lack of tension in this sequence is the peril of all concrete images of utopia: they always seem banal. The new version, with cuts across the Empire replacing the Ewok celebration, evokes the time of Carnival; yet because the general oppression had never really had proper filmic representation, the release depicted in this sequence rings false, seems too broad for the context of the film. In this sense the original ending was better. At least with that ending, the celebration had been confined to the representation; in the revised version, by contrast, everything is universalized, which magnifies the problem of the depicted utopia rather than containing it.

37. This is a loose paraphrase of Adorno's critique of Wagner: "The more triumphantly Wagner's music resounds, the less capable it is of discovering an enemy to subdue within itself; the triumphant cries of the bourgeois victory always drowned out its mendacious claims to have done heroic deeds. It is precisely the absence of any dialectical material on which it could prove itself that condemns Wagnerian totality to mere duration" (*In Search of Wagner*, 51).

38. Theodor W. Adorno, *Mahler: A Musical Physiognomy*, trans. Edmund Jephcott (Chicago: University of Chicago Press, 1992), 86–92.

39. The closest any of the scores comes to thematic transformation is the derivation of the Imperial March from the falling third of the storm trooper music and the Han and Leia theme from Leia's theme (Kalinak, *Settling the Score*, 194, 192).

40. Adorno, *In Search of Wagner*, 37.

41. The Main Title (a cross between the opening and the End Title music from *A New Hope*) moves from B♭ to G; Princess Leia's Theme from D to E; the Throne Room from F minor to G.

42. Even this illusion of development disappears in the later films, which at times suffer from a tedious piling up of themes, one right after another with little development. After the first film, there are also comparatively fewer summarizing statements that are not simply covering shifts of location. Sequences such as the Binary Suns sequence where the film pauses to take breath and reflect, allowing the music to come to the fore on its own, are actually rather rare in the series.

SCOTT D. PAULIN

Richard Wagner and the Fantasy of Cinematic Unity

The Idea of the *Gesamtkunstwerk* in the
History and Theory of Film Music

✳

Every man or woman in charge of the music of a moving picture theatre is, consciously or
unconsciously, a disciple or follower of Richard Wagner.
—W. Stephen Bush, 1911

The most important influence upon Hollywood film scoring . . . was that of late nineteenth-
century operatic and symphonic music, and Wagner was the crest of that influence.[1]
—David Bordwell, 1985

From early prescriptive writings on film-music practice to recent theoretical considerations of the status of music in cinema, the name of Richard Wagner has recurred with a regularity approaching inevitability. His sheer persistence as a figure in the literature has had a tendency to naturalize his position in the genealogy of cinema, making it difficult to assess the true nature and extent of his influence.[2] Wagner is cited as a model (or *the* model) for film-music composers and performers to follow, and concepts such as the *Gesamtkunstwerk, unendliche Melodie,* and the *Leitmotiv* circulate widely, frequently detached from Wagner's name and from his own theoretical treatment of them. Occasionally his influence is decried; more commonly, however, film music practitioners have received criticism for not being Wagnerian enough. In short, Wagner's relevance is taken for granted, but the paths through which his influence was passed down to film are unclear and disparate: Secondary and popular writings? "Common knowledge" about his practices? Live experience of the music dramas? Study of his scores? Close reading of his theoretical writings? In most cases, the rather vague nature of the Wagnerist texts suggests that less rigorous routes were probably most prevalent.[3]

A critical step back is necessary to determine the meaning of this particular species of Wagnerism. My purpose in what follows is not to deny the existence of elements in film and film music that can be described as Wagnerian. Rather, the pertinent question is "Why Wagner?" On one level I ask why Wagner's music was looked to as a model; but more interesting and potentially significant are the metatheoretical questions of why Wagner's name is inescapable and what function the name and notion of "Wagner" serves within the discourses on film and its music. A survey of the literature with these questions in mind reveals not only the ubiquity of Wagner but also the tendency among many theorists to overstate Wagner's influence in a totalizing manner, to misread both his own practices and the work of film composers, and to reify "Wagner" as a coherent, stable sign. The status of "Wagner" here is that of a fetish object, invoked ritualistically as a means of disavowal. Just as in classic psychoanalytic terms the fetish object functions to disavow a lack or absence (to repress the "knowledge" of castration), the fetishization of "Wagner"—the supposed unifier of the arts in *Musikdrama*—works to repress knowledge of the constitutional lack of unity in film, the material heterogeneity of the cinematic apparatus. It is also crucial in the positing of film qua art, papering over the stain of cinema's status as nonauratic, mechanically (re-)produced, low-cultural mass medium. The claim of unity and totality represents more of an ideological neo-Wagnerism than any influence on the level of technique or aural surface. To the extent that film music is or has been Wagnerian, it has largely been as a sort of wish fulfillment.

While leitmotivic technique, "endless melody," and other aspects of the Wagnerian music-dramatic apparatus have had crucial impact on thinking about music in the cinema, this essay is concerned most centrally with the role played by the notion of the *Gesamtkunstwerk* or "total work of art" in film history and theory. After briefly considering Wagner's own treatment of this concept, I shall examine it with respect to film accompaniment of the period from around 1910 (when attempts at codification of silent film accompaniment practice began), through the transition to sound, and into the "classical" period of sound cinema in the 1930s. The focus is principally American, but the work of several European theorists who have engaged either overtly or subliminally with Wagnerism will also be considered. The literature to be analyzed on this period, both practical and theoretical, demonstrates the ongoing tendency to overvalue Wagner, but also illuminates the importance of non- or counter-Wagnerian practices in the dialectical relationship with Wagnerism that has informed film music in theory and execution.

Wagner and the Collaboration of the Arts

Wagner's advocacy of some form of *Gesamtkunstwerk* in his effort to transform opera into *Musikdrama* is relatively constant across his writings from the early 1850s on: from expressing the hope (in *Oper und Drama* in 1851) that "by the collaboration of precisely *our* Music with dramatic Poetry a heretofore undreamt significance not only can, but *must* be given to Drama";[4] to the attempt in (in *Zukunftsmusik* 1860) to imagine an "Art-work in which all the single art-varieties should combine for their own highest completion";[5] all the way through to the 1879 formulation in which Music turns away from potential devolution into "boundless follies" by orienting itself toward Drama, whereby Opera can be redeemed and become the true "Musical Drama." In the latter "we reach sure ground for calmly reckoning the application of Music's new-won faculties to the evolution of noble, inexhaustible artistic forms."[6] If the need to redefine the relationship of the arts within some totality is a recurrent topos in Wagner's writings, however, the solution to the problem cannot be located at a stable point. Just in these brief quotations the change is clear: from an apparently equal "collaboration" between music and poetry in the 1851 passage, to the valorization in 1879 of music's active role in bringing about the transfiguration of opera into music drama.

The trajectory of Wagner's thought on the relations between the arts within a *Gesamtkunstwerk,* and the practical results thereof in his compositional practice, have been well charted; in particular, Jean-Jacques Nattiez has analyzed the gendered metaphors at work in Wagner's theories, with music moving from being a dominated woman to a dominating mistress and a procreative mother.[7] Initially Wagner posited the need for synthesis on an equal level, an integration of music and drama, in which music ought not attempt "of itself to prescribe the aim of Drama."[8] At this stage Wagner was particularly consumed by his reaction against Italian and French operatic styles, in which he saw dramatic integrity as being lamentably subordinated to text-distorting melody and vocal virtuosity (not to mention the required ballet sequences in Paris). His first prescriptive step is therefore to critique the putative abuses of music and demand that it retreat into a more self-effacing role of dramatic collaboration. Purely instrumental music, too, is considered lesser than vocal, texted music.

After encountering Schopenhauer's writings in 1854, however, Wagner gradually shifts the balance in music's favor, including new praise for the value of instrumental music, which for Schopenhauer was the highest art, the sonorous representation of will itself. The goal of integration is now superseded for Wagner by a less rigorous correspondence: music is to maintain an ongoing commentary on the drama but is not so strictly tied to language as proposed earlier in *Oper und Drama*.[9] Further, the poetry set in the operas from this period—the libretti written by Wagner himself— has itself been seen to take on characteristics of musical form, a concentration of linguistic repetition akin to the employment of musical motifs.[10] His use of alliterative verse, or *Stabreim,* also fosters a phonetic musicality. Broadly defined, it is clear both theoretically and perceptually that music's role in the *Musikdrama* was coming to the fore. The power attributed to music continues to grow, until the essay on Beethoven from 1870 asserts that "the union of Music and Poetry must . . . always end in . . . a subordination of the latter," and writings from shortly thereafter explicitly align music with maternal conception, active and creative.[11]

One means of assessing the relative importance of music in a Wagnerian opera is to consider the melodic ideas or leitmotifs and the extent to which they are linked to texts that thereby provide them with associative meanings that are then retained or developed on the motifs' subsequent appearances. In *Oper und Drama* the relationship prescribed is a close one: "A musical motif (*Motiv*) can produce a definite impression on the Feeling, inciting it to a function akin to Thought, only when the emotion uttered in that motif has been definitely conditioned by a definite object, and proclaimed by a definite individual before our very eyes."[12]

Music is given little theoretical freedom in its close bond to words. But by the operas of the *Ring* cycle it is quite common in practice for motifs to enter in the orchestra, not the voice, and in *Parsifal* (Wagner's final music drama and the limit point of the trajectory), only one thematic motif originates vocally, tied to a text; the rest are all introduced in the orchestra, "which develops them symphonically as an equal counterpart to the stage action in virtual independence of the words."[13] Music is at the fore, and is held to express the drama's essence, while any notion of a synthesis among equals has been explicitly repudiated. Even this cursory survey of Wagner's theory and practice reveals the vagueness of the concept of the *Gesamtkunstwerk*. In no way did it represent a coherent strategy, nor could Wagner ever have satisfied its requirements as an abstract concept of total unity. Simply put, it was a goal, the route to which Wagner frequently redefined.

Film: A fantasmatic Gesamtkunstwerk

The appeal of the notion of a Wagnerian *Gesamtkunstwerk* to theorists and makers of film is apparent. Occasionally a film-music historian or critic will note the debt of film music to opera in general, or state as Roy Prendergast does that composers in the early sound period wrote predominantly in the "mid- to late-nineteenth century symphonic idiom as exemplified in the stage works of Wagner, Puccini, Verdi and Strauss. . . . [They] looked . . . to those composers who had, for the most part, solved almost identical problems in their opera."[14] Note Prendergast's appeal to a "symphonic idiom" rather than an operatic one, revealing the knowledge that film music is of a different order than music drama because it mostly involves purely instrumental, nontexted composition; the synthesis desired in film therefore must take a different form than opera's words/music relation.[15] Nevertheless, it is Wagner who is almost always privileged in such discussions (even Prendergast lists him first), presumably because Wagner was known to have theorized about the relation of music to other artistic registers within a *Gesamtkunstwerk*. The latter notion seems to have been interpreted, however, as a rigorously codified principle for unity that had been successfully manifested in Wagner's stage works, rather than an abstract, unattainable goal. Wagner is seen uncritically as he envisioned himself, as the summit of the mutual development of music and drama.

Of course, Wagner ought not to be granted ultimate authority over the possible meanings and uses his ideas could acquire after he introduced them into our cultural vocabulary, any more than his theoretical statements can be taken as dependable keys to his own works. In transferring the concept from music drama to film, some modifications were—and had to be— made. Like opera, film is a heterogeneous form that combines a number of artistic practices. Unlike an opera, however, a film is also a heterogeneous body of material comprising separate shots of photographic footage edited together (after the invention of the splice), to which has usually been added either live musical performance, or (after the transition to sound at the end of the 1920s) a soundtrack including some combination of dialogue, sound effects, and music. The imperative for synthesis is therefore of heightened urgency in the case of film, almost always an art with "multiple authors" and the resultant risk of rupture. As much film theory argues, the spectator must not only sense the coordination of the artistic elements of the work toward a single end, but also must be led to perceive the fragments of film and sound as one continuous whole. Hence the development, for example, of "continuity editing," which renders the cuts and splices of visual material "invisible," and of equivalent techniques in sound editing. As Alan Williams notes in his critique of sound recording practices, "Spectators do not notice 'good' mixing, aural perspective, sound edits, and so on, but they are painfully, physically aware of 'bad' execution of these techniques. . . . 'Good' sound is 'inaudible.'"[16]

In addition to the need to create the impression of internal unity within both the imagetrack and the soundtrack separately, the two tracks must also cohere so as to invite perception as a unified whole. Sound and image must bear some relation of appropriateness or "realness" to each other, which can be extended to include the sort of transcendent or emotional realness often attributed to the use of nondiegetic music (defined as having no source within the "real" world as filmed). The question of what constitutes "appropriateness" in the relation of sound and image will be revisited shortly. At one extreme in the demand for a realistic audio/visual relation is film theorist André Bazin, for whom the foundational myth of cinema, implanted as the goal toward which the form progressed, was "a total and complete representation of reality; . . . a perfect illusion of the outside world in sound, color, and relief."[17] Bazin's idea of a mythical "total cinema" certainly has *Gesamtkunstwerk*-like overtones, but the centrality of realism in his theory—film as proto–virtual reality—tends to efface the artist's active construction of "realistic" representations. In a visually and aurally transparent cinema, a *Gesamtkunstwerk* can scarcely be a *Kunstwerk* at all, but is positioned as the conduit for reality itself as the ultimate and total work of art.

This rather simple idea that the relation of cinematic sound and image need only be one of verisimilitude is implicitly critiqued by later theorists who see a much broader and more laborious cinematic practice through which illusions of unity and reality are perpetrated. The end result of striving for unity in all dimensions has been theorized by Mary Ann Doane as constituting a "fantasmatic body" with which spectators, similarly desiring to see themselves as subjects marked by unity, are encouraged to identify:[18] "At the cinema, the sonorous envelope provided by the theatrical space together with techniques employed in the construction of the soundtrack work to sustain the narcissistic pleasure derived from the image of a certain unity, cohesion and, hence, an identity grounded by the spectator's fantasmatic relation to his/her own body."[19]

The project of film, as carried out in dominant cinematic practice, is thus intimately linked with the maintenance of an illusory, centered subjectivity; the import of this project can be inferred by inverting Doane's analysis to see that a differently organized film practice has the theoretical potential to provide not pleasure but *displeasure* and to promote a *loss* of identity. Michel Chion sums up this line of critical thought, asserting that the "question of the unity of sound and image would have no importance if it didn't turn out, through numerous films and numerous theories, to be the very signifier of the question of human unity, cinematic unity, unity itself."[20]

To be sure, it is a different question entirely whether audiences actually were bothered by nonunified cinematic practices, especially during the early years in which the medium was still defining itself. Both Rick Altman and Tim Anderson have recently suggested that audiences were little concerned with unity. Altman has demonstrated that the assumption that music was omnipresent in silent film projection, that "silent films were never silent," is misfounded, and that there is no evidence from the period that audiences were troubled either by silence, noncontinuous music, or music uncoordinated with the image.[21] Anderson has suggested further that audiences may have often especially appreciated musical accompanists who entered into a sort of ironic dialogue with the images rather than austerely respecting their integrity and meaning.[22] Practices with which neither Wagner's name nor the term *Gesamtkunstwerk* could be associated posed no problem to early mass audiences, for whom cinema was entertainment, not transcendent metaphysical art. While audiences today would surely be more alarmed by a willfully nonunified musical contribution to a film (unless an avant-garde approach was expected), given a cinematic horizon of expectations that has changed vastly since the days of the nickelodeon, this alarm only serves to highlight the effectiveness with which Wagnerism was belatedly imposed, and the lasting impact of the assumptions carried along with it.

Theorists such as Doane and Williams are therefore thinking through a Wagnerian paradigm even if they do not invoke Wagner in their analyses. The anxieties they identify as being at the heart of cinematic practice—and which have usually made producers of film more anxious than consumers—are the same concerns that have encouraged the appeal to the *Gesamtkunstwerk* as a concept transferable from *Musikdrama* to film: the need for unity, totality, continuity, fusion of some form among disparate elements.

The notion of film as a *Gesamtkunstwerk* dates back to the silent era. According to David Bordwell, the Wagnerian model, with which filmmakers including Sergei Eisenstein and the French Impressionists (such as Abel Gance) were sympathetic, allowed an analogy to be made from the relationship between music and drama in opera, to the relationship between cinema (defined as the visual elements and techniques specific to film) and narrative in the motion picture. Thus film's unique expressive possibilities—through montage, framing, and so forth—could "play precisely the role of orchestral accompaniment in Wagnerian opera by extending and intensifying feelings latent in the drama."[23]

Musical accompaniment itself, however, which most often—if not inevitably—would have been present in some form during the projection of any such cinematic *Gesamtkunstwerk*, is assigned no contributive role here in the production of aesthetic effect. This analogy was thus an early step in appropriating Wagner's concept and detaching it from its original context within a consideration of the relationship of music to words and drama on the operatic stage. It also thereby ignores the changes in Wagner's thought on the relationship of music to drama; the theory abstracted by Bordwell seems to imply that such a thing as "the role of orchestral accompaniment" has a static meaning for Wagner. Once the role of music itself in the cinematic *Gesamtkunstwerk* began to be theorized, the relationship to the Wagnerian precedent became even more problematic.

The Perfect Fit: Accompaniment and Appropriateness

"Wagner's theory of a synthesis of the arts is receiving a democratic ratification daily in every movie house throughout the land," according to Charles L. Buchanan, writing in 1926.[24] Presumably more from ignorance than deliberate obfuscation, Buchanan exploits the constitutional vagueness of the *Gesamtkunstwerk* concept. First, the content of the cited "theory" cannot be ascertained beyond the simple notion that the arts should, indeed, be synthesized. Second, as we have seen, the rhetoric of "synthesis" itself is always unclear as to the relative weight to be given to constituent elements, and Wagner gradually left it behind as a keyword as he retheorized the ideal relation between the arts. Buchanan's appeal to Wagner seems intended to confer legitimacy on the developing practice of silent film accompaniment, which by this time was more and more commonly taking the form of detailed original scores to be performed live by keyboardist or orchestra. Here the high-cultural aspirations of film are laid bare. The popular, "democratic" cinema is valorized for its artistic "progress" toward a sort of *Musikdrama*. The original score was one of many developments in the ongoing endeavor to supply each film with an appropriate musical accompaniment, one that "fit" the picture.

This goal had been advocated since roughly 1909 in industry circles. Earlier film accompaniment is generally described as arbitrary and unrelated to the content of the film. Martin Marks has taken issue with this consensus, however, showing that records from an 1895 film presentation in Berlin and an 1897 command screening at Windsor Castle indicate that music, at least on certain occasions, was chosen to fit the films. "Such music was apparently chosen partly for its simplicity, partly for its associative meanings, and partly for its rhythmic characteristics"; each short film was assigned a separate composition.[25] Evidence indicates, however, that this was by no means a universal practice (as Altman has shown, early film accompaniment was marked, more than anything else, by a lack of any universal practice) and by 1909 the need for appropriate music became a polemical topic.[26] An article in *Moving Picture World* from that year criticizes a Chicago pianist who "played a religious selection while an S. & A. rip-roaring farce was being enacted, and (this is fact) in another picture, while the father and son were parting in tears she set forth the strains of 'Don't Take Me Home.' Such work is bad—very bad. In my judgement, managers who do not make their pianist follow the film commit a very serious error."[27]

This desire to make good the perceived lack of unity in the cinematic experience soon spills over into explicit Wagnerism. A 1910 *Moving Picture World* editorial expresses hope that "just as Wagner fitted his music to the emotions, expressed by words in his operas, so in course of time, no doubt, the same thing will be done with regard to the moving picture."[28] In both of these quotations, note the subsidiary role of music: it must "follow the film" or passively be "fitted" to the picture. The evolving and eventually dominant role of music in Wagner's theory is effaced.

The literature from the period contains endless anecdotes about lack of coordination, "musical mishaps [that] began to turn drama and tragedy on the screen into farce and disaster," in the words of Max Winkler, who was consequently motivated to invent the "cue sheet" which contained specific musical recommendations for individual films. Winkler tells, for example, of a film screening in which just as the heroine "exhaled her last breath, to the heart-breaking sobs of her family, [the pianist] began to play the old, frivolous favorite, 'You Made Me What I Am Today.'" When Winkler asked why he had selected the song, the pianist responded, "I thought that was perfectly clear. Wasn't it the king's fault that she killed herself?"[29] In the sharpest satirical critique on the problem to appear in *Moving Picture World*, Louis Reeves Harrison condemned what he called "Jackass Music" and its archetypal practitioner, "Lily Limpwrist": "[W]hen Lily Limpwrist assails our unprotected organs of hearing with her loony repertoire it seems a shame to throw away ten cents on such a performance, to say nothing of the time wasted. . . . [N]o man will ever marry a girl who plays a dance while the pictured man is in a death struggle. . . . The girl of sympathy will play music in accord with the pictured story."[30]

These allegations against the accompanist may seem strangely and excessively gendered, but they should be considered alongside the tendency in Wagner (and other philosophies of music) to mark music as the feminine element. Here bad music is the scatterbrained girl, able neither to endow the "pictured man" with properly ennobled affect nor to serve him self-effacingly; as a result she will remain a spinster, Harrison asserts, never to join in procreative union. In focusing on the inadequacy of the individual musician, Harrison ignores the conditions under which Lily Limpwrist (and her male counterparts) labored, conditions that often mitigated against a musician's sensitive consideration of the relation of music to image or narrative. True, musicians were not necessarily of top caliber; as one step toward a solution, *Moving Picture World* made the somewhat self-evident point that "it is absolutely impossible to accomplish anything with a musician who has no ability."[31] But further, musicians were often on the job for nine to twelve hours a day, resulting in extreme fatigue.[32] While this was eventually alleviated by the introduction of a shift schedule (for instance, at large picture palaces like the Rialto and the Rivoli in New York, solo organ would alternate with full orchestra), this schedule was rigidly managed by the clock, not the logic of the films, and a break in continuity was inevitable when, in the middle of a picture, the orchestra would stop and the solo organ portion would begin.[33] These conditions were often criticized, and new ideas introduced to promote the unity of music and film, but as long as music in the cinema remained a performance medium—whether an on-the-spot improvisation, a score assembled by an individual theater musician, or later cue sheets and scores that were distributed by the studios but revised, ignored, or played selectively on-site—there was no way to ensure a coherent, institutionalized accompaniment practice among theaters with widely varying circumstances.

Parallel or Contrary?

Once it was established in theory that music should join with the film to form some kind of higher unity, a question remained: Exactly what form should the connection between the two take? How far should music go in seeking to relate itself to the images, and should the relationship be one of integration, parallelism, or something else? How much could music be free to add to the total effect? In their 1920 accompaniment manual, Edith Lang and George West argue that "nothing heightens the enjoyment and effect of a film more strongly than a close and minute following of every phase of the photo play, with due regard to musical continuity."[34] Five years later Erno Rapée, in the introduction to his *Encyclopedia of Music for Pictures,* explicitly and enthusiastically Wagnerizes this theme. Rapée's brief history of the union of music and action since 3000 B.C. leads teleologically to Wagner, and thence to film. After the birth of opera at the end of the Renaissance, Rapée leaps over a few centuries: "From this first crude attempt at an operatic performance, to the greatest dramatic Composer of all ages Richard Wagner, is a transitory period which we may neglect because it was Richard Wagner who established the fundamental principles of the music drama of today and it is his work which typifies to the greatest extent and in the minutest detail the accompanying of action with music."[35]

Wagner functions in Rapée's text as both the summation of the tradition and its founder; a duality that perhaps is not far removed from Wagner's own self-image. But to summarize Wagner's compositional technique as Rapée does, as the "accompanying of action with music," "in the minutest detail," is impossible. Wagner's music does not simply "accompany" anything, as we have seen. The slippage from Wagner's conception of a music/drama relation to Rapée's music/action dyad is more than semantic, as "action" is a purely external category and does not encompass the inner, psychological aspect of drama that Wagner saw his music as expressing.[36] Finally, the notion that Wagner's music is representational "in the minutest detail" is a common misreading of leitmotif technique as unambiguously denotative, whereas it can be more revealing to see the Wagnerian *Motiv* ("leitmotif" is a word not used by Wagner himself) as carrying a semiotic excess that resists strict denotation.[37]

The practical function of "Wagner" that emerges in Rapée's misreading of Wagner's theories and compositions is to justify the goal of his own film accompaniment practice: a minutely detailed musical accompaniment of action. Further, invoking the aura of Wagner camouflages Rapée's accompaniment practice as something quite other than what it was. In Wagner, especially when a motif is introduced in the voice, there tends to be the sense that a particular musical idea is uniquely wedded to a dramatic situation, character, object, or theme. The meaning of the motif may be unclear or seem to change across the course of the drama, but it presents itself, even draws attention to itself, as an integral part of the motivic web of a unique, auratic artwork. It could not simply be replaced by another combination of notes without altering the putative *Gesamtkunstwerk* as a whole; obviously, the Valhalla motif cannot be changed from one night's performance of *Das Rheingold* to the next, nor will it be any different in Boston than in Bayreuth.

By contrast, the fit between the cinematic image and Rapée's musical suggestions is far from one-to-one; there is not even an attempt to pretend that a fixed, necessary relationship beyond mere "appropriateness" exists between the coexisting musical and filmic events at this stage in the silent period. For Rapée, any preexisting composition, within a given "type" of music, will unambiguously suit the appropriate filmic situation or personage. For example: "The Villain ordinarily can easily be represented by any Agitato of which there are thousands."[38] Rapée's encyclopedia contains more than five hundred headings, compiling the situations an accompanist might be called on to represent. Some, such as "Cannibal Music," "Honduras," and "Aeroplane," are relatively specific and have only a few suggested pieces from the music library. Others are extremely vague, ranging from

"Happy Content" to "Mysterious"; these have long lists of presumably interchangeable compositions, all "appropriate" according to Rapée for accompaniment of such a scene. The fetishization of Wagner in this context occludes the fact that the musical elements chosen can have no more than a casual relationship to the film; they are not integrally connected as would be the elements of Wagner's ideal *Gesamtkunstwerk*.

Some commentators, however, believed that even a vague parallelism went too far, leading to formlessness and incoherence on a strictly musical level. In 1929, as fully recorded scores were becoming the norm, Harry Potamkin criticized the musical attempt to comment on, interpret, and augment film, arguing that "scoring approaches nonsense in its meticulous following of the action" and that "the notion that every trough and crest in the movie action must be followed or interpreted in the score is juvenile."[39] While earlier accompaniment had been criticized as nonsensical for its lack of concordance with film, Potamkin applies the same term to an overconcordant musical practice. Similarly reversing the conventional terms by which film music had come to be valued, Siegfried Kracauer, writing in 1960, reminisces about the silent cinema he frequented in his youth. As we have seen, industry insiders in the silent era became more and more frustrated with incompetent musicianship that was unsympathetic to the filmic events, but Kracauer remembers with some fondness the perverse pleasure he took in the accompaniment of the "Drunken Pianist":

And whenever he performed, he was so completely immersed in himself that he did not waste a single glance on the screen. His music followed an unpredictable course of its own. . . . This lack of relation between the musical themes and the action they were supposed to sustain seemed very delightful indeed to me, for it made me see the story in a new and unexpected light or, more important, challenged me to lose myself in an uncharted wilderness opened up by allusive shots. Precisely by disregarding the images on the screen, the old pianist caused them to yield many a secret. . . . I never heard more fitting accompaniment.[40]

Anti-parallelist and implicitly anti-Wagnerian, Kracauer theorizes that a photoplay of a basically theatrical nature can acquire cinematic qualities if placed in juxtaposition to music that does not fit it smoothly—a sort of montage effect—enriching rather than destroying the aesthetic experience unique to the medium.[41] This debate would continue well into the sound period, with an excessively representational music (as practiced especially by composers such as Max Steiner and Erich Wolfgang Korngold) being denigrated as "mickey-mousing" for its cartoonish mimicry of the image.

The parallelism question is closely tied to another Wagnerian inheritance alluded to above: the use of forms of leitmotivic techniques in film music. Such procedures are used with the goal of integrating music and image, with motifs being introduced and returning referentially to closely follow or duplicate the action onscreen. Beginning in 1910, *Moving Picture World* featured a regular column by Clarence Sinn titled "Music for the Pictures," which offered advice on film accompaniment, both in general and regarding specific films, and also printed letters from film musicians asking advice or providing hints of their own.[42] In 1911 Sinn enthusiastically embraced Wagner and the leitmotif, recommending Wagner's theoretical writings to his readers and summarizing them (in a diluted—but still totalizing—manner not uncommon to the Wagner reception of the day) as follows:

> Boiled down, it amounts to something like this: To each important character, to each important action, motif, or idea, and to each important object (Siegmund's sword, for example), was attached a suggestive musical theme. Whenever the action brought into prominence any of the characters, motifs, or objects, its theme or motif was sung or played. . . . Such a method of applying music to the pictures is the ideally perfect one, and if it could be universally carried out, would leave nothing to be desired.[43]

Sinn's description of what he called the "leit motif" is an extension of the general goal of fitting music closely to the picture. Any important element of a film will simply have its one-to-one musical analog that should always be played when its referent appears onscreen, and music and image are thereby fused into the desired totality. Notions of parallelism through leitmotivic technique continued into the sound era. Kathryn Kalinak has written of Max Steiner's musical practice in the 1930s that "the leitmotiv served as both a point of identification and as an embodiment of that which it accompanied, delineating important narrative elements such as character or situation."[44] Her assessment may be too generous in positing these desiderata as actually achieved by Steiner (an exaggeration complementing the high Wagnerist ambitions). Nevertheless, the importance of the *Gesamtkunstwerk* behind this technique is clear: a musical symbol gains dramatic weight and advances the narrative as an equal partner in the artwork.

Writing in the early years of sound cinema—and wary of the innovation—theorist Rudolf Arnheim endorsed a form of parallelism but took pains to delineate his meaning carefully. "Both elements conform to each other in such a way as to create the unity of the whole, but their separateness remains evident."[45] This is not the kind of parallelism in which one element mimics or supports the other; each must be a complete structure: "[A] 'double track' will make sense only if the components do not simply convey the same thing. They must complete each other in the sense of dealing differently with the same subject. Each medium must treat the subject in its own way, and the resulting differences must be in accordance with those that exist between the media."[46]

This notion has obvious affinities with Wagner's own of the "Artwork in which all the single art-varieties should combine for their own highest completion,"[47] and with a branch of Wagnerian scholarship typified by Karl Grunsky, who in 1906 defined *Musikdrama* as "a work shaped simultaneously according to a poetic and a musical plan," each a satisfying, comprehensive structure in itself.[48] Arnheim, however, makes a point of parenthetically dismissing Wagner's work, albeit in vague terms: Wagner's work "approaches an equilibrium of music and libretto, but this work is so debatable and so strongly influenced by theory that by itself it does not represent a valid counterargument" to the main tradition of opera, a genre Arnheim finds inadequate to his conditions for artistic unity.[49] Arnheim's theorization of film-music practice (which echoes a frequent critique of "mickey-mousing" in film scoring) zeroes in on the goal of avoiding redundancy: the components should "not simply convey the same thing." This approach is less radical than Kracauer's anti-parallelism, which takes positive pleasure in the nonconsonance of random or nonintentional audio/visual fusion. Arnheim is of course considering sound cinema, in which coincidental or chance events are less likely to occur in the audio/visual relationship, due to centrally managed techniques of sound-track production and mass reproduction. Nonredundancy must now be actively planned.

A critical debate has continued on the relative merits of parallelism versus counterpoint, synchronization versus nonsynchronization, audio/visual consonance versus dissonance, redundancy versus nonredundancy, as the opposition has variously been defined. To a certain extent this is a matter of differently valued semantic terms: critics in favor of a close sound/image relationship tend to valorize the "parallel" whereas those with a contrary viewpoint speak negatively of the same phenomenon in terms of "redundancy." In general, the latter terms in the above binaries are privileged by critics who advocate an oppositional cinematic practice, seeing a pernicious ideological manifestation in the endeavor to construct an illusion of unity and wholeness in which the techniques of production have been made invisible.

A major participant in this tradition is Theodor Adorno, who devoted texts both to film-music composition (in collaboration with composer Hanns Eisler) and to Wagner, drawing connections between the two topics. In the latter study, Adorno is critical of Wagner's impulse to create a *Gesamtkunstwerk*. "The basic idea is that of totality," he writes; "In the *Gesamtkunstwerk*, intoxication, ecstasy, is an inescapable principle of style; a moment of reflection would suffice to shatter its illusion of ideal unity."[50] The drive to totalism in Wagner goes beyond the combination of the arts to a protofascist mythic dimension that hails the audience as a homogenized *Volk,* as what Adorno and Eisler call a "sham collectivity" in their discussion of music's power to intoxicate and barbarize an audience into a false unity.[51]

But the underlying heterogeneity of *Musikdrama,* and by extension of film with its pretenses to *Gesamtkunst* status, is inevitably unveiled. The immense quantity of work that goes into sustaining the illusion of unity and totality is ultimately impossible to conceal, according to Adorno, and by this measure the Wagnerian work "falls to pieces."[52] Music, even if parallel or symbiotically linked to text or drama, still has the potential (frequently actualized in Wagner) to tip the balance severely in its own favor. Text may seem a mere appendage to the music that reinforces it. The sensuous dominance of music within the *Gesamtkunstwerk* can narcotize the audience into accepting the illusion of totality, but alternately, with the distanced "moment of reflection" held out by Adorno, music's foregrounding of its own importance can be seen to reveal the fallacy of unity, to call attention to the constituent arts as parts of a tenuously linked whole.[53]

In the sound film as well, according to Adorno and Eisler, a similar excess occurs. Not that music "takes over" the film as the main object of attention, but—continuing the critique of audio/visual redundancy we have seen above—in linking itself too closely to the image, music becomes an empty supplement that reinforces an already explicit message but adds nothing unique in its own voice. A principal target of this critique is leitmotifs, which "function as trademarks, so to speak, by which persons, emotions, and symbols can instantly be identified" in a parallelist interpretation of both music drama and film music:[54] "Illustrative use of music today results in unfortunate duplication. It is uneconomical." Film music represents a decline from Wagnerian music, which, despite its suspect characteristics, "was actually a means of elucidation" (13). The visual iconicity of representational film, always a problem for Adorno, is seen as rendering the musical illustration extraneous. "Why should one and the same thing be reproduced by two different media? The effect achieved by such repetition would be weaker and not stronger" (66).

For Adorno and Eisler, a potential solution lies in the same direction as Kracauer's valorization of the Drunken Pianist. Rather than trying to erase the heterogeneity of the multimedia artwork, this heterogeneity should be investigated: "The aesthetic divergence of the media is potentially a legitimate means of expression, not a regrettable deficiency that has to be concealed as well as possible" (74). Whether Adorno's proclamations are read as deliberately provocative overstatements or as genuine misapprehensions of the actual practice of "parallelism," they are certainly open to challenge. It is hard to imagine what form a truly "redundant" musical accompaniment would take; in its presence (or absence), music inevitably inflects the visual field in some way. The very use of music conveys a message about film's self-imputed status as *Gesamtkunstwerk*, and plays a role in legitimating it qua art. Music's ability to lull an audience into uncritical emotional involvement in and identification with a film, however ideologically problematic, is an augmenting function that cannot be reduced to a relation of mere redundancy to image and drama. Even "mickey-mousing" carries narrational force as a kind of aural "close-up," drawing attention to a particular event, object, or emotion in the frame that would be perceived differently with other or no music. The musical commentary always constructs (through semiotics of timbre, rhythm, meter, melody, harmony) a reading of the image no matter how "parallel" or "redundant" to the image it may seem. Adorno and Eisler may be on secure ground in encouraging nontraditional audio/visual relations that invite new means of expression and perception, but they underestimate music's intrinsic resistance to being reduced to mere additive superfluity.

Further, this "redundancy," such as it is, may in fact be a structural necessity in the cinema/music relationship. As Rick Altman has written, redundancy is not unproductive; rather, it creates "a functional supplement which invests its excess energy in the masking of cinema's multi-media status," precisely the fetishistic process I am hypothesizing.[55] Sound and image validate—not duplicate—each other, and together disguise the material heterogeneity of the "whole." Sound/image parallelism involves the mutual invisibility of visual "work" and inaudibility of soundtrack "work" in the service of creating a *realist* illusion that is nearer to Bazin's "total cinema" than to the more *mythic* illusion Wagner hoped to achieve.

Yet despite this gap between mimesis and myth, film may indeed be seen as more Wagnerian than anything Wagner himself could have conceived. Film, viewed in this way, represents a radical extension of what Adorno criticizes in the "Phantasmagoria" chapter of *In Search of Wagner:* the aspect he detected in Wagner's music dramas whereby "The product presents itself as self-producing."[56] Adorno and Eisler contest film's tendency toward phantasmagoria, insisting that when writing for the films, "one should not write a single sequence, not even a single note, that overlooks the social-technological prerequisite of the motion picture, namely, its nature as mass production. No motion-picture music should have the same character of uniqueness that is desirable in music intended for live performance."[57] What is really at stake is not just an aesthetically limiting redundancy of sound and image, but the way in which music conventionally hides its own mass-produced, materially heterogeneous character and simultaneously provides a cover for the imagetrack's equivalent constitution. What Adorno and Eisler require of a progressive cinematic practice, by implication, is that the film admit it can never be a *Gesamtkunstwerk*.

The Impossibility of the Cinematic Gesamtkunstwerk

Regardless of this strain of oppositional theorizing on the merits of counterpoint and nonsynchronization of film and music, the main stream of thought within the industry discourse on music for films is represented better by the excerpts from accompaniment manuals cited above. Recall Lang and West's recommendation of "a close and minute following of every phase of the photo play, with due regard to musical continuity." This counsel expresses one of the principal contradictions in film-music practice: the conflict between a close expressive parallel to the onscreen events and the need for a strictly musical continuity that does not admit of constant interruptions and radical shifts in tone. The impossibility of a filmic *Gesamtkunstwerk* can be seen precisely here, in the inability to create music (especially if one is improvising it on the spot) that supports both essential unities: of film and music in mutual relation, and internally within a strictly musical structure.

Wagner himself grappled with this issue. Carolyn Abbate has noted Wagner's rhetorical antithesis between mere "instrumental music . . . all logical, tidy, formal, musically explicable without reference to any text," opposed to "*his* music, semantically generated, musically audacious, and *au fond* inexplicable in purely musical terms."[58] This rhetoric of course represents a particular stage in Wagner's thought, in which music is generally conceptualized as responding to words, not as the expression and even generator of the drama's essence. But this is precisely the stage at which the cinematic use of music overlaps with Wagnerian theory. While theoretical debates have raged about the proper extent of musical synchronization to the film, it has not commonly been suggested outside of certain avant-garde practices that music should be anything other than a supportive, secondary artistic element within film. Despite the similarity in theory between Wagner's text-derived music and music that responds to visual elements and dramatic events in film, almost any film music, considered on a large scale, is more fragmented and less internally continuous than almost any operatic music, certainly more so than Wagner's mature work. Music is never conceived as the driving force behind film drama, but rather as responding to and supporting the narrative. Internal structural continuity of music always cedes importance to the continuity and mutual reinforcement of the music/image relationship. (Exceptions such as the Eisenstein/Prokofiev collaborations, in which scenes were often edited to fit Prokofiev's already composed music, are rare enough to prove the general rule.)[59] Hugo Riesenfeld, resident maestro at New York's Rialto Theater, discussed his practice in 1920:

There are millions of ways . . . of selecting music to serve as accompaniment for a picture, but there are only two ways that a good musician would choose. One is to select beautiful music that is appropriate for the scenes of the pictures, and the good musician, inexperienced in motion picture presentation, would undoubtedly follow this course. The second course, and the one that requires the hardest work, is to select music such as would be chosen in the first mentioned way, but *with an ear to subjugation*. There may be half a hundred waltzes that would go prettily with certain scenes, but the experienced scorer of motion pictures will, after listening to the piece know whether it is too striking—or even too beautiful.[60]

This need for "subjugation" of music is confirmed by Kurt London, the author of the first book-length study of film-music history and theory. For London, "the silent film without music had no right to exist," but the need for music did not mean that it had an actively creative input in the film: "The music cannot therefore develop any given process of thought logically according to its own forms, but must conform to the scenario, which is rolled off on the film without any consideration for the logical thought and form of the music. Music is no longer the mistress, but the servant, in the process."[61]

Here again is the familiar notion that music in the cinema cannot fulfill the traditional formal expectations of "autonomous" music, just as Wagner's composition in opera must depart from convention. But London's final sentence demonstrates a clear opposition to the Wagnerian trajectory, discussed above, which takes music from being a mistress fertilized by the poet to a more powerful maternal role in which it gives birth to drama—a role far from the status of servitude London posits for music in film. Adorno and Eisler, by contrast, critique the tradition of unobtrusive music (now in sound film): "Music thus far has not been treated in accordance with its specific potentialities. It is tolerated as an outsider who is somehow regarded as being indispensable."[62] Curiously, given their general antipathy to Wagner, the authors can be read here as articulating a (late) Wagnerian point of view, as their argument calls for a privileging of the role of music and its unique possibilities within a multimedia artwork. Here they seem simply to join the debate on the proper organization and interrelation of the arts within a *Gesamtkunstwerk,* rather than trying to topple the latter concept as they do elsewhere.

Further problematizing the *Gesamtkunstwerk* theory of film, especially in the silent period, are conditions of local variability and the lack of unitary authorship, both of which have been alluded to above. Surely for Wagner the *Gesamtkunstwerk* is unified in large part because it is a single, unique text; it has been engineered to produce its effect through the joining of drama and music regardless of the specifics of any given production; and it is the product of a single creator. Wagner himself single-handedly originated the most important composite elements—dramatic conception, music, poetry—and determined their relation to each other; eventually he created his own ideal venue for total control over the conditions under which his works would be produced in the Festspielhaus at Bayreuth.

In film, these conditions scarcely hold. Especially in silent film, the reality of practice dictated that an audience's experience of any given film would vary greatly from city to city and possibly even from screening to screening at the same theater. Even once studios regularly distributed cue sheets with films (after 1912), there was no guarantee that theaters would use them; the selections recommended might be too difficult for some musicians, or particular compositions might not be in a theater's music library.[63] And the attempt to distribute full orchestral settings to motion picture exhibitors also was problematic: parts were often lost or damaged; films were damaged or occasionally recut and edited by theaters (sometimes necessitated by local censorship boards), in which case the score no longer could be easily synchronized to the body of the film; and instrumentation in theater orchestras was far from standardized.[64]

As for the emanation of the *Gesamtkunstwerk* from the single, brilliant artist, this is a constitutional impossibility given the division of labor in any industrial film-studio production (auteur theory notwithstanding). In silent film practice the multiplicity of subjective contributions is foregrounded in the work of musical directors at the larger theaters and individual musicians at smaller venues, most of whom frequently violated the recommendations of the studios, whether through need or through believing themselves to have superior ideas about how to accompany a picture. Given the nonidentity of the film/music text in practice, it seems impossible to locate a *Gesamtkunstwerk* in silent film, despite the recurring rhetoric about the increasing sensitivity of music's relation to film. As for sound cinema, while there is but one mass-produced text, uniform wherever it is projected (barring print damage and varying theatrical audiovisual capabilities), the film is still the product of multiple authorship.

Even in the heyday of through-composed film scores of the mid-1930s, when many composers strove to re-create every filmic image and event in their music, their effort was still never more than an independently authored supplement to the images (and further, ultimately subject to directorial approval and the editor's shears).[65] Midcentury film-music critic Lawrence Morton discussed the further division of labor between Hollywood composers and orchestrators in one of his columns for *Hollywood Quarterly:*

In an ideal world every film composer would be a master, and he would have time, energy, and the desire to compose, orchestrate, and conduct his own scores. The artistic purpose of every score would be calculated along with the planning of the film as a whole. But the industry is still a long way from granting music the status of a sovereign art coöperating with other sovereign arts toward the creation of a *gesamtkunstwerk*.[66]

Morton's larger argument is concerned less with condemning the fragmentation of labor than with demanding an upgraded status for the whole sphere of musical production within film. Yet his wish must go ultimately unfulfilled, for the relationship between music and its fellow textual elements in sound film never even approaches theoretical equality, and so much the less does it rise to the privileged position Wagner eventually accorded music within his own idealization of the *Gesamtkunstwerk*. Rather, dominant film-music practice maintained the goal of parallelism tending toward overdetermination of the image, with music symbiotically linked but decidedly undervalued in relation to the picture (although in practice, the affective power of the film score can indeed fulfill its potential to overwhelm image and drama).[67] Like the name of Wagner itself, the concept of the *Gesamtkunstwerk*, whether directly referenced or merely implied by discussions of the relation to be encouraged between the arts, misrepresents the actual practice in film. The notion played a talismanic role in denying the fundamental disunity and imbalance that continued to characterize the field.

The Financial Imperative

It would be a mistake to see the widespread concern about the relation of music to the motion picture as a strictly aesthetic goal of bringing about a Wagnerian *Gesamtkunstwerk*. Film production was motivated largely by capitalistic concerns, and the Wagnerian rhetoric coexists quite comfortably, especially in industry trade papers like *Moving Picture World*, with the unapologetic articulation of economic reasons for innovation in musical practice. In the early silent era, any form of musical performance in a theater seems to have been enough to attract an audience, whether the music accompanied the films or came between them.[68] By 1910, it was seen as financially desirable to fit the music to the film more carefully: "It is in the interests of the moving picture first of all, and then of ourselves in the second place, because our prosperity is bound up in the prosperity of the moving picture."[69] Pilar Morin, herself a silent film actress, contributed an article to *Moving Picture World* in which she fantasized about the vertical integration of musical production into the film industry and the flow of money that would result: "The day will yet come when musicians will write for picture plays, manufacturers will print the music for such films, managers will gladly pay for same, pianists will be engaged to enchant the public, who are so willing to go and hear as well as see that which it craves for, good music in connection with silent picture plays."[70]

The need to attract a paying audience—and increasingly a more sophisticated, middle-class audience ("Better music means better patronage and more of it")[71]—was always behind the film industry's efforts to innovate, in musical matters no less than elsewhere.[72] Wagnerism was, among other things, one artistic justification through which film could hope to gain both prestige and profits, and the principles of the *Gesamtkunstwerk* were valuable for their potential to convince audiences that cinema was both aesthetically worthy and sufficiently entertaining to merit the repeated expenditure for admission tickets.

No less than serving the bottom line of financial profit, the idea of the *Gesamtkunstwerk* could serve to repress the awareness of that goal. Masquerading as an auratic artwork in spite of all signs to the contrary, the cinematic commodity is able to sell itself all the more effectively. False as this polar opposition may be, the closer film can seem to Bayreuth, the further it can seem from the mundane, exploitative world of dollars and cents (though naturally, writers are less coy about the importance of the latter in industry trade papers than in more widely circulating publicity). Appeals to Wagner must be understood as double-edged: a film joined with music to construct a *Gesamtkunstwerk* is made more marketable as high-quality entertainment; at the same time, however, it is allowed to illusionistically transcend its own commodification and nostalgically recapture a lost utopian culture of art for art's sake.[73] Filmmakers, musicians and composers, theorists and critics—all run the risk of participating in this fantasmatic erasure of the commodity when they appropriate Wagner. Only by self-consciously addressing the problematic entanglements of Wagnerist aesthetics with the ideological foundations of film production can sufficient distance be achieved from the Wagnerian myth to suggest why his name and ideas have had such currency throughout film history.

As a seminal figure in the (pre-)history and theory of film and film music, Richard Wagner should not be underestimated. The ecstasy so vividly expressed in Wagner's music reappears in the rapturously enthusiastic prose of film musicians and theorists who looked to him as an inspiration and claimed him as an ancestor since near the birth of cinema. But the fetishistic Wagnerism that developed was constitutionally vague, allowing an appeal to the composer as a master of the music/drama relation, without necessitating a close or doctrinaire understanding of Wagner's ideas and their evolution. Rather, film's agenda in appropriating the ideology of Wagnerism—whether we view its legacy as positive or follow Adorno and Eisler in condemning it—operated according to film's own specific logic and needs. The emblem of the *Gesamtkunstwerk* reinforces the use of Wagner's own name (along with concepts such as the leitmotif) as a talisman set up to ward off the ghoulish threats of film's material heterogeneity, discontinuity, mass production, and mechanical reproduction. The first two of these threats, at least, were issues for Wagner as well; his ideology of unity and totality in the artwork is first and foremost what would go on to constitute cinematic Wagnerism, now raised to an even more intense pitch thanks to the new conditions of artistic (re)production. Wagner's ultimate role in discourse on film and music is akin to that of the magic *Tarnhelm* in his *Ring* operas: draped rhetorically over the products of cinema, the figure of Wagner allows film's illusory transformation into an artwork that has succeeded in fulfilling its wish, achieving its goals of unity and totality.

Notes

1. W. Stephen Bush, "Giving Musical Expression to the Drama," *Moving Picture World* 9, no. 15 (12 August 1911): 354; David Bordwell, "Classical Narration," in *The Classical Hollywood Cinema: Film Style and Mode of Production to 1933*, by David Bordwell, Janet Staiger, and Kristin Thompson (New York: Columbia University Press, 1985), 33.

2. For the recent critical attribution of influence to Wagner, see for example Caryl Flinn, *Strains of Utopia: Gender, Nostalgia, and Hollywood Film Music* (Princeton: Princeton University Press, 1992), especially 13–50; a series of articles by David Huckvale: "Wagner and the Mythology of Film Music," *Wagner* 9, no. 2 (April 1988), "Twins of Evil: An Investigation into the Aesthetics of Film Music," *Popular Music* 9, no. 1 (1990), and "The Composing Machine: Wagner and Popular Culture," in *A Night in at the Opera: Media Representations of Opera*, ed. Jeremy Tambling (London: Libbey, 1994); and Claudia Gorbman, *Unheard Melodies: Narrative Film Music* (Bloomington: Indiana University Press, 1987), esp. 28–29. Charles Merrell Berg, *An Investigation of the Motives for and Realization of Music to Accompany the American Silent Film, 1896–1927* (New York: Arno, 1976) gives a thorough overview of debts to Wagner in silent film accompaniment practice (74–80) while not overstating it in relation to the many other fields of influence he discusses.

3. For an account of the vogue enjoyed by Wagner's music in late nineteenth-century America and the role played by the composer in shaping the period's cultural life, see Joseph Horowitz, *Wagner Nights: An American History* (Berkeley, and Los Angeles: University of California Press, 1994). Fascination with Wagner's work was widespread and doubtless played into his reception in the cinema.

4. Richard Wagner, *Opera and Drama*, in *Richard Wagner's Prose Works*, trans. William Ashton Ellis (London: Kegan Paul, Trench, Trübner, 1893), 2:20; emphasis in original.

5. Richard Wagner, "Zukunftsmusik," in *Richard Wagner's Prose Works*, trans. William Ashton Ellis (London: Kegan Paul, Trench, Trübner, 1894), 3:308.

6. Richard Wagner, "On the Application of Music to the Drama," in *Richard Wagner's Prose Works*, trans. William Ashton Ellis (London: Kegan Paul, Trench, Trübner, 1897), 6:182.

7. See Jean-Jacques Nattiez, "Music and Poetry: The Metamorphoses of Wag-

nerian Androgyny" in *Wagner Androgyne: A Study in Interpretation* (Princeton: Princeton University Press, 1993), 99–178; Carolyn Abbate, "Opera as Symphony, a Wagnerian Myth" in *Analyzing Opera: Verdi and Wagner,* ed. Carolyn Abbate and Roger Parker (Berkeley and Los Angeles: University of California Press, 1989), 92–124; Bryan Magee, "Schopenhauer and Wagner" in *The Philosophy of Schopenhauer* (Oxford: Clarendon Press, 1983), 326–78.

8. Wagner, *Opera and Drama,* 102.

9. Magee, "Schopenhauer and Wagner," 349–50.

10. See Abbate, "Opera as Symphony," esp. 102–3.

11. Richard Wagner, "Beethoven," in *Richard Wagner's Prose Works,* trans. William Ashton Ellis (London: Kegan Paul, Trench, Trübner, 1896), 5:104. On the maternal metaphors in Wagner's texts "On the Destiny of Opera" (1871), and "On Actors and Singers" (1872), see Nattiez, "Music and Poetry," 158–62.

12. Wagner, *Opera and Drama,* 329.

13. Magee, "Schopenhauer and Wagner," 371.

14. Roy M. Prendergast, *Film Music, A Neglected Art: A Critical Study of Music in Films* (New York: Norton, 1977), 39. Prendergast continues to argue for the fundamental similarity of film to opera beyond the simple dramatic concern they share: "If we equate the dialogue in a film to the 'sung words' of opera, we can see that there is little difference between opera and film. Indeed, the recitative of opera, like dialogue in a film, serves to move the plot forward" (40).

15. I am indebted to Carolyn Abbate for this insight.

16. Alan Williams, "Is Sound Recording Like a Language?" *Yale French Studies* 60, no. 1 (1980): 61. Williams argues as well that manipulations of sound are more easily hidden from spectators due to the tendency to hear an aural event as consequent of a visual one, not an independently constructed occurrence (60). This concealment of "work" through self-effacing technology has ideological effects as argued by Jean-Louis Baudry, and should be considered alongside Wagner's innovation of the "invisible orchestra," concealed in a pit during opera performances. See Baudry's "Ideological Effects of the Basic Cinematographic Apparatus" and "The Apparatus: Metapsychological Approaches to the Impression of Reality in Cinema," both reprinted in *Narrative, Apparatus, Ideology: A Film Theory Reader,* ed. Philip Rosen (New York: Columbia University Press, 1986), 286–318.

17. André Bazin, "The Myth of Total Cinema," in *What is Cinema?* ed. and trans. Hugh Gray (Berkeley and Los Angeles: University of California Press, 1967), 20.

18. Mary Ann Doane, "The Voice in the Cinema: The Articulation of Body and Space," *Yale French Studies* 60, no. 1 (1980): 34.

19. Ibid., 45. See also Bordwell, "The Introduction of Sound," in Bordwell et al., *Classical Hollywood Cinema*: "In the technical discourse of Hollywood during the 1930s, the link between sound recording and cinematography rests upon a biological analogy. Combined, camera and microphone resemble a limited but lifelike human body" (301).

20. Michel Chion, *Audio-Vision: Sound on Screen,* ed. and trans. Claudia Gorbman (New York: Columbia University Press, 1994), 97.

21. Rick Altman, "The Silence of the Silents," *Musical Quarterly* 80, no. 4 (1996): 656 and 677–82.

22. Tim Anderson, "Reforming 'Jackass Music': The Problematic Aesthetics of Early American Film Music Accompaniment," *Cinema Journal* 37, no. 1 (1997): 12–15.

23. David Bordwell, "The Musical Analogy," *Yale French Studies* 60, no. 1 (1980): 145.

24. Charles L. Buchanan, "Music and the Movies," *Outlook* (3 November 1926) 308, quoted in Berg, *Investigation,* 75.

25. Martin M. Marks, "Film Music of the Silent Period, 1895–1924" (Ph.D. diss., Harvard University, 1989), 79. For Marks's discussion of the Berlin and Windsor Castle screenings, see 75–82, and on the accompaniment of film in the earliest years of silent film projection, see 70–75.

26. See Altman, "The Silence of the Silents," 671 passim.

27. "Weekly Comments on the Shows: Among the Chicago Theatres," *Moving Picture World* 5, no. 13 (25 September 1909): 412, quoted in Marks, "Film Music," 148–49

28. "The Music and the Picture," *Moving Picture World* 6, no. 15 (16 April 1910): 590.

29. Max Winkler, "The Origin of Film Music," in *Film Music: From Violins to Video*, ed. James L. Limbacher (Metuchen, N.J.: Scarecrow, 1974), 17. Winkler's autobiographical narrative goes on to tell of his invention of the cue sheet, the overwhelming response of the industry to his invention, and the sudden collapse of his career with the coming of sound.

30. Louis Reeves Harrison, "Jackass Music," *Moving Picture World* 8, no. 3 (21 January 1911): 124.

31. Samuel L. Rothapfel, "Music and the Motion Pictures," *Moving Picture World* 6, no. 15 (16 April 1910): 593.

32. Berg, *Investigation*, 39.

33. Gillian B. Anderson, "The Presentation of Silent Films, or, Music as Anaesthesia," *Journal of Musicology* 5, no. 2 (Spring 1987): 266.

34. Edith Lang and George West, *Musical Accompaniment of Moving Pictures* (New York: Arno, 1970), 5. See Kurt London, *Film Music: A Summary of the Characteristic Features of its History, Aesthetics, Technique; and Possible Developments*, trans. Eric S. Bensinger (London: Faber and Faber, 1936), 66–70, for a description of various inventions designed to perfect synchronization between film and music in the silent period, including the music chronometer, the rhythmonome, and the cinepupitre.

35. Erno Rapée, *Encyclopedia of Music for Pictures* (New York: Arno, 1970), 8; punctuation and capitalization as in original. Altman has taken film scholars to task for constantly referring to the same sources for information on accompaniment practice in the period, including the Rapée and Lang/West volumes. I plead guilty to this—available in recent reprints, these are among the most accessible documents on the topic—and acknowledge the need to investigate the extent of Wagneristic rhetoric and ideas in a broader array of contemporary texts on film. See Altman, "The Silence of the Silents," 653.

36. Other polemecists did highlight the possibilities of extending the music/image relation in film to such internal dramatic states. For example, in *Moving Picture World*: "What is needed, then, in order that the silent drama can be made into the non-vocal music drama? . . . Simply that the music should be chosen to harmonize or synchronize with the emotions shown on the moving picture screen" ("The Music and the Picture II," *Moving Picture World* 6, no. 18 [7 May 1910]: 772). However, as Lang and West stress the need for the musician to "above all, learn to read facial expressions" in order to reflect them musically, it seems that the emotions at issue are precisely those that have been already externalized through iconic representation of the face, feelings that have become actions (*Musical Accompaniment*, 5). These are not the kinds of emotions, otherwise inaccessible to the operagoer, that are to be dramatically represented in Wagner's conception of music.

37. The term *Leitmotiv*, or "leading motive," is often attributed to Hans von Wolzogen, who compiled *Leitfäden*, guides containing lists of motifs from Wagner's operas, labeled with the names of characters, objects, or concepts with which he believed them to be fixedly associated; however, the word actually does

not appear in his guides, and had been used by other critics with respect to Wagner—and other composers—as early as 1860. See Thomas S. Grey, *Wagner's Musical Prose: Texts and Contexts* (Cambridge: Cambridge University Press, 1995), 351–22. As Wagner's ideas about the relation of music to words and drama changed, the motif became less easily decipherable. In the later *Ring* operas, the dense concentration and rapid sequence of motifs makes the associations nearly impossible to process; according to Carl Dahlhaus, "the real meaning of the leitmotifs never becomes apparent in the linguistically or scenically determined labels applied to them." Dahlhaus, "The Music" in *Wagner Handbook*, ed. Ulrich Müller and Peter Wapnewski, trans. and ed. John Deathridge (Cambridge, Mass.: Harvard University Press, 1992) 310. See also Magee, "Schopenhauer and Wagner," 354 and 369.

38. Rapée, *Encyclopedia*, 14.

39. Harry Alan Potamkin, "Music and the Movies," *Musical Quarterly* 15, no. 2 (April 1929): 287 and 292.

40. Siegfried Kracauer, *Theory of Film: The Redemption of Physical Reality* (London: Oxford University Press, 1960), 137–38.

41. "In other words, within uncinematic narratives [music's] dramaturgic maladjustment may easily turn out to be a virtue. There it stands a good chance of acquiring a cinematic quality, if it points up not the given story intentions but material phenomena passed over by them. Its merit there consists in neglecting rather than advancing the action. The drunken pianist who performed without looking at the screen was not far wrong after all" (Kracauer, *Theory of Film*, 144).

42. Other columns existed in periodicals including the *Dramatic Mirror*, *Metronome*, and *Melody Magazine* during the period (Berg, *Investigation*, 117–23). The *American Organist* was also the site of extensive discourse on accompaniment practice (G. Anderson, "Presentation," 257 passim).

43. Clarence E. Sinn, "Music for the Pictures," *Moving Picture World* 8, no. 3 (21 January 1911): 135. See also P. C. H. Hummel's letter to Sinn, quoted in Sinn's next column (*Moving Picture World* 8, no. 5 [4 February 1911]: 235), which advocates a much stricter adherence to Wagnerian style in film accompaniment. Sinn, however, saw this as an unworkably complex project: "I still hold that under present conditions the simpler form is the more practical for everyday use." The clarity of Sinn's conclusion shows that, at least initially, his reading of Wagner was less a misunderstanding than a pragmatic and deliberate adoption of certain limited aspects of Wagner.

44. Kathryn Kalinak, "Max Steiner and the Classical Hollywood Score: An Analysis of The Informer," in *Film Music I*, ed. Clifford McCarty (New York: Garland, 1989), 128.

45. Rudolf Arnheim, "A New Laocoön: Artistic Composites and the Talking Film," in *Film as Art* (Berkeley and Los Angeles: University of California Press, 1957), 207.

46. Ibid., 215–16.

47. Wagner, "Zukunftsmusik," 308.

48. Karl Grunsky, "Wagner als Symphoniker," *Richard-Wagner Jahrbuch* (1906): 1:231, quoted and translated in "Wagner, 'On Modulation,' and Tristan," by Carolyn Abbate, *Cambridge Opera Journal* 1, no. 1 (March 1989): 36.

49. Arnheim, " A New Laocoön," 222.

50. Theodor Adorno, *In Search of Wagner*, trans. Rodney Livingstone (London: Verso, 1991), 101 and 104–5

51. Theodor Adorno and Hanns Eisler, *Composing for the Films* (London: Athlone, 1994), 23–24. See also Andreas Huyssen, "Adorno in Reverse: From Hollywood to Richard Wagner," in *After the Great Divide: Modernism, Mass Culture, Postmodernism* (Bloomington: Indiana University Press, 1986), 39–41.

52. "The sound picture without montage would amount to a 'selling out' of Richard Wagner's idea—and his work falls to pieces even its original form" (Adorno and Eisler, *Composing for the Films*, 73).

53. Slavoj Žižek, drawing connections between Wagner and film music in an Adornian fashion, concludes similarly that "Wagner's attempt to synchronize music and poetry was doomed to fail: what we get instead of their organic harmony is a paradoxical double surplus. 'Too much theater' . . . seems to invert continually into 'too much music.'" See Žižek, "'There is no Sexual Relationship': Wagner as a Lacanian," *New German Critique* 69 (Fall 1996): 20. James Buhler and David Neumeyer have argued similarly, that "acting against musical necessity, the leitmotif . . . calls attention to itself and demands to be heard; it refuses to fade into that continuous and largely 'unheard' tapestry of musical unfolding. . . . Once freed of musical imperatives, however, the power of the leitmotif is not easily contained by the film. In fact just as Wagner's leitmotifs sometimes overwhelm the drama, so too the music of a film sometimes overwhelms the image" (Review of Caryl Flinn, *Strains of Utopia*, and Kathryn Kalinak, *Settling the Score, Journal of the American Musicological Society* 47, no. 2 [1994]: 377). One might question whether it is only leitmotifs or music in general that potentially disrupts the balance of the artwork— moments of musical excess can disrupt either film or opera regardless of whether leitmotivic technique is being used. Buhler and Neumeyer's privileging of the leitmotif betrays a continued reliance on a Wagnerian framework for understanding music in film.

54. Adorno and Eisler, *Composing for the Films*, 4.

55. Rick Altman, "Moving Lips: Cinema as Ventriloquism," *Yale French Studies* 60, no. 1 (1980), 76.

56. Adorno, *In Search of Wagner*, 85.

57. Adorno and Eisler, *Composing for the Films*, 128.

58. Abbate, "Opera as Symphony," 100; emphasis in original. The question of "continuity" must be considered alongside Wagner's technique of *unendliche Melodie,* a term occasionally brought up with regard to film music, if less frequently than *Gesamtkunstwerk* or leitmotif. Some film scores are practically through-composed but most are marked by discontinuity, exploring expressive effects in a syntactically free manner without having to fit into a unified musical structure; see Royal S. Brown, *Overtones and Undertones: Reading Film Music* (Berkeley and Los Angeles: University of California Press, 1994), 97. Continuity may be lent by music bridging an edit from one scene to another, and the soundtrack as a whole maintains continuity by a careful mixing of unobtrusive or dramatically motivated musical exits and entrances; nevertheless, a Wagnerian analogy is impossible to sustain, crediting film music with a coherence that is in fact antithetical to its conventional construction and to the role it is usually called on to play.

59. See Sergei Eisenstein, *Film Sense* (Cleveland: Meridian Books, 1957). "We turn now . . . to concrete methods of constructing relations between music and picture. These methods will not vary basically no matter how varying the circumstances: it makes no difference whether the composer writes music for the 'general idea' of the sequence, or for a rough or final cutting of the sequence; or, if procedure has been organized in an opposite direction, with the director building the visual cutting to music that has already been written and recorded on soundtrack. I should like to point out that in *Alexander Nevsky* [with music by Prokofiev] literally all these possible approaches were employed. There are sequences in which the shots were cut to a previously recorded music-track. There are sequences for which the entire piece of music was written to a final cutting of the picture. There are sequences that contain both approaches" (158).

60. T. Scott Buhrman, "Photoplays DeLuxe," *American Organist* 3, no. 5 (1920), quoted in G. Anderson, "Presentation," 271; emphasis added. Compare to this Claudia Gorbman's well-known discussion of the inaudibility often required of film music in her *Unheard Melodies,* esp. 76–79. Of course this is only one side of the picture—as Gorbman also acknowledges—and if film music were uniformly meant not to be heard, we would never understand Sam Goldwyn's exhortation: "Write music like Wagner, only louder" (quoted in Bordwell et al. *Classical Hollywood Cinema,* 34).

61. London, 37, and 52. Predating London's book by a year, Leonid Sabaneev's *Music for the Films: A Handbook for Composers and Conductors,* trans. S. W. Pring (London: Pitman, 1935) is primarily a practical manual for composers with occasional historical/theoretical passages.

62. Adorno and Eisler, *Composing for the Films,* 9.

63. Berg, *Investigation,* 124.

64. Ibid., 156–158.

65. For one such notorious case, see Kathryn Kalinak, "The Text of Music: A Study of *The Magnificent Ambersons,*" *Cinema Journal* 27, no. 4 (Summer 1988): 46–63.

66. Lawrence Morton, "Film Music of the Quarter," *Hollywood Quarterly* 5, no. 3 (Spring 1951): 288.

67. See Chion, *Audio-Vision,* 146, and Flinn, *Strains of Utopia,* 34.

68. Berg, *Investigation,* 239. On the likely prevalence of an "alternating" model between film and music in early theaters, see Altman, "The Silence of the Silents," 672–80.

69. "The Music and the Picture," 590.

70. Pilar Morin, "Silent Drama Music," *Moving Picture World* 6, no. 17 (30 April, 1910): 676. One of Morin's roles was as Carmen in a silent Edison adaptation of the opera. On Morin, see Marks, "Film Music," 153.

71. Harrison, "Jackass Music," 125.

72. See Berg, *Investigation,* 250–51: "As the film business shifted from an essentially working-class medium to a medium of entertainment for all the people and from the nickelodeon to the picture palace, music was instrumental in winning patrons from the middle and upper classes."

73. On Hollywood film music's perennial romantic engagement with utopic nostalgia, see Flinn, *Strains of Utopia.* Her analysis of the institutional circumstances of Hollywood film music production also arrives at a critical perspective on the meaning of Wagner to the film industry.

JUSTIN LONDON

Leitmotifs and Musical Reference
in the Classical Film Score

✴

It is often said that certain portions of the musical soundtrack of a film "refer" to characters or actions that may (or may not) be present on the imagetrack. That is, particular melodic and/or harmonic figures serve as sonic tokens for persons, objects, and/or ideas that have a significant role in the film's narrative. In standard and recent literature on film music, these tokens are called *leitmotifs* after Richard Wagner's elaborate use of a similar system of musical tokens in his operas.[1]

Indeed, although the view has its critics, the use of leitmotifs in filmic contexts is generally regarded as a stylistic continuation of Wagner's musical practice, one that links the musical techniques of late nineteenth-century Germany and the "classic film score." But how exactly do these leitmotifs refer? How do we sort out those themes that refer to specific characters or places in a film from music whose function is to provide continuity from scene to scene, or to underscore the events and emotions that occur in a given scene? Gorbman asks these very questions about the main title cue for *All About Eve* (see example 1): "Does this melody, first heard over the credits, and subsequently at most emotional moments when Eve (Anne Baxter) appears, signify Eve herself, or Eve's emotional impact on her 'audiences' (the characters and film viewers she manipulates), or is it simply a signature for the film *All About Eve?*"[2]

A foray into the philosophy of language on the nature of proper names will help us to sort out Gorbman's questions. Specifically, a consideration of the way that proper names function in language can provide a model for the referential function of musical leitmotifs. We also find that both proper names and musical leitmotifs have similar morphological constraints based upon their analogous referential functions. Taking note of these constraints allows for a more finely nuanced analysis of the usage and significance of

Example 1. Max Steiner, *All About Eve* (1950), main title cue.

musical themes in the classical film score. This essay concludes with an expansion of Gorbman's analysis of Max Steiner's score to *Mildred Pierce,* in which the relationship(s) between the referential uses and transformations of its leitmotifs are explained in terms of their particular rhythmic, melodic, and tonal properties.

Proper Names in Language and Leitmotifs in Music

In *Naming and Necessity,* Saul Kripke gives a critique of what had been the standard model for proper names.[3] Earlier philosophers, such as John Stuart Mill, treated names as "pointers" to things that designate their referents by ostension; proper names "denote but do not connote." This early model was superseded by the work of Gottlob Frege and Bertrand Russell. In the Frege–Russell model, names both denote and connote. That is, names function as abbreviated descriptions of their referents, for (as the argument goes) without such knowledge how can one make the connection between a name and the unique object to which it refers? Kripke dissects this view and shows how such abbreviated descriptions are highly problematic, especially when we consider counterfactual claims about a person or thing picked out by a proper name. As an alternative, he reinvigorates the Millian view of names with his notion of "rigid designators." The key to their "rigidity" is that the denotation of a name may remain fixed even when its "target" may change; to cite Kripke's example (40–49), "Richard Nixon" still refers to the same person even if we imagine a possible world in which he was not elected president. Thus, even though proper names are able to designate objects in the world, they are not yoked to any specific property or set of properties that their referents may have; in this sense proper names are said to be semantically empty or meaningless.

The idea that proper names are meaningless may seem counterintuitive, but consider the following example. Suppose you overhear the name "J. S. Brown" in a conversation. What can you do with this name? You know nothing about that person (other than that such a person exists); you don't know anything that would allow you to pick that person out of a lineup. Indeed, given the "J. S." as "first name" you cannot even give the sex of its bearer. Nonetheless, you could use that name in a linguistically proper fashion (that is, in grammatically well-formed sentences) and when you engaged in such usage it would be correct to say that you used "J. S. Brown" to refer to a person whom you knew very little else about. This is the main point made by K. S. Donnellan, namely, that it is possible to use names referentially even if you don't have the "descriptive backing" that Frege, Russell, and others claim is required of correct proper name use.[4] Similarly, as D. J. Allerton has pointed out, most proper names (save for the names of historically important persons) do not appear in dictionaries in the way that all of the other words used in ordinary language do; proper names are not defined in the same way as other members of the linguistic lexicon.[5]

The fact that proper names are semantically empty has important implications for reference in musical contexts. If there are linguistic structures that are semantically empty but are nonetheless able to refer, then semantic content is not a general requirement of reference. Thus, even though music lacks a semantic component, this lack does not rule out the possibility of musical reference. If rigid designation is good enough for proper names, then it is good enough for music.

The next step is to isolate those musical structures that can function as rigid designators from those musical structures that cannot, and again a consideration of the morphological and sociolinguistic properties of proper names will be useful. The connection between a proper name and its referent is not obvious; rather, one has to be told the proper name of a person, place, or thing (by way of introductions, for example). Furthermore, people and things get their proper names as the result of some act by a speaker or group of speakers in some linguistic community who are entitled, under certain conditions, to give proper names. As Kripke notes: "An initial 'baptism' takes place. Here the object may be named by ostension, or the reference of the name may be fixed by a description."[6] Subsequent to this baptism we pick up proper names through conventions of usage; we hear proper names used in coordination with the presentation or description of a person, place, or thing, and so we acquire knowledge of both the proper name and its referent.

In filmic contexts the introduction of musical leitmotifs is highly conventionalized. Usually this introduction involves the simultaneous presentation of the character and his or her leitmotif, especially when we are given a striking presentation of both early on in the film.[7] The conventions of opening title cues can also serve to fix the reference of a leitmotif. Main title cues were often cast in a two-part form. The opening "A" theme was associated with the title of the film. It may or may not refer to a specific character (that is, a male lead) or setting; it may simply signify the genre and tone of the picture.[8] However, the "B" theme, typically with reduced orchestration, dynamics, and more lyrical in character, is often associated with the female lead. The binary design of opening title music was well enough established so that audiences would be able to pick out these leit-motifs from the opening credits (and, of course, the stars' billing would tell them who to look for in their respective roles).[9]

Once the link is made between a linguistic name or musical leitmotif and its referent, a number of functional constraints apply to both sides of the semiotic equation. First, a name/leitmotif must be distinctive in its sound-shape, but no more so than is necessary: overlong and/or complex names and leitmotifs present a number of problems in both linguistic and cine-matic contexts. Because names are constituents of longer sentences they are usually brief, and they are morphologically distinctive. Indeed, there is a convention in language that one should not use a proper name in those in-stances where a longer, more discursive description of its referent is called for, and vice versa. That is (assuming we both know the referent of a proper name), if you are asked, "Who just called on the phone?" you would answer with a proper name such as "John Smith" and not "The man who is 5'7" tall who lives over on Elm Street and who drives a green Buick." Such an answer, while true, is inappropriate, as one of the reasons we have proper names is to avoid always having to use such long-winded descrip-tions in order to identify things in the world around us.[10]

Similarly, leitmotifs must be musically distinctive figures that themselves are not too discursive. In filmic contexts they must be quick enough to co-ordinate smoothly with the imagetrack and dialogue; it would not do to have a leitmotif/theme that takes five to ten seconds (or longer) to unfold.[11] Leitmotifs must also be musically distinctive; a rhythmically undifferen-tiated scale or arpeggio is less readily grasped as a significant musical figure than one with a distinct melodic and rhythmic profile. Thus, stock musical gestures, from cadences and generic chord progressions to stingers and se-quences that mickey-mouse the onscreen action, are to be avoided.

Another constraint on the sound-shapes of names and leitmotifs is that they must be reasonably stable so that every time they are uttered or per-formed they remain recognizable tokens of their name/leitmotif type(s). In musical contexts this means that while a leitmotif may be varied in a number of parameters such as orchestration, dynamics, accompanimental texture, and some small melodic or rhythmic variation (especially tempo), one can-not radically alter the basic shape of the musical leitmotif without risk of losing its designative function. In this sense musical leitmotifs might seem more variable than proper names, and perhaps they are in that the mood and character of a leitmotif can change so dramatically through variations in key (major versus minor), tempo, and orchestration—one can have seemingly antonymic presentations of the "same" leitmotif. But language is also quite variable in its phonological form, as a name can be spoken, whispered, screamed, or even sung, and still retain its linguistic identity. Thus, the primary parameters of music (melody, harmony, and rhythm) are like the categorical features of linguistic phonemes, and the secondary parameters of music (timbre, texture, orchestration, and dynamics) are akin to the paralinguistic features of language (intonation, dynamics, and pitch).

Leitmotifs and Musical Expression

Thus far, I have argued that leitmotifs can refer in a manner analogous to proper names in language: through broadly known conventions of usage, a particular musical fragment comes to be associated with a particular place, object, or (most often) character. The designative properties of musical leitmotifs explains how they can fulfill the narrative cueing functions such as giving point of view, indicating formal demarcations, and establishing setting and characters in the manner that Gorbman describes under her "'Principles of Composition, Mixing, and Editing' for Classical Film Music."[12] In fulfilling these cueing functions a musical leitmotif refers by putatively heralding the presence of a character, object, or locale; musical leitmotifs are always in the present indicative (that is, as if saying, "X is here"). Although the present indicative is the only tense/mood that a leitmotif can take, it is a very useful and powerful one in narrative-dramatic contexts. As such, a leitmotif can (1) underscore the obvious presence of a character, place, and so forth that is clearly visible on screen; (2) indicate the presence of someone/something that is otherwise obscure (out of the frame, hidden in the scene, in disguise, and so forth); and (3) indicate the "psychological presence" of a character or idea, as when character A is contemplating the absent character B—we see A while hearing B's leitmotif.

These uses of leitmotifs are doubtless familiar to moviegoers; my point here is not to belabor the obvious, but rather to note that these various functions are based upon the same referential capacity as a proper name. What is also familiar to most listeners is that musical leitmotifs, unlike proper names in language, do more than simply designate; they also contain an expressive content that is entwined with its musical structure.[13] Music has the capacity for signifying or expressing emotion; we routinely characterize musical passages as "heroic," "longing," "tender," "melancholy," and so forth, even in contexts of absolute music (for example, the opening of Beethoven's Fifth Symphony is "tempestuous"). Leitmotifs, as musical shapes embedded in larger musical contexts, are similarly expressive. They couple a capacity to refer with a sense of emotional expression. This is a powerful combination that allows the soundtrack to "comment" on the dramatic action of a film in the following way. First, it is established by extramusical cues that a certain motive is a referent to X. This same motive also has various expressive properties. Next, since the motive refers to X, and has certain properties, we are justified in believing that the composer thought that it was/is appropriate to associate those properties with X. In other words, there is a meaningful connection between X and its leitmotif. As a result, a leitmotif is both a reference to, as well as a statement about, X: "X is happy" or "X is melancholy." Finally, in some sense, because the musical shape of the leitmotif has to remain constant (to be intelligible, presentations of the motive must be recognizable designators of X), every presentation of the motive is a statement, a reassertion of some property of X. This is so even if X appears in different dramatic contexts. As a result, we may infer that X's leitmotif may state certain essential, unchanging aspects about X. In other cases, it is possible (through reorchestration, changes from major to minor and vice versa, and so forth) to retain a recognizable shape of the leitmotif (and hence continuity of reference) while altering its expressive properties. This allows for multiple statements about X; thus X's leitmotif can serve as a cue to character development and transformation.

Leitmotifs in Mildred Pierce

To conclude this essay I give a sympathetic critique of Gorbman's analysis of the score for Steiner's *Mildred Pierce*. First, Gorbman claims that the score to *Mildred Pierce* has the five major themes shown in examples 2–6.[14] Not all of these count as leitmotifs; that is, as leitmotifs with clear referential properties. Recall that in order to function as a name or a leitmotif the linguistic or musical figure should be both relatively compact and relatively distinct. Three of Gorbman's five themes are long-winded and/or musically generic. "Bert's theme" (example 3) consists of very common melodic material, a simple oscillation between two adjacent notes of the scale given in a common $\frac{6}{8}$ meter. Similarly, the "Mildred's Restaurant" theme (example 5), although melodically somewhat more distinctive, is again rhythmically undistinguished. Indeed, both of these themes sound like material that might readily be used for continuity cues. The "Monte and Mildred" theme is a bit better, as it has a distinctive shape, but it is long-winded as a result of the whole notes in the first and third measures combined with its relatively slow tempo; to recognize this theme one needs its entire presentation (which takes about six seconds). Though themes 3, 5, and 6 do not function very well in terms of musical reference, I hasten to add that they can and do serve quite well in terms of their connotative cueing as a result of their expressive properties.[15]

In contrast to examples 3, 5, and 6, examples 2 ("Mildred's Theme") and 4 ("Veda's Theme") are leitmotifs.[16] Not only is each theme-as-a-whole musically distinctive; the opening measures of each are also musically distinctive. That is, each theme opens with a characteristic melodic and rhythmic shape, and it is these opening shapes that function as referential leitmotifs for the two principal characters in the melodrama (the leitmotifs are marked with brackets in each of the two examples). Indeed, Gorbman notes that the opening measures of each of these themes are often used rather than the entire theme itself (93 and 97). This is a common stratagem in presentations of leitmotifs in both musical contexts (for example, Berlioz's *Symphonie Fantastique,* whose long-winded idée fixe is usually presented only in part) and in filmic contexts (for example, Korngold's score to *Captain Blood*). In my own tally of significant entrances of Mildred's leitmotif, the full (four-measure) theme appears only six times out of twenty-seven occurrences, two of which are the opening and closing credits.[17]

Example 2. Max Steiner, *Mildred Pierce* (1945), Mildred's theme.

Example 3. Bert's theme.

Example 4. Veda's theme.

Example 5. Restaurant theme.

Example 6. Monte and Mildred.

Thus, we may establish a rule of thumb for distinguishing referential from nonreferential themes in a score: a referential theme must have a short, distinctive opening that can readily and efficiently serve as a leitmotif, and it is the leitmotif that functions as the musical analog of the proper name. The clearest cases of musical reference, then, are precisely those in which only a portion of the original theme appears. Long-winded themes, which may be appropriate for underscoring an entire shot or scene, or for providing continuity between scenes, are far less apt for use as leitmotifs.

Gorbman claims that what I have labeled "Veda's Theme" (example 4) belongs to both daughters. She is aware of the referential problems of having a single theme for these two characters, as "each daughter is not only strongly differentiated, but is virtually the opposite of the other in terms of values in the mother-daughter constellation that the film assigns to them. In melodramatic terms, Kay is the good daughter and Veda the evil one. How, then, can the score use one theme for the two of them?" (94). Gorbman answers her questions pragmatically: example 4 first serves to refer to both children, but after Kay's death belongs solely to Veda, a sort of musical legacy, perhaps. However, I would argue (as my label for the theme implies) that, although we may initially think this motif refers to the children, over the course of the film we come to learn that it really only refers to Veda. Indeed, an oft-discussed scenario in the philosophical literature on proper names involves cases where one has misidentified the referent to a proper name, or a proper name has two referents (or two proper names have a common referent, and so forth). In such cases a distinction is made between what the name strictly refers to versus how a name may be used (co-opted by a speaker) in certain contexts. This is the essence of synecdoche; the proper designation of a name is stretched to encompass a broader range of reference.

Prior to the death of Kay we hear Veda's theme when both children are present, as well as when Veda is present without Kay; we do not hear it to underscore an appearance of Kay because Kay almost never appears without Veda. The imagetrack thus never gave Steiner an opportunity to provide Kay with a theme of her own. After Kay's death there is one point in the narrative when she is mentioned, the scene in the restaurant when Monte asks about Mildred's other daughter and Mildred answers that "she died." At this most telling point we do not hear a minor version of example 4, but rather Mildred's own leitmotif in muted strings. Consider also that the central narrative thread of the film is the interaction between Veda and Mildred. From the very beginning Veda gets the lion's share of Mildred's money and attention. Even at Kay's melodramatic death, when this theme is heard in minor, I would argue that its referential target is Veda, and not

Kay, as the culmination of the death scene is Mildred swearing to pour all of her love and effort toward Veda's safety and happiness; Kay's death isn't so much about Kay as it is a reaffirmation of Mildred's commitment to Veda. What we ultimately realize is that Kay has no theme of her own, a telling lack of musical underscoring that further indicates her marginal role in the narrative.

Mildred's and Veda's leitmotifs both have other interesting properties that have implications for the various guises in which they can and cannot appear. Mildred's theme starts on the tonic note of the scale, it then moves down to the leading tone (which may be lowered a half-step in minor) and then quickly skips down to the dominant, the fifth note of the scale. As a result Mildred's motif has a very clear tonal identity (that is, it makes plain what note is the keynote: D♭ in example 2). The harmonic mood of the leitmotif may change, but its tonal identity of theme remains the same. Veda's motif is harmonically quite the opposite. In Gorbman's transcription her theme begins on the mediant C, the third note of the A♭ major scale, and then climbs up to the dominant E♭ on the downbeat of the second measure. These same notes could be laid into a C minor context (starting on the tonic of the C minor scale and then moving up to the mediant). Alternatively these same notes could be put into an F minor context, with the opening Cs serving as the dominant note of that scale, moving up to the seventh scale degree of the minor scale (and indeed, this is how the major-to-minor transformation is achieved in the "dress scene" where Veda exclaims that she "wouldn't be caught dead in this rag"). One cannot resist commenting how the tonal stability or instability of each of these two themes is analogous to the constancy and steadfastness (or lack thereof) of the characters to which they respectively refer.

It is when musical leitmotifs are used to indicate narrative cues that we have the clearest sense of musical reference. Gorbman has noted a number of overt cases of narrative cueing in *Mildred Pierce*: Veda's theme is used when Monte and Mildred discuss Monte's relationship with Veda (here Veda's leitmotif refers to the character who is absent from the scene) (96); Veda's leitmotif is also used at the climax of the movie when Mildred discovers Monte embracing her daughter: though Veda's face is hidden in shadow at the beginning of the shot, the music telegraphs her identity—not that there was any doubt! (97). Mildred's leitmotif is also used for straightforward narrative cueing; for example, it is heard at the beginning of the movie when a dying Monte utters "Mildred."

There are some less obvious (though I would not go so far as to say "subtle") instances of narrative cueing as well. First, there are a few instances when we do not hear Mildred's leitmotif even though we would (by filmic convention) expect it to appear. One such instance is when Ida and Mildred exchange names at the end of the scene where Mildred is hired as a waitress. One might have expected to hear Mildred's theme immediately after this statement, but Joan Crawford's utterance of "Mildred Pierce" ends the scene; thus the demand for narrative cueing to frame the next scene outweighs the need to have musical emphasis to Mildred's answer to Ida's question. Another plausible reason for this is that the absence of nondiegetic music gives emphasis to this moment of dialogue.

Yet another reason may be to underscore the fact that at this point, when Mildred "was dead broke" she was also very much alone, without the support of her husband and marriage—in other words, she is no longer Mrs. Pierce in the usual sense of the name. Similarly, when Mildred and Monte break up, Mildred's theme is also absent. Instead we get a generic cue for musical tension, rather than an anguished presentation of the first three notes of Mildred's theme as we might expect. This is, of course, the other moment in the narrative when Mildred is alone; though she is no longer Monte's lover (and no longer in love with Monte, as the dialogue makes clear), she is not quite Mrs. Mildred Pierce again either.[18]

A big question in any narrative is, Who's who? What is the essential identity of each character? In this particular case, who is Joan Crawford's character? Throughout this melodrama the music answers this question again and again that she is Mildred Pierce, that is, Mrs. Bert Pierce—and, of course, in the end that is who she turns out to be (in a classic Hollywood instantiation of *das ewige Weibliche*) as she and Bert walk off into the sunrise under the closing credits. First, it is worth noting that the event which gave her the proper name "Mildred Pierce" was her marriage to Bert; we never know her maiden name. Throughout the film, the leitmotif reiterates this name (and note the none-too-subtle musical emphasis on PIERCE). Perhaps the most telling case of Piercean musical reference comes at the very end of the melodrama, when Mildred breaks under the pressure of police interrogation. Throughout this climactic scene (both before and after Veda makes her entrance), the detective continually refers to Mildred as "Mrs. Beragon," and at each instance the music counters with "Mildred PIERCE," telling the audience (who can hear the nondiegetic music) that the true identity of Mildred is that of wife (of Bert) and mother; the music gets it right even when the detectives get it wrong (though perhaps not; it seems clear they see through Mildred's ruse of trying to take the fall for the crime as motivated by a mother's instinct to protect her children). Though her legal name changed over the course of the melodrama, her musical name did not.

In a gloss on Kripke, D. Ackerman has noted that one way in which proper names are said to designate rigidly is that proper names in some way point to (but do not themselves describe) essential properties of their referent.[19] In Steiner's score Mildred's leitmotif seems to do just that. Its musical shape allows for a number of tonal and orchestral presentations that show temporary changes in her character (from the determined Mildred who bakes pies, to the mother mourning the loss of Kay, to the successful businesswoman, and so forth), all the while maintaining its underlying musical essence—a gestic, rhythmically halting shape appropriate for the tragic heroine of a Hollywood melodrama.

Notes

1. Claudia Gorbman, *Unheard Melodies: Narrative Film Music* (Bloomington: Indiana University Press, 1987); Kathryn Kalinak, *Settling the Score: Music and the Classic Hollywood Film* (Madison: University of Wisconsin Press, 1992); Roy Prendergast, *Film Music: A Neglected Art*, 2d ed. (New York: Norton, 1992). The terms *leitmotiv, leitmotive,* and *leitmotif* are used interchangeably (for example, Gorbman uses *leitmotif,* while Kalinak uses *leitmotiv*).

2. Gorbman, *Unheard Melodies,* 29

3. Saul Kripke, *Naming and Necessity,* 2d ed. (Cambridge, Mass.: Harvard University Press, 1980).

4. K. S. Donnellan, "Proper Names and Identifying Descriptions," in *Semantics of Natural Language,* ed. G. Harman and D. Davidson (Dordrecht-Holland: D. Reidel, 1972), 356–79.

5. D. J. Allerton, "The Linguistic and Sociolinguistic Status of Proper Names," *Journal of Pragmatics* 11 (1987): 61–92.

6. Kripke, *Naming and Necessity,* 96.

7. See Prendergast, *Film Music,* 40–41; and Kalinak, *Settling the Score,* 125.

8. Gorbman, *Unheard Melodies,* 82.

9. I am grateful for David Neumeyer for pointing out the conventions of main title cues to me.

10. J. E. Searle, "Proper Names," *Mind* 67 (1958): 171–72.

11. Royal S. Brown, *Overtones and Undertones: Reading Film Music* (Berkeley and Los Angeles: University of California Press, 1994), 39–40.

12. Ibid., 73.

13. This perhaps goes too far in giving a "purely Kripkean" account of proper names; various philosophers have noted that proper names (at least of persons) carry information as to their referent's sex, ethnicity, and class, and as such proper names are more than arbitrary designators (see Allerton, "Linguistic"). This may be even more true of proper names that are used in fictional contexts. Nonetheless, even if a proper name does contain this sort of nondesignative information, it does not, by and large, carry the expressive properties that are bound up with the musical structure of a musical leitmotif (discussed below).

14. Gorbman, *Unheard Melodies,* 93.

15. Indeed, the "Restaurant Theme" and (especially) "Bert's Theme" might be thought of as examples of "emotional mickey-mousing": rather than following the physical action of the characters on the screen these themes ape the emotional state of the character (a down-in-the-dumps Bert) or institution (a hustling and bustling restaurant).

16. Gorbman transcribes Veda's theme as beginning with three quarter-notes; I have lumped these notes together into a single sustained dotted half-note, as this is

the characteristic rhythm of the opening figure (and in m. 3 as well); the quarter-note pulses that Gorbman notates belong more properly to the accompaniment, and not to the theme itself. And though Veda's theme thus begins with a long sustained note, as does the "Monte and Mildred" theme, the former's quick tempo creates a different motivic structure; it takes only about two seconds to hear the first two measures of example 4.

17. In making this tally I did not count every single appearance of Mildred's leitmotif; I tried instead to count each significant entrance of the leitmotif. For example, if it appears a number of times in the same phrase I have counted this as only a single occurrence, as repetitions of a motif within a musical phrase are less salient than statements of a motif that begin the phrase.

18. One other telling use of proper names in the narrative is that her business is simply "Mildred's"—neither Pierce nor Beragon. One could make a great deal of this: that in the public/business sphere Mildred has only a partial identity (uprooted from her family, home, and hearth) whereas when she is with Bert (at the beginning and end of the movie) her name is complete.

19. D. Ackerman, "Proper Names, Essences, and Intuitive Beliefs," *Theory and Decision* 11 (1979):5–26.

PART TWO

✱

BEYOND CLASSICAL FILM MUSIC

✱

WENDY EVERETT

Songlines
Alternative Journeys in Contemporary European Cinema

✳

Aboriginal mythology recounts how, in the Dreamtime, totemic ancestors wandered across the Australian continent, singing the world into existence and scattering in their footsteps trails of words and musical notes. Thus were created the "Songlines" or "Dreaming-Tracks," that network of invisible pathways that criss-cross the Australian landscape and serve both as essential territorial markers and as sacred lines of communication between present and past. When an Aboriginal goes "Walkabout," he is making a ritual journey across the land, retracing the footsteps of the ancestors; in so doing, however, he is concurrently making an inner journey that leads via myth and subjective memory to personal identity. The starting point for each journey, and the direction it follows, are precisely determined by singing the right song: the song that has been handed down to an individual across the generations, sung to him or her from earliest childhood. As Bruce Chatwyn recounts in his fascinating study of Australian Aboriginals, "A song was both map and direction-finder. Providing you knew the song, you could always find your way across country."[1]

In theory, therefore, as Chatwyn suggests, the whole of Australia can be read as a musical score in which direction and distance are both perceived and measured as a length of a particular song, which is identified by its specific "taste" or "smell" (that is, its "tune"). Although the words of the song are important, having brought the universe into being, what really matters is the tune or melody: the songline it creates may cover vast distances and pass through the territories of many different tribes and languages, but it will always have the same tune, and it is this that links different tribes, generations, and individuals. And if it seems at first a little strange that an essay dealing with contemporary European cinema should begin with a detour to Aboriginal Australian mythology, my reasons will soon be clear. The latter's remarkable understanding of the fundamental role played by music in structuring an individual's perception of the world, and his or her sense of personal identity within that world, clearly predicts many current critical theories about music and has particular relevance to the autobiographical films this essay will consider, films in which the music and its essential link with memory and identity are paramount.

A few preliminaries. For the purpose of this essay, the films I shall be concerned with constitute a specific category of first-person narrative: autobiography. That is to say, they are essentially personal accounts in which a director is attempting to re-create, reexplore, and reevaluate elements of his or her own past. The memories the films explore—generally, but not necessarily, situated in childhood—may be painful, even partly repressed: the purpose of the film is not merely to reconstruct a nostalgic childhood world (though this may well be part of the process) but to reach behind conscious memory to what that world conceals. For this reason, and because of the element of personal exposure they involve, such films are frequently perceived as difficult to make. Because the process of remembering will inevitably change the rememberer in some way, and therefore his or her relationship with the past events being narrated, each of the films constitutes a sort of work in progress, an ongoing quest or journey. Their discourse is mobile, fragmented, and insecure, and the status of the scenes and objects they portray is subject to constant revision both at the level of the narrator's shifting viewpoint, and through the dialogue the films instigate between screen and spectator.

The concept of music as a subjective, nondiscursive, nonrepresentational discourse whose power lies in its ability to appeal directly to the emotions and, through them, to memory, has, of course, dominated the classical tradition of narrative filmmaking, in which music is seen to function primarily in relation to subjectivity, mood, and nostalgia. Therefore, it appears both predictable and entirely unremarkable that music should be accorded a central role within the essentially subjective and nostalgic discourse of filmic autobiography. Closer study, however, reveals that, while retaining the fundamental link between music and anteriority, such films— in which memory is perceived and articulated as an essentially dynamic process—accord music an equally dynamic role; in so doing, they radically subvert the very tradition they appear to support.

Nowhere is this subversion more clearly illustrated than in the popular songs that are a prominent feature of so much autobiographical filmic discourse. Imported directly into the soundtrack along with their personal and cultural baggage, they function as floating signifiers or *objets trouvés*, providing privileged access to the alternative fictions of memory, and serving as the locus of the complex interplay between past and present, truth and fiction, self and other, that structures an individual's search for personal identity. As we shall see, the songs tend to be foregrounded within the films' inevitably ironic and self-conscious discourse, where their essentially ambiguous status, simultaneously intra- and extradiegetic, private and public, mirrors that of autobiography itself, and draws the spectator directly into the remembering process.

By exploring some of the complex, multiple, and innovative functions of popular songs within such films, and by identifying the ways in which the songs simultaneously uphold and subvert accepted practice and theories of film music, I hope to establish a new understanding both of the relationship between music and subjective memory in film, and of the nature of filmic autobiography, which, despite its growing popularity and not inconsiderable importance in contemporary European cinema, is still imperfectly perceived by the majority of critics and theorists.[2]

It is important to explain at this juncture that I have chosen not to draw any distinction between films made for the cinema and those made for television, as this division reflects the attitude of the directors concerned: Dennis Potter, for example, normally favored television, which he perceived as more intimate and less likely to necessitate industrial compromise than film; Jean-Luc Godard's films have contextually explored and exploited the differences between film and video; and several recent French autobiographical films were originally commissioned for television by the channel ARTE, for a series called *Tous les garçons et les filles de leur âge* (All the boys and girls of their age), although some of them, including André Téchiné's *Les Roseaux sauvages* (The wild reeds, 1994), were in fact released in the cinema before being broadcast. What matters then, in the context of this essay, is not the format of the films but the fact that all of them have been acknowledged by their directors to be autobiographical, or at least predominantly autobiographical.

I am thus drawing a distinction between films that adapt first-person narrative or literary autobiography written by someone else, and those in which a director is actually dealing with his or her personal memories. While—as with Potter, who described his films as "fictive autobiography"[3]—the boundaries may not always be clear (for example, a director might well interpret someone else's memories of childhood through the lens of his/her own), the personal dimension of an autobiographical film does set it apart. If we look once again at the case of Potter, we see that, although he was not responsible for directing either of the two films we shall be considering, he did collaborate closely with the director in every aspect of the filming of his scripts, and throughout his life he repeatedly stressed the importance of personal control, of not having one's work taken over or compromised by a studio (92). Unlike the "heritage" films that have been so popular in Britain in recent years (and that are often carelessly confused with autobiography), in which the past is depicted as nostalgic and ideal-ized, as essentially safe and static, the remembered world of autobiography is both problematic and essentially open-ended—process, not state. Thus the two genres accord very different roles and functions to music. And if the specific demands of autobiography both foreground and self-consciously explore the relationship between music and memory, that relationship in-evitably recalls the link I established earlier between the director setting out on his or her filmic journey through personal and mythical memory in search of understanding and identity, and the Aboriginal who goes Walk-about. Not only are the dimensions of both journeys simultaneously spa-tial and temporal, public and private, but also—and this brings us to the central concerns of this essay—in both, the privileged role of music, partic-ularly song, as both "map and direction finder," key and structuring agent, is openly acknowledged.

That popular songs play a key role in autobiographical films is therefore linked with the personal nature of the journeys they trace. When, in the in-itiative I referred to earlier, the French television channel ARTE commis-sioned nine autobiographical films in which the nine directors involved were required to re-create their own adolescent memories, the main con-straint imposed upon them was that they should contain popular music of the period. However, one feels that this constraint was scarcely necessary; few people would not refer to music in some way in recalling their adoles-cent years. Nevertheless, it does reveal how central songs are perceived to be to the process of remembering and also highlights the fact that the music that recalls one individual's memories of a particular historical moment is likely to have a similar effect upon spectators who also remember that time. (This is a point we shall return to, but which already indicates that ques-tions of reception are quite fundamental.) Given that any piece of music can dramatically recall lost memories, for most of us, the songs that marked our own childhood or adolescence are particularly potent. Indeed, songs tend to be intimately associated with very specific places, people, events and feelings, hence the clichéd notion that "they're playing our song."

An individual's adoption of a given song as his or her own personal ter-ritory, appears to be entirely untouched by the fact that the song may well be creating an identical response in any number of those who hear it, a point that surely confirms the ability of song to bridge the personal/private dichotomy. However, while music has always been used to influence mood and emotion, to instigate temporal change and ensure narrative coherence, and to refer to, or re-create, the past, outside the somewhat specialized parameters of the musical, classical narrative film has tended to fight shy of including popular songs in its soundtrack. To understand this apparent paradox, we must briefly refer to the traditional principles governing film music in the context of memory.

In classical Hollywood practice, the traditional role ascribed to film music was, of course, that it remain entirely "inaudible" or at least inconspicuous. Even as early as 1936, Kurt London, for example, stipulated that the main requirement of film music was that it should be entirely "unnoticed," a view challenged in 1947 by Theodor Adorno and Hanns Eisler in their seminal book *Composing for the Films,* which criticizes film music that acquiesces to this "vanishing function."[4] Still, this view of music's "invisible" role has continued to inform contemporary film-music theory.[5] In *Unheard Melodies,* Claudia Gorbman, though drawing on Adorno and Eisler, actually enshrines the principles governing classical film music as: invisibility, "inaudibility," signifier of emotion, narrative cueing, continuity, and unity—in that order.[6] Once again the notion is proffered that while music powerfully influences our emotional response to, and interpretation of, a film, we are not supposed to be aware of its presence; its fundamental role is to support and protect the narrative without drawing attention to itself. "The classical narrative sound film has been constituted in such a way that the spectator does not normally (consciously) hear the film score," she comments (31). In practice, the main consequences of this notion that film music should somehow elude the spectator's perceptive awareness were, first of all, that film music should not be complicated or "difficult," as the attention such music demands would inevitably distract the viewers, drawing them outside the control of the narrative.[7] Second, "familiar" music (into which category popular songs must be placed) should be avoided because, similarly, it "runs the risk of drawing attention to itself as music," and again, in so doing, of distancing the spectator from the film's narrative.[8]

For his part, Ernest Lindgren, in commenting at length upon the "disturbing" potential of familiar music heard within a film, suggests that its main danger is that "it often has certain associations for the spectator which may conflict entirely with the associations the producer wishes to establish in his film."[9] In other words, by bringing the spectator's own personal memories and associations into the interpretative process, not only does popular music weaken the film's narrative hold, but also risks entirely subverting its intended meaning and affect.

Is this approach somewhat oversimplistic? In his article "Unheard Melodies?" Jeff Smith suggests that it is; whereas for Hollywood composers and early film-music theorists the idea of unobtrusiveness was only an implicit criterion governing the production of film music ("a kind of pragmatic guideline employed to create dramatically effective scores"), recent theorists, strongly influenced by the accounts of suture and enunciation that marked the 1970s and 1980s, have mistakenly extended that principle of unobtrusiveness to film reception and spectatorship.[10] He points out that if film music is to play any part in the text's construction of meaning, it must be to some degree "perceived and cognized by the film spectator"; that is to say, it must function at a level other than the unconscious one (235). This conclusion is undoubtedly true, although of course many of the problems film-music theorists have explicitly confronted over the years have concerned the difficulty of differentiating with any real precision between conscious and unconscious responses. Nevertheless, the whole tradition of the (Wagnerian) leitmotif in its cinematic interpretation(s) depends, to some extent, upon a conscious processing of the musical information we are given. Musical themes and motifs within a film enable us not only to recognize character, place, and period; in so doing, they construct memory patterns within the narrative, and our awareness of the connotative and, in particular, the ironic use of music, pinpoints the conscious processes at work.

Perhaps nowhere are these dichotomies more tellingly illustrated than in a film's use of popular songs, which, as we have already noted, appear sparingly in classical film narrative, despite—or possibly because of—their considerable emotive and nostalgic potency. Functioning as powerful triggers of memory and emotion, popular songs are likely to be easily recognized by the spectators, for each of whom they may well carry a complex range of intensely personal connotations. Instead of silently supporting the narrative, such songs thus weaken its control by drawing the spectator's attention away from the screen and into a realm of personal memory.

Yet the example Smith chooses to illustrate his case, *Love in the Afternoon* (dir. Billy Wilder, 1957), is discussed by him precisely in relation to its use of popular song. The film score, as he points out, adapts six popular melodies, one of which, the 1932 standard "Fascination," establishes its domination by accompanying the credits, and subsequently acquires the status of theme tune. Listing the various ways in which this song is heard (nondiegetic, diegetic, self-conscious, and ironic), Smith argues that the film teaches us to recognize both the melody and its textual function (244) and that therefore our conscious awareness of the music does not in any way harm the film's narrative impact. While these remarks are undoubtedly true, it must nevertheless be said that Smith is far from the first to recognize this fact: for example, in 1980 Gorbman commented that, through its repetition in a film score, a theme tune constantly acquires new diegetic associations for the spectator, who must therefore, one assumes, be in some way aware of it.[11] Similarly, in her analysis of the use of popular songs in *Penny Serenade* (dir. George Stevens, 1941), Caryl Flinn states that "although these examples appear to perform film music's classic function of emotional embellishment, they also foreground this affective function, making it noticeable and not 'invisible,' silent, or subconscious as classicists would have it."[12] Furthermore, in his own analysis, Smith leaves several fundamental questions unanswered or even unasked. He does not, for example, recognize that according "Fascination" the status of theme tune might well be little more than an attempt by the film to claim the music as its own, and in so doing, to tame its disruptive potential. Although it is true that we do hear familiar melodies that we may recognize and to which we may respond in a complex manner, nevertheless in each case these melodies have been specially "adapted" for the film, fairly drastically, in fact, since not once do we hear any of their lyrics.

Let us focus on this last point. A song is composed of melody and lyrics working in tandem, so why does *Love in the Afternoon* carry out such an amputation? Or, to put it another way, what is it about the joint articulation of words and music in song that accounts for Hollywood's apparent fear of including both? And why does removing the words make the song less dangerous, more easily controlled by the narrative? Smith's treatment of these questions is hesitant and unconvincing. In the footnote in which he raises the issue of the songs without words, he does acknowledge the "vexing question" of the way in which a song's lyrics may influence our reading of a film, adding that although *Love in the Afternoon* does not include any lyrics, "it is reasonable to assume that audiences would be likely to have some familiarity with them," presumably implying that they would in any case add what they knew of the words to their reading of the film, and concluding, somewhat disappointingly, that "though one can only speculate about the extent to which this awareness constrains or shapes a spectator's interpretation, it seems reasonable to assume that it did have some effect."[13] One might well wonder what sort of "effect" he means and, indeed, where this leaves his argument about the conscious analysis of film music by the audience.

Why does the fact that awareness of the lyrics may shape or constrain a spectator's reaction mean that they must be excluded from the soundtrack? Is Smith contradicting his earlier argument and implying that it is acceptable for the audience to listen "consciously" to music, but only up to a certain point? If so, his position seems fairly close to that of those theorists whose ideas he sought to disprove. Whatever the case, we have not advanced much in our understanding of the nature and function of popular songs in film.

Of course, there are films in which we do hear popular songs, words and all, even in their original recordings. Most prominent among such films are those that are historical or nostalgic in their intention and set in a relatively near past. Flinn notes the recent popularity of such films in the United States, particularly those aiming to reconstruct the 1950s and 1960s; in these, "music continues to play a key role in triggering this widescale yearning for yesterday."[14] Songs are often included on the soundtrack precisely because of their power to convey period; to bring the past to life. Given the sort of individual and slightly unpredictable response they may create in the audience, one might wonder how it is that the songs are not, in such cases, perceived as posing a threat to the narrative.

The answer is probably that, when songs are used in this way (that is, as a nostalgic device or historical signpost), they tend to be firmly anchored into the diegesis by some identifiable source, such as a gramophone, radio, or jukebox—visual symbols that enhance the historical "feel" or period setting. In other words, the songs have again been tamed, just as surely as they would have been by removing their lyrics. Thus, with regard to Flinn's analysis of the songs in *Penny Serenade,* it is significant that, although foregrounded, they are nevertheless diegetically contextualized. This is fairly typical: to ensure solid containment by the diegesis, frequently both the provenance and the artificiality of the song—the quotation marks that enable the spectator's illusions to remain intact—are emphasized by, for instance, its being heard as an old and inferior recording that contrasts starkly with the neutral status of the rest of the soundtrack. In this way, the spectator's response is again safely contained, the potential subversiveness of the song is reduced, and the supremacy of the narrative is protected.

We have seen that popular songs tend to be accorded a particularly important role within autobiographical films, where, in defiance of classical practice, they may be heard words and all, may frequently change status from intra- to extradiegetic, personal to public, and—essentially—will usually remain stubbornly self-conscious and foregrounded. This raised status is revealed by the fact that song titles are quite often used to provide the titles of the films themselves. Moreover, if we briefly compare the composition of the soundtrack of *Love in the Afternoon* with that of Terence Davies's *The Long Day Closes* (1992), we see that, whereas the former uses the tunes of six different popular songs, one of which is accorded the status of theme tune, and none of which is played in conjunction with its lyrics, the latter includes more than twenty different songs, all of which are heard, at least at some time, as original recordings, complete with words. Similarly, it is striking to note that, for example, the first episode of Potter's *Lipstick on your Collar* (first broadcast on Channel Four of British television, 21 February 1993), features six songs in under an hour; or that the soundtrack of André Téchiné's *Les Roseaux sauvages* contains, in addition to orchestral music by Barber, J. Strauss, and Wagner, some six different popular songs. Moreover, in these films, no one song is accorded a superior or identifiable status; instead they weave, in various and changing performances, in and out of the film, and they are perceived as an integral part of its narration.

In autobiographical films, the songs we hear are acknowledged as vital to the process of remembering, and they are always placed at the forefront of our awareness. It seems that the director positively wants us to be drawn into the remembering process on our own terms. Thus, even when the songs are being exploited merely for their nostalgic potential, in recognition of their emotive power to reawaken memories of a specific period, the spectator is not protected from his or her personal associations.

One such example (and of course there are many) is the recording of "Living Doll" that opens Diane Kurys's memories of her adolescence in a Parisian lycée during the 1960s, *Diabolo Menthe* (Peppermint soda; dir. Diane Kurys, 1977), a recording that powerfully and economically establishes the period in which the film is set. The song is heard extradiegetically and continues throughout the credits and the lengthy opening sequence, which shows the two sisters arguing on a beach. The song draws attention to itself and insists upon our attention by the length of time we hear it, by its extradiegetic status, and by the unclear relationship it has with the images we are watching on screen. In a way, it functions as narrative voiceover, not because of the meaning of the words (I have already noted that there is no apparent link between words and images and, in any case, it is an American song, with English lyrics, being heard in a French film), but because of its extradiegetic status. That its role within the filmic narrative is personal, part of the director's own past, is immediately established in the dedication that follows the credits: "To my sister who still hasn't returned my orange pullover." Thus, the song provides both the starting point and key to this retrospective and subjective film journey; inevitably, however, in so doing, it will also awaken a range of diverse but equally personal responses and memories for some proportion of the audience. Yet in autobiographical films, this overlapping of different subjectivities, this involvement of the spectator within the memory process, is not perceived as a threat; it is a fundamental characteristic of the genre.[15]

The ambiguous status and the emotional and nostalgic energy of popular songs can provide the director with an exceptionally potent device, as Dennis Potter acknowledges:

I knew there was energy in that sort of music, and I knew there must be a way of being able to use it in the way that I perceived people used it themselves, for example the way that they would say, "Oh, listen, they're playing our song." I was interested in the feeling that people have sometimes when they listen to the music of the past, the way songs wrap themselves around whatever emotion you happened to be carrying when you first heard them, the way a song can infiltrate the mood of a group of people.[16]

The potency of popular song—its ability to involve the spectator directly in the remembering process and to create the multiple levels of autobiographical discourse—is beautifully illustrated in the opening sequence of Terence Davies's *The Long Day Closes,* in which a song is one of the many devices being used to establish the historical moment and personal nature of the narrative. The film covers the period of one year or so of Davies's childhood in Liverpool in the 1950s. It does not present us with a straightforward linear narrative but a flowing series of memories, in which music—especially popular song—both instigates and structures the memories being explored. Some indication of the complex ways music is used to create and proliferate the multiple layers and viewpoints of autobiography, and also to draw the spectator into the memory process, is revealed by the film's opening sequence set in a deserted and derelict street, filled with rubble and decaying houses. Everything is very dark and partly shrouded by the heavy rain. The camera, at first static, very slowly advances part way down the street, then pans right into one of the ruined houses, where it pauses, focusing on the broken stairs. As the sequence ends, we see the figure of a boy (Bud, Terence Davies's alter ego) sitting on the stairs in the house now restored to its former state. Throughout this sequence, we hear a recording of "Stardust," a song that has marked personal connotations for Davies, as it instigates his memories and transports him from adulthood to childhood, to the solitude and isolation of that childhood. The first shot of Bud shows him sitting alone halfway down the stairs, separated from the adult world by the (imprisoning) banisters (in a shot that has its counterpart in a whole range of other autobiographical films, for example, *Hope and Glory* [John Boorman, 1987]).

The song is featured nondiegetically, so that it is not contained by the narrative but is presented as part of the process of remembering. As in the previous example we considered, it is to some extent functioning as a narrative voice-over—at least it seems to have that authority. However, unlike Kurys, Davies does not provide any explicit indication of the status of the film we are watching; instead, the complex nature of memory is approached entirely through the relationship of image and sound. This first song, which leads him (and us) back to the past, was extremely popular in Britain in the 1950s and beyond, and it is heard here in its original recording by Nat King Cole, an equally well-known singer. The song is likely to be recognized by a large proportion of the audience, for whom it will certainly awaken a wide range of personal memories and responses. Once again, filmic remembering becomes a function of the interplay between screen and spectator.

At this point, a brief comment is in order on the question of the gradations of response that result from the varying degrees of familiarity a group of spectators may demonstrate with regard to a given tune. I cannot develop this point fully here; I do, however, note that I have conducted some interesting work with groups of students between the ages of 19 and 24, for whom many of the songs will not be familiar. Yet there does seem to be a sort of group mythology based around the songs, a strong culturally acquired awareness they still share. Thus, even young English audiences respond to Piaf or Trenet, for example, as part of a particular and quite specific place and historical period. If a song is entirely unrecognized and unknown, the listeners seem to concentrate more actively upon the words, at least until they build up a relationship with the tune—an interesting phenomenon. Whatever the case, we can observe that, just like the Aboriginal songlines, popular songs foregrounded within a filmic narrative seem able, against all odds, successfully to cross barriers of age, nation, and language.

In *The Long Day Closes,* "Stardust," which is part of the personal memories of the director/protagonist and the spectators, is simultaneously used to reveal the essential artificiality or fiction of these memories. The voice is smooth and glamorous, by virtue of being American and therefore the product of an alien culture. That glamour, which is remembered by Davies as the positive side of childhood, is part of the film's explicit homage to the magic of childhood, namely those elements of it that were mediated and shaped by popular (and frequently American) culture.

At the same time, it is essential in film always to be aware of the relationship between sound and image; here, the camera briefly focuses on an old, tattered cinema poster advertising *The Robe,* the first Cinemascope film. The notion of America and glamour are now traced to the prime source of their mediation: the cinema. The state of the poster places this film in Davies's past, but our present historical awareness that it was a film to which all Catholic schoolchildren in Britain were likely to have been taken contributes to further layers of Davies's memories. At the same time, the artificiality of the set we are faced with, and the explicitly cinematic quality of the falling rain, carry us with Davies into a past we must recognize as partly fictional. Such indeed is the nature of autobiographical memory.[17]

Similar proliferation and confusion of elements result from the song's position in the soundtrack: it follows the Twentieth Century–Fox logo theme, and an extract from the soundtrack of *The Happiest Days of Your Life* (1950), in which the sounding of a gong is accompanied by Margaret Rutherford's voice saying (with heavy contextual irony): "Tap Gossage, I said 'tap'—you're not introducing a film." At the end of the sequence, the song cross-fades to an extract from the soundtrack of *The Ladykillers* (1956), where we hear the voice of Alec Guinness, another icon of British film of the period.

Of course, we hear the lyrics too, and they have a further and important contribution to make. Dealing with separation and distance, "Stardust" self-consciously refers to itself as "a song that will not die" and as "the music of the years gone by." Thus, song and film are both simultaneously using and ironically evaluating the power of nostalgia and its role in shaping the past. At the same time, the relationship between this song and the desolate images onscreen is frequently disturbing, while the status of the images themselves is unclear. Are they present or past, real or imaginary? Davies here underlines the impossibility of establishing clear boundaries in our memories; the rain we see and hear is falling both outside and inside the house, for example. And so the sequence announces the central concerns of autobiography: not the re-creation of a static past but an exploration of the process of remembering; the way the mind travels through the temporal and spatial landscapes of memory. Within this dynamic process music is accorded an equally dynamic role.

The relationship among music, memory, and identity is vital and, even in the somewhat checkered history of film-music theory, has received the most attention. Recently, music as longing for an irrecoverable past has been investigated (Adorno, Barthes, Flinn) in terms of its relationship with the pre-Oedipal, pre-linguistic state, and loss of plenitude. Because the infant hears long before it sees, it is argued, recognizing its mother's voice before it can identify her face, then the auditory realm must be central to the formation of subjectivity[18] (a particularly interesting development in film theory where Lacan's work on the importance of vision and the image in the formation of the subject—the mirror phase—has, not surprisingly, tended to dominate).[19] For Guy Rosolato, voice constitutes an acoustic mirror, as sounds are simultaneously emitted and heard by the subject. In this reading, the child's first sounds might be, at least in part, "a reprise, a hallucinatory evocation of the sonorous features of the maternal: a sort of auditory restaging of the *fort-da* game."[20]

Within this approach, music's soothing and comforting qualities are seen to emanate from its association with the mother, or (in Kristeva's terms) with the maternal *chora*.[21] On the one hand, therefore, music inspires feelings of joy by appearing to offer the restoration of plenitude and lost maternal objects (Blanchard, Vasse); but on the other, it creates a sense of loss and nostalgia by indicating their irrecoverability.

Music's function in returning the listener to "better, more perfect, times and memories," while simultaneously underlining the impossibility of any such return, leads Flinn to describe it as "utopian": music refers to a world outside "reality," passionately longed for but ultimately unrealizable.[22] It operates a process of constant referral within a film narrative; hence its ability to create feelings of nostalgia.

In autobiography, as we have seen, even this nostalgic function is ironic and self-conscious; a means rather than an end. As Potter explains: "Nostalgia is a means of forgetting the past, of making it seem cosy, of saying, 'It's back there—look how sweet it was.' But you can use the power of nostalgia to open the past up and make it stand up in front of you. That is why I use popular songs."[23] For Potter, therefore, the power of nostagia provides "a means to turn [fiction] inside out," to move inward from description to process.

Within this process, which transforms song from memory trigger to personal expression, we must indeed be aware of the importance of the joint articulation of music and language. Barthes thought that song, by adding voice to melody, gives music an essential *physicality:* "The materiality of the body speaking its mother tongue," which intensifies both the memory of the original experience, *jouissance,* and the keenness of its loss. Song, marked by the grain of the voice, thus occupies a privileged position in memory,[24] hence the importance to us of songs we remember from our childhood and early adolescence. But, as my own examples have shown, what is significant here about the use of popular songs is that they are both verbal and nonverbal, both music and discourse.

Just as the emotional impact of the melody is intensified by the presence of voice, so too it is mediated by the lyrics, which may well provide a commentary on, or counterpoint to, the narrative. The words can act as ironic distancing devices that draw attention to the gap between the adult narrator's understanding of them and the child's remembered perceptions. The film offers a rereading of the songs, and through this, an acknowledgment of the shifting relationship and distance between remembering and remembered, subject and object. The song both links and separates the different times of the narrative and draws attention to the processes at work.

I illustrate this by refering to a further sequence from *The Long Day Closes*. In the first part, we see Bud and his mother and sisters at a fairground; in the second, we see Bud, at home, sitting on his mother's knee. The two sections are linked by the song "She Moved Through the Fair," which we hear throughout. Like "Stardust," this song was popular both during and after the 1950s and is likely to be fairly widely remembered. It too is accorded, at least initially, a nondiegetic status. It is heard throughout the fairly long fairground scene, where it signifies Bud's happiness, although the slowness of its rhythm, echoed in the extremely slow pace at which the child and his mother walk through the fair, contributes a dreamy, nostalgic atmosphere. As we hear the words "And then she went homeward / With one star awake / As the swan in the evening / Moves over the lake," we move back into Bud's house and into the more intimate memory of his mother singing that same song to him. At the same time we see Bud on his mother's knee as she sings to him, we hear the recorded voice, which is first joined and then replaced by that of the mother.

The change of voice mirrors the gradual interiorization of the song, its changing status for Bud from public to personal. However, we can see that the mother's voice signals her interiorization of the song (as she recalls her father singing it to her) and expresses her sadness and loss. Bud, the child, is aware of her voice and interested by the information that his grandfather used to sing this song to his mother when she was small; unlike us, however, he is not aware of her sadness and does not see her tears. Nonetheless, Davies, the adult, in using the song to recall his own lost childhood, reaches through it to a new awareness of his mother's sadness and of her own lost past. So the song performs multilayered functions through the increasing internalization of its status; in so doing, it illustrates Potter's comments about using nostalgia to move inward from description to process. But equally important, it is foregrounded within the film, so that we, the spectators, are simultaneously emotionally involved in the process of remembering and intellectually required to consider the nature of that process.

Songs can therefore increase the multiple textualities of film and self by emphasizing the lack of distinct boundaries between past and present, fiction and reality, screen and audience. The insecurity of their temporal and narrative status mirrors the slippage and doubling we recognize as essential features of autobiographical discourse, an inevitable consequence of turning one's attention inward: "Self-scrutiny engenders self-estrangement";[25] the self you remember is both first and third person, both self and other. In film, this is illustrated by the representation on the screen of one's alter ego, in a narrative that articulates the distance between this self and the one who is remembering through devices such as authorial voice-over or the distancing irony of the camera. Popular song may be seen as another way of achieving this articulation, because song is able to capture the sense of disparity between self as historical phenomenon and self as something outside and perhaps at odds with history.[26] In other words, song provides the moment in the narrative when history and fiction, personal and public, present and past, intersect.

Here it is helpful to apply to autobiography Paul Ricoeur's concept of narrative as a response to the aporetics of temporality, to the discordance between inner and objective time.[27] Autobiography, like history, does not attempt to restore the past but to construct something in its place, and it does so using various connectors between past and present, one of which is trace. Lives, like historical events, leave traces (photographs, documents, songs) that signify, without actually reconstructing them, the circumstances of the original. Trace itself therefore occupies a hybrid time ("tiers temps"), since in it different time zones overlap and are stitched together. Deciphering a trace, or reconstructing the sequence of events that formed it, is a creative and imaginative process for both director and spectator. This process is illustrated in a well-known sequence from Dennis Potter's *Lipstick on Your Collar* (directed for British television by Renny Rye, in close collaboration with Potter, 1993).

The setting is the Foreign Office in London in the 1950s, at the time of the Suez crisis (described by Potter as "Britain's last imperial gesture").[28] For him, this period of unprecedented cultural and political change was perfectly encapsulated in the popular songs of the time, and in one scene in episode 4, he uses one such song, "I See The Moon," performed by the Stargazers, to re-create his memories of this doomed world. The song triggers and is part of an extravagant fantasy sequence in the imagination of the young Private Mick Hopper, transporting him from the fraught monotony of the detested office into a typical music hall and a highly clichéd representation of Egypt. Personal memory and national history are thus brought together for Potter through his associations with this song, but its non-naturalistic representation as carnival subverts the narrative (the characters in the office all join in with the dancing and singing in synchronization with the recorded songs). The distance thus gained allows the director to use the sequence to add his ironic and critical judgment of the remembered historical context.

Thus, song as historic trace and as subjective memory re-created within that trace simultaneously reevaluates and comments upon the memory and its representation (the pantomime camel defecates over the camera lens through which we are looking). The subjective framework contains multiple viewpoints and ironies, but it also provides self-conscious comment upon the nature of memory itself (truth and fantasy or fiction being inseparable), for when "reality" is restored again, Lieutenant-Colonel Harry Bernwood (whose mental breakdown symbolizes the breakdown of Britain's colonial status and of all the certainties that went with it) absent-mindedly kicks a balloon out of his way as he crosses the office: balloon as trace of (fictional) song whose "existence" is itself both trace and creation of memory.

If the songs in autobiographical films are placed in the foreground, and if their performance draws attention both to their position as memory trace and to the nature and process of remembering, it is because they are recognized as part of the personal act of narration (*énonciation*) of the director; in other words, they form part of the dynamic process of the creation of self: "Ecrire son histoire, c'est essayer de se construire, bien plus qu'essayer de se connaître" (Writing one's story/history, is an attempt to create oneself, rather than to know oneself), writes Philippe Lejeune, probably still the leading theorist on autobiography.[29] In *Jacquot de Nantes*, French director Agnès Varda sets out to make an "autobiography" of her dying husband, director Jacques Démy. That is to say, she attempts to create a portrait of her subject from the inside rather than the outside, and she does so by using songs from his films (which were musicals) as the key with which to open his childhood memories. In so doing, she hopes that the songs that structure her film will carry us into his memories and thus into his identity.

Potter too uses songs not merely to comment and illustrate but in order to explore and articulate the self, that interiority which cannot be expressed in either images or words. Such an attempt requires, as we have already observed, that the songs be accorded a central and determining role within the narrative. They must therefore be foregrounded. They cannot be permitted to remain unheard, unnoticed by the spectator, hence Potter's essentially non-naturalistic approach. In his films, the songs replace much of the dramatic dialogue; they never sit quietly in the background. The characters do not burst into song, as they would in a musical, but into a lip-sync performance of songs, whose essentially public theatricality creates destabilizing tensions with the subjective and intimate nature of their revelations. Writing of *The Singing Detective* (1986), he explains: "The purpose is not to illustrate with a song, but to use the song as though it had just been written for the occasion—in other words, to turn the song into quasi-autobiography, as though I had written the song, which is to re-see, re-hear what may be an extraordinarily banal tune and nonsensical lyric, . . . to give the song the meaning of the emotional and physical surround out of which you are made to re-hear it."[30]

Once the song is recognized as part of the actual process of recalling and articulating the past, and thus of creating the self, then its positive and dynamic role within an autobiographical journey becomes clear: it can actually lead to the deeper self-awareness and understanding that enables an individual to move forward, away from the past. Thus in *The Singing Detective*, perhaps the most famous of Potter's works, songs act both as journeys back to Philip Marlow's suppressed memories, and as psychological clues and floating signifiers in his attempt to reconstruct what Potter describes as his "sovereign self," a process that closely parallels that of the Aboriginal's journey along a songline.

I refer to a scene that provides a major turning point for the protagonist. Marlow has been in hospital for a long time, suffering—as had Potter himself since the age of twenty six—from extreme psoriatic arthropathy; unable to walk, or even move, he has been forced to live entirely within his head. In the scene in question, he is suffering extreme depression and is sitting with the psychiatrist in a small, bare hospital room. Suddenly, the psychiatrist stands up, with the words "It's now or never!" As he moves Marlow's wheelchair, locks its wheels, and clears a space around it, Marlow replies with another song title, "Into each life some rain must fall." "Metaphysics?" queries the doctor. "Music," replies Marlow, significantly. As he does so, the opening bars of this song are heard, and he makes his first attempts to get up out of his wheelchair. The song starts, and the lyrics we hear are performed in lip-sync by the psychiatrist and Marlow in turn, the camera cutting between them as if this were a normal conversation:

PSYCHIATRIST: Into each life some rain must fall, but too much is falling in mine (*cut to Marlow, still struggling to stand up*).
PSYCHIATRIST: Into each heart some tears must fall, but someday the sun will shine (*cut to Marlow, who nearly succeeds in pulling himself to his feet, and smiles*).
MARLOW: Some folks can rue the blues in their hearts.
PSYCHIATRIST: But when I think of you (*cut to Marlow still struggling*), another shower starts (*Marlow is standing; they both laugh wildly; the song ends*).

Thus Marlow's cure, the result of his having been forced to recognize what he was, to recall the repressed childhood memories that consigned him to paralysis and impotence, has been brought about by music. Throughout the narrative, songs have crept up on him, obliging him to remember. They have, in Potter's terms, acted like "hard little stones being thrown at [him]," but, as this scene illustrates, they must also be recognized as part of his very identity, his own subjectivity. "Into each life some tears must fall" is indeed both metaphysical cliché and popular song, both narrative comment and narrative impetus. In opening up Marlowe's past, songs have brought about healing and the possibility of continuation, which is of course the hidden agenda of the autobiographical urge.

So the autobiographer, just like the Australian Aboriginal, sets out on a journey through time and space, through personal memory and group mythology, in search of a new awareness of the self and a new beginning. The shape and length of both these journeys are inextricably linked to the songs that lie at their heart. In its self-conscious, self-referential, and essentially inventive use of popular song, filmic autobiography thus subverts expectations and involves the spectator's own memories within its processes. Recognition of this fact surely underlies Potter's last two works (called respectively *Karaoke* and *Cold Lazarus*), written during—and clearly reflecting—his desperate race against his own imminent death. The dialectic between memory and oblivion that structures them is, once again, predominantly articulated through the self-conscious use of popular songs and their ability (referred to in the title *Karaoke*) to become our own.[31]

Notes

1. Bruce Chatwyn, *The Songlines* (London: Jonathan Cape, 1987), 13.
2. For a more detailed development of the nature and significance of autobiographical film in Europe, see my "The Autobiographical Eye in European Film," *Europa, An International Journal of Language, Art and Culture* 2, no. 1 (Spring 1995): 3–10.
3. Dennis Potter, *Potter on Potter* (London: Faber and Faber, 1993), 95.
4. Kurt London, *Film Music* (London: Faber and Faber, 1936), 37; Theodor Adorno and Hanns Eisler, *Composing for the Films* (London: Athlone Press, 1994), chap. 7.
5. Royal S. Brown, *Overtones and Undertones: Reading Film Music* (Berkeley and Los Angeles: University of California Press, 1994), 1.
6. Claudia Gorbman, *Unheard Melodies: Narrative Film Music* (Bloomington: Indiana University Press, 1987), 73.
7. Tony Thomas, *Film Score: The Art and Craft of Movie Music* (Burbank, Calif. Riverwood, 1991), 72.
8. Max Steiner, "Scoring the Film," in *We Make the Movies*, ed. Nancy Naumberg (New York: Norton, 1937), 216–38; citation is from p. 225.
9. Ernest Lindgren, *The Art of Film*, 2d ed. (New York: Macmillan, 1963), 139.
10. Jeff Smith, "Unheard Melodies?" in *Post-Theory: Reconstructing Film Studies*, ed. David Bordwell and Noël Carroll (Wisconsin: University of Wisconsin Press, 1996), 230–47; citation is from p. 232.
11. Claudia Gorbman, "Narrative Film Music," in "Cinema/Sound," *Yale French Studies* 60, no. 1 (1980): 183–203; citation is from p. 192.
12. Caryl Flinn, *Strains of Utopia: Gender, Nostalgia, and Hollywood Film Music* (Princeton: Princeton University Press, 1992), 139.
13. Smith, "Unheard Melodies?" 247 n.
14. Flinn, *Strains of Utopia*, 151–53.
15. Indeed, the power of music to establish the direct link between spectators and screen that is fundamental to autobiographical discourse must also account to a considerable extent for the popularity of the genre. In autobiography, we use other

people's past as a mirror in which to see our own, and this explains the response that greeted films even as complex as Tarkovskii's *Mirror,* condemned as "avant-garde" by the authorities yet cherished as expressing their memories by those who saw it. Music's ability to work as a "socializing cement" (see, for example, Adorno and Eisler, *Composing for the Films,* 59) is clearly vital.

16. Potter, *Potter on Potter,* 84–85.

17. Wendy Everett, ed. *European Identity in Culture* (Exeter: Intellect, 1996), 109–110.

18. Guy Rosalato, "La voix entre corps et langage," *Revue française de psychanalyse* 38 (January 1974): 80.

19. Lacan does in fact also recognise the important (sexual) drive of the desire to hear, although he never fully investigates the way music functions in this context. See Jacques Lacan, *Ecrits: A Selection* (New York: Norton, 1977).

20. Guy Rosalato, "Répétitions," *Musique en jeu* 9 (November 1972): 42.

21. Julia Kristeva, *Desire in Language* (New York: Columbia University Press, 1980), 286.

22. Flinn, *Strains of Utopia,* 9.

23. Potter, *Potter on Potter,* 96.

24. Roland Barthes, "The Grain of the Voice," in his *Image, Music, Text,* trans. Stephen Heath (New York: Noonday, 1977), 179–89.

25. Michael Sheringham, *French Autobiography—Devices and Desire* (Oxford: Clarendon Press, 1993), viii.

26. Ibid.

27. Paul Ricoeur, *Temps et Récit* (Paris: Seuil, 1985), 3:204.

28. Potter, *Potter on Potter,* 101.

29. Philippe Lejeune, *L'Autobiographie en France* (Paris : Armand Colin, 1971), 84.

30. Potter, *Potter on Potter* 96.

31. *Karaoke* was first broadcast by the BBC in April 1996, and *Cold Lazarus* was first broadcast by Channel Four, also in April 1996. Dennis Potter died in June 1994.

CARYL FLINN

Strategies of Remembrance
Music and History in the New German Cinema

✳

The "young German cinema" is no stranger to themes of grief, loss, and the anxiety of personal, social, ethnic, and national histories. No other film movement has been so intimately tied to national, historical, cultural, and psychic losses—compare French surrealism, the Czech new wave, or even China's fifth-generation filmmakers. Indeed, thirty years after Alexander and Margarethe Mitscherlisch's influential study on Germany's "inability to mourn" was published, their notion of the culture's being unable to come to terms with the past still haunts textual production, not to mention academic, political, and critical discourse. As David Bathrick recently put it regarding the obsession with the Nazi past he observed in German and European films during the 1970s and 1980s, "Commercialization or genuine historicizing, nostalgia spectacle or critical reassessment, exploitative indulgence or *Trauerarbeit:* these are some of the parameters framing a debate which has sought to grasp the cinematic reenactment of that twelve year period of German history which simply can and will not permit closure."[1]

For Germanists more generally, *Trauerarbeit* has become a veritable latchkey with which to unlock the treasures of German aesthetic production. Although German culture was easily associated with the concept of *Trauerarbeit* prior to the war (recall Benjamin on the roots of German Tragedy) it is clear that "that twelve year period of German history" provides the generative center of these many sounds and images, all of this postwar mourning work. And the young German cinema, Germany's first significant postwar film movement, has been indelibly marked by that labor of grief and lack. Eric Santner describes the basic mechanisms of this labor, with films "cutting and subsequent shaping of organic material . . . to empower the mourner to survive his or her loss."[2] We see such losses and reconstruction explicitly undertaken in films like *Heimat; Lili Marleen; Deutschland, bleiche Mutter; Hitler, Ein Film aus Deutschland;* or Syberberg's documentary on Winifred Wagner, which closes upon the words "This film is part of Hans-Jürgen Syberberg's *Trauerarbeit.*"

Most of the more productive accounts of *Trauerarbeit* use the concept of mourning to frame psychic issues and subjectivity within larger questions of history and historiography—a few examples include Bathrick, Thomas Elsaesser, Santner, and Kaja Silverman,[3] and the cinema of Straub/Huillet, Fassbinder, and Kluge. For the majority of its scholars, however, the young German cinema's "special" relation to history and mourning has been construed largely as a visual phenomenon. Indeed, as I have noted elsewhere, the most influential pieces on the young German Cinema—and on Fassbinder most particularly—foreground vision, specularity, and the look.[4] Certainly this emphasis is justified: visually lavish films such as Fassbinder's *Chinesisches Roulette* and *Ein Reise ins Licht—Despair,* or Ottinger's *Bildnis einer Trinkerin* and *Madame* X feature elaborate framing devices, windows, mirrors, shimmering surfaces, splits in vision, splits in characters—all offering a stunning retreat from film theory's long-standing equation of looking with power, mastery, and enlightenment. Elsaesser connects this willed disempowerment, particularly in Fassbinder's case, to Germany's historical experience during and after the war, when identity was monitored by a succession of powerful "others"; for Kaja Silverman, Fassbinder's visual strategies manifest a willed relinquishment of conventional phallic authority. Vision, be it in terms of the films' actual look or the human looks and gazes that they elicit, is thereby the means by which German culture's assorted divestitures are articulated. But what of film sound?

To illustrate how the soundtrack in general and music in particular have been overlooked in this regard, consider Syberberg's titan *Hitler, Ein Film aus Deutschland.* Near the end, André Heller speaks to the Hitler puppet at great length: "You killed the Wandering Jew. You destroyed Berlin, Vienna. . . . You took away our sunsets, sunsets by Caspar David Friedrich. . . . You made old Germany kitschy with your simplifying works and peasant pictures." Heller even goes on to blame Adolf Hitler for fast food. Remarkably, in a film whose score is saturated with Germanic heavyweights like Wagner, Beethoven, and Mahler, Heller's list fails to include music; given music's enormous role in German culture, the omission is striking.[5] Moreover, the same omission is also reproduced in the critical literature on the young German cinema at large. North America film articles devoted to soundtrack of young German cinema of the 1970s and 1980s—especially outside of Straub/Huillet—can be counted on one hand,[6] and some of these concentrate on the plots, themes, and stories of famous operas, eschewing commentary on the music per se, much in the way that Clément approached opera in her influential *Opera, or the Undoing of Women.*[7]

My essay aims first to give the soundtrack, and music in particular, a place in the literature on German cinema of the 1970s and 1980s and second to begin to modify the model of mourning that still sticks to the young German film like glue. The intention is not to downplay the importance of longing and loss in our theoretical and personal encounters with film, music, or with historical representation, but to suggest that our critical models of the "inability to mourn" and *Trauerarbeit,* while once enormously important, may have outlived their use value. As Thomas Elsaesser has recently observed, "Germany, no longer disavowing fascism, Auschwitz, or its role in the disasters of the twentieth century, is simply adding their representations to its national heritage in order to move on."[8] Social, economic, and political exigiencies have changed since Fassbinder's death: "The changing balance of forces in Europe has brought Germany not only out of its political quarantine, but has also put an end to the morose, yet often enough self-laceratingly honest introspection which was one of Fassbinder's contributions to his country's cinema and—at the time—a reason for his reputation as a creative force."[9] Domestic German film production is up: current popular genres include comedies and action pictures. Certainly the sentimentalized regret that characterized much of the treatments of *Trauerarbeit* characterizes the way many critics and intellectuals may now look back to Fassbinder and to German film of the 1970s and 1980s. Yet there is no overwhelming reason today to preserve the hegemony of mourning and melancholia as *the* exegetic tool for discussing the young German Cinema's interest in the past; there are other ways of figuring social, political, and cultural histories, and one of them I believe is offered through film music.

The soundtracks of films of this time demonstrate a commitment to historical memory largely uninvolved with sentimental or romanticized mourning. A few reconfirm the model, to be sure, as even the brief example from Syberberg suggests, but given the vast number of directors using music in complex and innovative ways (for example, Straub, Schroeter, Ottinger), I think that music is well positioned to reformulate contemporary questions of history, mourning, and memory work. My focus here is primarily on the scores of films by Fassbinder and Kluge: the former, in order to widen the largely visual frame normally attached to his work; the latter, to explore what may be called a materialist musical archaeology. What is significant to the soundtracks of both directors is their borrowing, chopping, and combining of a wide variety of musical forms, and most of my attention will be paid to the uses of previously existing music. (Curiously, these films tend to bypass music from *cinematic* traditions, preferring those of high art [for example, Lieder, opera] and pop culture—often American, especially in Fassbinder's case—to make their points.) By using historically and emotionally meaningful pieces of the past, even noncinematically derived, German scoring practices show how directors, composers, filmgoers and scholars can redirect notions of history as an official series of events through contingent, partial, and personal objects without recourse to the totalizing perspectives that characterize so many discourses on film music.[10]

Acoustic Archaeology and Ludwig van B

As Miriam Hansen has described them, Kluge's films "engage in [and literalize] salvaging historical rubble from the drift of amnesia, taking on objects as cumbersome as the battle of Stalingrad"—or as small as a dead soldier's knee, the narrator of *Die Patriotin* (1979) an example of what Hansen compellingly calls "events breaking into discourse." "The method," she continues, "is allegorical . . . wresting fragments from petrified contexts and inserting them into a new discourse while preserving their strange and jarring character."[11] It is a description that, as we shall see, aptly characterizes Kluge's use of music as well. Ruins, in fact, have fascinated Kluge since his first film, *Brutalität in Stein,* which opens on the architectural debris of Nazi meeting spots surrounding Nuremberg. Here, as elsewhere, ruins function as material witnesses, something acknowledged in the film's accompanying voice-over: "The deserted structures of the Nationalist Socialist Party reactivate as stone witnesses the memory of that epoch, which ended in the most horrible catastrophe of German history."

If, for Kluge, film and television provide the forum for such witnesses to attempt to speak, the emphasis falls less overtly on the process of mourning-work than on a kind of excavation work, a project first literalized by Gabi Teichert, the history professor of *Deutschland im Herbst* (1978) and who subsequently struggles to "present history in a patriotic fashion" in *Die Patriotin.* Teichert's digging is conducted in libraries and in parliamentary meetings; the material basis of her efforts is comically depicted by the hammer and drills with which, in one scene, she attacks a pile of books. Not surprisingly, Teichert's search is unsuccessful, due partly to her devotion to a "patriotic" history full of carnage, and partly to "her" faith in the retrievability of truth *through* objects.

While ironized at Kluge's hands, the process of excavation nonetheless remains crucial, its labor made more important than its output. Indeed, excavations seem to be everywhere in German films of the 1970s and 1980s. Beyond Kluge's work, and with more productive results than those of the "confused" Gabi Teichert, is the female archivist-protagonist of Michael Verhoeven's *Das Schreckliche Mädchen* and the *Trümmerfrauen* in *Deutschland, Bleiche Mutter,* a text in which the women conduct their labor caring less for the correctness or authenticity of history than in reworking the concrete pieces of their collective and individual pasts in order to help rebuild their lives (see figure 1).

As Walter Benjamin famously wrote, historiography, along with digging, entails explosion: the historical materialist needs to "blast a specific era out of the homogeneous course of history." Underscoring his warnings against being absorbed by the interests of "historicism," with its "universal history" and official fictions, Benjamin preferred the lived moments of smaller counterhistories (a term I use with some caution).[12] I would like to illustrate how Benjamin's kind of historiographic blasting is achieved through three different appearances of portions of Beethoven's Ninth Symphony in German films of the 1970s and 1980s. Two of these instances participate in the strategies of historic reminiscences I am discussing here; the third is offered as a counterexample that elaborates a more nostalgic, sentimental approach to history and reminiscence:

1. The beginning of *Der Ehe der Maria Braun* most dramatically literalizes the "blast" of which Benjamin speaks. As Allied warplanes attack Berlin, Maria and Hermann Braun marry. The Adagio of Beethoven's last symphony is heard as the bombs rip the place apart.

2. Beethoven's Ninth is used for even more bombastic effect near the end of *Hitler.* Here the symphony's famous finale (sung by an off-frame nondiegetic chorus), accompanies—perhaps blesses—a lone figure in the frame, a child wrapped in celluloid. This young girl/muse/symbol of hope, purveys the cinema, what for Syberberg was the twentieth century's response to the heights of nineteenth-century music, the *Gesamtkunstwerk* of the twentieth century. Transcendence is in the air.

3. A somewhat humbler quotation of the Ninth Symphony's chorus appears in *Die Patriotin,* in which Gabi Teichert and her friends sit around drinking in her apartment kitchen on New Year's Eve. They sing along as the last movement of the piece is diegetically transmitted in the background.

In *Die Patriotin, Hitler,* and *Maria Braun,* Beethoven's renowned symphony is treated as a testament of high, official German culture. Such a function is, of course, entirely unsurprising; the finale alone in the Ninth Symphony perfectly illustrates the fetishization of canonical musical excerpts and the notion of Western music's "greatest hits" so condemned by Horkheimer and Adorno in their assault on the Culture Industry. (Indeed, K-Tel ads aside, there is every indication that the most official of high cultures

Figure 1. *Deutschland, bleiche Mutter* (1980). Photo courtesy of the Kobal Collection.

today relies on the same fragmentation and dismemberment of musical works that so concerned Adorno. The European Community, for instance, has adopted as its anthem the last ten measures of the Ninth Symphony—without Schiller's text—strikingly testifying to the endurability of Adorno's claims.)

The three films construct different relationships to the high (national) culture that Beethoven's finale metonymically suggests. What *Die Patriotin* highlights is the impartial and fragmented nature of the Beethoven excerpt. If the piece does constitute a portion of the "patriotic image" Gabi seeks, it is certainly not a romanticized image—indeed, as noted above, Gabi's quest for positive German images is treated with considerable irony, however affectionate it may be. And it is clear that Beethoven's Germanic "patriotism" is at best illusory in *Die Patriotin,* nothing more than a crutch. With her female friends, Gabi sings a reworked Schiller text while drinking schnapps in her modest kitchen. The performance of the music is thoroughly deprofessionalized; what we perceive most closely resembles a drunken kitchen reading of Schiller, or a karaoke singalong to scratchy, prerecorded accompaniment.

At this point Kluge effects a certain chipping away at the nineteenth-century mastertext rather than reproducing it whole—much as Benjamin had recommended combatting the lethal sanctimoniousness of official history.[13] In so doing, Kluge also chips away at musical institutions, which he believes impersonalize the feelings and desires of historical subjects. In his 1983 *Die Macht der Gefühle,* for example, he refers to the opera house as the "power plant of emotions," observing how industry and capital churn out and control something so nominally private, so presumably "uncontrollable" as human feeling. It is no accident that *Die Macht der Gefühle* positions nineteenth-century opera as a "factory" that "overcooks," overproduces emotions to such an extent that they become too big, too bombastic, simply too out of touch for actual use.

Our emotions, we are told in the same film, always want a happy end. Yet operatic stories cannot provide this, according to Kluge's voice-over. We are told that the "power plant" is a flawed apparatus from the beginning (the cables of the opera house never worked right, for instance), its emotional hardware associated with war. In fact, throughout *Die Macht der Gefühle,* a certain equivalence is drawn between narratives of conventional romance, war, and opera; their stories are all products of the same power plant, the same culture industry. "Operas are cruel by popular demand." Kluge narrates as he presents a young couple: "It begins with being in love and ends in a divorce. It begins in 1933 and ends in ruins. The great operas begin with the promise of intensified feeling and in Act 5 we count the dead."

The grimness of this recipe for musical and political stories has been noted by Miriam Hansen, who writes apropos of Kluge's later work that "romantic love itself appears complicit with the catastrophes of German history, because it nourishes fictions of fate that prevent any alternative course of action and usually lead to murder, suicide, mass psychosis and war."[14] Hansen's observation describes in equal measure films like *Deutschland, bleiche Mutter* and *Maria Braun,* and, as I shall discuss below, *Lili Marleen,* whose eponymous song, as well as the chanteuse with whom it is conflated, serve to prop up the desires of Third Reich officials. In one astounding scene "Lili Marleen" literally lures German soldiers to their deaths as it is being sung and transmitted on the battlefield, a "song of the siren" of truly epic proportions.

Instead of such deadly, grandiose, institutionalized, "operatic" emotions, Kluge states his preference to activate "small feelings." That is precisely how *Die Macht der Gefühle* works, with its near maniacal quotations of existing—mainly operatic—music. More than a dozen operas (such as *Aida, The Makropoulos Affair, Tannhäuser, Parsifal,* and the *Ring* cycle) are chopped into bits here, as if to make them smaller, humbler, more manageable and suitable for human consumption. Like an archaeological dig performed in reverse, with full disregard for linear, rational historicization or narrative, the film proceeds from wholeness to fragments. The raw "power of emotions"—which, in a somewhat dematerializing move, Kluge opposes to objects (to quote: "the opposite of emotions")—stubbornly resists the laws of conventional discourse. This Kluge illustrates in two humorous scenes: a protracted courtroom sequence features a woman who shot her husband who was sleeping with their daughter. Questioners are baffled by her lack of motivation, anger, or rage over the incident. In another sequence, an opera singer is questioned about his optimistic comportment in the second act of the performance: how can he do this when he knows, by virtue of playing the role many times, how badly it all will end? In Act 2, the singer responds, he does not know how things will finish.

Syberberg's attitude toward operatic desire is altogether different from Kluge's "militant distrust" of it, to deploy a phrase of Hansen's. In *Hitler*, music functions as a redemptive force, an aesthetic and national(ist) touchstone sullied by Hitler, a point I believe made clear in Heller's monologue mentioned earlier. Whereas in Kluge's work, music—even sacred cows such as Beethoven's Ninth Symphony—is used intermittently, as a series of interruptions, for Syberberg it is precisely *history* that interrupts *music* and the cultural continuity he believes it engenders. Music is positioned as an anchoring continuity while everything around it falls to ruin. Consider the film's mise-en-scène, its sets brimming with the clutter of German culture, with the big head of Wagner observing everything from its toppled position on the floor. While the detritus of history and the Hitler "phenomenon" may appear to have damaged the composer, there is a much greater sense in which the film establishes Wagner—along with other titans of Germanic high culture—as down, but not out. Once resurrected itself, German art will have the capacity to resurrect, something intimated by the pristine recording of the chorus of Beethoven's Ninth Symphony in *Hitler*.

It is no accident that the finale of the Ninth appears at *Hitler*'s conclusion, respectfully miming its place in Beethoven's own symphony. Following Heller's long monologue,[15] which itself closes on the final chorus of Mahler's Second Symphony (German Romanticism's grandiose last gasp, for some) and, even more important, opens with the Haydn string quartet whose second movement later provided the melody for "Deutschland über alles."[16] Placing Beethoven in such an elaborate and heavily coded musical frame, Syberberg offers the symphonic finale as a sign of hope for postwar German culture—an interpretation even more overdetermined by the inclusion of Syberberg's own daughter, wrapped in film celluloid, as the

Figure 2. *Hitler, Ein Film aus Deutschland* (1977). Photo courtesy of the Kobal Collection.

young avatar of the "future" (figure 2). Syberberg's sense of the future, of course, is decidedly backward-looking, a bittersweet (and indeed, ironic) nostalgia for the imaginary "unified" prewar national culture Hitler purportedly made impossible.

Despite an aesthetics of fragmentation that dominates the text, the film seems to long for the fictions of national coherence, for Romanticism's excesses and fantasies, its aesthetic heights and its isolated genius. In Elsaesser's early critique of Syberberg's work he writes: "The idea of a split tearing the universe, with which the film opens . . . points to the manifold divisions of German history in search of its Grail—the negative mythology of unity, redemption and reconciliation. Because these visions . . . imply desires of regression, self-oblivion and fantasies of the narcissistic ego, it is Melancholia and Narcissus as patron saints . . . calling for 'mourning work.'"[17] There is no question about the intensity of Syberberg's *Trauerarbeit:* in him, foreign critics can find their ideal, anguished (if kitschy) German mourner.

None of these things is apparent in the Ninth Symphony's brief appearance at the beginning of Fassbinder's *Der Ehe der Maria Braun.* There it appears mixed with enough other sounds so as to be very nearly drowned out entirely. Evoked from the past but coincident with bombs, fire, screaming, and destruction, the barely audible "masterpiece" suggests at best a certain impotence, an inability to help or matter, and, at worst, a complicity with the more destructive aspects of Western "progress." Certainly its status as masterpiece recedes amid the chaotic soundtrack, and even the film's credits are complicated and difficult to read. It is significant that Fassbinder selected not the triumphant finale but the third movement, which Susan McClary describes as a "negative image" to the first two "monomaniacal movements." For McClary, its gentleness suggests "arcadian recollection, the imaginary sublime, or a dream of utopia . . . [though] it can never be a reality."[18] This tranquil "arcadian" potential, of course, is completely shot apart by the military destruction of the scene (see figure 3). (In Roger Hillman's reading of the film, "Narrative, Sound, and Film," this signifies the impossibility of Maria's marriage-managed-by-fantasy.)

Accompanying the dissolution of *Maria Braun*'s various acoustic borders is another dissolution, one involving the blurred interweaving of official

Figure 3. *Der Ehe der Maria Braun* (1979). Photo courtesy of the Ronald Grant Archive.

high culture, of public and social space on the one hand (as represented by the marriage license bureau, Herman's Wehrmacht uniform, and political violence) and something as ostensibly private as romantic desire and courtship on the other. It was not uncommon for soundtracks of German films of the 1970s and 1980s to insist upon the intrusion of the war on supposedly "private" emotional arenas—something often depicted through other acoustic technologies such as diegetic radios, music, or other transmissions—in films like *Deutschland, bleiche Mutter, Redupers, Lili Marleen,* and *Heimat.*

In *Maria Braun,* the new context of the music is so cluttered—literally, with debris from the bombing—that any "purity" or integrity of Beethoven's work cannot remain intact, nor its meanings unaltered. Interestingly, the piece continues uninterrupted into the following scene, at Maria's place with her mother, and takes place some time later: Hermann Braun is lost at war and Maria is talking about selling her wedding dress to get some money for the household. The Beethoven is even quieter here, and hard to discern as it concludes on a radio (an announcer softly states, "that was Beethoven's Ninth Symphony," and then goes on to read a list of missing German soldiers, clinching the piece's connection to death). The temporal difference between the two scenes falsifies any sense of acoustic continuity initially generated by Beethoven's music, and suggests that the piece's ability to unify in other regards—say, as a token of national culture—is equally counterfeit.

We can see that while *Die Patriotin, Hitler,* and *Maria Braun* all deploy Beethoven's renowned symphony as a testament to high German culture, each film assumes a different position to that "high," official past through its metonymical musical (re)presentation through music, with Kluge attempting to rework it, Fassbinder to assail it, and Syberberg, in a very real way, to redeem it.

Musical Raids

During the 1970s and early 1980s, the young German cinema freely pillaged existing music, which it then put to very different uses. One of the interesting features of this extended culture raid is its refusal of stylistic unity: meshed musical styles of film soundtracks of the time are quite common. Fassbinder's *Die bitterein Tränen der Petra von Kant* features Giuseppi Verdi and the Platters back to back; Kluge's films, as one writer describes them in a partial list, move from: "military music . . . [to] barrel organ music . . . music from an out of tune piano, . . . German songs, American songs, music for winds, waltzes . . . , the funeral march from

Götterdämmerung from a merry go round organ"—everything, in short, but film music![19] (In fact, of his entire output, only Kluge's *Brutalität in Stein* had original commissioned music, by Hans Leopold Posegga.)

Combining different types of music—say, popular and classical—has been common since the movies began, but the trend experienced a real boom after World War II, coinciding with the mushrooming of recording industries and rock and roll. Today, the mixed scores of a movie like Wenders's *Until the End of the World* are almost *de rigueur,* required by corporate culture to maximize a film's profit through tie-in products. For this and other reasons, it cannot be claimed that the plundering and mixing of existing music guarantees an alternative film scoring practice. But young German films used musical citations in such exaggerated ways that they generate the impression of inculcated, clichéd codes rather than the sense of something emotionally expressive or "original" being articulated.[20] "Originality" emerges solely from the new context, the deracination of the work from its original aesthetic, cultural, and historical circumstance, as in Kluge's *Die Artisten in der Zirkuskuppel: Ratlos* where the Beatles' "Yesterday" is played in Spanish as documentary footage of the 1939 festivities for German Art Day in Munich is shown.[21]

One senses that all is uprooted and then chucked back together. It is worth contrasting this practice to a more conventional film citation of a musical piece. In Hitchcock's *Shadow of a Doubt,* the "Merry Widow Waltz" is repeatedly used as a clue to the murderer's identity. You know the melody is Lehár's, and in fact its effect in the film comes from that association, emphasized all the more when a character misidentifies the tune as the "Blue Danube" at one point. The boundaries of the musical citation are in this way clearly demarcated. Compare this practice with the entirety of a score being constituted by a mélange of borrowed, partial, interrupted music. The sheer weight of quotations in Kluge, the intensity of their revision, or the variety of musical forms and styles in Peer Raben's compositions makes it impossible for any singular piece (or composer) to stand out on its own.[22]

Here, then, are some of the ways previously recorded music is reworked in the postwar German cinema. First, it is reframed, and given new meanings, by its different context, like the Beethoven at the beginning of *Maria Braun* or the Spanish Beatles in Kluge's *Artisten.* Second, it is mixed with other, disparate musical forms. *Chinesisches Roulette,* for instance, features Mahler, Kraftwerk, melodramatic thriller motifs, and liturgical forms. Third, previously recorded music is altered or "damaged" in some way (the imperfect transmission of Beethoven's Ninth symphony in *Die Patriotin* is a good example here). Fourth, the music may not be played in its entirety. As in the sound design of art directors like Godard or Ackerman, who turn music on and off like so many spigots, any tonal resolution of a work is left frustrated, melodies undeveloped. Finally, there is often little time to identify even the most renowned pieces (this is particularly true in Kluge's work). When they are recognized, as Rudolf Hohlweg believes, they are "familiar to the point of being clichés, popular to the point of becoming obnoxious,"[23] worn-out fragments of official cultural history.

This list of practices, I should note, is not exhaustive, nor are its items mutually independent. The truncated performance of works like Beethoven's Ninth Symphony, say, or their being overlaid onto additional music and sound effects, or their distortion and manipulation in other ways collectively frustrate the "totality," the uniqueness, the originality of the performance. Their historicity, as Bathrick puts it, emerges from the tensions among "coexisting, intertextual histories" that may have less to do with German cinema's thematic preoccupation with the past than with, to paraphrase him apropos of *Lili Marleen,* the day-to-day terrors of the Third Reich; the relationship of music to the state, power, and control; the industry of glamour; the story of singer Lale Anderson; and Hollywood's popular iconography of Nazism.[24]

To be sure, other musical strategies exist that do not rely on previously existing music and that also suggest different connections between music and remembrance. One strategy reduces music to little more than primal sounds and effects, something perhaps best exemplified by Ottinger's *Madame X* and *Trinkerin.* The latter is an acoustically sparse but visually extravagant staging of the death drive; the glamorously dressed drinker tours the spots in Berlin she believes best suit her plan to drink herself to death. The soundtrack relies largely on exaggerated sounds (some diegetic, some not). Not unlike a film by Jacques Tati, we hear amplified sounds of the drinker's high-heeled footsteps, the crinkling of her dress; there is very little language, with music erupting in the most unusual places. In a diegetic nightclub, for instance, punk performer Nina Hagen sings a song to the tune of Frederick Loewe's "On the Street Where You Live" from *My Fair Lady.* The drinker herself, in a rare foray into language, performs a song in English, but by and large Peer Raben's music for the film (actually more sound design than score) creatively parallels the formal deterioration of image that progressively "undoes" the unnamed protagonist. Any sense of memory invoked by this particular film relates less to a political or historical event than a cultural ideal, one wrapped in the signs of old Hollywood studio glamour. *Trinkerin* in general unwraps the conventions of bourgeois, heterosexual femininity through a variety of means (for example, the character's inability to live up to the idealized glamour of her outfits; her cross-class intimacy with a "street woman"; the inappropriateness of a Broadway musical love song to her circumstances) and also suggests a disintegrated identity through the character's excessive consumption as both drinker and tourist. Retreat and disintegration mark both text and character, but it is a retreat that refuses the refuge of established visual and acoustic models, no matter how elaborate—or minimal—they may be.

Repetition is another device frequently used in scores of the New German Cinema. The pop song "Sugarbaby," for example, in Percy Adlon's *Zuckerbaby* appears frequently enough to duplicate (quite playfully) Marianne Saegebrech's obsessive passion for food and for the young male subway conductor. In the same way, the song "Lili Marleen" is obsessively repeated in Fassbinder's film to the point of sadism—a sadism comically acknowledged when it is used in the "torture" sequence of Giancarlo Giannini.[25] Repetition, as Freud argued, is borne out of a compulsion to master a past trauma, and that is largely the way the young German Cinema has been approached: tearing around in circles, unable to purge its Nazi past.[26]

One could alternatively depathologize the process somewhat and consider how musical repetition more productively unsettles the notion of originality (Benjaminian aura), making every sound a copy uninvolved in romantic myths of creativity, or of "expressing" anything original from inside the text, or encrypted within the past. To return to *Petra von Kant,* for example, when records such as "The Great Pretender" or "Smoke Gets in Your Eyes" are played on the phonograph, there can be no question that these songs—and the sentiment they might express—have been previously manufactured. While they may provide some commentary on Petra's emotional polarities (given that, as she says, "these records are from my youth [and] either make me very happy or very sad"), there is little to attach them directly to any sense of an "inner" character. The pieces are borrowed, imported not only from a different period in her life but from a different culture, another set of kitschy mementos not unlike her many wigs or "Midas and Dionysus" mural—all objects that refuse to "add up."

Utopia: Partial Challenges to the Whole

> The very idea of an authentic national experience or a mythic hero points to a culture singularly obsessed with wholeness, unification, and identity. These cultural motifs are themselves symptomatic of a history marked by division, particularisms, regionalism and decenteredness, punctuated by brief and usually disastrous periods of centralised military-bureaucratic rule. —Thomas Elsaesser, *New German Cinema: A History*

If opera supplied the "power plant of emotions" in the nineteenth century, cinema, as Kluge has maintained, has provided the same for the twentieth. That we should distrust such an industry, with its imposing mass production of overpowering narratives, is very much in evidence in German films of the 1970s and 1980s, through their emphasis on the smaller slivers of reminiscences, their accusations, uncertainties, and desires. Such partialities, much like the musical fragments and the disunified, heavily quotational film scores, formally articulate both the division—and revisioning—Elsaesser and others observe. The intelligence of composers such as Peer Raben working within such a markedly quotational framework emerges from their own music working in a similar way; that is, of *not* reinforcing or unifying the image, but of showing a different potential altogether, new combinations that, Raben, along with Fassbinder, Kluge and even the later Adorno, have associated with the utopian. Raben, for instance, has stated that music, "supports something that isn't yet in the image, nor in the mind either . . . that *isn't yet true*."[27] In his score for Fassbinder's *Berlin Alexanderplatz*, for instance, he composed several different themes for "Franz B": the first is a tango, the second a sort of false waltz (the standard waltz form is given unconventional accentuation, added beats, and so forth). The forms Raben deploys in this and other films like *Lola* and *Veronika Voss* are most aptly described as "off," suggesting simultaneously the inadequacy of dominant forms as well as their endurability—and, again, the potential for something that lies beyond them.

Fassbinder's work, known for its unrelenting pessimism, does not immediately invite comparisons to utopia. Yet no shortage of critics have pursued his intricate relationship to the utopian.[28] In one particularly insightful piece, "Fassbinder, Spectatorship, and Utopian Desire," Peter Ruppert argues that Fassbinder's utopia doesn't offer blueprints for social or psychic escape so much as the possibility of alternatives: "Unlike the classical models of the utopian tradition . . . Fassbinder's do not provide us with a utopian vision that ameliorates social tension and social contradiction."[29] Instead, they "intensify our perception of the gap that separates social fact from utopian desire"[30] and "plant the seeds of utopia negatively: they arouse utopian desire by making manifest the need to displace images of human misery and exploitation with more desirable alternatives."[31] Ruppert's emphasis on negativity receives provocative and convincing elaboration by Kaja Silverman, for whom Fassbinder's complex relationship to utopia stems from his refusal of the comforting fictions by which we usually live our lives. Siverman suggests that "a psychic 'elsewhere' . . . which is synonymous with . . . masochistic ecstasy" emerges precisely out of that refusal and negativity.[32] It is important to add that Fassbinder's utopian "aesthetics of pessimism" is unfathomable without a consideration of memory and history in their many forms: official, antagonistic, psychic, political, and socioeconomic.

Lili Marleen—a film subtitled "the story of a song"—offers several ways to explore how music participates in the construction of a sense of alterity and of a historically conceptualized utopia. From the very outset, the text announces its fascination with music both formally and diegetically. As Bathrick argues (in a comment that could be extrapolated to other New German films), "By inundating us with an excess of sound collage, *Lili Marleen* forces the issue of sound itself, and music in particular into the foreground as a historical, self-defining thread," a function made all the more intense when considered against classical narrative's more covert use of (mainly nondiegetic) music.[33] Thematically, the film depicts Willie's survival and endurance of fascism by virtue of her relationship to popular music, specifically, through the song with which her identity virtually fuses. Robert Mendelssohn, on the other hand, the Jewish lover from whom she is separated, survives through his alliance with music of the artworld, something none too subtly suggested by his name. For him, however, performance is "tragically" deferred until after the war, when he is free to conduct once-banned Jewish Gustav Mahler at his bombastic best: the Eighth Symphony, Mahler's "symphony for a thousand."

In this regard, the Mendelssohn/Mahler combination initially suggests a kind of resisting ideological propriety denied the popular music associated with Willie, who is willing to work within fascist circles if it will help her love affair. Yet that high-culture propriety is ultimately rendered questionable and even ironic (consider that the Eighth is based on the Faust story). Even without access to Raben's or Fassbinder's intentions, it is difficult to imagine their selection of music here as much else but parodic. The intense Romanticism of Mahler's late nineteenth- and early twentieth-century work made him somewhat of an anachronism even at the time, emerging as it did on the cusp of atonal and serial music, and the composer's work can easily suggest a nostalgia for outmoded, Romantic ways of composing and conceptualizing music.

Such an associative link was made—uncritically if artfully—through the Mahler score in Visconti's *Death in Venice*, just as it was established through Visconti's transformation of von Aschenbach from writer to composer.[34] I imagine that much more to Fassbinder and Raben's liking would have been Ken Russell's campy send-up of Visconti's sentimental invocation of the composer in an early scene of *Mahler* that wordlessly and viciously lampoons its cinematic predecessor, washing us in the famous Adagio as we see a little Tadzio teasingly weaving in and out of several sun-drenched columns.

By contrast, *Lili Marleen* shows distrust for the classical endeavors of Mendelssohn as well as for Willie's vulgar tunes. Neither high nor popular

Figure 4. *Lili Marleen* (1980). Photo courtesy of the Kobal Collection.

music finally enables the characters to establish relationships with the objects they want (namely, each other) nor offers any real refuge from the difficult political and historical circumstances that surround them. At the same time that Mahler is finally and climactically being performed, for instance, Willie, back after the dramatic separation from Robert during the

Figure 5. *Lili Marleen*. Photo courtesy of the Ronald Grant Archive.

war, encounters the woman whom he has married in her absence. Even before this romantic disloyalty, the film controversially questions the nobility of Mendelssohn and his family (involved in the Jewish underground resistance) by drawing firm parallels between the family's methods, values, and attitudes—especially toward Willie—and those of the Reich officials.

At first glance, the popular music of *Lili Marleen* seems to offer, if not the full sanctuary or refuge denied to Western art music, at least the idea of an unofficial sphere in which desire might flourish. During Willie's first performance of "Lili Marleen" in a small cabaret, for example, a barroom brawl erupts. And in her first performance of the song sponsored by the Nazi party, she wears a colorful dress exposing much of her throat and chest, leaving her arms free to gesticulate and add other emphatic weight to it. In this way the first two performances suggest an association among the popular tune, anarchic energy, and unimpeded movement, but it is a kinetic freedom that diminishes each time Willie sings. Her costumes become increasingly constrictive as well: her second "official" performance of the number, for instance, features her in a stark, colorless outfit. In her last performance (made under duress after her failed suicide attempt when Nazi officials insist that she must be made to look more beautiful than ever to dispel rumors that they had killed her), Willie's metallic costume is like a kind of chintzy armor whose mechanistic clinks are audible on the soundtrack. Her outfit covers nearly all of her body, and she can barely move (compare figures 4 and 5). Any explicitly utopian affect the song might have had fully recedes; its political function as spectacle takes over.

The catchy song that thus moved hearts and minds during the war is turned into deadening artifact, something visualized during this final, elaborate production number. The scene is cross-cut between images of German soldiers lured into enemy fire because of the latter's broadcast of the song, meeting profoundly literal deaths. The writer of "Lili Marleen," Norbert Schultze, criticized Peer Raben for having "turned [his] song into a helmet" (to which Raben replied, "precisely"). Through the song's affiliation with the militarism of war, and through its equally militant repetition at the hands of a massive state apparatus and colossal entertainment industry, Fassbinder's film weakens the affiliations it might have had with romance, nostalgia, utopia, and the fulfilment of desire or utopia. In this regard, its sadistic function (for example, the acoustic torture of Mendelssohn) elaborately mirrors its political and ideological function to manipulate the masses.

At the same time, the above reading does not account for all meanings of the song, and the film finally suggests the irreducibility of music to fixed functions, objects, or desires of any sort. Diegetically used by both Allied and Axis forces alike and initially sung out of Willie's idealistic belief in the power of love, the song remains at the intersection of conflicting functions, subjectivities, and discourses. Its repetition does not work to overdetermine a singular function, but to destabilize meaning into a plurality of effects. Bathrick's recent analysis reframes the question of musical repetition further still, arguing that it offers productive critique, if not an out-and-out utopia: "The repetition of the song in *Lili Marleen* thus serves as a kind of inverted critique of ideology: its insistently overbearing restaging indulges us to the point of revulsion [Giannini's torture again], transforming its meaning from the inside out and mutating before our very ears into an object of political subversion."[35]

Read in this way, as an articulation of the importance—and frequent impotence—of human utopias, the film engages the kind of negative critique for which Fassbinder is renowned. Indeed, such a reading would doubtless have been embraced by Fassbinder himself, who in his well-known repudiation of the charge of fatalism in his work, argued that "film, possessing a fatalistic ending, creates a need on the part of the audience to search for the idea of a utopia. The more fatalistic the film is, the more hopeful it is."[36]

It is important to stress the considerable role played by emotions in any "political subversion" or utopian direction suggested by films such *Lili Marleen*. The "story of a song" shows the characters' passion, however thwarted and misguided, aiming toward the idea, if not the practice, of an alternative and hope for fulfilment.[37] It also demonstrates the contestatory and partial nature of utopian alternatives and the social and historical elsewheres they intimate. That the integrity of the utopias suggested by the film's musical forms are severely compromised indicate that the future is every bit as circumscribed and constrained as the past. Nevertheless, though compromised, they are not without affect, and emotions are very much on the table. Fassbinder does not hesitate to take advantage of music's emotional impact. As Bathrick writes: "Unlike Brecht's [use of] music, Fassbinder's [and Raben's use of] music indulges in affect—excessively."[38]

Not unexpectedly, Alexander Kluge also places considerable weight on the "power of emotions," irrationality, imagination, and dreams, which he believes to be suppressed by prevailing conventions and social, political, and discursive institutions. His is not a desire simply to unleash the forces of irrationality (as, say, in surrealism) so much as acknowledge them in material and unconventional ways. In a significant revision of the claim in *Gefühle*, which opposes objects to emotions, he writes, "Desires are no less real than real events."[39] It becomes a matter of excavating them: because, as Kluge states, like his patriot, the materials and imagination necessary for change lay hidden in fragments "buried under a thick layer of cultural garbage. [They have] to be dug out. This project of excavation, not at all a utopian [that is, impossible] notion, can be realized only through our work."[40] Curiously, the idea is not dissimilar to Novalis's notion of constructing utopian paradise: "Paradise was the ideal of earthly life, and the question of the whereabouts is not unimportant. It has been scattered all over the world and has become unrecognizable. Its scattered traits must be collected, its skeleton filled in." One might add that only considerable labor (including psychic) is required in order for objects to function in this way.

History/Memory

These are some of ways that music, through its new contexts and unusual forms, can articulate alternative ways of history-making. Although the alternatives it suggests do not, and cannot, exist removed apart or in any pure state, music's partial, fragmentary, and even contradictory presentation is important. The prerecorded, non-German pieces at the end of *Petra von Kant,* the truncated Mahler that opens *Chinesisches Roulette,* the endless operatic citations of *Die Macht der Gefühle*—all distance us from the possible fullness that their earlier contexts, identities, and fantasies may have offered. But their affect, and meanings are not voided. As portions of the past, these fragments become materialized and reactivated in much the same way as the dead Colonel's knee that narrates *Die Patriotin.* Like Gabi Teichert, the knee tries to make sense of the pieces and ligaments of the past that aren't "dead," that still speak, and speak differently from the bigger histories enframing or embalming them. And as these former bodies—human or musical—become fragmented, it could be argued that so too do they fragment and blast away at the "homogeneous course of history" Benjamin warned against: pieces of the past, while lifted out of official versions and stories, are not reducible to them.

Emphasizing partial remembrance over totality and changed contexts over lost origins, music can challenge notions of *Trauerarbeit* that have focused on totalized, mass-psychologized and even romanticized notions of loss, German nationhood, and history. Music can put the past into new contexts, moving it forward instead of only facing backward. What is more, postwar German cinema's frequent, often hyperbolic presentation of the past—with its elaborate restagings and musical playbacks—further attenuates the aging claims of a national "inability to mourn." In the scores of Kluge, Fassbinder, and others, music works not to provide the illusion of reunified reminiscences but to acknowledge their incomplete nature. Its presentation in material bits and pieces, collages and modified forms establish the endurance, if not the continuity, of the past in new circumstances and meanings, all of which give evidence of sundry histories taking form in the present. These small struggles of reactivated remembrance are important amid contemporary voices proclaiming the "end of history" or that

Germany has now remembered "too much." As Kluge's ironic—yet still earnest—voice-over tells us about his patriot, "We must change history in order to get new material." Perhaps listening is one way to do that.

Notes

The author would like to thank the Social Sciences and Humanities Research Council of Canada for support that made researching and writing this essay possible.

1. David Bathrick, "Inscribing History, Prohibiting and Producing Desire: Fassbinder's *Lili Marleen,*" *New German Critique* 63 (1994): 35.
2. Eric Santner, *Stranded Objects: Mourning, Memory, and Film in Postwar Germany* (Ithaca: Cornell University Press, 1990), 22.
3. See Bathrick, "Inscribing History"; Thomas Elsaesser, "Primary Identification and the Historical Subject: Fassbinder's Germany," *Cinetracts* 11 (1980): 43–52, and *New German Cinema: A History* (New Brunswick: Rutgers University Press, 1989); Santner, *Stranded Objects;* and Kaja Silverman, "Fassbinder and Lacan: A Reconsideration of Gaze, Look, and Image," *Camera Obscura* 19 (1989): 54–85, repr. in *Male Subjectivity at the Margins* (New York: Routledge, 1992).
4. Some of the more influential articles include Elsaesser's "Primary Identification"; Anna Kuhn, "Rainer Werner Fassbinder: The Alienated Vision" in *New German Filmmakers: From Oberhausen through the 1970s,* ed. K. Phillips (New York: Ungar, 1984); Judith Mayne, "Fassbinder and Spectatorship," *New German Critique* 12 (1977): 61–74, repr. as "Fassbinder's Ali: Fear Eats the Soul and Spectatorship," in *Close Viewings,* ed. Peter Lehman (Tallahassee: Florida State University Presses, 1990); and Silverman, "Fassbinder and Lacan." I make the comment about vision-based approaches to New German Cinema in my essay "Music and the Melodramatic Past of the New German Cinema," in *Melodrama: Stage/Picture/Screen,* ed. J. Bratton, J. Cook, and C. Gledhill. (London: BFI, 1994), 106–18.
5. We shall see below that by omitting music from the list of German cultural achievements "ruined" by Hitler the film also suggests its possible transcendence or imperviousness to the atrocities of the Shoah. At the same time, the centrality of Wagner (fragments) to *Hitler*'s image and soundtrack acknowledges the impossibility of that fantasy.
6. See, for example, Bathrick, "Inscribing History"; Timothy Corrigan, "Werner Schroeter's Operatic Cinema," *Discourse* 3 (Spring 1981): 46–59; Gertrud Koch, "Alexander Kluge's Phantom of the Opera," *New German Critique* 49 (1990): 79–88. By contrast, a full-length study exists in German, Norbert Jürgen Schneider, *Handbuch Filmmusik: Musikdramaturgie im Neuen Deutschen Film* (Munich: Ölschläger, 1986). Australian scholar Roger Hillman has written a delightful analysis of the role of classical music in *Der Ehe der Maria Braun* in his essay "Narrative, Sound, and Film: Fassbinder's *The Marriage of Maria Braun,*" in *Fields of Vision: Essays in Film Studies, Visual Anthropology, and Photography,* ed. L. Devereaux and R. Hillman (Berkeley and Los Angeles: University of California Press, 1995), 181–95.
7. Plot summaries aside, powerful parallels exist between Clément's text and Kluge's *Die Macht der Gefühle,* discussed below. As Clément writes, "on the opera stage women perpetually sing their eternal undoing," and in Kluge's work we hear that "in every opera that deals with redemption a woman is sacrificed in Act 5." See Catherine Clément, *Opera, or the Undoing of Women* (Minneapolis: University of Minnesota Press, 1988), 5.

8. Elsaesser, "Historicizing the Subject: A Body of Work?" *New German Critique* 63 (1994): 33.

9. Ibid., 15.

10. See my *Strains of Utopia: Gender, Nostalgia, and Hollywood Film Music* (Princeton: Princeton University Press, 1992) for a fuller discussion of totalizing discourses that have historically surrounded film music.

11. Miriam Hansen, "Alexander Kluge, Cinema and the Public Sphere: The Construction Site of Counter-History," *Discourse* 6 (Fall 1983): 70.

12. Walter Benjamin, "Thesis on the Philosophy of History," in *Illuminations: Essays and Reflections* (New York: Schocken, 1969), 262–63.

13. Beethoven's Ninth reappears briefly at the close of the film. For critics like Hillman, this signals an effort to "regain the original impetus of the Ninth's idealism"; "Beethoven, Mahler, and the New German Cinema," *Musicology Australia* 20 (1997): 101. Yet even Hillman acknowledges that such restorative efforts are fraught with ambivalence, ambiguity, and even criticism.

14. Miriam Hansen, "Introduction," *New German Critique* 49 (1990): 9.

15. At the same time, the image of the eye that follows Heller's long monologue is accompanied by excerpts of *Tristan und Isolde,* an opera whose impulse toward transcendence—not to mention death—is well-known: "Oh descend night of love . . . release me from the world!" The intense Romanticism of these fragments matches those of other details Syberberg makes available: we see a small, weeping figure of Ludwig II; his winter garden (depicted with the same nostalgic sensibility as Charles Foster Kane's boyhood home as seen through the toy globe of shaken "snow"); playing at film's end is the "Fanfare" from Beethoven's *Fidelio.* In my view, the sentimental aesthetic nationalism of such details is unmistakable, though others have debated such a reading of the film.

16. The second movement, the "Kaiserhymne," written after Haydn's exposure to English music glorifying the monarchy, was later integrated into the string quartet, opus 76 no. 3. This music was thus *already* inscribed with nationalist fervor even before its reincarnation as the notorious "Deutschland über alles."

17. Elsaesser, "Myth as the Phantasmagoria of History: H. J. Syberberg, Cinema and Representation," *New German Critique* 24, no. 5 (1981–82): 152.

18. Susan McClary, *Feminine Endings: Music, Gender, and Sexuality* (Minneapolis: University of Minnesota Press, 1991), 128.

19. Rudolf Hohlweg, "Musik für Film–Film für Musik: Annaeherung an Herzog, Kluge, Straub," in *Herzog/Kluge/Straub,* ed. Peter Jansen and Wolfram Schuette. (Munich: Carl Hanser, 1976), Reihe Film 9:45–68. All citations are from an unpublished manuscript translation by Rebecca Harries (1994).

20. See my essay "Music and the Melodramatic Past" for an elaboration of this point in terms of melodramatic expression and interiority in the scoring practices of West German film from the 1970s and 1980s.

21. Hohlweg, "Musik für Film," 7.

22. Also ibid., 6. The difference here is what many theorists maintain separates modernist from postmodernist aesthetics: whereas the modernist piece still has a stable point of origin, an artist behind it, and clear boundaries, even as it quotes, postmodern texts have no definitive sense of where citations end and "new" material begins, or who indeed has "created" the work at all (compare the modernist music of Charles Ives, for instance, to postmodern rap sampling).

23. Ibid., 5.

24. Bathrick, "Inscribing History," 39–40.

25. Raben confirms this was precisely his and Fassbinder's intention.

26. Repetition in the New German Cinema can be situated in a melodramatic tradition to which Fassbinder in particular is heir (the cyclicity of narrative events is the

key thing here). The principal difference is that the repeated use of music in Fass-binder's work goes against conventional (post-Victorian; Hollywood) melodrama's belief in the possibility—however remote, artificial, or forestalled—of happy endings. (Hohlweg offers a lovely analysis of *Fitzcarraldo*'s score in this regard.) See also my "Music and The Melodramatic Past."

27. Peer Raben, "Musique et cinéma, ou la cantate de Bach dans l'érable," *CinémAction* 1984. (English translation forthcoming in *Canadian Journal of Film Studies*.)

28. In addition to those mentioned here, other critics who have identified and explored Fassbinder's relationship to the utopian include Timothy Corrigan, who argues that the director's works gives us a "clear view of missing historical landscapes" ("Fassbinder's *Bitter Tears of Petra Von Kant,*" in *New German Film: The Displaced Image* [Austin: University of Texas Press, 1983], 47); Ruth McCormick, who sees in Fassbinder the failed utopia of love ("Fassbinder's Realism: Imitation of Life,"in *Fassbinder* [New York: Tanam, 1981], 85–97); Brigitte Peucker, for whom Fassbinder's characters are motivated by "an urge to utopia," which she identifies as "bourgeois individualism run wild," suggesting less an alternative to social realities and more their grotesque intensification ("Political Paradigms in Fassbinder and Herzog," *Purdue University 6th Annual Conference on Film West Lafayette* [1982], 31); and John Sandford, who argues that his work offers "a principle of hope that gives an inkling of a better world" *(The New German Cinema* [London: Wolff, 1980], 103). Thomas Elsaesser, in *Fassbinder's Germany: History, Identity, Subject* (Amsterdam: Amsterdam University Press, 1996), pursues the term largely, though not exclusively, in terms of Fassbinder's radical reworking of notions of exchange, economics, and contracts.

29. Peter Ruppert, "Fassbinder, Spectatorship, and Utopian Desire," *Cinema Journal* 28, no. 2 (1989): 33.

30. Ibid., 34.

31. Ibid.

32. Silverman, *Male Subjectivity*, 252.

33. Bathrick, "Inscribing History," 49.

34. Adorno's influential study of Mahler offers a convincing and much more nuanced assessment of the composer's work, arguing that its active use of outmoded material indicates an awareness of what musical forms could no longer deliver in a changing aesthetic, social, economic, and political atmosphere.

35. Bathrick, "Inscribing History," 52.

36. Norbert Sparrow, "I Let the Audience Feel and Think: An Interview with Rainer Werner Fassbinder," *Cinéaste* 8, no. 2 (1977): 20.

37. A similar, ambivalent response to the film might be expected from contemporary audiences familiar with the history of the song "Lili Marleen,"since the release of the 1993 documentary on Norbert Schulze, *Den Teufel am Hintern Geküsst* (Kissing the devil's arse) by A. Bondy and M. Knapp.

38. Bathrick, "Inscribing History," 49.

39. James Acuff, "Toward a Realistic Method: Commentaries on the Notion of Antagonistic Realism: A Translation of Alexander Kluge's *Zur realistischen Methode*" (M.A. thesis, University of Texas, 1980), 22.

40. Alexander Kluge, "On Film and the Public Sphere," *New German Critique* 24, no. 5 (1981–82): 210.

KRIN GABBARD

Kansas City Dreamin'
Robert Altman's Jazz History Lesson

✳

Just after the release of *Kansas City* in August 1996, Robert Altman told several interviewers that his jazz-infused film was constructed *like* jazz.[1] Altman has been justly celebrated for his ability to coax memorable performances out of actors by turning them loose without a script. Contrast, for example, Elliott Gould's extraordinary improvisations in Altman's *California Split* and *The Long Goodbye* with his wooden performances in most of his other films. In *Kansas City,* as in all of Altman's films, there was much jazz-inspired ad-libbing during the rehearsal process. As a totality, however, *Kansas City* has been carefully planned and scrupulously researched in ways that barely resemble the in-the-moment improvisations of a jazz performance.

As with his earlier film *Short Cuts* (1993), Altman co-wrote the screenplay for *Kansas City* with Frank Barhydt, like Altman a Kansas City native. Altman and Barhydt created a handful of fictional characters for the plot of the film, but they also carefully reproduced many of the details of Kansas City in 1934. The soft-spoken boss Tom Pendergast, the ineffectual Governor Guy Park, the respectable criminal John Lazia, and the shootings at a polling place on election day are all presented with as much attention to the history books as can be expected from a Hollywood film.[2] The automobiles, the hairstyles, the telephones, the storefronts on Eighteenth and Vine, and the old Beaux-Arts Union Station all look much as they did in 1934. Carolyn Stilton (Miranda Richardson), the wife of a fictional politician, even gives a little speech about "Goats and Rabbits," although the film never explains that these were nicknames for local political factions.[3]

With similarly understated fidelity to jazz history, *Kansas City* represents the artists who invented a distinct style of music in that wide-open city. Count Basie, Lester Young, Mary Lou Williams, Ben Webster, and Jo

Jones, all of whom were in Kansas City in 1934, are played by real-life jazz musicians in the film. According to Geri Allen, who appears as the legendary pianist/arranger Mary Lou Williams, the filmmakers went out of their way to make the musicians feel comfortable in *Kansas City,* providing them with well-tuned pianos and rehearsal facilities even in their dressing rooms. Altman then took the unusual step of filming their performances "live," eventually accumulating enough footage for a separate sixty-minute video featuring only the musicians.[4]

Altman relied on Hal Willner to assemble the jazz musicians who dominate the soundtrack in *Kansas City.* Willner had previously convened the jazz group around Annie Ross for Altman's *Short Cuts* (1993), a film based on several unrelated short stories by Raymond Carver. Drawing upon the work of Robert T. Self, I have argued that the jazz singer Tess (played by Annie Ross) and her daughter Zoe (Lori Singer) provide a key to understanding how the many narratives of *Short Cuts* might fit together.[5] On the one hand, Tess the jazz singer and Zoe the classical cellist represent, respectively, those who wear their emotions on their sleeves and those who repress their feelings until they explode. On the other hand, some characters in *Short Cuts* are improvisers like Tess while others seem to need scripts such as Zoe reads when she performs. Tess and Zoe then provide multidetermined paradigms for understanding almost all the characters in the film. Throughout *Short Cuts* the music of Zoe or Tess is often the "glue" that holds together disparate scenes involving unrelated characters. Significantly, Tess and her daughter are the only two characters in the film who do not grow directly out of stories by Carver.

For *Kansas City,* Willner brought in an array of mainstream and avant-garde jazz artists, sometimes with stunning results. For example, when pianist Allen appears as Mary Lou Williams with her hair worn up, she bears an uncanny musical and physical resemblance to a woman whom Allen herself has admired and studied. In the same spirit in which they wrote the Goats and Rabbits speech, knowing that only a handful of viewers would catch the reference, Altman and Barhydt have unobtrusively introduced many small details from jazz history. They accurately place the real-life Addie Parker (Jeff Feringa) at a Western Union office and at her home where boarders occupy rooms on the second floor. Most viewers were probably unaware that this woman's son is Charlie Parker, who is also faithfully portrayed as a fourteen-year-old saxophonist in his school's marching band. In another carefully researched moment, Kevin Mahogany sings "I Left My Baby" from behind a bar, a reference to the blues shouter Joe Turner who originally worked as a singing bartender at the Sunset Club in Kansas City. At no point in the film, however, does anyone in the film mention Turner by name. When the black gangster Seldom Seen (Harry Belafonte) does in fact speak the name of a jazz musician, he refers to "Bill Basie." Basie has said that he did not become *Count* Basie until 1936 while working at the Reno Club.[6] At its most esoteric, the film has Seldom ask about "that doctor friend of Bennie Moten,"[7] a reference to the successful Kansas City bandleader who employed musicians such as Basie, Webster, and Jimmy Rushing. Moten died in 1935 while having his tonsils removed by the same doctor with whom he had socialized the night before.[8]

Nevertheless, *Kansas City* takes a few liberties with jazz history. Seldom Seen and the musicians are situated at the "Hey Hay Club." There was in fact a "Hey Hay Club" in Kansas City, but it was too small to accommodate all the musicians and dancers who appear in the film's spacious Hey Hay Club. The club is clearly a composite of several of the city's better known clubs, especially the Reno. In the film's musical centerpiece, Coleman Hawkins (Craig Handy with his dreadlocks concealed inside a large hat) wages a tenor saxophone battle with Lester Young (Joshua Redman in a modified porkpie). Hawkins did in fact square off against Young in Kansas City, but the legendary encounter took place in December 1933, at the Cherry Blossom Inn while Hawkins was in town with Fletcher Henderson and his orchestra.[9] Hawkins left Henderson early in March 1934 and sailed for England a few weeks later at the end of the month, not returning to the States until 1939.[10] He could not have been in Kansas City on election day in 1934 when the action of the film takes place. The film might also be criticized for a scene at the end when Ron Carter plays Duke Ellington's "Solitude" as a solo for pizzicato string bass. The most innovative bassists of the period, such as Milt Hinton and Jimmy Blanton, did not begin recording bass solos until 1939; it is unlikely that the bass was regarded as a solo instrument in 1934.[11]

But these are not the kinds of complaints that jazz purists have lodged against the film. Peter Watrous, at that time the principal jazz writer for the *New York Times,* spoke for many when he made two basic criticisms. He charged that the film "has turned the music and musicians into servants of the plot and the film's ambiance," and that the music "isn't particularly idiomatic of the time and place . . . as if rock-and-roll predated it, not the other way around."[12] This second complaint must be answered in terms of how jazz musicians today could successfully perform and improvise in a style that is more than sixty years old. According to Michael Bourne, Wiliner did in fact start out directing the musicians to imitate recordings from the 1930s, but he soon realized that "if we concentrate on that, it'll end up dull."[13] There have long been "ghost bands" touring the United States that

Figure 1. Robert Altman, *Kansas City* (1996): Harry Belafonte as Seldom Seen. Photo Eli Reed. © New Line Home Video. Courtesy Photofest.

play note-for-note imitations of old Swing Era recordings by Glenn Miller or the Dorseys. Jazz, however, especially the music of Basie, Ellington, and Henderson that is performed in *Kansas City,* was not meant to be played the same way every night. The handful of repertory jazz orchestras that have re-created this music in recent years often succeed more in embalming the music than in bringing it back to life. Willner and the musicians who came to Kansas City for location shooting eventually agreed to play in their own, more extroverted styles while trying to suggest the "flavor" of their predecessors' playing.

There was probably no solution, however, that would have pleased the more implacable jazz aficionados. I have maintained that the discourses of jazz writing during the last several decades have almost always cast the music as an autonomous art outside of history and cultural circumstance.[14] Jazz enthusiasts are not likely to be swayed by arguments about the specific purposes the music has actually served, whether it be accompaniments for drinking, gender coding among musicians, or background for a Hollywood film. Watrous's first complaint—that the musicians were only "servants" of the plot—is thus related to the second. In both cases he appears unwilling to acknowledge established cinematic practice or the validity of any other attempt to recontextualize the music. Watrous also overlooks the many subtle ways in which the musicians are in fact closely related to the action and are frequently essential to the meaning of the film. In fact,

Kansas City may have succeeded more than almost any other Hollywood film in folding jazz performance into a cinematic narrative.

The musicians in *Kansas City* play throughout the day and night at the Hey Hay Club, the domain of Seldom Seen, an articulate but sinister gangster based on a real-life figure from Kansas City history, who carried his money and drugs in a cigar box.[15] The plot of the film is built around the attempts of Blondie (Leigh) to retrieve her husband Johnny O'Hara (Dermot Mulroney) from the Hey Hey Club where Seldom holds him captive. Earlier Johnny smeared burnt cork on his face and robbed Sheepshan Red (A. C. Smith), a wealthy black gambler on his way to the Hey Hay Club. Seldom quickly figures out the ruse and informs the victimized gambler, "You've been robbed by Amos and Andy." Johnny is brought in by Seldom's henchmen following the confession of his accomplice, a black cabdriver named "Blue" Green (Martin Martin). While Seldom contemplates how he will punish Johnny, Blondie kidnaps Carolyn Stilton in hopes that her husband can use his influence to set Johnny free. Henry Stilton (Michael Murphy), however, is on a train to Washington, and Blondie and Carolyn spend most of the film together waiting for messages to get through. All of this happens during the last moments of an election campaign when the politicians who might have been able to intercede with Seldom are distracted to say the least. And almost all of the action takes place while the Hey Hay Club musicians perform throughout the night and into election day. Although this music shifts between diegetic and extradiegetic registers, there is no other music in the film except for a high school band playing in the train station early in the film.

As in *Short Cuts,* the music occasionally "glues" scenes together and provides ingenious moments of continuity, as when Carolyn and Blondie begin to relax with one another at the film's halfway point just before the camera cuts to reveal Mary Lou Williams playing piano at the Hey Hay Club. The scene at the opening of the film when the two women first meet in Carolyn's bedroom is accompanied only by the occasional rumble of diegetic thunder. Although the music of the jazz musicians plays regularly behind most other scenes—even those that are far away from the actual music—Carolyn and Blondie usually interact without musical accompaniment. After Carolyn lights Blondie's cigarette and the two begin to chat for the first time without hostility, music swells up behind them. Significantly, this music features the lone female musician, Geri Allen, who is performing when the scene changes to the Hey Hay Club but the music from the previous scene continues uninterrupted. The sympathy that gradually develops between Blondie and Carolyn is one of the most intriguing elements in the

Figure 2. Robert Altman, *Kansas City* (1996): Blondie (Jennifer Jason Leigh) and Carolyn (Miranda Richardson) at the telegraph office where Addie Parker (Jeff Feringa) dwells in the background. Photo: Eli Reed. © Fine Line Features. Courtesy Photofest.

film, and Altman has achieved much by allowing Miranda Richardson and Jennifer Jason Leigh to write most of their own speeches. As was the case in *Short Cuts,* the music allows an emotional aspect of one scene to carry over into another that would otherwise seem entirely unrelated. In many ways this is standard Hollywood practice—what Claudia Gorbman has called "narrative cueing"[16]—but Altman's film uses the technique to emphasize the realities of the women's discourse in contrast to the more direct statements of the male characters. Surprising the audience by showing them that Geri Allen/Mary Lou Williams has been playing behind the first moments of bonding between the two female leads is typical of how Altman, Barhydt, and Willner have rethought the conventional practice of cinema sound in both *Short Cuts* and *Kansas City.*

Kansas City is especially inspired in its use of music when Seldom's men take Blue out to an alley and stab him repeatedly with their knives, finally leaving him to a pack of hungry dogs. This scene is punctuated by the tenor battle between Young and Hawkins. The two tenorists engage in some fancy cutting of their own (as do Altman and his editors), trading phrases and choruses in a flamboyant show of phallic competitiveness. Altman has expressed admiration for Craig Handy, who *acts* the part of Coleman Hawkins even though he speaks no dialogue. Says Altman, "Handy could be a movie star. Craig does that look when Joshua starts soloing. Craig does that look at him like, 'Who is this bird?' And then he takes his coat off. And people get it, even people who don't know what a cutting contest is."[17] Yet all of this happens within the inherently collaborative context of a jazz performance. When the combatants finally put down their weapons, they shake hands as a sign of mutual respect. The tenor contest and Blue's journey to death are "cut" together so that the black men in the alley are killing one of their own at the same time that the black men at the Hey Hay Club are engaging in the richest kind of cooperation.

In fact, no two people in the film ever connect so exquisitely as do the musicians. Virtually no nonmusical schemes are realized: Johnny's blackface holdup is a failure; Blondie's attempt to rescue Johnny is equally disastrous; phone calls to political cronies never produce results; even Pearl, the young black girl who has come from a town outside Kansas City to give up her baby, does not meet the white women from the Junior League who arrive at the train station too late to meet her. Without a trace of didacticism, Altman has held up jazz as a vivid contrast to everything that was wrong with Kansas City in 1934.

Nevertheless, Altman has also subtly implicated the jazz musicians in the city's racial and sexual politics. An early scene features a solo by tenor saxophonist James Carter who is meant to be the young Ben Webster. After reeling off an especially flamboyant phrase, Carter defiantly thrusts his horn to the side and juts out his chest and lower lip. Although he does not play in a style much like Webster's, Carter may be "sampling" the bravura that often characterized the older musician's playing. Late in his career Webster was a master of the romantic, heavy-breathing ballad. But, as Rex Stewart has written, "during his early period, he blew with unrestrained savagery, buzzing and growling through chord changes like a prehistoric monster challenging a foe."[18] Carter/Webster's musical and macho posturing accompanies Johnny O'Hara's arrival at Seldom Seen's inner sanctum at the Hey Hay Club. Johnny's first words are "I thought we could talk this over like gentleman," but Seldom resists all his overtures. The jockeying for power and masculine superiority among musicians parallels the game played out between Johnny and Seldom. Although Seldom obviously has control over whether Johnny lives or dies, Johnny still has room to assert his masculinity, especially in the scene near the end when he arrogantly explains to Seldom why a black man ought not to kill a white man.

Nonetheless, as Eric Lott has convincingly argued, this is a game that white males, especially working-class white males, seldom win in competition with black men. Although real economic and social power has always been kept out of the hands of blacks in American culture, African American men have been gender role models for most white males at least since the 1840s when minstrelsy became the dominant form of popular entertainment in American life.[19] In the twentieth century, the comportment of white athletes on the court or playing field has become increasingly based on the body language of black athletes, just as white jazz musicians and then popular musicians have engaged in studied imitations of how black men make music. In *Kansas City*, Johnny O'Hara effectively adopts both aspects of minstrelsy's legacy. He transgresses against law and custom after blacking up, not unlike the minstrel man (and his audiences) for whom the practice authorized antisocial behavior. But Johnny also adopts the swaggering, hypermanly comportment of the working-class white man who unconsciously mimics black masculine display. Or as Lott has phrased it, the imitation of African American styles of masculinity rooted in minstrelsy "is so much a part of most American white men's equipment for living that they remain entirely unaware of their participation in it" (53).

Altman has dramatized male anxiety about being male in films such as *McCabe and Mrs. Miller* (1971), *Thieves Like Us* (1974), *Buffalo Bill and the Indians* (1976), *Come Back to the Five and Dime, Jimmy Dean, Jimmy Dean* (1982), and *The Player* (1992), to name just a few. His white and his black male characters run the gamut in terms of how they play out their masculinity. Unlike the vast majority of Hollywood directors, Altman neither romanticizes nor pathologizes blacks and their interactions with whites. He seldom employs familiar myths such as the loyal black retainer we know so well from mainstream films such as *Driving Miss Daisy* (1989), *Robin Hood: Prince of Thieves* (1991), *Dave* (1993), *Die Hard With a Vengeance* (1995), and *The Long Kiss Goodnight* (1996). Although he has often put angry black men on the screen (*M*A*S*H* [1970], *Nashville* [1975] *Streamers* [1983]), he has also depicted the complexity and ironies of even the most casual interactions among people of different races (*A Wedding* [1978], *H.E.A.L.T.H.* [1979], *Short Cuts* [1993]). One of the most remarkable aspects of *Kansas City* is its representation of the wide range of interactions between blacks and whites. Some of these interactions are tense; some are completely matter-of-fact; sometimes blacks have the upper hand; other times whites are in control; and sometimes no one is in control.

Altman took an almost perverse pleasure in bringing black characters into his work as early as 1959 when he directed episodes of a syndicated television program *The Troubleshooters,* a weekly series starring Keenan Wynn and the Olympic decathlon champion Bob Mathias as glorified construction workers. Altman told me that in one episode he had cast a black actor as the owner and bartender of a saloon frequented by the regulars in the series. The sponsor objected on the grounds that the actor was not right for the part. When Altman hired a second black to replace him, the sponsor again objected, and Altman asked that any objections be put in writing. The producer of the program then told Altman that the sponsors would never put such statements into a written document, that they did not want to show a black man as the owner of a saloon, and that a white actor must play the part. Altman then tried something else: "So I hired an actor and I tattooed him—every bit of his skin, like Queequeg in *Moby Dick.* . . . I put him in tails and a top hat, gave him a German accent and an Indian name. It was so bizarre that it didn't make any sense, but they [the sponsors] just loved it."[20] Later on, too many episodes provoked clashes, and Altman was asked to leave *The Troubleshooters,* as was often the case in his career as a director for television.[21] Altman would later see to it that African Americans played a regular role in his repertory panoramas.

The black and white characters in *Kansas City* have few interactions typical of the Hollywood mainstream. Seldom's imperious reception of the audacious but dim Johnny O'Hara is as unusual as the scene when Blondie takes Carolyn into Addie Parker's house on Olive Street for a few hours of rest as they hide from the police. When Blondie awakens from a nap, she finds the elderly black women in the Parker living room nodding politely while Carolyn, stoned on laudanum, holds forth on race relations. Earlier, in a minor but revealing subplot, the young Charlie Parker (Albert J. Burnes) latches onto the pregnant Pearl (Ajia Mignon Johnson). Parker takes her along to the Hey Hay Club where he adoringly points out Lester Young. They watch in amusement as Seldom's men unceremoniously expel Blondie after she has demanded the return of her boyfriend.

The scene in which Blondie is carried out of the Hey Hay Club shows that Altman is more interested in the complexities of race relations than in an uncritical celebration of *Kansas City* music and musicians. The black players laugh and make fun of Blondie with their instruments as she passes the bandstand kicking and screaming. The wide-open politics of Kansas City gave blacks some degree of autonomy in their own domain; Altman and Barhydt have suggested that the musicians relished the situation in which they could publicly display their power in the face of a white person. In fact, the constant foregrounding of power imbalances in the film involves much more than race and gender relations; it is everywhere in a film that chronicles an election campaign fought with bullets and clubs as much as with ballots. As Robert T. Self has written, *Kansas City* is one of several films that Altman made during presidential election years that tie personal dramas to larger political dramas.[22] The connection is explicit in *H.E.A.L.T.H.* (*1979*), *Secret Honor* (1984), and *Tanner 88* (1988). Although not so overt in its political foregroundings, *Buffalo Bill and the Indians* from 1976 features an appearance by Pat McCormick as President

Figure 3. Robert Altman, *Kansas City* (1996): Lester Young (Joshua Redman) and Coleman Hawkins (Craig Handy) in the midst of a cutting contest. Courtesy Photofest.

Grover Cleveland and dramatizes the power struggles between whites and Indians. Altman contributed to the nation's bicentennial celebration when politics and patriotism became entertainment with a film that problematizes this same combination. *Kansas City* holds up the city's jazz as the great unintentional monument of the Pende rgast era, but the film is more sophisticated than *Buffalo Bill* in finding parallels between politics and an especially meaningful form of entertainment.

Although I began this essay by suggesting that Altman exaggerated when he attributed a jazzlike structure to his film, I return to that statement in my conclusion. Until now I have treated Altman and his collaborators as scrupulous professionals, fully in control of the meaning of their film. But there is material in the film and in Altman's post–*Kansas City* interviews that justifies a more overtly psychoanalytic reading of the film. In particular, I see Altman unconsciously returning to the scene of an idealized childhood and forging an identification with the young Charlie Parker.

In his interviews, jazz itself seems related to a sense of maternal plenitude for Altman. He has spoken of a love for jazz that began when when he was nine years old and first heard a 1934 recording of Duke Ellington's "Solitude." Altman told Leonard Lopate that Glendora Majors, the family's black housekeeper "who raised me," sat him down next to the phonograph and said, "Bobby, now you listen to this. This is the best music there ever was." He then said that "Solitude" is still his favorite song. Altman has also told interviewers that he started going to the jazz clubs in Kansas City when he was fourteen, exactly the same age as the Charlie Parker of *Kansas City*. If there is any character in the film with whom Altman is likely to identify, it is Charlie Parker, and if there is a noncinematic art form to which Altman aspires, it is surely jazz.

Not surprisingly then, *Kansas City* offers an idealized view of Parker, not to mention his mother, whose portrayal in the film may have some relation to Altman's fond memories of Glendora Majors. But as always, representations in cinema are "massively overdetermined."[23] The view of Parker in particular and jazz in general may also have been affected by Matthew Seig, listed as one of *Kansas City*'s two co-producers. Seig has been involved in a number of jazz documentaries, most notably *Thelonious Monk: American Composer* (1991), which he directed for PBS. The documentary is almost hagiographic when compared to Charlotte Zwerin's *Thelonious Monk: Straight, No Chaser* (1988), a film that foregrounds the pianist/composer's mental illness. Thelonious Monk Jr., for example, takes on different personae in the two films: while he reminisces warmly about cherished moments with a loving father for Seig's camera, he soberly tells Zwerin about looking into the eyes of a father who didn't recognize his own son. Seig also directed *Lady Day: The Many Faces of Billie Holiday* (1991), a similarly idealized look at the legendary singer, especially when compared to Robert O'Meally's thoughtful book on which the video is based.[24] Along with Gary Giddins's videos on Louis Armstrong and Charlie Parker, the work of Seig represents a revision of the dominant modes of jazz biography on film. Clint Eastwood's *Bird* (1988) is much more typical of a well-established tradition of jazz narrative in which a genius musician, usually black, is brought down by drugs, alcohol, and an audience of Philistines.[25] While the Parker of *Bird* is a cipher, Altman's Parker is devoted to the music of his hometown, especially the work of Lester Young. Seig may have played a role in giving us a more charitable view of the young Parker.

Altman, however, has gone a bit farther than simply rejecting the familiar story about Charlie Parker the drug addict and ne'er-do-well. The fourteen-year-old Parker of *Kansas City* even appears to have honorable intentions toward Pearl. He looks after her by taking her to the Hey Hay Club to hear Lester Young, unquestionably the major influence on Parker's early style. The real-life Parker spent a good deal of time in the balcony of the Reno Club where he could sit undisturbed and listen to Young soloing with the Basie band or at after-hours jam sessions. Although he has certainly idealized the young Parker, Altman has chosen a moment in the artist's life when he was merely another listener in the world of Kansas City jazz, not unlike Altman's description of himself as a fourteen-year-old.

Kansas City is very much about imitation. In some ways it is a film about a woman who behaves like a woman in a film. As Blondie, Jennifer Jason Leigh does a sustained impression of her role model Jean Harlow, who appears on screen with Clark Gable in a climactic scene from *Hold Your Man* (1933) while Blondie and Carolyn wait in a movie theater for Henry Stilton to call. At the end when Blondie has returned to her peroxide Harlow look and is finally reunited with Johnny, the lovers play out a desultory version of the Gable/Harlow scene before they both end up on the floor dead. Imitation is also at the heart of Johnny's misadventures in blackface. When he wipes the burnt cork off his face, Johnny looks at himself in the mirror and says, "So long, Amos."[26] Accordingly, Seldom Seen repeatedly mentions Amos and Andy as he taunts Johnny. Seldom also says, "You come swinging in here like, like Tarzan. Right in the middle of a sea of niggers. Just like in the picture show. You like picture show?" When Johnny replies, "I can take it or leave it," Seldom says, "I recommend you leave it." This is advice that both Johnny and Blondie should have observed; it also touches on a major theme in the works of Altman—the discrepancies between the images presented by the entertainment industry and the realities behind them. Although Altman has not exactly imitated what he sees in the picture shows, he has on some levels imitated Charlie Parker.

Kansas City is unique for marking the first time in a long career that Altman has clearly turned to his own experience as a consumer of entertainment. His affinity to Charlie Parker goes well beyond their common experience as young men listening to jazz. Like Parker, Altman is an artist who assimilated a body of material that few regarded as art and then went on to create his own brilliant but eccentric brand of that art. Altman further resembles the jazz artist in his regular reliance on improvisation throughout his career. Although Parker succumbed to his addictions at a young age, Altman has battled various forms of addiction for most of his life.[27]

If Lott is right that black men have long provided models of manliness for white American males, it is also true that the male jazz musician expresses his masculinity in more subtle ways than does the athlete, the rock and roll star, or the white suburban teenager with his baggy shorts and loping walk. The jazz musician expresses much more than just manliness. In fact, as I have suggested elsewhere, black jazz musicians have even developed codes for problematizing received notions of masculinity.[28] Putting aside for a moment the hyperbole of Norman Mailer's "The White Negro,"[29] I would argue that black improvising musicians have inspired many of America's most important white artists, including filmmakers as diverse as Martin Scorsese, John Cassavetes, Henry Jaglom, Stan Brakhage, and Dennis Hopper. Like Altman, they all practice a "jazz aesthetic." Like the others, and like jazz musicians such as Parker, Altman has also learned much from the great artists who preceded him. But by identifying with a black jazz musician, Altman has gone even farther than the others. Perhaps unconsciously, perhaps not, Altman has sought "the cool, virility, humility, abandon, or *gaieté de coeur* that were the prime components of white ideologies of black manhood."[30]

At Addie Parker's, Pearl tells Blondie that she dreamed about her the night after she witnessed her expulsion from the Hey Hay Club. Pearl says that in her dream Blondie was dancing and Charlie Parker was playing the piano. Blondie is nonplussed by this confession but has other things on her mind. She does not pursue the issue. One wonders if the dream ends as disastrously for Blondie as does her brief adventure with Carolyn. At the end of *Kansas City*, Blondie and Johnny are dead. Carolyn has pointed a gun at Blondie in her negligee just as Blondie had held a gun on the negligee-clad Carolyn at the beginning of the film. Carolyn and Henry return to a marriage that is emptier than ever. Seldom Seen, the one character who has had anything at all to say about the music, counts the money he has made from his gambling tables. An alto saxophone hanging from his neck, Charlie Parker is back at the Hey Hay Club, having drifted off to sleep on the balcony, perhaps like the historical Charlie Parker after a long night at the Reno Club. As the credits role, a small jazz ensemble performs Altman's favorite song, "Solitude." The film does not reveal what Parker is dreaming about, but it is likely that his dreams, like Altman's, resemble those of few other artists.

Notes

1. Altman explains this comparison in some detail in the interview with Leonard Lopate and in the article by Bourne: Leonard Lopate, "interview with Robert Altman, New York Public Radio, WNYC, New York, 16 August 1996; Michael Bourne, "Goin' to Kansas City and Robert Altman Takes You There!" *Down Beat* (March 1996): 22–27. In writing this paper, I have also benefited from my own conversations with Geri Allen, Loren Schoenberg, and Dan Morgenstern.

2. Altman says that he himself recalls most of what happened in Kansas City in the 1930s and has not mentioned if he or anyone else looked at history books. In researching the music and politics of Kansas City in the 1930s, I have consulted Barnes, Dance, Dorsett, Giddins, Murray, Pearson Jr., Porter, Reddig, Russell, and Shapiro and Hentoff: Harper Barnes, *Blue Monday* (St. Louis, Mo.: Patrice, 1991);

Stanley Dance, *The World of Count Basie* (New York: Scribners, 1980); Lyle W. Dorsett, *The Pendergast Machine* (New York: Oxford University Press, 1968); Gary Giddins, *Celebrating Bird: The Triumph of Charlie Parker* (New York: Morrow, 1987); Albert Murray, *Stomping the Blues* (New York: McGraw-Hill, 1976); Nathan W. Pearson Jr., *Goin' to Kansas City* (Urbana: University of Illinois Press, 1987); Lewis Porter, *Lester Young* (Boston: Twayne, 1985); William M. Reddig, *Tom's Town: Kansas City and the Pendergast Legend* (Philadelphia: Lippincott, 1947); Ross Russell, *Jazz Style in Kansas City and the Southwest* (Berkeley and Los Angeles: University of California Press, 1971); Nat Shapiro and Nat Hentoff, *Hear Me Talkin' to Ya: The Story of Jazz As Told by the Men Who Made It* (New York: Holt, Rinehart and Winston, 1955).

3. The speech is even accurate in terms of how a character such as Carolyn might represent her situation as the wife of a man who emerged from local politics to become an advisor to Roosevelt in Washington. Disoriented from a large dose of laudanum and speaking for no particular reason to the bewildered cleaning woman Addie Parker, the aristocratic Carolyn carefully distances herself and her husband from the corrupt Goats and Rabbits while hinting at their sympathy with the more powerful faction.

4. Since the 1930s, the vast majority of Hollywood movies have filmed actors and even real-life musicians miming performances to prerecorded music. A rare exception was the French/American co-production *Round Midnight* (1986), unlike the musicians in *Kansas City*, however, the players in *Round Midnight* often appeared uncomfortable playing on camera, and their performances suffered as a result.

5. Robert T. Self, "Adapting Centers Elsewhere/13 Short Cuts: 'Raymond Carver' and 'Robert Altman,'" Florida State University Conference on Literature and Film, Turnbull Conference Center, Tallahassee, 26 January 1995; Krin Gabbard, *Jammin' at the Margins: Jazz and the American Cinema* (Chicago: University of Chicago Press, 1996), 283–93.

6. Shapiro and Hentoff, *Hear Me Talkin' to Ya*, 300–301.

7. The doctor in question is not identified by his real name in the film, probably to avoid legal complications. After Johnny O'Hara offers "his guts" to Seldom Seen, the doctor is presumably the one who surgically removes them before sending Johnny home to die.

8. Barnes, *Blue Monday*, 208–9.

9. Walter C. Allen, *Hendersonia: The Music of Fletcher Henderson and His Musicians*, Jazz Monographs 4 (Highland Park, Ill.: Walter C. Allen, 1973), 290.

10. John Chilton, *The Song of the Hawk: The Life and Recordings of Coleman Hawkins* (Ann Arbor: University of Michigan Press, 1990), 96.

11. Various other complaints might be made about the film's representation of Kansas City jazz. The musicians at the Hey Hay Club play carefully arranged compositions for large jazz orchestra, such as Fletcher Henderson's "Queer Notions," although they also seem to be engaging in a jam session. Dan Morgenstern has pointed out that a poster that appears early in the film

The Hey Hay Club

Battle of
Jazz
All Day • All Nite
MONDAY
Lester YOUNG vs. Coleman HAWKINS
Plus!
Noteable Appearances

was completely inconsistent with KC practice. If nothing else, there could have been no guarantee that Hawkins would show up at an after-hours place while on tour with the Henderson Orchestra.

12. Peter Watrous, "The Movies Miss Another . . . ," *New York Times,* 11 August, 1996, sec. 2, 26.

13. Bourne, "Goin' to Kansas City," 25.

14. Krin Gabbard, "Introduction: The Jazz Canon and Its Consequences," in *Jazz Among the Discourses,* ed. Krin Gabbard (Durham: Duke University Press, 1995), 1–28.

15. Bourne, "Goin' to Kansas City," 24. According to von Ziegesar, the "real" Seldom Seen was a Kansas City gangster named Ivory Johnson (12): Peter Von Ziegesar, "Robert Altman's Journey Home," *New York Times,* 27 August 1995, late ed., sec. 2, 9 ff.

16. Claudia Gorbman, *Unheard Melodies: Narrative Film Music* (Bloomington: Indiana University Press, 1987), 73.

17. Bourne, "Goin' to Kansas City," 22. These aspects of the cutting contest between Hawkins and Young are somewhat consistent with the account of the event that Mary Lou Williams gave to the jazz periodical *Melody Maker* in 1954: "The word went around that Hawkins was in the Cherry Blossom and within half an hour there were Lester Young, Ben Webster, Herschel Evans and one or two unknown tenor players piling into the club to blow. Bean [Hawkins's nickname] didn't know the Kansas City tenormen were so terrific and he couldn't get himself together though he played all morning . . . when we got there Hawkins was in his vest taking turns with the KC men. It seems he had run into something he didn't expect" (quoted in Chilton, *Song of the Hawk,* 91).

18. Rex Stewart, *Jazz Masters of the '30s* (New York: Macmillan, 1972), 128.

19. Eric Lott, *Love and Theft: Blackface Minstrelsy and the American Working Class* (New York: Oxford University Press, 1993), 89–107.

20. Robert Altman, personal interview, 2 December 1982.

21. Patrick McGilligan, *Robert Altman: Jumping Off the Cliff* (New York: St. Martin's, 1989), 274.

22. Robert T. Self, "*Kansas City:* Story, Subject, and Entertainment in the Films of Robert Altman," Florida State University Conference on Literature and Film, Turnbull Conference Center, Tallahassee, 26 January 1996.

23. Robert B. Ray, *A Certain Tendency of the Hollywood Cinema: 1930–1980* (Princeton: Princeton University Press, 1985), 14.

24. Robert O'Meally, *Lady Day: The Many Faces of Billie Holiday* (Boston: Little, Brown, 1991).

25. Significantly, Eastwood also produced Zwerin's Monk documentary. I discuss jazz biographies on film at some length in Gabbard, *Jammin' at the Margins,* 64–100.

26. The original "Amos 'n' Andy" radio show became hugely successful during its second year on NBC in 1929. The eponymous characters were played by the white actors Freeman F. Gosden and Charles J. Correll, who would later play the same roles in blackface in the 1930 film *Check and Double Check.* In his interview with Lopate, Altman said that he and Harry Belafonte were working on a new film based on "Amos 'n' Andy."

27. McGilligan, *Robert Altman*, 272.

28. Gabbard, *Jammin' at the Margins*, 138–59.

29. Norman Mailer, "The White Negro," *Advertisements for Myself* (New York: Putnam, 1959).

30. Lott, *Love and Theft*, 52.

PART THREE

✳

STYLE AND PRACTICE IN
CLASSICAL FILM MUSIC

✳

MARTIN MARKS

Music, Drama, Warner Brothers
The Cases of *Casablanca* and *The Maltese Falcon*

✳

Ask an audience to recall the music of *Casablanca,* and chances are that the great majority would point to one, two, or three moments. First would be Sam's playing of "As Time Goes By" for Ilsa, as she sits in Rick's Café Américain; second, the scene later that evening, when Rick demands that Sam play it ("for me"); third, the contest of anthems in Rick's the following night, when a group of German soldiers gathered around the piano attempt to sing "Wacht am Rhein," only to be drowned out by the café's international crowd of refugees, led by Victor Laszlo in a stirring rendition of the "Marseillaise." Ask the same audience to discuss the music of *The Maltese Falcon,* and most will probably respond by saying that if there was music, they didn't notice. Of course, such a survey would only confirm something we already know: that most people don't really hear most film music most of the time, unless it is made an essential part of the narrative. (Even people who are deeply experienced as listeners miss a great deal of music in films, unless they force themselves to pay close attention.) All the same, Adolph Deutsch composed music for nearly half of *The Maltese Falcon*—that is, about fifty minutes of background score—and Max Steiner provided about forty minutes of music for *Casablanca* (not including the segments already mentioned). One might well want to ask these composers why they bothered—or, more positively, what purposes or functions they intended their music to serve.

These questions are by no means new: they have been discussed virtually since the advent of recorded sound, in a body of literature that has grown steadily and become increasingly complex. Early on, much of the most informative writing was undertaken by film composers themselves.[1] Indeed, both Steiner and Deutsch were among those who occasionally took pen in hand to discuss the nature of their work, although they tended to confine their remarks to pragmatic observations based on individual experience, and to description of technical procedures.[2] Implicit in their thinking were three fundamental ideas shared by most professionals: (1) film was a new medium in need of music; (2) the work posed special problems for the composer, who had to accept a subordinate position in a collaborative process that was less than ideal; (3) musical precedents could be found in older dramatic genres, including opera, plays, and other types of musical theater. (For Steiner and Deutsch the last point could be taken for granted, given the course of their careers: after receiving classical training, each had acquired considerable experience as a composer, arranger, and conductor for pit orchestras — Steiner in Vienna, London, and New York, Deutsch in London — before moving to Hollywood and devoting themselves to careers in the film industry.)[3] At present the leading scholars of film music tend to focus much more on the first two points than on the third, and to carry on the discussion in largely theoretical terms, mostly derived from innovative work in cinema studies. They have done much to deepen our understanding of music's place in studio films of the 1930s, 1940s, and 1950s — the so-called classical Hollywood cinema of the period when Steiner and Deutsch were most productive.[4]

Yet for all the recent advances, detailed analyses of music's dramatic functions in landmark Hollywood films are still in short supply; that is why I bring up the cases of *The Maltese Falcon* and *Casablanca,* two films that make for compelling comparison. Produced at a single studio a year apart (in 1941 and 1942), they show the polish of their era and feature the same charismatic star. Moreover, both achieved cult status decades ago. *Falcon* continues to be appreciated both as a brilliant film in its own right and as "a model of adaptational fidelity,"[5] while *Casablanca* remains an icon of popular culture (as Aljean Harmetz argues, "no other movie better demonstrates America's mythological vision of itself").[6] Most important for the present essay: although the scores by Deutsch and Steiner follow similar formal schemes, they offer sharp contrasts in style and function, owing partly to the inclinations of the composers, partly to fundamental differences in the filmic narratives. These differences emerge most clearly if we turn first to *Casablanca,* the easier of the two scores to comprehend; but ultimately it will be through the eye of the falcon that the distinctive qualities of each score are best perceived.

Casablanca

Let us begin with some basic points about Steiner's autograph that reflect common practices of the period. First, it contains sixteen discrete segments (headed Reel 1, Part 1; Reel 1, Part 2; Reel 4, Part 1, and so forth), mostly running about two to three minutes in length. Steiner composed these cues by following detailed timing and breakdown charts—"cue sheets," in Hollywood parlance—prepared by the film's music editor. (Figure 1 gives an overview of the entire score.) Second, the music is laid out in a short score of four staves per system, the top two usually containing melody lines, the bottom two (treble and bass clef), given over to accompaniment figuration and harmonies, in the manner of a piano-vocal score.[7] This was an efficient, standard format, which combined the gist of the music with a good deal of important subsidiary information. In particular, as can be seen in examples 1–3, Steiner penciled in numerous indications of instrumentation, along with occasional verbal comments, addressed to his orchestrator of long standing, Hugo Friedhofer—such division of labor being customary in Hollywood, then as now. (For instance, in example 1, the chord in the first measure is marked for woodwinds, vibraphone, harps, piano, celeste, and horns; above the chord Steiner has written that it should be orchestrated "like Reel 5, Part 4"—an intriguing comment because it suggests that he wrote the latter cue, or at least decided upon its scoring, prior to this one, which comes earlier in the film.) Third, there are other sorts of markings, too, like the prompts placed above and within various systems. (See, for example, the partial lines of spoken dialogue in example 1, mm. 5, 8, and 9.) Originally these had appeared on the cue sheets that had guided Steiner while he composed; once copied from the composer's manuscript into the final conducting score, they helped to ensure precise synchronization during recording.

In addition, despite the composer's frequent reliance elsewhere upon mechanical "click tracks" to help the synchronizing process,[8] the *Casablanca* autograph is laced with conventional terms for tempo and expression throughout: "Slowly" and "molto espressivo" in example 1, "Appass[io-nato]" in example 2, and "Tragic" at the head of example 3. I shall give attention to the expressive, passionate, and tragic nature of these segments below; for the moment the main point is to realize the dual nature of the autograph. On the one hand, it served as a blueprint for the production of music within a highly industrialized and technologically complex system; on the other, it shows that Steiner approached his task like a composer of traditional dramatic music, constantly thinking about music's ability to interpret what is depicted on screen.

The same duality of old- and newly fashioned features is apparent at the outset of *Casablanca*, in the "main title." As in earlier genres, this music functions like an overture and introduces two of the score's key themes.[9] However, film music often being an art of compression, this is at best a mini-overture; unlike, say, an operatic prelude or an overture to a Broadway musical, one of its essential features is that the musical structure is entirely dependent upon the film's visual content. Specifically, the main title contains six distinct bits of music smoothly linked, ranging in length from a few seconds to more than a minute. Each new section is cued by an important change in what is seen onscreen, and each works in musical code, designed to indicate something about the setting and other particulars of the narrative. Each of these six segments is described in turn below.

1. *Fanfare* (for the Warner Brothers logo). Steiner had originally composed this noisy, memorable signal for the film *Tovaritch* (1937); in the version used in *Gold Is Where You Find It* (1938), it quickly became his (and Warners') signature. One thing that made it so serviceable was its rapid motion through a number of triads without a unifying tonal center. (Starting firmly in C major, it lands as firmly on a B-major chord after a measure and a half, or about five seconds later.) In effect, such a sequence of harmonies can be manipulated to lead to any key one wishes, and in this case the goal turns out to be F minor. (Steiner reaches the goal enharmonically, first by respelling the B-major chord as C♭, placing it over an F pedal, and holding it long enough to define it as a dissonance needing resolution, then by changing the chord to an open fifth, F and C, holding that, and finally filling in the minor third).

The harmonic sleight-of-hand is a convincing match to the transformation accomplished onscreen, in that the fanfare reaches its dissonant C♭ chord just as the logo dissolves to an image of a map, showing the continent of Africa. While the music vamps, the names of three principal cast members (Bogart, Bergman, Henreid) appear in superimposition. Precisely as those names dissolve to the film's title, a flourish sweeps the music to F and C, and after four bars, while the credits continue, the next theme begins.

2. *Frenzied exotic dance.* "Lots of tom-tom," Steiner asks of Friedhofer, and "very rythmic" [*sic*]. The instrumentation (which also includes bells and xylophone) and the unyielding ostinato accompaniment could be construed as elemental symbols of the film's "African" setting, just as the sinuous stepwise melody, colored by triplets and by augmented seconds, is pseudo-Arabian. All these elements are highly clichéd—and really too savage for a film about such sophisticated characters. In fact, Steiner recycled this music from his main title for *The Lost Patrol* (RKO, 1934), a more truly Arabian story, set in another part of the desert. Yet the music has its place in *Casablanca:* the flailing theme and pounding rhythm work to prepare us for a breakneck story of desperate people trapped in a dangerous locale. Fittingly, like a dance on the verge of going out of control, the structure of the segment moves ever ahead, in urgent fashion: there is one eight-bar

Max Steiner's Score for *Casablanca*: An Overview of Structure and Thematic Content

[Note: "Reel" and "Part" numbers are given as they appear in Steiner's manuscript. Timings are mine, and approximate.]

1) Reel 1, Part 1 (0:00–2:35) = Beginning of film.

WB logo	main title (credits)	"Music by Max Steiner," etc.	narration + montage	Scene 1, shot 1	shot 2
fanfare	*frenzied exotic dance*	*Marseillaise*	*impassioned lament*	Casablanca	teletype machine in
			street scene	police station	
				pseudo-Arabian	*"Deutschland*
				fragment (like	*über alles"*
				source music)	

2) Reel 1, Part 2 (2:35–5:30) = Plot preliminaries.

roundup of "usual suspects"—courier shot	outside Palais de Justice: tourists + pickpocket	airplane lands
agitato (tuneless)	*Marseillaise + funereal phrases . . . misterioso*	*impassioned lament*

Source Music (performed in Rick's café, by Sam and the band, etc.)—not in the Steiner score:

1) It Had to Be You
2) Shine
3) Crazy Rhythm
4) Knock on Wood
5) The Very Thought of You
6) Baby Face
7) I'm Just Wild About Harry
8) Heaven Can Wait
9) Parlez-moi d'amour
10) Love for Sale
11) Tango della Rose
12) Avalon
13) As Time Goes By (chorus 1st half [A A] sung)

3) Reel 4, Part 7 (33:30–36:05) = first meeting of the four principal characters.

eye contact—Rick sits at table	conversation	Victor and Ilsa depart
CASA chord 1 + ATGB var. 1	*ATGB var. 2 versus Dtsch*	*. . . ATGB fragments*

Source Music:
14) [Sam: "just a little something of my own."]
13a) As Time Goes By (1st phrase [A] on piano, joined to next cue)

Figure 1. *Casablanca*: An overview of musical structure and thematic content.

4) Reel 5, Part 2 (38:15–41:50) = Paris flashback.

close-up Rick	dissolve to Paris	Rick & Ilsa driving	aboard ship	together in hotel room
ATGB A' . . .	*Marseillaise*	*ATGB var. 3*	*barcarole*	*ATGB fragments*

dancing in night club	in hotel room at night—kiss	Germans enter Paris
Perfidia	*ATGB fragments*	*dissonant march*

Source Music (which Steiner wrote into the beginning of the next segment, then eliminated):
[deleted] 13b) As Time Goes By (second half [B A'] sung)

5) Reel 5, Part 3 (43:05–47:50) = Paris flashback, concluded.

La Belle Aurore	German voice on loudspeaker	conversation resumes	kiss—glass spills
ATGB var. 4	*Dtsch*	*ATGB var. 5 with lyric extensions*	*Doom*

(cont.)

at the station	Ilsa's note	train departs	dissolve to close-up of whiskey bottles
Marseillaise	*ATGB fragments*	*Doom*	*return to Sam's piano version of ATGB (cut short)*

6) Reel 5, Part 4 (48:04–51:00) = Ilsa returns to Rick's.

she appears	his bitter dialogue	she tries to explain, he drives her away	fade to Renault's office sign
CASA chord 2	*Doom—ATGB var. 6*	*Laszlo ATGB fragments—Doom*	*Marseillaise*

Source Music:
15–16) Arabian music for scene at the Blue Parrot (no musicians seen on screen)
17) If I Could Be with You
18) You Must Have Been a Beautiful Baby
1a) It Had to Be You
13c) As Time Goes By (fragment)
5a) The Very Thought of You
19) Watch on the Rhine (sung by Germans in Rick's café), overpowered by:
20) The Marseillaise (sung by others, played by the café band, and enhanced by the studio orchestra)

7-8-9) Reel 8, Parts 4 & 4A. Reel 9, Part 1 (1:13:45–1:18:40) = focus on Victor and Ilsa.

Renault is forced to close café and Strasser confronts Ilsa	she and Victor leave café	enter hotel room	discuss danger	discuss the past	he affirms his love	she watches him go, then leaves
Dtsch (cf. accompanied recitative)	*Laszlo*	*misterioso*	*Watch on the Rhine*	*ATGB fragments*	*Laszlo*	*misterioso + ATGB fragment*

Figure 1. (*continued*)

10) Reel 9, Part 2 (1:19:21–1:23:00) = Ilsa's second return to Rick's.

he sees her	she pleads with him	pulls gun	breaks down—embrace, kiss and fade
CASA chord2	*Doom + ATGB fragments*	*Agitato + ATGB + Laszlo + Doom*	*ATGB car. 5*

11) Reel 9, Part 3 (1:24:45–1:26:50) = intensification of the central conflict.

Ilsa asks Rick	Carl & Victor elude police	they enter café—	Carl leaves with Ilsa, Rick goes to Victor
to take charge		*Rick summons Carl*	
ATGB car 7	*agitato*	*Laszlo*	*ATGB fragments*

12) Reel 9, Part 4 (1:28:20–1:28:50) = further intensification: Laszlo's arrest.

police break in	take Laszlo away
dramatic chords	*ATGB fragment*

Source Music (scene at the Blue Parrot):
16a) Arabian music

13) Reel 10, Part 3 (1:32:00–1:32:30) = preparing the denouement: Renault's arrival at Rick's.

"Closed" Sign	knock—Rick at desk	lets Renault in
CASA chord 1	*ATGB fragment*	*misterioso*

14) Reel 10, Part 4 (1:32:50–1:35:15) = dramatic reversal: Rick's trap.

Victor & Ilsa arrive	Renault arrests Laszlo	Rick holds gun on Renault	Renault phones Strasser, who leaves	dissolve to airport
drum roll + Laszlo + ATGB	*pause!*	*ATGB*	*Watch on the Rhine*	*pause!*

15–16) Reel 11, Parts 1 and 2 (1:36:00–1:42:00) = further reversals and denouement.

"Mr. and Mrs. Victor Laszlo"	Rick tells Ilsa she must go	cut to Strasser	Rick reassures Victor	propellers
CASA chord 3 (= dim. 7th)	*ATGB var. 5, then var. 4*	*interruption!*	*Laszlo [= end of Part 1]*	*CASA chord 2*

(cont.)

goodbyes	Victor and Ilsa exit	Renault chides Rick	propellers	Strasser arrives	Renault's decision	
				—Rick shoots Strasser		
Doom	*ATGB:*	*Laszlo*	*low chords*		*Watch on the Rhine*	*ATGB*
	apotheosis of cadence phrase				*versus Disch*	

(cont.)

policemen leave—Renault discards Vichy water	plane takes off	exit Rick and Renault = "The End"
Marseillaise in minor	*low chords to cadence*	*Marseillaise (ethereal, then exit march)*

Figure 1. (*continued*)

Example 1. Steiner's score for *Casablanca*, reel 4, part 7, beginning. Used by permission of Warner/Chappell Music, Inc.

phrase, which is repeated and then extended in a modulating phrase of six more bars. In this way Steiner makes another seamless musical link, parallel to the continuing credits on screen.

3. *"La Marseillaise."* This familiar music probably has the most powerful impact of any in the main title for at least four reasons: (1) it is a clear

Example 2. Steiner's score for *Casablanca*, reel 11, part 1, beginning. Used by permission of Warner/Chappell Music, Inc.

melody, and very evocative: a nationalist anthem and a stirring march, it immediately comes to symbolize French—and by extension, Allied—resistance to Nazi oppression; (2) set in A major, it sounds particularly brilliant after the previous material, and thus brings the cue to a conventional, "brass-blasting" climax;[10] (3) the convention has been given a surprising

Example 3. Steiner's score for *Casablanca*, reel 11, part 2, beginning. Used by permission of Warner/Chappell Music, Inc.

twist: whereas normally the producer's credit was the one that summoned a new fanfare, in this case the music heralds Steiner's own name, followed by separate cards for the executive producer and director; (4) the final chord is a jarring dissonance: the bass, instead of leaping from F to A, steps down from F to a minor chord on D♯, a tritone away from its expected goal; an augmented triad on A sits above. For two bars the dissonance holds, while the march beat of the previous music carries forward through the director's credit, a fade to black, then into a new image. Thus, the avoidance of closure is deliberate and obtrusive: we are alerted to understand that the struggle for freedom is still in doubt.

4–6. *Impassioned lament to pseudo-Arabian source music to "Deutschland über alles."* The credits have ended, but before the story begins comes a lengthy prologue. "With the coming of the Second World War," the narrator eloquently begins, "many eyes in imprisoned Europe turned hopefully, or desperately, toward the freedom of the Americas." As he speaks, the first image is that of a spinning globe—a symbolic expansion of the story's range to suggest its worldwide significance. While he continues, another map is used to track the movement of the refugees toward Casablanca; on this is superimposed wartime newsreel footage in rapid montage. Finally comes an aerial view of the city—a frozen shot (taken on a studio set) through which the camera suddenly begins to move down, bringing us closer to the bustling street scene. With this shot and the next one emerge the first sounds of the film's diegetic world: a hubbub of voices from the crowd in the marketplace, the teletypewriter in the police station, the paper ripped cleanly from the machine, and finally the voice of the policeman, who speaks directly into a radio microphone and announces the murder of two German couriers. "Important!" he concludes; we are directed to sit up and take notice as the action begins.

In short, the fusion of image, spoken word, and other select sounds gradually becomes rich enough to claim our full attention; yet the music persists. What is Steiner's aim? Simply put, to move us completely into the film's world, via three contrasting segments, each with its own role to play. The first is lyrical and clearly expresses sympathy for the refugees: a string melody of two broad phrases (one closing in D minor after eight bars, the other in A minor after ten). It also depicts their weary trek: each phrase begins high in range, meanders more or less chromatically, and ends at a low point; and every two bars the melody pauses, while the march rhythm pushes forward in dissonant chords. In the second segment, for the opening scene in the city, Steiner returns to the sinuous melodic style of his "African" dance, but the feeling here is more relaxed: the melody winds about in triplets, the pulse is weak, the harmony unchanging (the bass reiterates A minor throughout), and the orchestration dominated by oboes, with soft cymbals for color. (Steiner's direction: "Hugo! Sort of misterious [*sic*] shimmer.") If we consciously hear this music at all, we are meant to perceive it as a kind of Arabian source music, emanating from the city, even though no musicians are to be seen.[11] But with the dissolve to the police station comes a final dramatic gesture from outside the scene: in antipodal contrast to the "Marseillaise," the German anthem begins, played loudly by brass. There is time only for the tune's ominous opening—the melody that we hear corresponds to the words "Germany, Germany o[ver all]"— because Steiner knows that the music must give way to the policeman's announcement. So he primes us for action, by making a suspenseful pause in midphrase and then resorting to a favorite melodramatic device (used at many points in this score and others): a rumble of timpani continues under the words, until the next shot begins.

Even though "this connects to Part 2," as Steiner writes at the end of the main title, we shall pause here a moment in order to return to larger issues that concern the score as a whole. We have seen evidence of the composer's ability to deepen our perception of the world onscreen and draw us in, as well as his interest in both linear continuity and disruption, depending upon the context. Three topics that remain to be discussed are the nature of Steiner's thematic material, the uses of source music, and music's role in crucial segments from the film's middle and end.

As the main title suggests, Steiner liked simple themes, direct in their emotional expression: the *Casablanca* score has six such themes, each recurring at several points to intensify key aspects of the drama. These include the initial phrases from the "Marseillaise" and "Deutschland über alles": after being introduced in the main title, they reappear throughout the film, whereas the rest of the opening music, having served its function, is discarded. (The theme of lament does return briefly once, at the end of Reel 1, Part 2, to remind us of the refugees' plight. It underscores the moment when a crowd in the street gets a glimpse of an airplane overhead, and a minor character utters their collective wish, saying to her husband, "Perhaps tomorrow we'll be on the plane." After the plane lands the cue fades away, and, for the next several minutes, important characters and plot exposition are presented without benefit of dramatic music.) Later Steiner derives prominent themes from the beginnings of two more songs, "As Time Goes By" and "Wacht am Rhein"—but only after those memorable performances that have already been mentioned. In Steiner's hands the themes borrowed from "Deutschland über alles" and "Wacht am Rhein" are a matched pair of grotesques: what were stirring major-key melodies are distorted into open-ended fragments in minor, the former symbolizing the Nazi menace in general, the latter standing for Major Strasser in particular.[12] As for the remaining two themes, both are Steiner originals, one a descending fragment of the chromatic scale, whose steady marchlike tread seems to threaten the lovers with doom, the other a warm hymnlike melody with elemental diatonic harmonies: associated with Victor Laszlo, it sounds like the national anthem for his unidentified homeland and serves to represent his noble, forthright character.[13]

Of these four themes, only "As Time Goes By" is introduced as part of the film's abundant source music. In the lore of *Casablanca*, the story is often told that Steiner disliked having to use the song, which had been written in 1931 by Herman Hupfeld, a minor Broadway composer; that he asked to compose a love theme of his own for the score (as he had successfully done for *Now Voyager*, the film he worked on just prior to *Casablanca*); and that his request was denied, mainly because Hupfeld's song was written into the story, perhaps, too, because the executives liked the idea of a familiar "theme song."[14] Steiner's response was to make a virtue of necessity by keeping the melody out of the main title, indeed out of the score altogether until after Sam begins to sing it, "for old time's sake." In the meantime, whether by the composer's own choice, or by dictate of studio executive, for almost half an hour the music of *Casablanca* consists of a dozen vocal and instrumental numbers performed at Rick's.

Most of these were familiar popular songs of the 1920s and 1930s, and very likely other personnel in the Warner music department were involved in their selection and arrangement: they are not part of the Steiner score, and there is no direct evidence of his involvement in the process.[15] No matter who did the work, however, the songs deserve our attention, because they are used to make narrative points, sometimes obvious, sometimes subtle, through association of melodies and lyrics with the story unfolding on-screen. Occasionally the association is ironic, as when Sam plays "It Had to Be You" the moment Ilsa and Victor walk back into Rick's. Harder to catch is the verbal irony of the scene in which we are introduced to Rick: while he stands in the inner doorway to his casino and refuses admittance to a pompous German banker, the energetic fox-trot heard on the background piano is "Crazy Rhythm," whose chorus begins "Crazy rhythm, here's the doorway, I'll go my way, you'll go your way."

Then there is the peculiar case of "Knock on Wood"—a Dooley Wilson original, and the first number that puts him at the center of a scene: this song works at more than one level, partly in opposition to what we see. Led by Sam, almost everybody sings but Rick and Ferrari. The former uses the moment to hide Ugarte's letters of transit on the piano, the latter, once he enters, merely sits and eyes Rick suspiciously. (He is too cool a customer to be bothered by music.) Meanwhile the crowd sings "we're unlucky"; and Sam tells them to "knock on wood"; the jaunty music enables them to make light of their troubles, but the song's superstitious lyrics also anticipate impending turns of fortune's wheel: Ugarte's arrest, Ilsa's arrival.

In other cases the songs are more directly apt and atmospheric, and in context quite moving. Here are two of the richest examples. First, when Victor and Ilsa enter Rick's and pass by Sam, he is playing a favorite sentimental waltz of the 1930s, "Parlez-moi d'amour" (sometimes known by its English title "Speak to Me of Love"). The music emphasizes the moment with a poignant change of mood (it follows a breezy rendition of "Heaven Can Wait") and brings to mind thoughts of Paris and romance in preparation for the flashback scenes to come. Second and no less telling is the performance of the "Tango della Rose" by Corinna Mura as a backdrop to the scene of Laszlo's conversation with Berger. Given the song's highly emotional flamenco style, it makes us more than ever aware of the multicultural milieu at Rick's; probably, too, the Spanish flavor is meant to be symbolic, as we learned only a few minutes previously that Rick fought in Spain against the Fascists, just as Berger and Laszlo are now trying to carry on the fight in "the Underground." Finally, the "Tango" is the saddest, most expressive source music heard thus far: it adds weight to the scene under way and contributes to the rising tension that must culminate with the performance of the one song Rick has told Sam never to play.

Taken on its own, as sung by Wilson and played by Elliot Carpenter (who dubbed Sam's piano playing), "As Time Goes By" is far less expressive than these numbers—less so even than the waltz version of "Avalon," of which Sam plays a fragment just before. Yet "As Time Goes By" is clearly the most significant song of all—the only one to be discussed by the film's characters, and the one given the greatest meaning through its manner of presentation. The opening words speak of the trifles of love ("a kiss is just a kiss, a sigh is just a sigh"), and the music has a free and easy swing; but Sam's performance is only momentarily in view. Most of the time while he sings, we are shown Ilsa, listening, and it is the triple counterpoint of words, music, and photography—the soft lighting that perfectly captures the gleams of her hair and jewelry, her beautiful face a frozen, introspective mask—that makes for such a powerful effect.

Accosted by Rick, Sam breaks off singing, and the interruption is Steiner's prompt: with a dissonant chord, he accents the moment when Rick and Ilsa first make eye contact and thereby brings his music back into the picture. Thereafter, Steiner's score dominates the picture (except for a second lengthy stretch of source music for scenes at Rick's the following evening that culminate in the singing of the "Marseillaise"). Moreover, much of it is based on "As Time Goes By," which he subjects to a number of contrasting variations as well as looser transformations. In other words, from this moment on, Steiner strives to make his score the site of true music drama.

The composer's dramatic range is shown by comparing what may be called the first and third variations of "As Time Goes By" (in Reel 4, Part 7 and Reel 5, Part 2): both are far removed from Sam's rendition, and each has a different function. In the first (see example 1), the song becomes a lament, owing to the music's slow tempo, the sustaining of the opening dissonant chord, the use of plangent woodwinds, and the solemn half-cadence in D minor with which it concludes. The effect of this music on the viewer is subliminal: when it is being played, the story has brought together all four of the principal characters (Rick, Ilsa, Victor, Louis) for the first time. The dialogue crackles, the music is subdued; if we perceive it at all, it comes through in counterpoint to the dialogue, serving to convey the unexpressed sadness of the two lovers. Quite the opposite effect is made by the theme's appearance in the next segment, in which it helps to move the film from present to past: from the close-up of Rick in his darkened café, listening to Sam "play it" (again), through a dissolve to a shot of the Arch of Triumph in Paris, then to one of Rick and Ilsa riding together in the French countryside, and so forth. This entire sequence is accompanied by the score's happiest transformations of the song, punctuated, as in the main title, by a single phrase of the "Marseillaise" (when the Arch comes into view). Moreover, the bright music is the sole element on the soundtrack for about two minutes, and for good reason. Without it the sequence (which includes some standard process shots that appear quite crude) would be utterly unconvincing; and just as opera composers often relied upon music to accompany scene changes, so it became routine for Hollywood composers to supply music to cover lead-ins to all flashbacks along with other highly artificial devices, such as voice-overs and newspaper montages.[16]

From the moment the studio orchestra usurps Sam's playing of "As Time Goes By," the flashback segment exemplifies Steiner's fondness for blending source and background music in merging streams, the apparent intent being to keep the music's entrance and exit unobtrusive, and to enhance the unity of the whole.[17] We may note, as another instance, the way the background music flows smoothly into and out of "Perfidia," the number to which Rick and Ilsa briefly dance in a nightclub. Steiner had used the same music in virtually the same arrangement the year before, as part of a parallel sequence in *Now Voyager*: there, too, a scene of nightclub dancing was preceded by a montage of the couple riding in an automobile, and followed by a romantic scene for the couple alone. His decision to reuse the music in *Casablanca* could thus easily have been a time-saving expedient. Yet how appropriate it is! The song was first published in 1939, the year in which the flashback takes place; moreover, the (unsung) lyrics resonate with the plot. ("To you, my heart cries out 'Perfidia'; for I found you, the love of my life, in somebody else's arms.")[18]

Even more resonant are the lyrics of "As Time Goes By," and in their connection we may note the pointed way the background score stops in midflashback, for the scene in which Sam sings the second half of the song. Earlier, when Sam began to sing the song for Ilsa, Rick rudely yet conveniently interrupted him at the very moment its first half had gone by; the new performance thus provides balance and closure—though in a manner at odds with the chronology of the narrative. In any case, we should keep in mind that such formal principles may not have meant very much to Steiner, as the only part of the song he ever used was its first eight measures, over and over. (Indeed, after Sam's second performance is finished, the next segment of the score, Reel 5, Part 3, begins almost immediately, with a new variation of the song; then, as the flashback concludes, with a dissolve back to Rick's, Steiner leads the music back to the song's opening measures on the piano once more—back, that is, to the moment when the flashback began. It is as if Sam were going to play the tune yet again, until Rick knocks over a whiskey bottle and cuts him off.) These considerations aside, *somebody* working on the film understood that hearing the whole song was important, because a key point is voiced near the close: "it's still the same old story, a fight for love and glory, a case of do or die." At the film's end, these are the fundamentals that continue to apply, though with implications far from what Hupfeld had in mind.

As the film reaches its climax, Steiner's treatment of the song culminates in three variations—or rather, two plus one, sharply contrasting in style but complementary in effect. The first two variations are paired at the start of the score's final segments (Reel 11, Part 1, followed directly by Reel 11, Part 2) under the scene at the airport, where Rick makes clear that he means to give Ilsa up and send her off with Victor. We have heard both of these variations before, albeit in reverse order, during the second segment of the Paris flashback (Reel 5, Part 3), and that in itself counts for a lot: hearing them again, even without realizing it, we may come to feel the song much as Rick and Ilsa do; that is, as a melody that triggers remembrance of things past, things that are painful to recapture. In keeping with such feelings, the first variation, whose beginning is given in example 2, is the score's most passionate. After another harmonic shock (this time a diminished seventh, one of the staples of opera and melodrama), the melody spins itself out in free extensions, reaching ever higher and modulating widely with no cadence. But when Rick attempts to console Ilsa, the music subsides into the next variation, a sweet waltz; and by the time he closes his speech (repeating the famous phrase, "Here's looking at you, kid"), the tempo of the music has slowed and the triple meter broadened to duple. In this way Steiner seems to point the cue and the scene toward resolution via a major key close—except that the expected final chord of the cadence phrase is never reached, owing to a brutal interruption: an abrupt cut to Strasser in his car, honking his horn. (So absorbing is the film at this moment, we might not register the symbolism of the strident blast: someone at Warner Brothers was inspired to have it imitate the rhythm of the "fate" motive that opens Beethoven's Fifth Symphony.)

The interruption is the first in a series of musicodramatic deceptions that Steiner uses to keep us in suspense until the very end of the film; it is also the first of several key sound effects that figure prominently in the film's closing minutes, and the next one, the shrill sound of airplane propellers, cues the start of Reel 11, Part 2 and leads to the final variation of "As Time Goes By" (see example 3). The sight and sound of the propellers is followed by an altered version of the tense chord we first heard when Rick saw Ilsa in his café—an appropriate parallel because once again Rick and Ilsa gaze at one another, this time as they prepare to part. Then, delaying the inevitable, there comes a restatement of the sinking chromatic scale, the motive of doom. Finally the song is heard once more; and this time, unlike the previous two variations (and unlike the first scene at Rick's), no dialogue gets in the way. Knowing that his music would be out in the open, Steiner saw his opportunity to create a climactic variation in the manner of tragic opera; accordingly, the theme is now played by the whole orchestra at full volume, it is anchored to weighty minor key harmonies, and it is slowed down and extended with the most solemn of cadence formulas. (By way of precedent, consider the endings of *Carmen, Otello,* and *Tosca,* to name only a few famous examples.)

Ilsa and Victor exit nobly, and, as they do, the song undergoes an apotheosis; but again the music presses on, because the film's denouement is not complete. That is why, at the end, Steiner brings all of his other important themes into play; he thereby creates a more elaborate musical design, its climax delayed until we hear the "Marseillaise."[19] The anthem returns only after the key moment when Louis has decided to join with Rick; then, like "As Time Goes By," it undergoes three variations, culminating in another apotheosis. Initially it is subdued and in a minor key—the sort of tentative music we need, if only for a moment, to accept the Frenchman's change of heart (as he puts it, "his least vulnerable spot"). When Louis casts aside the bottle of Vichy water, Steiner emphasizes the symbolic gesture with one more dissonant chord—and at last the dissonance resolves to a stable cadence (quietly, in D major, under the noise of propellers), as Victor and Ilsa's plane takes off. Finally, while the two men walk side by side into the fog, the anthem takes off, too. Having relaxed into C major, the song is at first ethereal; but it quickly becomes a triumphant exit march that carries through "The End." At this moment, as he has done so often in this score, Steiner shows his control of pacing and turns compression to advantage. Within the space of a minute and a half, the anthem leads us out of the film's world just as efficiently as the main title had led us in; moreover, the speed with which this happens precludes our worrying about the details of the plot, or the implausibly quick resolution.[20]

Thus, from beginning to end, Steiner's approach is mostly to be a helpful subordinate, to catch as many cinematic details as he can, and to keep the music moving forward, with an ear for linear continuity if not for coherent musical form. Along with the best dramatic composers in any genre, he shows a keen understanding of the narrative's overall design and music's ability to enhance it. Moreover, whether or not we like to admit it, Steiner's scores often move us deeply. The fact is, just as the writers of *Casablanca* counted on our being overwhelmed by nostalgia when we hear "some of the old songs" (no matter whether they are all that good), so Steiner knew that very simple themes, skillfully constructed, connected, and repeated in deft transformations, could work magic on an audience and make the most improbable melodrama more convincing.

The Maltese Falcon

As for *The Maltese Falcon,* it is in many respects the richer of the two films, and its ambiguities are matched by Adolph Deutsch's music, which floats beneath, above, and through the story. As stated at the beginning of this essay, most of us have a hard time remembering any of this score, even though there is more music here than in *Casablanca:* twenty-four segments, lasting about fifty minutes.[21] One basic reason why is that we never hear diegetic music; thus, no songs are the basis for the background score. No character ever turns on a radio, plays a record, or goes to a club like Rick's, where music is to be sung, listened to, or ignored. What these corrupt and captivating characters *do* do is talk, mainly in lies and riddles, using lines taken mostly verbatim from Dashiell Hammett's novel.[22]

To be sure, *Casablanca* is also crowded with enjoyable, cynical talk: frequently quoted lines are legion, and there is no one whose voice offers more purely musical delight than Claude Rains's; but, to a greater degree, talk in *The Maltese Falcon* is virtually the whole story. It has no flashback like the one at the center of *Casablanca* and no climactic shoot-out. True action segments are quick and dirty, as when Archer is abruptly murdered or when Spade brutally robs Cairo of his gun, and the only complete scene that transpires outdoors is a brief shot of a burning ship. Otherwise such action as occurs in the film is mostly a matter of showing Spade's movements: riding in taxis, getting in and out of cars, walking, climbing up stairways, going through doors, and turning on lights—these are the segments that take us from one chapter of the story to the next. The director obviously thought that they must not be allowed to slow the story down, so they are virtually all depicted in montages of quick dissolving shots. (Dissolves, it should be noted, suffuse this film from start to finish and contribute both to its fluidity, and also to its ambiguous tone.)

These matters have been emphasized to suggest the stylistic qualities of the film that must have impressed Deutsch when he first saw it without a note of music; just as Huston did his best to keep out of Hammett's way and let the story speak for itself, so Deutsch's music is self-effacing to the point of inaudibility. This is due less to the way the music is mixed into the soundtrack than to the composer's, and director's, approach. "Deutsch and I ran the picture many times," wrote Huston, "discussing where music should be used and where not." He continues with what was then one of Hollywood's most widely received ideas: "As with good cutting, the audience is not supposed to be conscious of the music. Ideally it speaks to our emotions without our awareness of it, although, of course, there are moments when the music should take over and dominate the action."[23] Following these dictates, Deutsch usually keeps music out of conscious range in two ways: (1) most of the cues come and go with the transitional montages, fading out at the start of each dialogue scene, fading back in near its end; (2) the melodic material is utterly elusive. At the heart of the score lies a group of five or six thematic fragments, each lasting two or three measures at most. None of them deserves the label of tune, and all are subjected to so many transformations that they seem to have no prime form. As a result, with one exception, it is almost impossible to assign them precisely differentiated symbolic meanings of the sort that seemed so clear in *Casablanca*.

The exception is the theme with which the film begins and which is stated five times in the course of the main title, as well as dozens more thereafter. Example 4 shows the beginning of the main title. Following Deutsch's imaginative version of the Steiner/Warner fanfare in measures 1 and 2, the theme appears twice, in measures 3 and 4, marked to be played by the horns. It should be noted that the theme is chromatic and that the harmony of this passage consists of complex chords with no clear tonal center; moreover, the harmonic ambiguity continues through the main title, while the theme undergoes changes of rhythm, instrumentation, and starting pitch. Here, *pace* Steiner, is a truly "mysterious shimmer." More metaphorically, we might say that the theme is both exotic and menacing; ultimately, it proves as hard to pin down as the falcon itself. Such an association must have been intended: while the opening music plays, we see the credits superimposed on the image of the falcon statuette. Moreover, throughout the film, as the characters scheme to find the object, the theme comes and goes; but at the end, once the statuette is exposed as a fake, it disappears. Indeed, even though the image of the black bird reappears during the end credits, its theme does not. The point is a subtle one, and, typical of this score, one that is achieved as much through absence as through presence.

The falcon theme is heard for the last time during Spade's final scene with Brigid a few minutes before the end, when he tells her why she is going to "take the fall." The scene merits our attention because it is so close in narrative significance to its counterpart in *Casablanca*, yet so different in musical effect. In both scenes, the hero tells the woman he loves that he must give her up, and he explains why; in both the act is a painful one, difficult to live up to. We have seen how Steiner chose to emphasize that pain and the bittersweet sense of triumph that went with it. Deutsch's music gives support to the anguish of his characters, too, but in a manner that is much more nebulous. Perhaps the most important point is that this particular dialogue gets music at all: as Sam sits and makes his case, the music is always *there*, commenting subtly in the manner of melodrama (to use the word in its original sense). About one-third of the way into the cue, the falcon theme makes its appearance, played on the bass clarinet—an expression of Spade's physical and mental dejection—but the cue's most striking effects are themeless and come near the cue's end: the music swells up to convey the desperate passion of two physical gestures, Sam's sudden rise (lifting Brigid to her feet) and Brigid's kiss. These musical surges break in a flash; at the end an uncertain chord holds steady for a moment, then is punctuated by a door buzzer that brings the music and the conversation to an inconclusive halt. Thus a sound effect ends the cue, as does the blast of Strasser's horn in *Casablanca*. Unlike the latter, however, the buzzer's sound is a hazy, colorless monotone (not an allusive motive), and no music follows to support the next stage of the action.

The falcon, Spade tells a policeman in the last line of the film, is "the stuff that dreams are made of"; so is the music. Although a final grand cadence is brought in to coincide with the words "The End," for the preceding shots there is no stirring apotheosis *à la Marseillaise*, and of course none would be appropriate. We see Brigid behind bars in her elevator cage, being carried downward, as if to hell. As for Spade, holding the worthless falcon, he descends a staircase in the foreground of the shot—a descent, it would appear, to nowhere; as far as we can tell, he has nowhere left to go. That at least is Huston's visual construction of the story's ending, and Deutsch's music is a suitable, if somewhat frustrating, match.[24]

Example 4. Deutsch's score for *The Maltese Falcon*, main title, beginning. Used by permission of Warner/Chappell Music, Inc.

Conclusion

In summary, we might say that one of these scores sings, the other doesn't; that one speaks a language we can easily understand, the other whispers secrets; and that, following pathways both parallel and far apart, each finds a different way to move with its film, from beginning to end. We do well to analyze their effects, because they have so many to offer, and they give us so much to ponder of a more general nature. For one thing, the more we look at such scores, the more we realize how easily they can be misconstrued when labeled "classical," no matter how we choose to refer to the films. Simply put, to those familiar with musical terminology, the word carries the wrong connotations. It suggests models of formal perfection (which most film scores are not) using the restrained musical vocabulary of the later eighteenth century (foreign to most film scores). In point of fact, as Buhler and Neumeyer have stated, Hollywood composers of this period chose mainly to communicate using post-romantic idioms, together with styles learned from the popular theater, because such a mix was best able "to accommodate stylistic diversity"—the sort of diversity demanded by each film on its own and by the range of films assigned to composers one after the next.[25]

Writing at the time of *The Maltese Falcon*'s release, Léon Kochnitzky, though not sympathetic to the score, pointed us toward recognition of its diverse stylistic origins from another perspective, by summing up the music as follows: "Scarpia announces to Mélisande the death and transfiguration of the Fire-Bird."[26] We may laugh at the joke even as we reject the author's point: the promotion of modernist art as crafted by film composers like Hanns Eisler, whose score for *The Forgotten Village* receives considerable praise in the same review. *The Maltese Falcon,* according to Kochnitzky, is not art at all: it is just one product of the "smooth working of the astonishing machinery [in Hollywood] that sells pleasure and forgetfulness all over the world." In today's world, this scholar and countless others find such rhetoric far from persuasive, if only because our agendas have grown more inclusive. Is it not curious that in Kochnitzky's summation he belittles the score to *The Maltese Falcon* by suggesting its indebtedness to four landmarks of nineteenth- and mainly twentieth-century theater music (by Puccini, Debussy, Wagner, and Stravinsky, respectively)? Could not this just as easily be a point of neutral observation?

Let us go still further and make the point one of affirmation. To Deutsch and Steiner, indeed to all talented composers of film music, such great works, together with others that are more conventional, will always provide models to imitate and inspire. Even so, each new score, when conceived as an integral part of its film, can work in infinitely diverse ways. For this reason the astonishing mix of music and drama at Warner Brothers, as at every studio that housed instruments for the production of pleasure, remains richer than we yet comprehend. If at present our understanding of the subject is what Rick might call "a story without an ending," that is perhaps good: we do not want to reach the end of the story so much as to continue discovering treasures of film and music. They enrich our lives and enable imagination to take flight.

Notes

This essay was previously published in *Michigan Quarterly Review* 35, no.1 (1996): 112–42.

1. For a sampling, see Fred Steiner, "What Were Musicians Saying about Movie Music During the First Decade of Sound? A Symposium of Selected Writings," in *Film Music 1,* ed. Clifford McCarty (New York: Garland, 1989), 81–107. Many more sources can be found in A *Comprehensive Bibliography of Music for Film and Television,* comp. Stephen D. Westcott, Detroit Studies in Music Bibliography, no. 54 (Detroit: Information Coordinators, 1985). See also my survey "Film Music: The Material, Literature, and Present State of Research," *Notes* 36 (1979–80): 282–325: repr. *Journal of the University Film and Video Association* 34, no. 1 (Winter 1982): 340. A revised and updated version of this article appears in my book, *Music and the Silent Film: Contexts and Case Studies, 1895–1924* (New York: Oxford University Press, 1997).

2. These are their most important essays: Max Steiner, "Scoring the Film," in *We Make the Movies,* ed. Nancy Naumberg (New York: Norton, 1937), 216–38; Adolph Deutsch, "Collaboration between the Screen Writer and the Composer," in *Writers' Congress: Proceedings of the Conference Held in 1943 under the Sponsorship of the Hollywood Writers' Mobilization and the University of California* (Berkeley and Los Angeles: University of California Press, 1944), 240; and Deutsch, *"Three Strangers," Hollywood Quarterly* 1 (1945–46): 214–23.

3. There is no book-length biography of Steiner (b. Vienna 1888–d. Los Angeles 1971), but there are many reliable sketches: see especially Rudy Behlmer's notes for the recording *Now Voyager: The Classic Film Scores of Max Steiner* (RCA album conducted by Charles Gerhardt, 1973; reissue on compact disc, 0136–2-RG); Christopher Palmer, *The Composer in Hollywood* (London: Marion Boyars, 1990), 15–50; and Tony Thomas, *Film Score: The Art and Craft of Movie Music* (Burbank, Calif.: Riverwood, 1991), 56–78. (The last two authors both cite material from Steiner's unpublished autobiography; other sources containing extracts are listed in Westcott, *Comprehensive Bibliography,* 232–36.) Far less has been published about Deutsch (b. London 1897–d. Palm Desert, Calif. 1980); the most detailed sketch remains Lawrence Morton, "Film Music Profile: Adolph Deutsch," *Film Music Notes* 9, no. 2 (November–December 1949): 45. See also the obituary in the *New York Times,* 3 January 1980, sec. B, 19; and William Darby and Jack Du Bois, *American Film Music: Major Composers, Techniques, Trends, 1915–1990* (Jefferson, N.C.: McFarland, 1990), 186–87. (The latter contains various references to Deutsch's work as an arranger, passim.)

4. See especially these books: Claudia Gorbman, *Unheard Melodies: Narrative Film Music* (Bloomington: Indiana University Press, 1987); Caryl Flinn, *Strains of Utopia: Gender, Nostalgia, and Hollywood Film Music* (Princeton: Princeton University Press, 1992); and Kathryn Kalinak, *Settling the Score: Music and the Classical Hollywood Film* (Madison: University of Wisconsin Press, 1992). Both Gorbman and Kalinak contain chapters on scores by Steiner, the former focused on *Mildred Pierce,* the latter on *The Informer.* See also the review essay by James Buhler and David Neumeyer in the *Journal of the American Musicological Society* 47 (1994): 365–85: the books by Flinn and Kalinak serve as points of departure for a systematic overview of the whole corpus of theoretical literature.

5. See Stephen Cooper, ed., *Perspectives on John Huston, Perspectives on Film* (New York: G. K. Hall, 1994); the quoted phrase is from the opening sentence of Cooper's own essay, "Flitcraft, Spade, and *The Maltese Falcon:* John Huston's Adaptation," 117–33. A somewhat different approach to the same topic is found in

James Naremore's essay, "John Huston and *The Maltese Falcon*," in *Reflections In a Male Eye: John Huston and the American Experience*, ed. Gaylyn Studlar and David Desser (Washington, D.C.: Smithsonian Institution Press, 1993), 119–35.

6. Aljean Harmetz, *Round Up the Usual Suspects: The Making of* Casablanca— *Bogart, Bergman, and World War II* (New York: Hyperion, 1992), 6. See Ronald Haver's assertion that the film "crystallized and encapsulated a whole generation's idealistic view of itself," in the concluding paragraph of his essay, "Finally, the Truth about *Casablanca*," *American Film* 1, no. 8 (June 1976): 11–16. Harmetz has a useful chapter on the creation of the score for the film: "Play it, Sam," 253–66.

7. Steiner's scores and papers are now held at Brigham Young University, Department of Special Collections and Manuscripts, in the Harold B. Lee Library. (I am grateful to James V. D'Arc, curator, for his assistance, and to Warner/Chappell Music, Inc., for permission to publish photographs from Steiner's manuscript score for *Casablanca;* I also express my gratitude to the late Mrs. Lea Steiner, who allowed me to obtain a microfilm of the score at the time when Steiner's collection was still in her personal possession.) Other copies of the *Casablanca* score are in the Warner Bros. Archive at USC, School of Cinema-Television, Stuart Ng and Bill Whittington, curators. My analysis of the film is based on the "restored and digitally remastered" videotape version, MGM/UA Home Video, M302609 (1994).

8. Steiner's ideas about click tracks underwent changes over the years: in "Scoring the Film" (1937), 236, he writes of using them "in long sequences, when the tempo is more or less unvarying." Much later, in the excerpt from his autobiography cited by Thomas (*Film Score*, 76–77), he takes them for granted, and describes himself as "one of the first conductors to adapt [the click track] to my own use."

9. See Gorbman, *Unheard Melodies*, 82, and Kalinak, *Settling the Score*, 98–99. Both make important general points, but also some questionable ones. For example, there is nothing in *Casablanca* or *The Maltese Falcon* to support the former's assertion that "conventionally for melodramas, adventure films, and comedies, composers wrote opening music 'full of joy and gladness.'" (The quote is Dimitri Tiomkin's, cited from a book by Tony Thomas, *Music for the Movies.*) Similarly, we may question the latter's statements that it was common to turn the job of writing the main title over to an arranger, "saving the composer for more important work," and that "typically, the main title was conceived in terms of the structure of concert music." (Kalinak analyzes the main title of *Captain Blood*, arranged by Ray Heindorf from Erich Korngold's themes as a "variation of the sonata-allegro" form.) In the present cases, the composers created their own main titles and made use of no preexistent forms.

10. The phrase is from Lawrence Morton, "Film Music: Art or Industry," *Film Music Notes* 11, no. 1 (September–October 1951): 4–6.

11. Cf. Gorbman, *Unheard Melodies*, 83.

12. Though Steiner treats these two melodies in similar fashion, their histories are distinct. The melody of "Deutschland über alles" was composed in 1797 by Haydn to another set of words ("Gott Erhalte Franz den Kaiser"), to honor the Austrian emperor on his birthday; hence it first became widely known as the "Emperor's Hymn." In 1922, the tune was officially adopted by Germany with the poem beginning "Deutschland, Deutschland über alles" (which had been written by Hoffmann von Fallersleben in 1841), and the Nazis continued to use it, together with the "Horst Wessel Lied," from 1933. As for "Die Wacht am Rhein," the text was a patriotic poem written and published in 1840, when German territories on the left bank of the river seemed threatened by the French, and its melody was composed in 1854. Subsequently, historical circumstances remained such as to make the song popular, but there is no evidence to suggest that the Nazis considered the song to be one of their own. That the makers of *Casablanca* chose to have it sung in Rick's café may

have been due to two factors: (1) "Watch on the Rhine" first had captured the attention of American audiences in 1941 as the ironic title of Lillian Hellman's World War II play; (2) the melody fits rather neatly in overlapping counterpoint with the "Marseillaise," at least for the short time the two songs compete in the film.

13. As can be seen in figure 1, "Doom" is introduced in segment 5 of Steiner's score, Laszlo's theme in segment 6. Harmetz's label for the former theme is "Bitterness."

14. See Haver, "Finally, the Truth about *Casablanca*," 16, and Harmetz, *Round Up the Usual Suspects*, 253–55.

15. According to Ken Bloom, *Hollywood Song: The Complete Film and Musical Companion* (New York: Facts on File, 1995), 1:146–47, the Warner Brothers cue sheet listing the songs of *Casablanca* attributes them jointly to Jack Scholl and M. K. Jerome, as composers and lyricists. Possibly these men selected and/or arranged the songs, but none of the songs listed was their own composition. Bloom also lists the titles of two songs supposedly written for the film ("That's What Noah Done," and "Muse's Call"), which he says are not on the cue sheet. Perhaps these are heard as part of the background music at Rick's: there are segments of source music that have yet to be identified, including the melody that Sam describes as "just a little something of my own."

16. See Kalinak, *Settling the Score*, 82: "It was almost impossible to allow a montage to exist without accompaniment."

17. Whatever Steiner's rationale, Aaron Copland objected to the technique, arguing that once we become aware of it, the narrative illusion is lost. See Copland, *Our New Music* (New York: McGraw-Hill, 1941), 267–68 (in the chapter "Music in the Films").

18. "Perfidia" was composed and given Spanish lyrics by Alberto Dominguez; in 1941, the year that *Now Voyager* went into production, English lyrics were written by Milton Leeds, and a hit recording of the song was issued by Glenn Miller, featuring vocals by Dorothy Claire and the Modernaires. See The *Best of Latin Music / Lo Mejor de la Musica Latina* (Miami, Fla.: Belwin, 1990), 62–65, and the album Glenn Miller: *A Memorial, 1944–1969* (RCA, VPM-6019, n.d.).

19. Shortly before the end of the film, after Rick has killed Major Strasser and Louis must decide what to do, Steiner quotes the opening phrase of "As Time Goes By" once more, in dissonant counterpoint with the opening of "Deutschland über alles." (The same passage had been heard in Reel 4, Part 7, under Rick's bitter conversation with Ilsa.) This is the only spot in the film in which "As Time Goes By" does not function explicitly as a love theme (unless one wants to stretch a point and read the new relationship between Rick and Louis in such a light); the simplest explanation for Steiner's use of it here is that he wanted to give voice to Louis's dilemma with conflicting theme, and these were the two that came most readily to hand.

20. The speed of the film's ending also evidently reinforced Steiner's habit of paring source material down to essentials. In the penultimate, ethereal variation of the "Marseillaise," he makes use only of the song's opening three phrases (that is, its initial eleven measures), which come to a pause on the dominant; this he resolves with a reprise of the first phrase (the initial four measures) as the final exit march, which closes firmly on the (local) tonic, G. In short, the song's long and asymmetrical melody has been nicely abridged and rounded; whether or not we hear the result to be an improvement, there was a famous precedent for it in Robert Schumann's "Die beiden Grenadiere"—a song that Steiner more than likely knew.

21. My analysis of *The Maltese Falcon* is based on the videotape version of the film released by MGM/UA Home Video, M201546 (1992), and on the conductor score which is held in the Warner Bros. Archive, USC. (I am grateful to Stuart Ng

for his assistance, and to Warner/Chappell Music, Inc., for permission to use the conductor score.) The holograph score is at the American Heritage Center, University of Wyoming, in a collection of materials that belonged to Deutsch. For further information on the latter, see Edgar J. Lewis, "The Archive Collections of Film Music at the University of Wyoming," *Cue Sheet* (Journal of the Society for the Preservation of Film Music) 6, no. 3 (July 1989): 89–99, and no. 4 (October 1989): 143–61.

22. For a detailed study of what Huston's film does and does not take directly from the novel, see the whole of Cooper's essay, "Flitcraft, Spade, and *The Maltese Falcon*," as well as Naremore, "John Huston and *The Maltese Falcon*," 121–22, and Marcus's introduction to Hammett, *The Continental Op*, xiv–xix. Cooper observes that, while "it has been remarked that *The Maltese Falcon* (both novel and film) consists largely of dialogue, it has not been sufficiently emphasized how much of that dialogue consists of characters telling stories" (119).

23. See John Huston, *An Open Book* (1980; repr., New York: Da Capo, 1994), 79: the director writes of working with Astor on the characterization of Brigid O'Shaughnessy, "her voice tremulous, hesitant and pleading, her eyes full of candor."

24. As was often the case, when the film ends there is a dissolve from the final shot to a cast list, and new music begins immediately. It consists of a band arrangement of a tune in pop style, with three phrases, each lasting eight measures (like a compressed version of a thirty-two-bar song form). I have detected no thematic relationship between this music and the score proper; very likely it was composed by one of the studio's specialists in end titles, not by Deutsch.

25. Buhler and Neumeyer, Review of Flinn and Kalinak, 383.

26. Leon Kochnitzky, "On the Film Front," *Modern Music* 19 (1941–42): 132.

RONALD RODMAN

Tonal Design and the Aesthetic of Pastiche in Herbert Stothart's Maytime

✳

Herbert Stothart and the "Operetta" Musical

With the advent of sound on film in the late 1920s, composers who worked in the cinema found themselves having to formulate new conceptions of structure and function of music in the new medium. Composers of sound-film music were largely conservatory-trained musicians steeped in the tradition of Western art music, particularly the art music of the nineteenth-century symphony and opera. As conceptions of the role of music in sound film developed in the 1930s, composers found themselves with an aesthetic dilemma: how can film music best serve the narrative of a film and yet retain some of the characteristics of unity and organicism that were venerated in the tradition of Western art music? As George Antheil put it: "It must be plain to everyone that if the music constantly follows its picture's action, a spotty and choppy score will be the natural result. But . . . if motion picture music attempts a purely symphonic solution it will find itself in the same hot water as the symphonic music which has so misguidedly appeared in various modern operas of the past."[1]

Fred Steiner has chronicled the thoughts of film composers in the early 1930s—George Antheil, Marc Blitzstein, Carlos Chavez, Maurice Jaubert, Walter Leigh, Leonid Sabaneev, Virgil Thompson, among others—who wrestled with the role of music in the new medium of sound film. As the quote from Antheil intimates, these composers struggled especially with the issue of how music can serve the imagetrack without sacrificing its own intrinsic properties of form and tonal design. Composers sought answers to this dilemma in different ways. In *Cinema Quarterly*, Walter Leigh expressed a view more common than we might think when he suggested that anyone who composes for films would "do well to abandon many musical conventions on which he was brought up, and attempt to approach this new problem of film-sound as a fresh art with many unexplored possibilities, which is only now starting to make its own conventions."[2] Antheil, on the other hand, expresses the problem without resolving it: how can music serve the narrative of a film and yet retain some semblance of the thematic and/or tonal unity traditionally characteristic of symphonic music?

By the mid 1930s, the issue of thematic unity in the narrative film, at least, seemed to be solved: the adaptation (or misapplication) of the Wagnerian leitmotif served as the primary element for musical unity in early sound films. Karlin and Wright maintain that using the leitmotif is a solution for the film-music composer; that the "development of motifs is a powerful compositional device for the film composer, allowing him to bring an overall sense of unity to his score and still leave room for variety."[3] Claudia Gorbman, on the other hand, cites the psychological denotative properties of the leitmotif and its repetition as a means of unifying a film musically for the film's auditor.[4] However, Gorbman goes on to describe a musical "envelope" that encloses a film, "announcing genre, mood, and setting, and then providing musical recapitulation and closure to reinforce narrative closure" (90). Along with thematic unity of the leitmotif, implicit in her account of this "envelope" are additional parameters of scoring, instrumentation, style and genre, and tonal design.[5]

While the authors listed above and others have developed various theories of music in the narrative sound film,[6] a theory of music in the American film musical remains largely unexplored. The genre of the film musical draws upon a complex of origins of the American musical stage, including Broadway, vaudeville, operetta, Savoy opera, and pasticcio. Traditionally, film musicals do not use leitmotifs in the same manner that the narrative sound film did in the 1930s. Consequently, composer/arrangers interested in the issue of musical structure had to seek different solutions for the film musical, mainly by working with the primary unit of the musical: the musical number. Using two areas for study suggested by Gorbman—tonal design and the use of style and genre—I address how Herbert Stothart's 1937 adaptation of Sigmund Romberg's *Maytime* is an attempt at creating a stylistic and tonal design that, while not immediately perceived by the listener/auditor of the film, may nonetheless be understood as a framework on which the composer organized the film's music to support the narrative.

Herbert Stothart was a key figure in reconciling these disparate sources with the needs of narrative film. Born in Milwaukee in 1885, Stothart attended the University of Wisconsin. After teaching at the university for a few years, he moved to New York to pursue a career as a conductor for

Broadway musicals. By 1920, he was composing music for the Broadway stage, beginning with *Blue Kitten*. In 1924, Stothart collaborated with Rudolf Friml in the stage production of *Rose Marie,* for which he contributed the incidental music as well as many of the songs. *Rose Marie* turned out to be his greatest Broadway success, running for 557 performances.

With Hollywood turning to sound and desperate for composers with practical theatrical experience, Stothart moved west in 1929 to become music director for MGM studios. He quickly went to work adapting Lehar's operetta *Gypsy Love* for sound film. The result was *The Rogue Song,* one of the first films to exploit an opera star, Lawrence Tibbett, as a screen attraction.[7] Following the success of this and other early projects, Stothart was appointed music director for a series of musical films starring Jeanette MacDonald and Nelson Eddy—MGM's answer to RKO's couple of Fred Astaire and Ginger Rogers. The MacDonald/Eddy films were loosely based on popular operettas of the 1910s and 1920s. Like the Astaire/Rogers series at RKO, MGM's "operetta musicals" proved a successful formula: from 1935 to 1942, MGM produced eight films in the series.[8] Yet the success of these films was arguably due less to MacDonald and Eddy singing old favorites of Herbert, Friml, and Romberg than to Stothart's clever adaptations. Indeed, Stothart jettisoned many of the original musical numbers, especially the more old-fashioned ones, and replaced them with material in a variety of styles ranging from popular tunes in the public domain to grand-opera arias that showcased MacDonald's voice. The new musical numbers in the films helped delineate character even as it was tailored to the specific talents of the two stars.

Stothart himself never saw musical adaptation as "hack" work; far from it. Stothart's son notes: "Although my father never liked living in California he liked composing for films, and also liked a task at which he became preeminent. This was adapting the music for stage hits to film needs. He was the musical adapter and director on some of the most financially successful filmusicals [*sic*] there have ever been."[9]

Stothart's working procedure in adaptation was pastiche, which critics of film music often deride as an artistic weakness. Stothart, on the contrary, considered it a strength, even in a purely dramatic film. Writing about his score for *Mutiny on the Bounty,* Stothart states:

I saw in the scope and magnitude of the story an opportunity for something new in music of the screen. I approached the task with the intention of having the score actually tell the story in psychological impressions. The listener can, without seeing the picture, mentally envision the brutalities at sea, the calm, the storms, the idyllic tropics, mutiny, clash of human wills, and retribution.
I drew on ancient ship chanteys, music of old England, carols, and other authentic sources, and used these as a pattern to weave together my musical narrative.[10]

Pastiche allows music to contribute to the narrative, to "tell the story in psychological impressions."

Stothart realized, of course, that the film musical requires a different approach to music than does narrative film. In an article for the *New York Times*, he states:

> Musical scoring falls into two divisions. One is the so-called musical, of which the "Chocolate Soldier," "Naughty Marietta," and other operettas or such musical presentations, not in the operetta category, as "Babes on Broadway" are typical. The other division is the providing of background music to create audience moods in dramatic pictures.[11]

Stothart stresses the importance of placing musical numbers in a film musical such that they add meaning to the narrative and not detract from it.

> When musicals first came to the screen, songs were interpolated haphazardly. But it was soon found that, interesting as a song or singer might be, a song carelessly interpolated hampered action of the play as a whole. Audiences and exhibitors protested. Music began to become unpopular in pictures. We learned that a musical episode must be so presented as to motivate a detail of the plot and must become so vital to the story that it cannot be dispensed with. . . .
>
> In other words, we now know that any music in a musical must have definite value as story point and be so presented. The operetta form, its story dramatically heightened, is ideal for this treatment, but, conversely, it can be handled in whimsical comedy with a like result.

By advocating a variety of music in the film, Stothart, whether consciously or not, draws on the tradition of the pastiche (or pasticcio) of the American musical theater. Pasticcio developed from the seventeenth- and eighteenth-century Italian practice of borrowing music from other operas to accommodate visiting singers to a particular opera company. Lawrence Levine notes that nineteenth-century American opera companies frequently inserted "popular airs of the day either as a supplement to, or as a replacement for, certain arias."[12] The practice was also done to adapt a particular opera to satisfy a particular audience, or a guest artist (thus the use of the term "baggage aria"), both of which would certainly enhance box-office revenues.[13] According to Julian Mates, pasticcio found its way into these American opera companies due to, among other things, a long-standing disdain for the pretentiousness of European grand opera. From the outset, European opera was continually being adapted in the United States, with spoken dialogue replacing recitatives and complex ensemble finales transformed into strophic airs and homophonic choruses.[14] By the early 1900s pasticcio was a popular form of musical theater and utilized a vast array of musical styles.

Having worked within the tradition of pasticcio on the Broadway stage, Stothart developed his pastiche aesthetic gradually in the MacDonald/Eddy musicals, replacing more and more of the original music with his own varied tapestry as the series progressed in order to strengthen the narrative function of the musical numbers. The first of these, *Naughty Marietta* (1935), for instance, retains much of Victor Herbert's original score. By *Maytime* (1937), the third film in the series, only one complete song ("Will You Remember?") and a few fragments from the original 1917 production remain.[15] Stothart replaced Romberg's material with a selection of opera arias, chansons (mostly French), and popular songs such as James Bland's "Carry Me Back to Old Virginny" and Teodoro Cottrau's "Santa Lucia." Pastiche, which is indifferent to the niceties of musical unity, serves as a sign that Stothart was willing to sacrifice whatever unity existed in the musical surface of the original operettas for a more unified narrative. Yet the issue is not quite so simple. In *Maytime* especially, Stothart forges a score that, despite its pastiche quality, functions in the film as more than a simple compilation of songs.

A Reading of Maytime

Maytime is told as a flashback of the life of Marcia Morney (portrayed by Jeanette MacDonald), a rising opera diva in the court of Louis-Napoléon and the Third Empire who falls in love with Paul Allison (Nelson Eddy), a struggling American opera singer also residing in Paris. The romance is complicated by Marcia's loyalty to her vocal coach, Nicholai Nazaroff, whom she marries early in the film as a token of her gratitude for furthering her career (though she is not in love with him). Marcia and Paul fall in love, but Marcia decides to call off the affair to pursue her career. After a long separation (portrayed in the film in a stunning audio montage of opera arias and scenes), Paul and Marcia are reunited in the United States in a production of the opera *Czaritza*.[16] During the climactic performance, Paul and Marcia realize that they are still in love and decide to run off together. However, Marcia remains forthcoming and seeks her husband's consent to separate. Nazaroff at first agrees to the arrangement but later changes his mind; in a fit of jealousy, he goes to Paul's apartment, shoots and kills him. The film flashes forward to the United States in 1906, where, after many years of loneliness, Marcia is reunited with Paul in death—but not before she counsels her young friend that love is more important than a career in the opera.

MUSICAL PASTICHE AS A STRUCTURAL DEVICE

Structurally, the film follows closely Rick Altman's concept of dual-focus narrative.[17] For instance, both lead characters are opera singers, but they have very different personalities that are played off of each other. Marcia represents "highbrow" opera; she is contemplative, articulate, graceful, loyal, calculating, elegant, somewhat humorless, passive, and career-oriented. Paul's traits are matched, but directly opposed to hers: though also an opera singer, he is "lowbrow," preferring popular song to opera; he is also spontaneous, clumsy, vivacious, tenacious (hyper)active, and floundering in his career. While their personalities are different, they are both budding opera singers who both have close relationships with their respective vocal coaches, each of which has only one student—Nicholai Nazaroff (John Barrymore) by choice, and August Archipenko (Herman Bing) by circumstance. The dual focus described here is more complex than may first appear: while Marcia is career-driven and focused on becoming an opera diva, in her personal life she is acquiescent and passive; while Paul is energetic and dynamic in his desire for love and pleasure, he is without direction in his career aspirations.

The mise-en-scène of the film is also crafted in a way to reflect the dual-focus narrative of the characters. The manner in which the characters are introduced in the film serves as a good example. MacDonald's first musical scene of the film occurs in the well-lit, expansive court of Louis-Napoléon. Eddy's first musical scene occurs in a crowded and somewhat dark Paris bistro (see figure 1). Other settings of the film likewise contrast the two characters, for instance, Marcia's plush and roomy hotel accommodations versus Paul's crowded one-room flat; Marcia's elegant costumes versus Paul's one threadbare suit, and so forth.

As Altman's schema predicts, it is only through their interaction and the eventual conjoining of traits in a (symbolic or real) marriage that the characters can alleviate their respective shortcomings. In *Maytime,* this process occurs gradually. As a "bittersweet" tragedy, *Maytime* consummates the union of its couple only in death, but the process of "dissolving" the two personalities begins much earlier in the narrative. For instance, with Marcia as a source of inspiration, Paul becomes a great opera singer like her. In the "lunch" scene, Paul begins to sing "Carry Me Back to Old Virginny" several times in several different keys. It is only when Marcia sits at the piano and they sing together that Paul at last finds his "voice." Marcia, on the contrary, learns how to have fun with Paul's help at the May Day festival at Saint-Cloud. She confides in Paul that she "has never known such fun, such happiness." This scene is followed by Paul's profession of love for Marcia in the song "Will You Remember?"

However, both of these narrative events have tragic consequences in the film. Had Paul not heeded Marcia's admonitions to become a great opera star, then surely he would not have been in the position to meet his

Figure 1. *Maytime* (1937). Paul (Nelson Eddy) entertains habitués of a Paris bistro.

demise after his opera performance. Had Marcia not agreed to meet Paul in Saint-Cloud, then she surely would not have fallen in love with him, and thus raised Nicholai's jealousy. The romance between Marcia and Paul leads to Paul's death and Marcia's lonely life. But their love is grounded in different personal circumstances. For Paul, it means a renunciation of his carefree lifestyle, while heeding Marcia's advice to become an opera star. For Marcia, it means letting go of responsibility and enjoying the pleasures of life that Paul has introduced to her. Ultimately, the film teaches that choices have real consequences that cannot simply be undone after the fact. This is Marcia's point to the young Barbara at the end of the film.

The genius of Stothart's pastiche is the way it draws music into the same dual-focus structure. Figure 2 illustrates the song pairings in the film. Every musical number sung by one of the protagonists has a corresponding number sung by the other protagonist, and the solo numbers also form pairings with the numbers in which Eddy and MacDonald sing together. Hence, Marcia opens the singing with a performance of works by Delibes and Planquette at Louis-Napoléon's ball.[18] The elegance here contrasts sharply with Paul's corresponding sequence: Stothart's "The Student Drinking Song" and a folk song, "Vive l'opéra," sung in a dark, candlelit bistro. It is notable that the scenes balance each other with two songs each.

Style Topics:

Opera	Operetta	Popular Song
		1. MayDay Scene I ("Now is the Month of May," "The Tabor and the Pipe," etc.)
	2. Paul "Will You Remember?" (excerpt)	
3. Marcia "Les Filles de Cadiz" "Le Regiment de Sambre-et-Meuse"		
		4. Paul "Student Drinking Song" "Vive l'Opera"
5. Paul's "Viginia Ham and Eggs" Opera "Montage" (*Barber of Seville, Faust*, etc.)		
		6. Paul and Marcia together "Carry Me Back to Old Virginny"
7. Marcia *Les Huguenots*		
	8. May Day Scene II ("Will You Remember?" orchestral)	
		9. Paul and Marcia together "Santa Lucia"
	10. Paul singing for Marcia "Will You Remember?" **Marcia** responding to Paul, "Will You Remember?" "Will You Remember?" Duet	
11. Marcia's **opera career montage**		
12. Marcia and Paul together *Czaritza*		
	13. Marcia and Paul together "Will You Remember?" (reprise)	

Figure 2. Deployment of musical numbers in *Maytime*.

The next number in the film is Paul's ecstatic "Ham and Eggs" aria sequence, sung in the streets of Paris to an unappreciative audience trying to sleep in their homes.[19] This is Paul's "illegitimate" opera montage, which is paired with Marcia's "legitimate" montage later in the film. These two montage sequences are divided by the first duet, "Carry Me Back to Old Virginny," sung in popular style in Paul's apartment.

The second duet, "Santa Lucia," is followed by the number "Will You Remember?" signaling the first climactic scene of the film. Paul sings for Marcia (in the key of C), and Marcia sings the song back to Paul (in D), with Paul singing an accompanying obbligato. Marcia's opera-career montage, which strikingly illustrates her rise to fame through several brief excerpts, follows this number. The scene from *Czaritza* is the second of two opera scenes shown in their entirety. It is paired with Marcia's rendition of "The Page's Aria" from Meyerbeer's *Les Huguenots* (see figure 3). Only Marcia is featured in the Meyerbeer example, though Paul is present in the audience. "The Page's Aria" signifies the beginning of the romance between the characters, while the scene from *Czaritza*, in which both leads appear onstage, signifies the tragic end of the romance. In fact, the story of the "opera" mirrors the narrative of Paul and Marcia, as an illegitimate lover of the Czarina is put to death by the Czar. The scene from *Czaritza*

Figure 3. *Maytime.* Marcia (Jeanette MacDonald) performs the Page's aria from Meyerbeer's *Les Huguenots.* Photo courtesy The Museum of Modern Art/ Film Stills Archive.

may also be paired with "Carry Me Back to Old Virginny" in the sense that the latter was a performance sung completely in Paul's world, while *Czaritza* is sung completely in Marcia's world.

Besides arraying the songs in such a way as to strengthen the dual focus of the main characters, Stothart also uses three distinct singing styles in the film: the original operetta music, opera, and folk (or popular) song. Not only do the various styles lend musical variety to the film; they also function to create what Gorbman calls a "denotative tag of cultural musical properties."[20] In other words, each musical style is used as a kind of musical topos, which serves to signify a property of the characters or the situation.

The columns of figure 2 illustrate the three style topics, with opera as the left column, popular song as the right column, and operetta as the center column. As figure 2 shows, Marcia Morney is initially identified with opera and classical chanson literature. She sings arias from highbrow composers such as Delibes, Meyerbeer, Donizetti, Verdi, Wagner, and Gounod. The pinnacle of her career is her performance of Trentini's *La Czaritza,* an opera composed especially for her.[21] "Opera" signifies high culture in this film, a standing that is reinforced visually by MacDonald's lavish costumes, the extravagant sets on which she sings, and the constant grace and charm with which she portrays her character. The opera-style topic also points to the character of Marcia Morney herself, a woman driven to the career of a diva, remaining loyal to her vocal coach, Nicholai, even to the point of marrying him and sacrificing her opportunity for personal happiness with Paul. Thus, while "opera" stands for Marcia and her highbrow lifestyle, it is also a tragic musical plane, because Paul and Marcia find not happiness there but death.

Paul Allison, on the contrary, is at first associated with popular song, which throughout the film is linked with comedy, fun, and the simple pleasures of the common life. "Popular song" thus signifies Paul's whimsical and undisciplined character, his "lowbrow" nature. Recall that we first meet Paul in the small Parisian bistro where he leads the crowd in singing a student drinking song (a song that not coincidentally lampoons opera divas). He is introduced in the bistro among "commoners," dressed modestly in street clothes (see figures 1 and 4). Though he has the talent to become a great opera singer, he prefers his Bohemian lifestyle, much to the chagrin of his vocal coach. Paul's potential as an opera singer is evident in his spontaneous quodlibet—a structural parallel to Marcia's elaborate opera montage later in the film—where he strings together excerpts from such operas as Rossini's *Barber of Seville* and Gounod's *Faust.* Paul not only runs the music together; he also replaces the lyrics with silly words extolling his joy that Marcia will be joining him for lunch.[22]

Figure 4. *Maytime.* Contrasting characters: Marcia and Paul meet in the bistro. Photo courtesy The Museum of Modern Art/Film Stills Archive.

While opera and popular song are structured within the film as opposite cultural extremes ("highbrow" vs. "lowbrow"), these two topics are mediated by a less obvious middle term: operetta. The operetta-style topic appears in the film in the last vestiges of Romberg's original music, the song "Will You Remember?" Though the operetta-style topic appears only in this one song, Stothart deploys it to good strategic effect. The song reflects the singable, sentimental nature of popular song, but it is performed bel canto, a style of singing associated with the opera tradition but also with the team of MacDonald and Eddy. "Will You Remember?" is the structural centerpiece of the film, an intersection of high and low, or opera and popular song, and, ultimately, of Paul and Marcia.

The operetta-style topic also represents the musical place in the film where both characters can exist happily together. In this sense, "operetta" is a utopian musical space: it does not really exist except as an opportunity missed or a realm outside of the world. The song is first performed in its entirety during the second May Day scene in which Paul declares his love for Marcia. He sings the song for her and she sings it back to him: love offered and returned. But the operetta-style topic does not appear outside this utopian May Day setting, which gives the sequence the feeling of an

Figure 5. *Maytime*. The ghostly union of Marcia and Paul.

"as if." The song is only reprised in the gentle finale of the film, as the ghostly images of Marcia and Paul, reunited in an eternal May Day after death, strolling down the garden path singing "Will You Remember?" (in D♭) as a duet.[23] Mistakes insurmountable in life proved redeemable in death (see figure 5).

Because operetta represents a middle ground between the highbrow of opera and the lowbrow of popular song, in a sense combining aspects of both styles, it serves as a point of synthesis: both elevated popular song and popular opera. At the same time the musical synthesis of *Maytime* extends beyond this (to coin a term) "stylistic dissolve." Indeed, it reaches down even to the specifically musical plane of tonal planning, which operates as another arena structured by dual-focus narrative, an arena in which the narrative is emplotted musically. The choice of musical key for the final duet is no accident. It is a tonal dissolve that musically reinforces the basic dual-focus narrative.

KEY CONSTELLATIONS AND TONAL DESIGN

In addition to the diachronic interplay of musical styles, the deployment of keys for the musical numbers in *Maytime* reveals another means by which Stothart used musical structures in the film. In this regard, music can be viewed in a similar fashion to the narrative of the film itself.

As opera composers before him, Stothart certainly chose the tonal areas of the musical numbers in *Maytime* for a variety of reasons: personal preference, conventional or idiosyncratic association between affect or topos and key or mode, and (probably most important from a pragmatic standpoint) the vocal ranges (and abilities) of Jeanette MacDonald and Nelson Eddy. However, in constructing a tonal design for the film, Stothart went beyond the mere pragmatism of suiting the singers' voices, as the selection and arrangement of keys takes on narrative significance.[24] The tonal structure of the film is one in which "key constellations" are established for each character as a means of identifying them "tonally." Once the two constellations are established, the tonal design of the film takes on a progressive or teleological dimension, with the two constellations "resolving" to a new key of synthesis at the end of the film.

MacDonald's versatility and virtuosity allow her to sing in a variety of keys. However, on a narrative level the wide range of keys also signifies her weak character, as she willingly permits herself to be led around by Nazaroff. As the film progresses, however, her musical numbers tend to gravitate toward D major, the key she uses the first time she performs "Will You Remember?" but also the key of the excerpt from *Czaritza*. D major proves to be a good key for MacDonald's soprano voice, as she can exploit the strong F♯ and A of her high register. Eddy's numbers, on the other hand, are somewhat more tonally constrained. He sings mostly in and around C major, a key well suited to his baritone voice.

Marcia's (MacDonald's) constellation of keys is illustrated in example 1. (Open note heads refer to numbers sung in duet with Eddy, while closed note heads refer to solo numbers.) Marcia's first performance of the film is Delibes's "Les filles des Cadiz" in F♯ minor, followed by the patriotic "Le Régiment Sambre-et-Meuse," which begins in E minor and ends in G major. Next she sings "Carry Me Back to Old Virginny" in G major with

Example 1. Marcia's constellation of keys.

Paul. She then performs the "Page's Aria" in a staged scene from Meyerbeer's *Les Huguenots*. The excerpt begins with a chorus in D before modulating to B♭ for the aria itself. In the "Santa Lucia" duet, she sings with Paul at the May Day celebration in Saint-Cloud in E♭. Most strikingly, when Paul sings "Will You Remember?" to her in his key of C, she responds with her key of D. The excerpt from *Czaritza* recapitulates the tonal trajectory toward D, moving from E minor to D minor before ultimately culminating in D major. As is evident from the graph, Marcia's "home" key of D does not occur until the midpoint of the film, when she articulates her love for Paul in the first rendition of "Will You Remember?"

Paul's constellation of keys is illustrated in example 2. As the graph makes clear, Paul also sings in a variety of keys, primarily major. Unlike Marcia, and in contrast to his unfocused character, Paul's music lies in close tonal proximity to C major. This key is established at the very beginning of the film as the old Ms. Morrison's (Marcia's) reminiscence brings Paul's disembodied voice, ghostly and distant, onto the soundtrack singing "Will You Remember?" Paul's voice is first linked to his body in the bistro, where he sings the "Student Drinking Song" in E, and "Vive l'opéra," which begins in C. The song modulates three times (to D, E♭, and F) in "encore" verses as a drunken patron shots "Higher!" after each verse. Next, Paul sings the "Virginia Ham and Eggs" aria in the keys of E♭, G, and finally C. In his first attempt at "Carry Me Back to Old Virginny," he sings an unaccompanied excerpt of the song in C♯, perhaps searching for a common key with Marcia. When they both sit at the piano, they sing a distant tritone away in G, which also happens to be closely related to both his key of C and hers of D in tonal terms. As mentioned above, Paul's first full rendition of "Will you Remember" is in C with Marcia answering in D, and the *Czaritza* excerpts begin in E minor and end in D.

It is clear from example 2 that Paul remains firmly grounded in C throughout the early portions of the film. The ascending verses of "Vive

Example 2. Paul's constellation of keys.

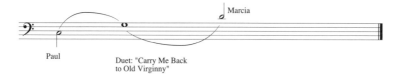

Example 3. G as midpoint in the circle of fifths.

l'opéra" provide a stepwise motion from C to the subdominant, F, which finally culminates in "Carry Me Back to Old Virginny" in G. Following "Santa Lucia" in E♭, the next song is "Will you Remember?" in C. The keys of F and G are closely related to C, while E♭ is associated with C minor. One might even make the case that the inflection toward C minor in the tonal background here reveals a musical premonition of Paul's tragic death to come. Paul's "tonal migration" to D in *Czaritza* is pivotal, as it is Marcia's "home" key of opera, but it proves fatal to him.

Marcia and Paul intersect musically at every narratively crucial turning point in the film, which means that the tonal plan here reinforces the narrative. The first intersection occurs in the scene of Paul's apartment. Here, the characters sing together for the first time, joining for a duet of "Carry Me Back to Old Virginny" in the key of G. As example 3 shows, G represents a middle point in the circle of fifths between C and D. In this context, G represents the first tonal confluence of the two characters. At this point their relationship is tonally proper, indicating a growing warm relationship between Paul and Marcia, but at a stage at which they merely enjoy each other's company. However, in addition to being a convenient "meeting point" owing to its proximity on the circle of fifths, G also foreshadows the "dominance" of Paul (his activity) and the "plagalness" of Marcia (her passivity).

The second intersection of key constellations occurs in the rendition of "Santa Lucia" at the second May Day festival. Here, the key is E♭; while perhaps chosen primarily for how the song lay in MacDonald's and Eddy's vocal ranges, the key serves, on a tonal level, as a comfortable, nonthreatening medial point in the narrative. However, as intimated above, E♭ also foreshadows Paul's demise because it represents the tragic minor third of C minor. In addition, Stothart associates E♭ with the May Day festival itself in the film, as he uses the same key for the orchestral version of "Will You Remember?" in the sequence of the American May Day festival of 1906 that opens the film.

Leaving aside the important sequences involving "Will You Remember?" for a moment, the next intersection comes in the performance of

Czaritza. Here, Paul enters directly into Marcia's tonal world, an attempt at a tonal dissolve that proves unsuccessful, that indeed leads directly to his death. This is a tonal arena where, as *Czaritza* illustrates, only tragedy is possible. As Paul has strayed onto Marcia's stage and in her home key, he has also "strayed" into her affections; because she is married to Nicholai, however, he must ultimately die. Marcia's "operatic" key of D is the tragic "death key" for Paul, the sacrifice on a tonal level of what he is; the narrative punishes this self-sacrifice through the intervention of Nicholai, who kills Paul after the performance in a fit of jealous rage.

Ultimately, the tonal dissolve, the tonal reconciliation of Paul and Marcia, occurs in the mediate tonal space of Db, the key of the reprise of "Will You Remember?" In a sense, this denouement is a transfiguration from tragedy to triumph. In life, Marcia's and Paul's keys were C and D, two key areas with many pitch-classes in common. The tonal area of Db represents a drastic shift in pitch-class content from the keys of C and D. Thus, while this shift in pitch class is prepared at some level by the introduction of the "tragic" Eb of the idyllic "Santa Lucia" duet, it does nothing to undercut the status of Db as a kind of iconic tonal sign of "otherworldliness" that matches the narrative shift to the afterworld. Db signifies the meeting of the two characters (by half-step), and ultimately the literal "elevation" of Paul (up a half-step), and Marcia's renunciation of opera (descending a half-step) for Paul. At the end of the film, then, tonal synthesis is achieved at the same moment that the character dissolve is completed. Moreover, this tonal synthesis, shown in example 4, is replayed on a local level as the music in the scene modulates from C to D before finally settling in Db. Any question about the perceptibility of this long-range tonal plan is answered in this final resolution of keys.

Stothart's tonal design in *Maytime* in fact has antecedents in nineteenth-century opera as the work of Walter Kindermann, Bryan Gilliam, and Scott Balthazar, among others, makes evident.[25] Indeed, the tonal design of the film is quite similar to the directed tonal scheme described by Balthazar for

Example 4. Long-range tonal design with key of synthesis.

Verdi's *Il trouvatore*. Each character is provided a separate constellation of keys that serves to distinguish the plot lines, underscore convergences, articulate shifts from one event to the next, and connect related events.[26] Whereas Verdi works with the unit of the aria, Stothart likewise works with the unit of the musical number. Stothart's design diverges from its European counterparts, however, by the particular tonal dissolve he uses: a new key that synthesizes and mediates the two constellations rather than resolving one pole into the other, as is the case most strikingly in sonata form. Where sonata form structures two keys in a dialectical opposition that is ultimately resolved in the favor of the principal key, Stothart's tonal design breaks new ground, where the two keys are assimilated, not by resolution but by establishing a new key of synthesis.

Such a design is reminiscent of the "progressive tonality" of Mahler but differs from it because Mahler continues to resolve the dialectic of the double-tonic complex in favor of one pole or the other. Indeed, *Maytime* explicitly rejects the latter, more European conception when it refuses to accede to D major as a point of synthesis. Stothart's solution is thus reminiscent of the narrative structure of the musical, where two characters are synthesized into one "romantic couple" through a process of mediating differences rather than one side simply yielding to the other. This solution reproduces on a tonal level the structure of the dual-focus narrative but has the consequence of demanding a tonal innovation that is perhaps uniquely American. The D♭ tonal area achieves its synthesis by opening new ground, expanding the tonal horizon; in this sense, it represents something like a "New World" of tonal relations, a tonal synthesis that displaces the Old World tonal dialectic of resolution characteristic of European sonata form.

The MacDonald/Eddy operetta films were ideal opportunities for Stothart's aesthetic of quotation and pastiche, while also reflecting his desire to unify films through the interaction of narrative and musical designs. Stothart derived the pastiche elements from the American musical theater, especially the comic opera and pasticcio of the early twentieth century, but elevated these pastiche elements by integrating different musical styles into the narrative of the film. Stothart's use of tonal design can be seen as derived from the double tonic-complexes and associative networks of nineteenth-century opera and symphony, while adapting to the narrative requirements of the musical. Stothart's tonal design is quite different from that of the eighteenth- and nineteenth-century symphonic tradition. While this tradition, with sonata form as its epitome, depends on a dialectical relation of musical tension, Stothart's tonal design breaks new ground, relying on a directional tonality in which two key constellations are assimilated within a new key of synthesis. Such a design can be viewed as not only a musical solution to the dual-focus narrative, but also an innovation of tonality that is uniquely cinematic and American.

Stothart thus solved (at least for himself) the dilemma of musical unity for films in the 1930s. This solution satisfies the aesthetic of the composer; his desires for tonal and thematic unity in a work. And the solution satisfies the audience as well, particularly in the denouement of the film as the tonal constellations are brought in close proximity and then resolved to the new key of synthesis. The use of musical pastiche also serves a double function: while it provided Stothart the opportunity to experiment with a new formal process based on stylistic contrast, it also provided the audience a wide variety of musical styles to enjoy.

Notes

1. George Antheil as quoted in Fred Steiner, "What were Musicians Saying About Movie Music During the First Decade of Sound? A Symposium of Selected Writings," in *Film Music 1*, ed. Clifford McCarty (New York: Garland, 1989), 92.

2. As quoted in Steiner, "What Were Musicians Saying," 89.

3. Fred Karlin and Rayburn Wright, *On the Track: A Guide to Contemporary Film Scoring* (New York: Schirmer Books: 1990), 176.

4. Claudia Gorbman, *Unheard Melodies: Narrative Film Music* (Bloomington: Indiana University Press, 1987), 26–30.

5. The issue of tonal design in film was addressed by Leonid Sabaneev in 1935, who provided a rule of thumb that "if music has been absent for more than fifteen seconds, the composer is free to start a new music cue in a different and even unrelated key, since the spectator/auditor will have sufficiently forgotten the previous cue's tonality. But if the gap has lasted less than the requisite time, the new cue must start in the same key (or a closely-related one)." Cited in Gorbman, *Unheard Melodies*, 90.

6. Others include Kathryn Kalinak, *Settling the Score: Music and the Classical Hollywood Film* (Madison: University of Wisconsin Press, 1992); Caryl Flinn, *Strains of Utopia: Gender, Nostalgia and Hollywood Film Music* (Princeton: Princeton University Press, 1992); George Burt, *The Art of Film Music* (Boston: Northeastern University Press, 1994); Royal S. Brown, *Overtones and Undertones: Reading Film Music* (Berkeley and Los Angeles: University of California Press, 1994).

7. Stothart's first film score was actually a commission from Hammerstein for *The End of St. Petersburg*, a Russian film shot in the USSR without music. See Herbert Stothart Jr., "Herbert Stothart," *Films in Review* 21 (1970): 625.

8. Stothart was involved in music direction for all eight of the MacDonald/Eddy operetta films: *Naughty Marietta, Rose Marie, Maytime, The Girl of the Golden West, Sweethearts, New Moon, Bitter Sweet,* and *I Married an Angel*. He also served as music director for other operetta vehicles, notably, *The Merry Widow* (1934, starring MacDonald), *The Firefly* (1937, starring MacDonald), and *The Chocolate Soldier* (1941, starring Eddy).

9. Herbert Stothart Jr., "Herbert Stothart."

10. Herbert Stothart, "Film Music," in *Behind the Screen: How Films Are Made*, ed. by Stephen Watts (New York: Dodge, 1938), 141.

11. Herbert Stothart, "Film Music Through the Years," *New York Times*, 7 December 1941, sec. 10, pt. 2:8.

12. Lawrence Levine, *Highbrow/Lowbrow : The Emergence of Cultural Hierarchy in America* (Cambridge, Mass.: Harvard University Press, 1988), 90.

13. For more background in the history of the pasticcio, see also Reinhard Strohm's article "Pasticcio," in the *New Grove Dictionary of Music and Musicians*.

14. Julian Mates, *America's Musical Stage: Two-Hundred Years of Musical Theater* (Westport, Conn.: Greenwood, 1985), 56–57.

15. Other Romberg fragments in the film include the song fragment "Reverie," and "Dancing Will Keep You Young," performed only as an instrumental background number. Stothart also contributed an original song, "The Student Drinking Song," which introduces Nelson Eddy's character. See James Robert Parish and Michael R. Pitts, *The Great Hollywood Musical Pictures* (Metuchen, N.J.: Scarecrow, 1992), 415–16, for a complete list of musical numbers in the film.

16. *Czaritza* is a "ghost opera" based on music of Tchaikovsky's Symphony no. 5, with a libretto written in French. Stothart writes in 1941: "I expected criticism when I adapted Tchaikovsky's Fifth Symphony into an opera sequence, 'The Czarina' for *Maytime*, but other musicians were good enough to agree that it was a permissible procedure, and that it opened the whole symphonic field for future opera sequences on the screen." The adaptation of the "opera" along with two stunning musical montage sequences undoubtedly were responsible for Stothart's Academy Award for the film.

17. Rick Altman, *The American Film Musical* (Bloomington: Indiana University Press, 1987). According to Altman, the film musical progresses through a series of paired segments matching male and female leads, with each separate part of the film (plot, mise-en scène, costumes, lighting, makeup, and so forth) recapitulating the film's overall duality. This duality is reconciled in a marriage (real, implicit, or symbolic) that resolves the duality of characters in a "character dissolve," in which characters take on characteristics of each other in a sort of synthesis.

18. Although Marcia's style topic is portrayed as opera, neither of these songs are truly operatic. "Les filles de Cadiz" is a chanson composed by Delibes around 1875, while "Sambre-et-Meuse" is the famous French "National Défilé," the anthem of the Napoleonic regime. I am grateful to Rick Penning of the Carleton College music faculty for informing me of the source for the Delibes song.

19. The "aria" consists of excerpts of opera arias from Rossini's *Barber of Seville* and Gounod's *Faust* with new words added to reflect Paul's joy that Marcia has accepted his invitation to lunch. This scene is one of only two in the film that utilizes what Altman describes as an "audio dissolve"; that is, the spontaneous, diegetic singing of the characters with a nondiegetic orchestral accompaniment that takes over the action and soundtrack of the film. Although audio dissolve was used even in the earliest film musicals (in such films as "*The Love Parade* [1929] and *The Broadway Melody* [1929]) and becomes common in film musicals, it is used cautiously in *Maytime*. Even when Paul first sings "Maytime" to Marcia, he prepares her (and the audience) for the song by stating that he is going to sing for her before actually breaking into song.

20. Gorbman, *Unheard Melodies*, 28.

21. "Trentini" is the fictional, Toscanini-like composer of the film. The character's name may have been chosen as an homage to Emma Trentini, a popular singer who starred in stage versions of *The Firefly* and *The Merry Widow* in the 1910s.

22. Stothart adapted and arranged the opera music for Paul's "Virginia Ham and Eggs," while the lyrics were contributed by Robert Wright and George Forrest, two lyricists for many popular pasticcios of the 1920s. The lyricist team also composed the "libretto" for *Czaritza*.

23. This reprise uses an "audio dissolve" for only the second time in the film, which emphasizes our sense of this being another world.

24. Here, I use the term "tonal design" in the same sense as David Beach: as the layout of keys in a composition ("design") as opposed to harmonic-tonal voice-leading structure in a Schenkerian sense ("structure"). See David Beach, "Schubert's Experiment with Sonata Form: Formal-tonal Design versus Underlying Structure," *Music Theory Spectrum* 15, no. 1 (1993): 1–18.

25. William Kinderman, and Harald Krebs, *The Second Practice of Nineteenth-Century Tonality* (Lincoln: University of Nebraska Press., 1996); Bryan Gilliam, *Richard Strauss' Electra* (Oxford: Clarendon Press, 1991); Scott Balthazar, "Plot and Tonal Design as Compositional Constraints," *Current Musicology* 60–61 (1996): 51–78.

26. Balthazar, "Plot and Tonal Design," 78.

MURRAY POMERANCE

Finding Release
"Storm Clouds" and
The Man Who Knew Too Much

✳

> Even sad music requires absolute happiness.
> —Galway Kinnell, "The Choir"

> The Jesuits taught me organization, control and to some degree analysis.
> —Alfred Hitchcock, to Peter Bogdanovich[1]

In the popular imagination, the name of Alfred Hitchcock (1899–1980) is ineradicably marked by a group of scathingly chilling, often violent, sometimes ghoulish, and always provocative films that have tended to be classified in the suspense genre. For somewhat fewer viewers and critics, however, Hitchcock's work showed that he had what François Truffaut pointed to in a letter of 2 June 1962 requesting cooperation in the production of what would turn out to be *Hitchcock* (1985): "a love of celluloid itself."[2]

Close analysis of even the select body of work Hitchcock made from 1950 onward will show, I believe, that it was produced by the greatest film technician of the century, the man best able to use the skills and strategies implicit in the filmic process for achieving depth of expression, sophistication of argument, ambiguity of evocation, and fineness of form. Hitchcock's mastery of the screen has been made evident by many critics, from Astruc to Žižek, but very few observers have paid keen attention to his ways of marrying image and sound.[3] Later in that same letter, indeed, Truffaut himself shows a lapse of attention of this sort, promising Hitchcock that "If, overnight, the cinema had to do without its soundtrack and become once again a silent art, then many directors would be forced into unemployment, but, among the survivors, there would be Alfred Hitchcock and everyone would realize at last that he is the greatest film director in the world." What, one might profitably ask, would everyone say if the soundtracks didn't have to be discarded?

Hitchcock was not only a creative artist who collaborated with ambitious musicians—Franz Waxman, Dimitri Tiomkin, Bernard Herrmann, Arthur Benjamin, John Williams, to name but five—but a composer of sorts himself, following Wagner and Scriabin in binding tonal development to graphic figuration. At least from *The Thirty-Nine Steps* (1935) onward, there is deep interpretive significance in the use of sound, but *The Man Who Knew Too Much* (1956) is arguably not only his most accomplished work but a profound statement about the role of music in private and social life. Nevertheless, this film has received insufficient critical and precise attention, given the subtleties with which it is filled and the astonishingly rich expressions Hitchcock has been able to make with music and film at his disposal together.

While this film contains a complex score—including both orchestral, chamber, cabaret, and folk material, mostly either written by Herrmann or arranged by him for the screen[4]—an especially fascinating and uncommon element is a full-length cantata, "Storm Clouds," performed (diegetically) at the Royal Albert Hall.

There are no analyses of *The Man Who Knew Too Much* that fail to place the cantata performance—the "absurd" cantata, as Pascal Bonitzer perversely puts it—at the dramatic center of the film.[5] Often, the performance at the Albert Hall is viewed as the scene in which Jo is able to overcome a personal devotion to her own family in order to take a socially responsible action that protects the life of a stranger: "They are ready to let an assassination happen, in order to get their child back. But during a concert at the Albert Hall, as the cymbals are about to crash (and as they do), they find a sense of human dignity and solidarity again: they prevent the assassination."[6] I, however, would not urge such an interpretation. If Fereydoun Hoveyda's statement explains the political outcomes at various moments in the story, it fails to address Jo's state of confusion in the Hall; the fact that we were present at the cue rehearsal for the shooting but Jo and Ben were not; Ben's relentless search for Ambrose Chappell and his entanglement with the Assassin *at a time when Hank is still missing*; the exact emotional "tonality" of Hank's absence for the viewer; and the rather brutal fact that we never receive enough information to ensure that any human redemption is achieved by saving this particular Prime Minister's life.[7]

But the simplest, and for me the greatest, critique of the Hoveyda position is that, even if its supposition that the McKennas achieve some "humanity" as Jo screams is accepted, the cantata, by its light, must be seen as a decorative musical setting for action that is not intrinsically musical in itself and could just as well have been set somewhere else. The McKennas can perform heroically in the grand lobby of the Savoy, on any street—in Hyde Park for that matter. If all they are doing is relinquishing their selfishness for the sake of another person's life, there is no need to have a choir singing as they do it. Hitchcock does not use his settings in a facile, purely decorative, way (although some other directors certainly do), and it is far from inconsequential that the confrontatory action takes place in the Albert Hall. If it is clear in some analyses (for example, Weis's; see note 3) that the civilized harmony of the cantata is an ideally ironic setting for the violating wildness of the scream, it is less apparent why viewers should hear *this* cantata, performed in *this* way, in *this* place. Bach wrote some very moving—and civilized—cantatas, for example, and one is advertised on a billboard Jo passes as she enters this location; why not that? Why could the nefarious Draytons not have taken Hank to Vienna so that we might hear "Wachet auf" in the Konzertverein? I believe this cantata must be considered with serious devotion for the film as a composed entity.

Like film, music is the metrically unfolding probability of resolution in play, and the suspense of that probability is a function of harmony, poetic ambiguity, facial expression, phrasing—the stuff of cinema, of symphony, of social life. Jo Conway is as aware of these relations as is "Bernard Herrmann"; Doris Day as aware as Bernard Herrmann.

Nothing that happens filmically in the Albert Hall is unrelated to the performance of the music. An attempt to experience the sequence closely, noting in detail not only what is sung but what is revealed optically at the same time, perhaps reveals a great deal about Hitchcock's filmmaking—and surely his intents—in this strange film. For oddly here one needs not only to hear but also to read, and to have rehearsed the score earlier in the company of the intended killer. Like the conductor, the Assassin has a score—in the hands of an assistant, Miss Benson, who knows how to read it. Evaluating the impact of the cantata scene in the context of the whole, one realizes that, rather than producing a murder, the Assassin in fact manages to kill the performance of the music—an act of central importance in a Hitchcock film but, I suspect, unthinkable in any other.

The cantata "Storm Clouds" was composed by Arthur Benjamin (1893–1960) with a text by Dominic Bevan Wyndham-Lewis (1891–1969) specifically for the 1934 version of the film[8] and "in such a manner as to reach a climax involving a cymbal crash at the very instant that a murder was being committed."[9] For the 1956 remake, "Storm Clouds" was reorchestrated by Bernard Herrmann: he involved himself by "doubling several parts and adding expressive new voices for harp, organ, and brass"[10] and also (as will be seen), alone or with Hitchcock's help, by slightly altering the text.[11]

> There came a whispered terror on the breeze,
> And the dark forest shook
>
> And on the trembling trees came nameless fear,
> And panic overtook each flying creature of the wild.
>
> And when they all had fled
>
> Yet stood the trees
> Around whose head, screaming,
> The night-birds wheeled and shot away.
>
> Finding release from that which drove them
>   onward like their prey,
> Finding release the storm clouds broke and
>   drowned the dying moon.
>
> Finding release the storm clouds broke,
> Finding release the storm clouds broke,
> Finding release the storm clouds broke,
> Finding release!

Further, about one and a half minutes of material was added to the original score because Hitchcock wished "to elongate the playing time."[12] Although the release of the final chord is drowned out by the audience hubbub subsequence to the Assassin's plunge from the box circle railing, the cantata is heard in its entirety here, running 9:07 on the screen. (A 34-measure portion of the allegro agitato [mm. 108–42] is repeated.) With only the one pungent exception that makes this film famous—Jo's scream—there is dramatic dialogue neither during the music, nor for some time previous as Jo scans the auditorium and the concert gets under way.[13] The actual performance of the cantata occupies 124 shots in the cut film.

Herrmann had recommended as conductor, "both for recording and photography,"[14] Muir Matheson, but by 3 May 1955 Richard Mealand, managing director of Paramount British Productions, and Unit Production Manager C.O. "Doc" Erickson were being asked in London by night wire from New York, "Does Bernard Herrmann have work permit as conductor?"[15] If he didn't yet, he had one within a few weeks, because "Storm Clouds" was prerecorded 26–28 May 1955 at the Festival Hall, London with the London Symphony Orchestra and the Covent Garden Choir under his direction.[16] For some of the scenes shot with the orchestra and chorus at the Albert Hall (30 May, 31 May, and 5 June), an audience was not present, and the conductor was Richard Arnell.[17] But it seems the recording session booked for 6 June may well have coincided with an actual concert performance; such an item is certainly posted outside the hall as Jo makes her approach:

London Symphony Orchestra
CONDUCTOR BERNARD HERRMANN
Cantata Storm Clouds
by ARTHUR BENJAMIN
Monday 6 June at 8
Tickets 21 15 10/6 7/6 5 3/6.

A second poster reveals that two nights later Arnell would conduct the LSO in Bach's *Art of the Fugue*.

But the "Storm Clouds" cantata is itself a prelude and fugue—indeed, a prelude and fugue *about* a prelude and fugue: a prelude to a storm and a desperate attempt at flight from it (fugue). Because the work is organized grossly into two sections, I consider them separately.

Section 1

(a) The introductory Lento orchestral passage in the somewhat abstract, if not eerie, key of C, is set in $\frac{3}{4}$ at a metronome tempo of sixty to the quarter, or one second per beat, providing a kind of clock for real and narrative time and a superb "ruler" for cutting purposes: seventy-two frames of film, or three seconds, would pass in each measure of music.[18] The repeated trumpet fanfare on a fortissimo string ground, broken by an appassionata passage in the violins, gives an opportunity for Hitchcock to set out the majestic spatial parameters of the hall and the august technical parameters of the performance, in case his audience is not especially familiar with the workings of an orchestra. Before the action, the scene. Though a very high establishing shot from near the ceiling was presented earlier, as the music begins, the viewer drops to a position near the top row of the upper balcony, thus entering the concert frame as a "typical" listener in place. A second view is from equally high, but over the stage, so that a closer view can be offered of the display of forces. Then, we jump to a close shot of the conductor seen from among the violinists, a suggestion of the serious, personal commitment with which the performance is undertaken. It will be clear soon that this film is in many ways principally about the musicality of life, the shifting formality of social organization, and the importance of individuated passion in resolving the clash between them.

It is worth saying at this point that although a number of motion pictures have depicted classical concert performance, *The Man Who Knew Too Much* offers a rare opportunity to see the filmic role of "performers" played not by actors pretending to be musicians (by which I mean persons who do not normally identify themselves as musicians, now, for us, selectively doing so, to the accompaniment of a prerecorded track) but by the actual (backstage) musicians who under other nonfilmic circumstances might make exactly such music as this. Of all the performers available to Hitchcock for filming over music that had been prerecorded, he chose Bernard Herrmann and Barbara Howitt themselves to play their scenes. The conductor, "Bernard Herrmann," being performed by the music director of the film, Bernard Herrmann, the viewer is opened to the thought of seeing a real-life conductor actually conducting; and that thought can constitute a surface reading of the scene. Steven Smith, indeed, rhapsodizes that "Herrmann was given the choicest screen appearance by a real-life conductor since Stokowski shook hands with Mickey Mouse."[19] But in *Fantasia*, Leopold Stokowski conducts in shadow when he is seen conducting at all. And *Fantasia* is not about his performance, but about what one could imagine if inspired by it. Here, viewers are meant to think they are seeing a perfectly faithful, because real, depiction of how a conductor waves his arms to the music. Both Hitchcock and Herrmann cared profoundly about music and accomplished the scene with a precision unique in motion pictures; musicians will be delighted to find that the "downbeats," which are not actual— the music having been prerecorded—make sense, and that the "conducting" is in general related, and responsive, to the "music-making" of the orchestra and chorus.[20]

But of course, in the sense that whatever sound was produced in the Albert Hall was not for ultimate public consumption, the concert sequence was a colossal mime.[21]

(b) Another fanfare (m. 10) echoes softly in the muted brass choir, suggesting distance and preparing viewers to anticipate the entrance of the voice—to be ready to listen to what is sung. Shots of the audience, which draw closer and closer as the preamble of the music comes to a hush, intensify expectations and lead thoughts to focus on the human response to the music. A signal is thus given that this music is in the film to show a human response in the audience and to produce a human response in Jo and in us; that in fact it *is* a human response, an "integrated and passionate human endeavor"; and that human response is what ultimately counts as time goes by. It will be worth recollecting that Hitchcock's method brings his viewer again and again to a character's response to a situation: the odd confrontation at the hotel in Marrakech, the festering marketplace, the bleak London chapel, the Savoy hotel, and, now, the Albert Hall. We will see, too, that human response is not *all* that music is.

(c) The first entrance of the harp (m. 24), which provides a gilded little ripple, accompanies a long, and then a close, shot of Jo McKenna standing against scarlet curtains at the back of the hall. Behind her are doors with light—slightly amber—filtering through. She looks forward toward the stage, just off-camera, and twists her gloves, ruffled. She has come here to seek the help of Inspector Buchanan, not to find music, but now she is caught up in concert formalities. Being a performer herself, she is an insider; indeed, she is in partial turn-out, as a singer might be who is ready to perform, and therefore she seems to answer the expectation produced in (b) that we will encounter a voice. Her eyes are serious, intent. She is ready to apprehend the music. Seeing her in this musical trance a viewer learns, in a swift moment, that all the turmoil of the film is behind her. This music will be an apotheosis. Her trance lasts two measures, six seconds. We turn now to the orchestra she is seeing onstage.

(d) In the solo flute's arpeggio over the pianissimo tremolo of the violins (m. 26), it is possible to catch the first whispered imagination of something strange and beautiful on the mythical "horizon." But then:

(e) There is a troubled passage of descending sixths, scored for strings *divisi* and *sul ponticello*. The camera cuts back to Jo: she is clasping her jacket at the waist and looking around. She looks up to her right, in the Assassin's direction. (But she has no way to know at this point that he is an assassin. He has accosted her in the lobby and warned her about her child, although in the press of his attention she may very well not quite recollect where she has seen him before.)

(f) We follow her gaze, first to a long shot of the box circle where the Assassin is, and then to a close-up of the Assassin, in half-profile looking camera-left, whose eyes slowly turn toward us as the tympani and bass drum strike a signal beat and the strings reach their ominous nadir. He slowly continues to turn his head as a muted, soft fanfare from trumpets is heard (m. 32). But now we are relieved to realize it is not us he is looking at, but the Prime Minister, across the hall. We occupy his point of view and see the Prime Minister sitting pompously. The strings play a sad, swelling descending motive in A minor harmonized in sixths, as:

(g) We cut to Jo looking up to her left (camera-right), in the Prime Minister's direction, concern and anxiety etched on her face. As the strings hit a low E, resigned, and the fanfare is echoed elegiacally by the French horns (m. 34), Jo slowly turns to look behind her for a moment of private thought, fingering her white gloves. "What can be happening here?" she must wonder. Now a most exquisite and moving C major obbligato is heard in the celli, prepared by flute triplets, and echoed by an appassionata solo violin in E (mm. 35–37). Jo very slowly revolves, lifting her eyes in an apotheosis of hope, as the celli hit their high and very optimistic E (m. 37). The full orchestra is seen from her viewpoint, brightly lit, and then, as the celli reprise their obbligato, this time in a C minor variant that prepares a relatively strong cadential motion (mm. 38–40), the camera frames (i) the celli up close, and (ii) the conductor and soloist. The music is an instigation for sensing meaning and feeling a response; but it is also a socially organized technical production. As the violins play an octave passage, passionately (m. 40), the frame isolates the celli, the conductor, and soloist again, as reminders: music is experience, but also order, status, meaning.

(h) As the violin passage is repeated more painfully (m. 42), the conductor is seen in long shot from high up at the rear of the orchestra. Beneath is a whole panoply of musical forces, and the precision of his beats, along with the roll of the music and the extent of the productive force on display, lulls the listener into a measured, growing, anticipatory kind of breathing. The music crescendoes through measure 45. Next, Hitchcock shows various groups of musicians in close shot, to introduce with precision the idea that this complex and large mechanism, controlled by one man, is in fact a well-organized interplay of activities (like a film, or at least the plot of this one) undertaken by individuals who are different, who are trained to capacities, who are cued. At measures 46 and 47, for instance, we can see a piccolo player, a flautist, clarinetists, horn players, and an unmanned xylophone at the rear. At measure 48, an A minor solo for the principal oboist appears. It is a picture of social organization, with the music as a kind of program providing topical direction for the time. But one person can change everything. Now, as if to emphasize this thought, one man is shown sitting at the rear in the percussion section, with his hands on his lap, as the B♭ clarinets play a passionate octave passage (m. 49).

This man is seen again, closer, when this passage is picked up by the flutes in the next measure. The music builds rapturously here, and there are two cymbals on chairs next to him. The succeeding shot, as the flutes repeat the octave passage at a new pitch level and now harmonized with a deliciously anticipatory second (m. 52), shows the cymbals alone. Vibrating from the cymbals as they rest on the dark scarlet chairs are shimmering patches of gold and white light as well as reflections of the pale blue plasterwork and of the rich burgundy of the chairs (figure 1). These brass orbs are instrumentalities (weapons) not yet in use; but also visual purities—glowing, reflective, circular, elemental, symbolic.

The musical passage ends with a crescendo: the flute trill and tympani roll at measure 53 are intensely preparatory, and the view turns to:

(i) Jo, standing with her eyes closed and clasping her belly. As she opens her eyes it is clear that she is strained, that the beauty of the music is capturing her, but she is exhausted. Her lips seem dry. Led by an ascending violin glissando we see what she sees—the stage—and there is a sumptuous descending G minor passage for the strings during which the mezzo-soprano

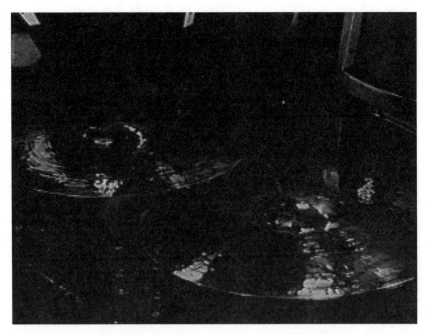

Figure 1. Shimmering patches of gold (h).

soloist slowly stands up. The opulent, gathering movement of the conductor's baton (marking out the seconds of our attention here) nicely echoes,
and is echoed by, the sawing movement of the players' bows. It is a slow
and oceanic movement, suggesting that Jo might be on the verge of a kind
of seasickness. This lasts a fulsome twelve seconds, so that viewers can
hardly fail to participate.

(j) Now, from the front row, the camera looks up at the soloist and conductor as, with a reprise of the flute arpeggio as preparation (m. 58), she
readies to sing. There are pink hydrangeas ranged in front of her and she
wears sapphire blue: summer vegetation and the sky, an invocation of nature. And behind, the tuxedoed and white-gowned chorus and orchestra
are a social mechanism. Not without drama, she sings (in A minor): "There
came a whispered terror on the breeze—." The melodic line is invocational,
as though she is recounting a great and mythic tale beyond human proportions. The architectonics of the music as a whole suggest that all of what is
happening in this plot can be seen to fit into a mythic organization that is
greater than human life, and yet foreknown.

(k) "And the dark forest shook," she continues.[22] The conductor and soloist are visible from the lip of the stage, with the chorus behind and
higher: the lens is just at the top of Herrmann's head and his black back

Figure 2. From the lip of the stage (k).

dominates the screen, at right (figure 2). The shaking, the trouble, comes out of the music; and in a filmic sense, it also comes out of the score of the film. Herrmann here stands in for Hitchcock, bringing out what is latent. For punctuational emphasis, the trumpet fanfare sounds, muted (m. 64).

There is no doubt that, in all of their collaborations, Hitchcock uses Herrmann's presentations as signals of himself; of his attitudes, his fears, his sensibilities at the moment. But in this film, he overtly announces that he is doing so. *The Man Who Knew Too Much* is therefore an artist's statement; a public discussion about the architectural principles that underpin his work. Even as much as the film is made musical, Herrmann is made filmic.

(l) The chorus is about to make an entry, piano, at measure 65 with the quasi-recitative, "And on the trembling trees came nameless fear," so we are cued just at the same time the chorus itself is, by means of a close shot of the conductor looking up and raising his hand in a preparatory upbeat. As the chorus continues with "And panic overtook each flying creature of the wild," the visual image of the chorus is fragmented; various groups of singers are shown, but from a position, each time, within the orchestra. As viewers we are part of the music-making, because we are cued; but we are separate, too, because we stand just outside and watch. We thus mimic Jo's position, as singer who must not sing. Panic, it seems, overtakes us singly.

It is important to keep in mind that Jo is not only the mother of a kid-napped child; she is herself a child of the stage and music, kidnapped by Ben and social propriety. Her panic is that of both the mother and the art-ist in restraints.

(m) The fanfare sounds again now (m. 72), isolated, admonitory, against silence: a muted trumpet trio in A minor. A close shot of Jo at her position prepares a gaze upward at her. Her mouth is open; she is gasping for breath; her eyes are alert and yet unseeing. She is in the middle of a perfor-mance, in every sense of the word. As violins and violas play a cautioning descending arpeggio passage (m. 73), she looks up toward the Assassin.

He sits placidly, with Miss Benson, fixed upon the stage. His lips, too, are parted. The horns echo the fanfare, pianissimo, and he takes a pair of opera glasses from Miss Benson, who has the score unfolded on her lap. He raises them slowly to his eyes as the flutes play their introductory triplets for the cello obbligato again (m. 75). This time the chorus joins the stun-ning cello obbligato heard earlier (m. 76, cf. m. 36), sopranos echoed by tenors, singing "And when they all had fled." Here, a close shot reveals the Assassin with the glasses to his eyes, slowly, as on a lubricated dolly-head, revolving toward us like a monitor. "And when . . ." suggests that some-thing is about to be narrated; that we are on the border of an event. The Assassin turning with his double lenses is a great dark camera (figure 3). His movement is smooth, almost mechanical. We note his jarring jawline, his terrifying fluidity. For this shot alone Reggie Nalder's performance should be judged superlative. Intercut is a single shot of Jo watching him, gasping, but not grasping.

(n) "Yet stood the trees," sings the mezzo. The view is through the Assassin's binoculars now in an iris shot, and we are implicated again as perpetrators even as Hitchcock has implicated us in virtually all of his films.[23] But the shot is curious. It is trained up one level, both across the hall and to the balcony above—except that in the earlier establishing shot the Assassin looked directly across to the far side of the box circle. This sub-jective angle, then, puts viewers down with Jo, who does not have opera glasses, letting us imagine *her* imagination of what the Assassin can see: his iris, her point of view.

If we might not wish to put a bullet in the Prime Minister (directly be-neath whom designer Henry Bumstead has kindly seen fit to hang a banner with an X),[24] we would certainly wish to spy on him. Below is an EXIT sign: when all the creatures had fled, when all the narratively insignificant hu-mans flooding this concert hall had been negated by concentrated focus and filmic framing—yet stood the trees, yet stood the central narrative ele-ments. In this case, for the Assassin, the trees are the Prime Minister and his

Figure 3. A great dark camera (n).

party. And the exit, the way out of here, is by way of some kind of treatment to that party.

Jo is still looking up at the Assassin's box as the mezzo sings "Yet stood the trees" in an octave leap in C, ending on B♭ (m. 80), and she is panting, her eyes closing, her head thrown back. At this moment she is outside rational, semantic, analytic knowledge; indeed, her response to the music might be called belief. That an event is about to occur in this hall to the accompaniment of this cantata is something *we* know, not something *she* does; while Jo is carried off in an aesthetic response we struggle as best we can to enjoy the music, knowing that it is a harbinger of death. On the other hand, as music is its own form of knowledge, she is swallowing and inhaling knowledge that is musical, and the music is leading her onward into darkness. Something will happen soon, the music says. Something is on the verge of happening. Music is a lip of experience.

(o) "Yet stood the trees," repeats the singer, with another octave leap, now a step higher on D, ending on C (m. 82). "—Around whose head screaming": on "head" (m. 85), an ascending fourth (C♯ and F♯), as the mezzo bares her teeth. The conductor and orchestra at this point are deeply engaged in their playing, carried away, oblivious to what is "around their heads." The view cuts to Jo in extreme close shot at the doorway on "screaming," with the mezzo's white teeth still traced in the viewer's memory. Jo's eyes are closed, her lips barely parted, her head back. As the singer continues with "The night-birds wheeled and shot away," ending on a high sustained G (m. 87), Jo wheels and backs away against the wood-paneling of the wall at the entrance. The camera dollies with her, almost pushing. She is sobbing into herself with feeling (she is in mortal fear for her son's life, she has not slept, she has been running the streets of London), with loss, with the apprehension of sublimity all at once. The music, for this moment, is too much for this woman—who is a night-bird, a stage performer. She has wheeled and shot away.

(p) But the music is also too much for the Assassin, now seen in a close shot as, with his eyes lowered, he has withdrawn from musical appreciation and musical movement to a calculation, a utilitarianism. He looks off-left, over Miss Benson's shoulder, to catch a quick glimpse of her score. There is a moment to spare, in which the chorus will repeat "Yet stood the trees"; and so the line of inquiry can be developed in a close shot of Miss Benson, seen from below. She is looking down, somewhat sleepily, but her finger is moving across the pocket score on her lap.

As the chorus rather emphatically repeats "Yet stood the trees," there is a very close shot, looking down on the score. It is a minature study score,[25] and her finger, with brilliant scarlet nail polish, is moving rightward with the words. The polish on the thumb (figure 4) catches the eye in the middle of the screen (as did the indigo stain on Louis Bernard's hand in Morocco as he died) defining what could be a confusing and meaningless shot without that image; it holds us and draws us along with the music, much as we can imagine it might also be doing for the Assassin, who is musical but sitting at some distance from the printed notes.

Three more times the women sing "Yet stood the trees," as if to taunt. The Assassin looks slowly over toward the Prime Minister, off-right. That man "yet stands," although in fact he sits, stiffly. As he is not seen below the waist, he might in fact be standing, so straight is his back. There is as yet no sign of pleasure on his face (m. 92), if in fact he is enjoying the concert at all. (Like the Assassin, he is at work.)

Now, as a glissando brings forth the full orchestra for a statement of this thematic line (m. 94 ff.), we cut to the Prime Minister moving forward in his seat with his back stiff and his attention rapt. He seems wooden as a tree.

The choir is repeating the lines slowly, fully, with full orchestral accompaniment. The rhythm suggests the great broad sweeping shifts of a rolling sea building for a storm. In close shot Jo, against the wooden wall, is sobbing. The musicians announce "Yet stood the trees" three times more, descending each time into relative stillness, as though a wind were dying down.

Figure 4. Polish on the thumb (p).

(q) Now, in an innocent, almost sugary, plainness, the altos and sopranos sing "Yet stood the trees" in F (m. 98). The harp, innocent and beatific, is seen at left. The singers are all in white. The sense is, everything will be all right now: the trees yet stood. But they go on: "Aaaa——", and on the syllable "—round" the note shifts abruptly from F to D♭ (m. 100). "Around whose head" something is yet to be narrated, because it is not the trees that are important but the event that is happening, the event that hasn't been told yet, the event around their heads.

(r) On "—round whose" (sung with a self-reflexive rounding swell of amplitude), the percussion section is glimpsed again, with the man sitting peacefully; on "head" (m. 101), there is a shot from above him, looking down at the player on his left, the cymbal part on its stand on his right, and the cymbals to his left. He is bald. The lighting of the shot draws the eye of the viewer first to his head, which is perfectly still, then to the perfectly still cymbals (one of which is partially in shadow), and finally down to the open pages of the part at right. Suddenly, urgently, he jerks forward to examine the score. This rouses us in preparation for:

(s) From the cymbalist's point of view, we see a very close shot of the actual cymbal part to the cantata, as the choir hisses, in D♭ again, "screaming" (m. 102). The part is headed "CYMBALS | THE STORM CLOUDS | ARTHUR BENJAMIN" and indicates a sforzando cymbal crash at the bottom of the right page. Before this, 186 measures of rest are clearly marked.

In his *Fire at Heart's Center*, Steven Smith suggests this shot is a "last visual joke" of Hitchcock's,[26] but I think it is not. The alarming speed with which the man leans forward to check his score puts us on edge. The fact that the choir sings "screaming" as it is looked at further heightens the anxiety. The manner in which they sing it, emphasizing the sibilant and elevating the amplitude of their sound, adds still more tension.

Further, this is the ultimate visual statement of a theme Hitchcock has announced many times: that in a complex and hectic world the action of an individual can have far-reaching consequences. "There are times when all of us need a little help," Louis Bernard told Ben McKenna on the Casablanca–Marrakech bus. "No one will know—No one, but only one," the Assassin told Drayton as they rehearsed all this. We will see Jo alter narrative history with her scream. But here, unknowingly, the cymbal player is preparing to collaborate in a murder using his score. "The man is unaware that he is the instrument of death," Hitchcock told Truffaut, "He doesn't know it, but in fact, he's the real killer."[27] The score neatly sets out how he can and must act, giving him the smallest conceivable window of opportunity: that is, one beat in an entire work, at the conclusion. So all he has to do is count and smash—which is to say, wait patiently and then bring together the two sides of the world.

But the cymbalist's counting signals something beyond a hiatus. In his private access to the score—now revealed to us—with its meted and numbered measures of rests, he is the apotheosis of the actor behind a role, appearing to act naturally and spontaneously but working all the while from a script that has set out all of his actions, in linear sequence, in advance. He knows, then, as does every actor in this film,[28] considerably more about what is going to happen than we think he knows, and the score in front of him is an overt admission of this piece of theatrical magic. Goffman is the master on this subject:

Turn . . . to the inner realm of a stage play in progress. Obviously the playwright, the producer, the prompter, and the players all share a single information state concerning the inner events of the play; they all know what will prove to be involved in the happenings and how the happenings will turn out. Rehearsals make this all too clear. Further, this knowing is much more appreciable than real persons ordinarily share about their world, since the playwright has decided in advance just how everything will work out. Just as obviously, during a performance the characters projected by the peformers act as if they possess different information states, different from one another and, of course, less complete than the one the actors and the production crew possess. Note, the make-believe acceptance of different information states, different from one's fellow characters and different from the production staff, is an absolute essential if any sense is to be made out of the inner drama on the stage. Any utterance offered in character on the stage makes sense only if the maker is ignorant of the outcome of the drama and ignorant about some features of the situation "known" to the other characters.[29]

The cymbalist in this case, for example (by which I mean, the man contracted by Herbert Coleman with the accession of Herrmann and on behalf of Hitchcock to play the cymbals in the London Symphony Orchestra during certain shots for this film—a stuntman named Charlie Quirk)[30] knows, or can be taken to know (to be working on the level of reality where it is known), that he will be preempted, before he plays that one beat, by Doris Day screaming. Perhaps in fact Quirk does not know. After all, the entirety of the sequence could have been accomplished in an editing suite. So in this case, there might well have been an instance of naive or "sincere" performance, in which the performer really does happen to "know" just what we, the viewers, "know" that he "knows." But as I say, it is known—and precisely by the sorts of people who are in contact with the Charlie Quirk who is at a remove from us.

In the way that the cymbalist has this score, Doris Day has her script, and she surely knows that while Jo is sobbing in this scene she will be smiling happily in another to come much later. The latent effect of the extreme close-up of the cymbal part is to provide a view of the kind of script that lies behind a production like this, without in fact breaking the spell of this production. And the very insertion of the whole cantata into this film gives such a chance for a performance within this performance, in which issues bearing upon the production and perception of this performance can be stated and played out on a fictional, interior, and isolated stage within this stage. So, we have the play-within-the-play.

One last nuance: it is interesting to see how much "resting" the cymbalist can sustain in the midst of stormy turmoil. The "turmoil," therefore, is not "stormy" in reality but only in imaginative effect, like Ariel's in act 1, scene 1 of *The Tempest*. In reality, for the musicians, it is the manufacture of music; it is work. And this cymbalist may represent a limiting condition of a man working. All he has to do is count and smash, but he had better smash brilliantly and he had better count with absolute precision. He is laboring very hard, just sitting there with his hands in his lap.

It is evident, then, in reflection, that Miss Benson is working very hard in exactly the same way. The Assassin is working hard, too, as he calmly enjoys the music. A thought backward reveals that the Draytons, peaceably enjoying Marrakech, were working very hard, and that Louis Bernard, making flippant conversation on a bus about snails, was working as hard as anybody. We may recollect that Hitchcock, the man who *really* knew too much, stood lazily looking up at entertaining acrobats for his cameo—apparently doing nothing.

The use of the single cymbalist here, by the way, is a visual accommodation of Hitchcock's. Had there been two cymbalists, not one; holding four cymbals, not two; it would have been necessary to have shown some interactional signals between them in order to visually and emotionally understand the mechanism whereby they could operate together to produce a single crash. And this mechanism would detract, emotionally, from the drama of the climax. But in fact, the cantata "Storm Clouds" is scored for two cymbalists playing four cymbals for the climactic moment in measure 171. Just as the role of the cymbalist is here played by a stunt man, the "role" of the pair of cymbals is "performed"—and is an index to—something greater. The percussion section of Benjamin's original score called for three timpani, bass drum, cymbals, large gong, triangle—that is, *one* pair of cymbals.[31] But Herrmann had decided to "sweeten" them, which is to say, to enhance the sound, both for the concert and for the snippet of the recording played in the "rehearsal" scene between Drayton and the Assassin. In the score, therefore, the end of measure 171 is clearly marked: "4 CYMBS. 2 PAIRS." What is heard (and not seen) both here and in the rehearsal takes is twice the cymbalism, twice the symbolism, twice the labor that is now in front of our eyes. The word "screaming," at any rate, trails off now, and then is followed by:

(t) "The night-birds—": at which are seen, frontally, the two cymbals sitting beside one another, like sleeping owls, on two chairs.

(u) The next shot is stunning (figure 5). The sopranos sing, ethereally, ascending a celestrial triad in F (m. 104), "Whee–ee–ee–eeled . . ." and

Figure 5. Miss Benson wheels (u).

while they do, Miss Benson folds her score, rises up, wheels in a graceful movement. "And shot—." She climbs quietly up to the back of the box and retreats behind a swag of scarlet drapery. The Assassin has not moved. She is not quite invisible, not quite an absence of reminder.

There is a pause, as the word "shot" diminishes to a point and ends. The Assassin stands. He turns. "Aaaa——," the singers sing, oh so quietly. His dark form moves up to the back of the box, past the near swag. The voices trail off: "——way." He vanishes, reaching up to touch the draperies affectionately as he passes. We see the double curtain swag, with Miss Benson hiding back at the left. Two hot-spot reflections of auditorium lights beam from the wooden tops of two now-empty chairs. This marks the end of the first half of the cantata.

Section 2

Like the film, which begins in Marrakech and ends in London, the cantata itself has two general settings. The first, lento appassionato, is moody, evocative, lyrical, majestic, and sweeping. The second, allegro agitato, is about action, not place; pulse, not harmony. The passion had been Jo's but the succeeding agitation is Ben's. In the allegro, the meter changes from triple to duple, and the increase in tempo creates urgency, presses forward: the wind is being whipped. The tempest that was approaching, and the approach of which constituted a pretext for narrative, would seem to be here.

(aa) The two light reflections from the shot of the cymbals become the white padded heads of tympani mallets of the next shot. This close shot of the tympani roll observed directly from beside the drum heads introduces the second half of the piece (m. 108). Hitchcock's conviction that the emotional value of a shot is given by its size is nowhere more evident than here, where he wants to stun us into a fast-paced racing mentality that will call to mind the chase sequence in the Marrakech market.[32] To have only the sound of the tympani roll called for in the Benjamin score would be insufficient. Hitchcock wants the tympani roll as a first enunciation of thunder, not merely in the cantata but in the frame that holds the film. These "storm clouds" are themselves only indications of the more ominous ones on the narrative horizon. To show the tympanist at a distance, or have the roll merely heard, would place the event inside the cantata score but give it no particular filmic weight. Constructing an extreme close-up brings the thunder visually to the fore.

(bb) As the trombones and horns sound the ominous and repetitive storm motive—an eighth note followed by a quarter, then an eighth followed by a half (m. 109)—there is a spasm of urgency, compounded by a sense that things have gotten out of control and help is needed. At the same moment, in a long shot, the narrative has jumped away to the lobby of the Royal Albert Hall, where Ben McKenna is dashing in from the street. The brass motive is stated four times in a rising sequence, twice by the tubas and trombones, twice by the horns and trumpets. On the first Ben enters and, dazed, looks around. On the second he approaches two elderly chatting ushers. On the third he talks to them, gesturing. On the fourth, in a closer shot, he looks up past them to something he sees off-camera to the right. We catch his view and see that it is Jo, leaning in anguish against her wall. He moves through connecting doors to her, accompanied by frenetic sixteenth notes in the violins.

A bass drum figure—a rest followed by seven even strokes on the beat (mm. 115–116)—signals an end to the first statement of the extended brass motive; Ben is seen to enter the auditorium and come up to Jo.

(cc) The brass motive sequence from (aa) is now repeated altogether. The first statement (trombones) accompanies Ben and Jo clutching one another at the back of the auditorium. At the second (trombones), she quickly turns and gestures with her hand to the box circle where the Assassin had been. A close shot of the empty box follows her gaze. On the third enunciation (horns), she is still clutching Ben and guiding his eyes up to the Prime Ministerial box. Loyal to Ben, but not to Jo, the balding usher standing at the curtain leans forward and takes a peek up to the Prime Ministerial box. On the fourth (trumpets), we are regarding that box. At this instant in the narrative, Ben and Jo know there is to be an assassination; they believe it is to be in London; they are missing their son. Jo knows she has seen the man with the opera glasses before, in Marrakech, but he has not been identified for her as an assassin (nor, except by innuendo, has he yet been identified as such for us). He frightens Jo and she has seen his interest in someone across the hall. The Prime Minister is across the hall. Though we may assemble these logical fragments into a coherent reading of action (and of course we *do* if we have seen the film before), our direct and immediate sense of the moment is that it is pregnant with happening, sensuality, ominousness, fear, and disconnection. As the music brings us forward in time, and as dissonances in the harmony are progressively resolved, the pieces of the puzzle will meld.

Meanwhile, listeners sitting in the aisle seats in the last row, just near Jo and Ben, continue to stare forward, oblivious to the pantomime that is going on behind them. In other words, the aesthetic sanctity of the performance has not been violated by Jo's agitated demonstrations; even though it is possible to see Ben's lips moving, and also Jo's, their "talk" is only for themselves. Cinematically, they are mute through the sequence.[33]

It is a delicious little pantomime. As the orchestra picks up the frenetic sixteenth-notes again, Ben tries to run out but Jo holds him back with a quick second glance back to the Assassin's box. While their backs are turned, the usher leans further forward for a look. Again the cumulatively slowing bass drumbeats are heard (mm. 123 and 124) as the two remonstrate silently with one another, arm in arm, with the usher as audience. Ben pulls away and exits. "Finding release," sing the basses in A minor (m. 125).

(dd) "Finding release from that which drove them onward like their prey," continue the basses and tenors. Ben is in the lobby now, racing to the staircase the Prime Minister had ascended and quickly climbing it (mm. 128 and 129).

(ee) As the men hold the E on "prey," the women interpose, "Yet stood the trees," with an octave leap on E. Ben is arriving in the corridor of the box circle. It is dark. Police bobbies and inspectors stand around alone or in small groups chatting, wooden and stultified as trees. Ben heads into the "dark forest."

The lyric "All save the child" is struck from Herrmann's score here and replaced by "Yet stood the trees."[34] What the change accomplishes, beyond allowing reference to the stodginess of certain character types such as the police and the diplomatic corps, is of great narrative interest. Had the original lyric been retained at this moment of acute narrative tension, we should have been listening, along with Jo, to agitated high female voices singing, "All save the child around whose head, screaming, the night-birds wheeled and shot away." Certainly, taken on its own, this is a chilling and profoundly disturbing image; but in the filmed context of a cantata performance, which "just happens"[35] to be the one being heard by our protagonist as she thinks of her own lost child, perhaps terrified by night birds screaming around his head, it becomes irritatingly pat, maudlin, and then thin. Rather than really supporting the filmmaker's narrative concerns, the concert would only seem to have been arranged to do so and would consequently be flattened, rendered cinematically impotent and musically trite. It must therefore be the listener who makes the connection between the cantata lyric and poor Hank, not Hitchcock.

(ff) "Finding release," the men sing, and echo, again (mm. 130 and 131). This time the nearest bobby seizes Ben to prevent him from getting ahead to the area where the Prime Minister's box is. Ben remonstrates but the bobby will not release him. "Finding release from that which drove them onward like their prey." Ben and the bobby are clearly arguing, face to face (m. 134), but again in cinematic muteness. "Yet stood the trees," sing the women, leaping an octave on G (m. 134). The bobby raises his hand as if to say, "Wait here, I'll check for you. Trust me. Wait here." Now the women are chanting, "Finding release, finding release," and the men echo them. The bobbies are chatting sociably in the background, with Ben pinioned in open space, unable to take a step forward or backward to find release.

(gg) The camera is close to Jo, back in the auditorium. She is looking up to the Prime Minister's box, profound anxiety washed over her face. Her body is tense. She holds her breath. "[Re-]lease, the storm clouds broke," sing the women, ascending chromatically upward F–F♯–G. At "The storm clouds," she turns to the Assassin's box.

(hh) "Broke, and drowned—": the women descend by step from a high G (m. 141), as we see the virtually empty Assassin's box. Miss Benson's hand holding a score is peeping out from the curtain swag at left. Something moves behind the curtain swag at right.

"The dying moon" completes the descending scale (mm. 142 and 143). The voices become sullen and quiet; upstairs again, a second bobby approaches Ben in the corridor. Clearly frustrated, Ben starts to explain all over again: the consternating game in which musical recapitulation is imitated in business life.

(ii) There is now a full musical repeat of the second "movement," from its inception (mm. 109–143). The repetitive brass motive is once again sounded four times, as, from Jo's position, a view of the full orchestra is presented. At this juncture, a master shot such as this one is helpful, since, for the viewer, engagement with the protagonists who act to make up the whole has in fact obscured perception of the whole. (We cannot see the forest for the trees.) This setting, we must not forget, remains a summer's evening concert at the Royal Albert Hall. But, of course, we have forgotten. We have been subtly led into believing that we are attending a murder attempt, magnificently choreographed and performed to full orchestral accompaniment. The stabilizing view that Hitchcock now provides is essential to the moral turnout of the picture.

At a passage of frenetic sixteenth-notes, which suggest impending serious action, the percussion section is shown again, backed by a handsome piece of robin's-egg blue and white plasterwork that suggests neoclassical restraint and elegance. The cymbalist decorously stands.

(jj) As the frenetic passage concludes sharply with the slowed drumbeats, the cymbalist gathers the nearer cymbal into his hand. He is bending for the second as the fourfold repetition of the brass motive is heard again. At the first iteration of the storm motive (in the trombones), he stands up straight and the light catches the inside, the reflective surface, of the great brass ear. For the second, third, and fourth iterations (in trombones, horns, and trumpets respectively), we cut to the Assassin behind his swag. He is lit obliquely, half his face in shadow. A swarthy hand reaches inside the jacket and withdraws a pistol. The cuff, the collar, the folded handkerchief in the breast pocket, and the flower in the lapel—each of these is translucent in its whiteness, like the milk Cary Grant carries in *Suspicion*. Equally white are the whites of his eyes, but the light that gleams off the side of the brutal, squarish gun is blue-white.

As the string section takes up the sixteenth-note figure, we see Miss Benson, furtive in a shadow. Slowly she breathes, sweetly indifferent: a perfect apprentice.

(kk) Ben is still in the corridor for the summative slow bass drum tattoo and has been having no luck persuading anybody to let him pass, perhaps because, as much in the dark as Jo, yet full of foreboding, he does not yet have an articulate theory to sell. As the men start chanting "Finding release" again, he again tries (soundlessly) to explain to a bobby what is going on. There is a cut to Jo, downstairs, still looking anxiously up at the Prime Minister's box. She turns to see if Ben is at the door behind her but then comes back and looks quickly up at the Assassin's box.

(ll) As if to interrupt now, as if peremptorily and audaciously to impose an irritation on the overriding and more elevated dramatic needs of the plot, the sopranos sing, "Finding release," and there is suddenly a side shot of the whole range of them, in seraphic white gowns, innocently pressing forward with their "insignificant" performance. In short: we are so wrapped up in Ben's helplessness with the police, the Assassin's preparation, and Jo's anxiety (even though she does not know fully what we know) that the music has become transparent, utterly trivial. We wish, in fact, to find release from the music in order to enjoy the drama. Yet the music is what Hitchcock has brought us on this filmic journey for. The men, in medium shot, from the side, now echo with "Finding release from that which drove them onward like their prey."

The women, once again: "Yet stood the trees."

More women: "Finding release."

But there are numerous releases, to summarize, that cannot at this moment be found.

1. The Assassin does not have license yet to liberate his bullet. Drayton has been both precise and dictatorial about a dramatized assassination that makes full use of the musical scheme of the evening.

2. The Prime Minister, who is an aesthetic boor present at this concert only for political and ceremonial reasons, cannot find release as yet from the tedium of the music. It is clear elsewhere in the film that he is also fatigued

with the demands of his very ceremonial job, and he has not yet been able to find release from that. Ironically, the Assassin's bullet could free him but will fail to.

3. Ben cannot find the understanding that will bring him release from the tyranny of the London police. Nor, because his son is implicated, can he find release from the deathbed promise he implicitly made to Louis Bernard.

4. Jo cannot find release from the precarious position her family is in because of the obligation her husband incurred to Louis Bernard. Nor can she find release from her own needs as a musician, as they are exemplified and magnified by the quality of this music. Nor can she, a former performer, find release from her proper duty as a concertgoer, which forbids her to make a stir. The trip from America has become a nightmare for her, and she cannot find release by waking from this nightmare.

5. We cannot find release from our knowledge that as the powerful music proceeds, as it builds dramatically and engages our ears, as it begins to culminate and to evoke a natural sense of culmination; the awful assassination draws ever nearer, and inexorably so. So we cannot find release from the music. Nor can we find release from the musical, expanding, culminating development of the film. We are trapped.

(mm) One group of female singers is now seen chanting, "Yet stood the trees"; and then a second, from the reverse angle, chanting, "Finding release." They are all tied to their scores, which are boldly open in front of them. And they stand like trees in a dense wood, unmoving, unchangeable. The suggestion is that the current high-tension standoff will be prolonged forever. But when "Finding relea[se]" is repeated, there is a close shot of the cymbalist holding his cymbals, and looking up from his score which he has been reading. He will, we know, shortly bring release. Behind him is the morning-glory blue plaster, which suggests the receding, liberating sky that was behind Ben's head when Louis Bernard died and again as he clung to the steeple of Ambrose Chapel and found release to come to this concert.

Because we know about the musical cue the Assassin will follow—indeed, that he *is* following one—but Ben and Jo do not, we are as much actors in the play they are watching as the Assassin, and the Assassin is therefore our collaborator. Ben and Jo mimic our position with respect to the film as a whole, as an audience keenly aware that something is afoot, sniffing the oncoming thunderous destruction, yet powerless to fix it in time and space and thus to take action to prevent it.

It is a curious, and wonderful, filmic construction: that the protagonists should be pinned in a temporary paralysis relative to the viewer of the film. One can recollect Starobinski's dictum to look so that one may be looked at.[36] We, in their place (we think), would know precisely what to do. They know only that somewhere, relatively nearby for each, there is grave danger; and that at a moment they cannot predict it will break loose. In Jo's ears must also be ringing the Assassin's gracious threat (though she did not know who he was when he delivered it): "You have a very nice little boy, madam. His safety will depend upon you tonight."

This quality of being frozen in one's knowledge, stunned by it into a state of pure vigilance while action flows all round, is the "suspense" that is at the heart of Hitchcock's intent. He suspends not our belief, or disbelief, but our whole power in a trance of vision: seeing is better than doing. Thus, the filmic enterprise is redeemed by our commitment to seeing it transpire. Of all fifty-four films Hitchcock made in his long career, no one piece more complexly or elegantly establishes the framework and formula for suspense than *The Man Who Knew Too Much*.

(nn) The choir proceeds with "[Re-]lease, the storm clouds broke, the storm clouds broke and drowned the dying moon." At the first "storm clouds broke," Ben breaks away from the police enclave and heads in the opposite direction, toward us, where he will find the Assassin's box. His first impulse had been to give sufficient warning to have the Prime Minister's box evacuated, which is a roundabout approach but a safe one. His self-protective constraints are now eclipsed. He moves into relative darkness on the screen, a glare of fixed purpose in his eyes.

On "moon" the Assassin is behind his drapery. He is lifting the gun into position, staring off at an angle toward the Prime Minister. If Jo McKenna, with her golden hair and brilliant personality, is the sun; surely the Assassin, swarthy in darkness and highlit vaguely blue, is the moon, dominator of night and night-birds. Spiritually, he is the Ben McKenna who keeps her locked away from her stage career, and she must free herself by triumphing over him.

(oo) To a persistent side-drum pattern (m. 143), the orchestra speeds up and the choir sings, building chromatically from a low F♯ (see example 1). In the next measure, the Prime Minister sits bolt upright (figure 6.1), as though suddenly aware. He may be experiencing the music for the first moment. He may be realizing that he is in danger, or intuiting it. He may just feel curiosity for a closer view of the stage. But he awakens.

In measure 146, Jo, who has been watching him, has a remarkable experience. The "dying moon" is now her own aesthetic dreaminess, her ability to swoon at, and be carried by, the music. It drowns. She, too, awakens. She suddenly turns 180 degrees and looks up toward the Assassin's box but with a sharp and fully realizing intake of breath (figure 6.2). It is now, for the first time, that Jo knows not only that something evil is going to happen in this place, that the Prime Minister is somehow involved, and that the man with the gaunt face and the menacing voice is engaged as well, but that there is a line from one box to the other, from one man's eyes to the other's chest. She can see the action in her mind's eye.

As measure 148 begins a repetition of mm. 144 ff. a step higher, we see the Assassin's whole box, empty in the front, with the drapery swag at right being ruffled by action from behind (figure 6.3).

At measure 150, Bernard Herrmann in close-up delivers a furious down-beat and looks down (figure 6.4). A matching shot brings a view of the score on its music stand, with the conductor's hand jumping in to turn the page swiftly (figure 6.5). The music, in short, is hurtling forward in time, and the future is swooping toward us.

3 (pp) The music is louder and most urgent now. At measure 152 there is a very close shot of the conductor's score, with the notes inked in black (figure 6.6). The repeating arpeggios suggest furious activity and urgency. The shadow of the conductor's baton, moving up and down metrically but with great emotional pressure, overlays the page.

Let me take a moment here to suggest again that this is a film about both music and theatricality; about both the urgency to voice and the need to

1 2

3 4

Figure 6.

5

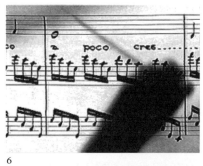

6

7

8

9

10

11

12

Figure 6 (*cont.*)

13

14

15

16

17

18

19

20

Figure 6 (*cont.*)

21

22

23

24

25

26

Figure 6 (*cont.*)

stage. The shot of the conductor's score here is *not*, in fact, the conductor's score for measure 152. Marked "poco cres-cen[-do]," it does not quite mirror the actual "crescendo poco a poco" in the score at this moment; moreover, there are no descending sixteenth-notes here. The "score" that we are now seeing with such "fidelity" is yet another construction, believable as we see it, yet standing in for its counterpart in the real world as so many stand-ins do in this film. What has been interpolated here is a bit of the harpist's part for the finale, ten measures and some thirty seconds later, so that we skip forward in time, impatient, even as we focus more dreamily and the music swells all around.

Measure 153 coincides with an extreme close-up in which three groups of sixteenth-notes occupy the whole screen (figure 6.7). This close-up both exaggerates the pressure and urgency of the musical moment and expands it to fill the screen. The expansion is a visual reflection of the temporal plasticity being employed in the editing, where a brief moment, examined in minute detail and from up close, swells to fill a large context. This shot renders self-conscious the filmic editing process through which we are seeing all of the picture and the concert-hall sequence in particular, wherein events expand to occupy the time dramatically needed. In musical terms, the tempo here is taken ad libitum (with liberty) so that the music might slow, swell, and expand to form the grand finale. During this shot, by the way, the metric beating of the shadow baton remains in view, and there are four distinct beats. This allows viewers to keep the measure of the developing event metrically—to count out a procedure to the finale.

At measure 154, as the voices rise a third from D to F♯, the cymbalist raises the cymbals near his face (figure 6.8). The cymbals are the storm clouds, and they are about to clap together (audiences, such as the one we constitute, also clap) to make sound.

In measures 155 and 156 Ben finds the doors to some boxes, opens them desperately, peers inside, backs out, closes the doors, and keeps on down the corridor (figure 6.9).

Measures 157 and 158 are divided between two complimentary shots as the storm clouds break again from D, through F♯, to high A. In the first (figure 6.10) is a bank of female singers enunciating the word "broke," their mouths open and their gazes fixed forward. This is the last gasp of civilization before the takeover of nature. Then, with a jump, there is a shot of Jo, extremely close up, her mouth open in the exact same way, her hands raised together at her bosom (figure 6.11). She is clearly not holding her breath: she is singing.

(qq) The rising melodic third in measure 159 coincides with a shot of the Assassin's face (figure 6.12). The camera then drops down to his elbow. The next measure begins a step higher on the mediant; the camera moves rightward along the Assassin's arm to his cuff, ending with the dark hand holding the dark gun, all bathed in blue light (figures 6.13–14). In measure 161, a dominant seventh chord arrives, the second scale degree emphasized melodically. It is a perfectly unresolved chord, anticipating a perfect resolution. As we move beat by beat, the filmic motion is itself

Example 1. Arthur Benjamin, "Storm Clouds" Cantata mm. 143–72.

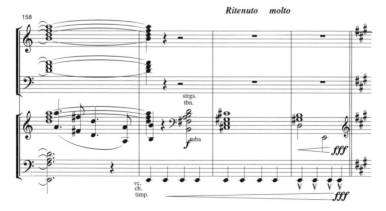

Example 1 (*cont.*)

Example 1 (*cont.*)

slowed and swelled to fill the screen with new information on each beat of the measure:

Beats 1–2. The cymbalist, seen from directly in front and below, with the two instruments opened (figure 6.15). One reflects light, the other darkness. His expression is impassive, suggesting dutifulness and technical adeptness. The simple appearance of the shot suggests how simple the clash of cymbals will be; and one is reminded how a small movement, perfectly calculated, can have great effect. (But throughout the film, small movements have had great effect. This man is dressed more formally than Hank was on the bus, and is more trained to do what he is about to do, but Hank's grasping the

Example 1 (*cont.*)

Arab woman's *yashmak* was also a small, simple movement with a great out-come. Lucy Drayton's gentle question in the marketplace as Ben and Jo pre-pare to depart Bernard's corpse for the Commisariat de Police, "You . . . don't want your little boy to go, do you?" is yet another.)

Beat 3. The conductor, opening his arms as he gives the beat, so that his movements are huge and spherical (figure 6.16). This cues the viewing au-dience that the finale is impending; but it also suggests the balloonist going up at the county fair that excited Ben McKenna as a kid.

Beat 4. Ben, trying the doors of yet another box, with the same fervid emotion, now that another "balloon" is "going up." The box door will not open (figure 6.17).

(rr) The finale (m. 162) is marked "molto meno mosso quasi maestoso" (much less motion, as though majestically). The organ that accompanies the finale, sonically recalling the hymn service at Ambrose Chapel, is heard behind the orchestra sustaining an A major triad, as Ben manages to get the box open. Peering quickly inside he withdraws and races to the right. The music is now slower, rising sequentially for each of three repetitions of "Finding release, the storm clouds broke."

The first statement begins with a shot of the orchestra, the conductor on his podium, and the audience behind him, all seen from between the two cymbals, which frame the margins of the screen (figure 6.18).

As we hear the second statement, Ben tries another locked door, box 31, and moves on. There is a cut to Miss Benson still in her shadows, the whites of her eyes gleaming; and we see the dark swag hiding the Assassin, with the tip of the gun beginning to protrude on "broke" (figures 6.19–21).

The frame stays on the gun for the third musical line. It moves outward from the curtain a few more inches, and then slowly swivels until the barrel is pointed our way. The swivel echoes the one in the finale of *Spellbound* and, of course, the earlier moment here with the opera glasses. On the ultimate "broke," the orchestra breaks off. We see Miss Benson again, and then, quickly, Jo, but now expressing an astonishing sensibility, produced by the sensuousness of that note. Having migrated from C to A minor and then to A major for the finale, the music now prepares its culminating A chord by means of a subdominant on "storm clouds," so that an A chord is expected on "broke." But what is delivered is something else—C major again. C major is a key at once elementary, childlike, primitive, and abstract, easy to play but unnatural, and the tendency to depart from it for accidentals is to desire fervently to return.[37] Yet here the return takes us off guard and raises attention to—Jo (figure 6.22).

(ss) This is a new Jo. The camera is above her, looking down on her head and shoulders. She looks off, camera-left. She knows she must act. There is complete silence, a fermata. She moves her head quickly to the Prime Minister and then to the Assassin. The score reads "ALMOST TWICE AS SLOW" (m. 170).

(tt) The choir sings and holds the first syllable of "finding": "find—." The triangle sounds an alarm fortissimo, as the camera looks directly into the face of the Assassin, one eye shut in darkness, the other taking aim along the gun barrel to "find" his release (figure 6.23).

The Prime Minister poses, a naive small smile on his broad face. Our view drops down his chest, guided by the helpful blood-red ribbon pinned across his white waistcoat. A gold and blue medal hangs nicely in the middle of the chest (perfect for aiming) and a monocle dangles uselessly around it, dropping to the belly (figures 6.24–25).

(uu) As the choir pauses to take in breath, Jo, in a close shot, lets loose with her scream, rending the musical tissue. The choir joins in with "Re-[lease]" as the Assassin, looking away a little, jiggles his gun.

Jo's scream is long and hideous. Though her head is made up as a model of civilized containment—cropped bangs, bunned hair, reticent little black beret, understated earrings, finely drawn eyebrows, immaculate collar, and Italian linen suit—her mouth is now animal, wild, untamable, vicious in its pure power. The scream is the last thing anybody would expect from this epitome of vocal focus and skill. It is purely terrifying in its effect, even though for Jo it is a release and relief. Thus, even a killer as cold-blooded as this dark Assassin will believably be jarred when he hears it. And there is the additional effect of social displacement produced when a scream of any kind is uttered in the middle of a concert. Thus, the concert serves not only Drayton (as camouflage) but also Jo McKenna (as civil ground). If the concert hall is a perfect place for an assassination because nobody will hear the shot, it is also the perfect place to foil an assassination: nobody will be able to shoot who hears something when there should be silence.

(vv) As the choir sings "[Re-]lease" fortissimo, there is an extreme close-up of the cymbal crash (figure 6.26) followed immediately by a long shot of the Prime Minister standing and, aghast, clutching at his arm. Given that he would have heard no shot, his "innocence" is both a caricature of his fatuousness and situationally accurate.

Why, it is interesting to ask, must we hear the cymbal crash? Hitchcock's emphatic close-up must dispel any notion that this event holds status, for the filmmaker, predominantly in the cantata frame. The cantata is dissolved with the scream. But the cymbals crashing when the music is not there to support the sound (itself an elegant joke) indicate filmically—and for Hitchcock, I believe, film was the true music—the elemental conflict between the aspects of Jo's life as singer and as mother. This is one of the central themes of *The Man Who Knew Too Much*. If Drayton has required the cantata for staging a murder and Jo has required a violation of the music in order to prevent one, Hitchcock has required a cantata—indeed, this cantata—to set up the explicit cymbal crash (read duality) that has been implicit throughout.

(ww) As the orchestra draws the cantata swiftly to a close with repeated cymbal clashes on the tonic, the action moves quickly from audience reaction shots to Ben breaking into the Assassin's box, fighting with him, causing the gun to drop, then hurling the man forward to the camera. From outside the box we see him try to walk the balcony rail, as hands reach up to him. He slips and falls to his death. The last note of the cantata is interrupted as the audience breaks out into screams and the orchestra and choir stand to see what is going on—performers who until this moment have dutifully refused to behave like an audience under the most strenuous of conditions.

*   *   *

If we analyze the composition of the cantata sequence carefully, we can see that Hitchcock composes filmically by integrating dramatic moments, visual setups, and acoustic "backgrounds" into a coherent, fluid, rhythmical musical whole. This effect can be perceived, as well, in Jo's duet with Hank, "Que Sera, Sera"; in the Marrakech dining sequence; in the marketplace sequence; in the Ambrose Chapel hymn service; and in Jo's performance at the embassy, which involves two songs. There is never a moment in this film when the sung material, or musical ground of any kind, is either extraneous or marginal to the central meaning of the shot and the sequence in which we experience it.

Further, we can see the "Storm Clouds" as a microcosm of the film itself. If we consider that it is written in two main sections, and that the second is itself subdivided—that it is a prelude and fugue, and that the fugue itself contains a prelude to a fugue—there are three musical passages: (1) lento (mm. 1–107) (2a) allegro agitato (mm. 108–61), and (2b) [quasi] maestoso (mm. 162–77). In terms of the Albert Hall footage, these are roughly equivalent to (1) Jo's enthrallment; (2a) Ben's excited entry and attempt at action; and (2b) the aim-taking, the scream, the shot, the confrontation, and the finale. But if we conceptually withdraw from the Hall we see that in the film itself we have (1) a lento appassionato exploration of Marrakech, leading to Louis Bernard's death and its aftermath; (2a) an agitato race around London in search of Ambrose Chap(p)el(l), culminating in this concert; and then (2b) a maestoso, even pompous, foray into a glittering soirée at the foreign embassy in search of Hank, involving Jo taking aim with her voice, Lucy's redemptive scream, Drayton's gun use and the shot that kills him, the joyful reunion of Jo and Hank, and the film's true finale in the Savoy Hotel. Structurally, the cantata is a version, or performance, of the film as well as of itself, embodying simultaneously the vocal and the representational themes that are intertwined throughout. The release is at once Jo's—so that as a mother she can sing again; Ben's—so that he can be freed from knowledge into experience; Hank's—so that he can rejoin his family; and ours—so that we can voyage into performance and return home whole. The yet-standing trees are the over-formal obstructions to true and feelingful experience: stuffy Ben Mckenna, the stuffy Prime Minister; the stuffy Draytons. The prey: not only children, but artists, singers, all those who are night-birds in a businesslike world.

The musicality of this film should not surprise us. "I was greatly interested in music and films in the silent days," Hitchcock said to Stephen Watts in 1933,

and I have always believed that the coming of sound opened up a great new opportunity. *The accompanying music came at last entirely under the control of the people who made the picture.* That was surely an advance on having a separate score played by cinema orchestras. . . .

"Do you believe, then, that every film should have a complete musical score before it goes into production?" I asked.

"I do," Hitchcock replied emphatically. "Though by 'complete' I do not mean continuous. That would be monotonous. Silence is very often effective and its effect is heightened by the proper handling of the music before and after."[38]

Slightly later in the same interview, Hitchcock says that music can make it possible to express the unspoken in a film:

For instance, two people may be saying one thing and thinking something very different. Their looks match their words, not their thoughts. They may be talking politely and quietly, but there may be a storm coming. You cannot express the mood of that situation by word and photograph. But I think you could get at the underlying idea with the right background music. It may sound far-fetched to compare a dramatic talkie with opera, but there is something in common (82).

In *The Man Who Knew Too Much,* filmed twenty-two years after this interview, the music is far more than background, as an intimate reading of the cantata sequence shows. If, as Barthes suggests in *S/Z,* the codes mobilized by reading "extend *as far as the eye can reach,*"[39] it must be true that those engendered by film viewing also extend as deep as the ear can draw. "Storm Clouds," indeed—and by implication, a good deal of Hitchcock's work—can be seen as having been strictly choreographed, with the dramatic action either mirroring, or echoing, or metaphorically playing off the lyrical expression and the musical composition phrase by phrase. Ben's harried entrance to the Hall at the precise moment of the inception of the allegro agitato and the Assassin's stately gliding departure from his box the moment before, as the chorus softly sings "the nightbirds wheeled and shot away," are only two examples of the continuous byplay of music and filmic action that I have mapped above.

The Man Who Knew Too Much is far more than a notable and under-read Hitchcock masterpiece; it is signal in the history of film. Here Hitchcock advances a step further than any other filmmaker has done, dramaturgically shifting the music on occasion to a foreground role as important as any other roles in the film. No longer a visual form merely decorated by music, the film is here transformed into visual music itself, even opera, in which the director's profound contemplation of our dramatic condition finds release.

Notes

1. Peter Bogdanovich, *Who the Devil Made It?* (New York: Knopf, 1997), 486.
2. François Truffaut, ed. Gilles Jacob and Claude de Givray, trans. and ed. Gilbert Adair, *Letters* (London: Faber and Faber, 1989), 178–79.
3. Two striking exceptions are Elisabeth Weis, *The Silent Scream* (Rutherford: Fairleigh Dickinson University Press, 1985); and Royal S. Brown, *Overtones and Undertones* (Berkeley and Los Angeles: University of California Press, 1994).
4. Not by Herrmann are two songs "Que Sera, Sera (What Will Be, Will Be)" and "We'll Love Again" by Jay Livingston and Ray Evans. See Murray Pomerance, "'The future's not ours to see': Song, Singer, Labyrinth in Hitchcock's *The Man Who Knew Too Much* (1956)," in *Soundtrack Available: Essays on Film and Popular Music*, ed. by Arthur Knight and Pamela Robertson (Durham: Duke University Press: forthcoming).
5. Pascal Bonitzer, "The Sin and the Straw," in *Everything You Always Wanted to Know About Lacan (But Were Afraid to Ask Hitchcock)*, ed. Slavoj Žižek (London: Verso, 1992), 179.
6. Fereydoun Hoveyda, review of *The Man Who Knew Too Much*, in *Cahiers du Cinéma* 60 (1956): 13. Hoveyda's theme here is developed at length in Weis.
7. Here and at other points in this essay, I use the word "we" to mean viewers as positioned by the framing of the narrative, and thereby indicate a certain playful affiliation the director strikes with his audience. Careful viewers of the filmic unfolding, who take account of everything given upon the screen to be taken, are included in this aggregate. At other moments, which I hope are clearly and sufficiently distinguishable, the "we" is simply editorial and stands for a mannerly extrapolation outward from my own discursive self. It is worth noting that for Hitchcock, the narratively present viewer/observer is very typically invoked and catered to in the exquisite progression of vision through shots, involving both editing and movement and placement of camera.
8. The present essay is not substantially concerned with the earlier film. Yet it should be noted that the Cantata sequence of the 1956 film is no carbon copy of the one shot in 1934. The later sequence is considerably longer, containing at least twice the number of shots, only one of which—and that, inaccurately—reproduces a matching shot from the early film (a view of the whole from above, as the conductor begins to conduct). Jill Lawrence is seated in the stalls several rows from the rear, while Jo Conway stands; the Assassin is unaccompanied and does not tumble; and the slowly protruding gun is densely backlit in the early film, floating in a bright field, while later it is keylit and oozing out of a darkness. Throughout, in fact, it is evident that the 1956 film was made by a creative artist with a wholly different visual sensibility. (I am grateful to Brian Carr for his observations in this respect.)
9. Roy Fjastad, music director of Paramount Studio, letter to Benjamin, 11 February 1955. Fjastad refers to the Cantata as a "Choral Symphony" in a letter dated 8 February 1955 concerning the rights. All correspondence cited in this essay, except that in note 17, are housed in the Margaret Herrick Library, Center for Motion Picture Study, Academy of Motion Picture Arts and Sciences, Beverly Hills.
10. Steven Smith, *A Heart at Fire's Center* (Berkeley and Los Angeles: University of California Press, 1991), 196.
11. But Bernard Herrmann did not write a cantata himself as some have suggested; nor was he invited or encouraged to by Hitchcock or anyone else on the production staff of the film.

12. Fjastad, letter to Benjamin, 11 February 1955.

13. Not only dialogue but natural sound, too, is eliminated during the "performance," a token, in Benjamin's estimation, of Hitchcock's "admiration" of the Cantata. The admiration was mutual. Recorded on 9 October 1956 for broadcast on the BBC North American Service, Benjamin expressed himself "lucky" that his first big film score should be for Hitchcock, "for I don't think that any great director appreciates the use of music as much as he does." This appreciation required an intensive labor of a large production team. Though the Royal Festival Hall had been booked for three days to prerecord the Cantata, "the Americans were so impressed with the excellence and efficiency of the British team of sound engineers under the leadership of that real artist, Ken Cameron, that after two days the chorus and orchestra were dismissed and handsomely paid for the unwanted third day." The Albert Hall concert we see in the film was in fact mimed to the prerecording, almost a whole week being spent setting up equipment and "rehearsing orchestra and chorus so that they appeared to sing and play in absolute rhythm with the play-backs of the records made the previous week" (Arthur Benjamin, "Talk on Music for the Film 'The Man Who Knew Too Much,'" Tape No. TOX 46805, transcript from the composer's private collection, shared in communication by Vernon Duker, June 1998).

14. Night wire from Paramount New York to Paramount Hollywood, 28 March 1955.

15. Night wire.

16. Herbert Coleman, letter to Bernard Herrmann, 26 April 1955.

17. Vernon Duker, personal correspondence, 8 September 1995.

18. Here and in what follows I utilize the Herrmann conductor's score as edited by Christopher Palmer. For sight of it, and of Palmer's early notated version, I am deeply indebted to both John Waxman and the Estate of Sir Arthur Benjamin.

19. Smith, *Heart at Fire's Center*, 196.

20. I am grateful to Herbert Coleman for information about prerecording, which was typically done on wax disks.

21. A respectful tribute of sorts is to be found in George Roy Hill's *The Sting*, where, albeit with sound included, we see depicted another fabulously complex choreographic execution of what turns out to be a "false" reality.

22. Music can inspire us to create, and this passage can be seen as a prevision of the Redwood sequence in *Vertigo*.

23. To give but two examples: in *Rear Window*, we are eager for Lisa Fremont to commit robbery in Thorwald's apartment; in *Rope*, we were hopeful Brandon and Philip, the lover-murderers, would not be caught. Hitchcock was very often delighted to place his viewer in a morally questionable position.

24. In the 1934 film the banner had a dragon—far more exciting, yet less plausible, and certainly less filmic. The present flag is an optical space, after all. And the Prime Minister was more dramatic, too; thus, self-consciously "realistic," with a tiny goatee. "They sent me a lot of small men with little beards," Hictchcock complained to Truffaut (François Truffaut, *Hitchcock*, rev. ed [New York: Simon and Schuster, 1985], 228). The present actor, Alexei Bobrinskoy, beautifully conveys a man whose power is all in his exterior presentation—his ribbon, his medallions, his retinue.

25. The pocket score here bears the same relation to Herrmann's conducting score as the razor Roger O. Thornhill borrows from Eve Kendal does to the razor being used at a neighboring sink in Chicago's Central Station in *North by Northwest*.

26. Smith, *Heart at Fire's Center*, 196.

27. Truffaut, *Hitchcock*, 134.

28. Due to the exigencies of motion-picture production schedules, film actors

working "together" do not share information states with one another quite as stage actors do; but in the sense that they stand as agents of the writer and director they can be said to be "knowledgeable."

29. Erving Goffman, *Frame Analysis: An Essay on the Organization of Experience* (New York: Harper and Row, 1974), 134.

30. A movie horse stunt man and friend of producer Herbert Coleman, Quirk was not only "filmic" in professional commitment; his particular expertise went back to the very early days of film, and so he was a kind of talisman of the history of movies and is here "cymbalizing" crucially. Like other "musical performers" in the film—which is to say, others whose performances could be characterized as contributing to the production of the orchestral score—Quirk's casting was approved by Bernard Herrmann (Herbert Coleman, in conversation, 19 July 1995).

31. In a letter dated 25 February 1955, Benjamin wrote to Fjastad that he had at long last located the "Full Score" for the 1934 film. "The Orchestral Material, Chorus Parts have been destroyed but you may be interested to have the orchestration for the 'Oratorio Section.'" He then provides the scoring, which includes the percussion listed above.

32. "The size of the image is used for dramatic purposes, and not merely to establish the background" (Truffaut, *Hitchcock,* 218; see also 290).

33. Royal S. Brown, who is rather partial to the 1934 film, makes the point that the cantata sequence is reminiscent of a silent film (*Overtones and Undertones,* 75–80). I think he misses one of the key points of *The Man Who Knew Too Much,* however: for Hitchcock, film and social life together were reminiscent of music.

34. On 18 April 1955, Herbert Coleman wrote to Herrmann, asking: "Will you please check the text of the enclosed for accuracy before we sent [*sic*] it on for censorship approval." At the bottom is penned, 'BERNIE SAID O.K.' and "All save the child, all save the child" is changed to "yet stood the trees, yet stood the tree" (Coleman, letter to Herrmann).

35. It should be noted that like the usher, the Assassin, the Prime Minister, the Ambassador, the Assistant Manager, Buchanan, and the performers onstage, Ben and Jo have not come to the Albert Hall to listen to music; unlike everyone else, they have no prior knowledge of the concert program. All of the protagonists in the film action are here for their own "concert."

36. Jean Starobinski, *L'Oeil vivant,* trans. Arthur Goldhammer (Cambridge, Mass.: Harvard University Press, 1989).

37. I am indebted to Michael Doleschell for this observation.

38. Alfred Hitchcock, "Alfred Hitchcock on Music in Films: In an Interview with Stephen Watts," *Cinema Quarterly* 2, no. 2 (1933): 80–83; citation is from p. 81 (my emphasis).

39. Roland Barthes, *S/Z,* trans. Richard Miller (New York: Hill and Wang, 1974), 5–6.

JEFF SMITH

That Money-Making
"Moon River" Sound

Thematic Organization and Orchestration
in the Film Music of Henry Mancini

✳

"When Henry Mancini passed away in the spring of 1994," wrote Timothy Scheurer in a recent overview of the composer's work, "I expected to see a flurry of valedictories as well as concerts and tributes to honor this popular composer and musician. None of that happened."[1] As Scheurer points out, although Mancini penned some of the most familiar melodies in the history of film music, his death produced only a few minor obituary notices and little in the way of serious criticism. This was despite the fact that Mancini's record of achievement included four Oscars, twenty Grammy Awards, several gold records, and work on more than eighty film scores.

Yet the relative indifference to Mancini's death is not surprising when one considers his critical reception among contemporary film-music scholars. Unlike many of his contemporaries, Mancini is often regarded as a gifted songwriter, but a glib and limited film composer. Mathias Büdinger, for example, lauds the composer's melodic facility, but also admits that "Goldsmith fans and those who love full-blooded orchestral music are not likely to be that much affected by Mancini's music."[2] Similarly, William Darby and Jack Du Bois write that, "apart from his pop-oriented films, Mancini's music emerges, for the most part, as a pale imitation of more potent forerunners."[3] Ironically, even Mancini's defenders sometimes damn the composer with faint praise. Donald Fagen, for instance, notes Mancini's influence on New Wave and No Wave bands, like the Lounge Lizards, but then argues that this influence derived from his role as a middlebrow popularizer of "fake jazz."[4] In sum, while Mancini's work pervades our contemporary popular culture landscape, it often does so in forms that are far less respectable than film, such as television commercials, Muzak, figure-skating programs, and sporting events. As the Capital City Goofball says to Homer Simpson in the classic episode of *The Simpsons* entitled "Dancin' Homer," "Ah, Mancini. The mascot's best friend."

Contemporaneous commentary on Mancini's work was equally disparaging. Although Mancini won several awards for his work on *Peter Gunn* and *Breakfast at Tiffany's* (1961), film-music critics often used the composer as a symbol of the film score's decline into crass commercialism. In 1962, for example, Bill McCutcheon described the score for *Breakfast at Tiffany's* as "frivolous music" and claimed that Mancini is not the composer "his admirers like to think him."[5] Similarly, with the emergence of pop music in early 1960s film scores, critics also carped that arrangers like Mancini were taking jobs away from more talented composers, men who had refined their craft after years of working in the studio system. Noting this changing of the guard, Page Cook observed:

In filmusic[*sic*] circles, 1964 is chiefly memorable for the sad fact that Alfred Newman, Miklos Rosza [*sic*], Franz Waxman, and Hugo Friedhofer composed no film scores and movie audiences' ears were belabored by the non-filmusical improvisations, haphazardries, banalities, and auditory disturbances of Elmer Bernstein, de Vol, Nelson Riddle, and "king of the trade" Henry Mancini.[6]

If anything, the low regard for Mancini's work has resulted in a camp or ironic appreciation of it among the subcultures surrounding the recent "Cocktail Nation" movement.[7] Over the past few years, cuts from *Breakfast at Tiffany's* and other Mancini scores have been turning up in anthologies like Rhino's *Cocktail Mix, Vol. 3: Swingin' Singles* and Capitol's Ultra-Lounge series. Along with Esquivel, Mantovani, and other composers of "easy listening," Mancini has been tapped as a musical symbol of Kennedy-era optimism and leisure. In his liner notes to *Shots in the Dark*, a collection of Mancini themes covered by various alternative rock bands, Joseph Lanza writes, "Henry Mancini, like Walt Disney, helped to usher in the Cold War escapism that satisfied an over-worked and over-anxious middle class sold on suburbia, satellites, stereophonic sound, super-sonic travel, and armchair screen adventures involving espionage and transnational romance."[8] Lanza's assessment of Mancini's cultural import nicely summarizes the reasons for his appropriation by the Cocktail Nation, especially the music's "environmental" qualities. Lounge music's environmental qualities should be understood here in two senses: to the music's functional aspect (its use as a form of aural wallpaper for the bachelor pad) and its ability to "transport" listeners to exotic and picturesque settings. Unlike rock and roll, which has developed codes of authenticity through its appropriation of

African-American musical styles, idioms, and modes of emotional expression, cocktail music is currently celebrated for its falsity, its kitschy "Orientalism," and its evocation of middle-class retro cool.

Both of these representations of Mancini prove to be problematic insofar as they ignore the specific historical and industrial pressures on the composer's work. The former simply inserts Mancini into earlier mass culture debates by casting him as the villainous "king of the trade," the enemy of true musical art in film. The latter representation simply negates historical factors by adopting an ironic, postmodernist stance to Mancini's work. As such, neither of these views considers the various kinds of factors that mark film and film music as the product of an industry. As Janet Staiger notes, these factors include both the need for standardization and differentiation, and the desire to satisfy consumer demands.[9]

By participating in a broader shift toward the use of pop music in film, Mancini's place within the industry represents a particular historical configuration of the ongoing demand for music that is both dramatically effective and commercially astute. While this has been a concern for film composers since the silent era, the late 1950s and early 1960s were marked by the appearance of several new industrial developments, all of which combined to create a new constellation of economic pressures on film music. These include the trend toward diversification and conglomeration in the entertainment business, the growth of the record industry, and the film industry's acquisition and development of new record subsidiaries.

Taking up where Scheurer's essay left off, I argue that these industrial pressures are most apparent in two features of Mancini's work, namely his approach to thematic organization and his use of orchestration. To show the effects of these pressures, I illustrate each with examples drawn from several scores written during the height of Mancini's popularity as a recording artist. These examples do not encompass all aspects of Mancini's style, but they do provide a representative survey of his work in different genres and with different directors. Finally, I conclude with a more detailed analysis of Mancini's music for *Experiment in Terror* (1962) to demonstrate how each of these stylistic features operates within the context of an entire score. My purpose here is to offer a more balanced perspective on Mancini's career, one that situates both his theme writing and his evocation of 1960s cool within a broader historical context.

Thematic Organization

As Scheurer points out, Mancini's career was shaped by several industrial factors related to Hollywood's interest in exploiting film music in ancillary markets. During the late 1950s, when virtually all of Hollywood's major studios began buying or starting up their own record subsidiaries, film music underwent a major transformation in terms of its form and function. With film music emerging as an important site for industry diversification and cross-promotion, producers hoped that the circulation of film titles via records, radio, and retail displays would give their product greater name recognition and bring more people into theaters. In return, a successful film usually generated additional revenues for the studio's record and music-publishing subsidiaries by spawning a hit single or hit album.

Much of the impetus for this current cycle of songplugging came from Hollywood's growing interest in the recording industry. Between 1955 and 1959 aggregate record sales nearly tripled; by the end of the decade, retail sales of records amounted to more than a half billion dollars worth of business.[10] This economic growth prompted several film companies to either purchase or start up recording subsidiaries in 1957 and 1958. Paramount initiated this trend with its purchase of Dot Records in early 1957, but it was soon followed by start-up ventures at Twentieth Century–Fox, Warner Bros., Columbia, and United Artists.[11] As *Variety* noted in January 1958, "The film companies want in to the record business for more than just pic tie-in reasons. They realize it's a booming business and they want a share."[12]

These new record subsidiaries faced several problems, however, the most serious of which was their lack of established rosters of artists and repertoire. With little or no musical talent under contract, these new labels developed a myriad of strategies to compensate for this lack. After some lean years in the early 1960s, Warner Bros. Records adopted an aggressive strategy of label and talent acquisition, signing acts such as Bob Newhart and the Everly Brothers, and buying out established record labels such as Atlantic and Reprise. Columbia's subsidiary, Colpix, added several teen idols to their label, such as James Darren and Shelley Fabares. By far the most common strategy, however, was to emphasize the subsidiaries' links to their parent companies and the latter's substantial repository of film music. As such, the release of film scores on soundtrack albums not only served the cross-promotional aims of these labels' parent companies; they also provided them with a regular supply of musical product.

The impetus toward commercially exploitable film scores resulted in a number of changes in Hollywood's scoring practices. Among these were an increased interest in title themes and a growing reliance on source music (that is, music that was diegetically motivated). For Scheurer, the latter was especially important to Mancini's career, as it provided an entrance into the big time. In his work on *Touch of Evil* (1958) and the television series *Peter Gunn*, Mancini displayed his facility with both the source music currently demanded by producers and the more conventional underscoring characteristic of the classical Hollywood score. By 1963, Mancini was so in demand, he was able to turn down nine of every ten films that were offered him.

While theme songs and source music were certainly central to Hollywood's growing interest in commercially viable film music, Scheurer's account overlooks the extent to which this phenomenon was driven by record-industry economics. For record companies, singles, and hence title themes, were far less profitable than albums. For the most part, their chief utility was in promoting sales of their more lucrative counterparts. Consequently, the soundtrack album emerged as the linchpin of Hollywood's system of cross-promotion, and record companies initially responded to their parent companies' demand for product by editing a film's actual musictrack and releasing it in the form of a 12" LP. As such, there was not so much an inherent interest in source music as there was an interest in using it to enhance the commercial prospects of soundtrack albums.

The conflict between the interests of film companies and record labels is especially evident in many of these early soundtrack albums. As Mancini pointed out in the early 1960s, the majority of these "background music" soundtracks succeeded only in establishing a main theme, usually on the first track of the album.[13] The rest of the album emerged as an assortment of fragments, a collection of bits and pieces that were worthless both musically and commercially. The development of title themes for these albums may have helped producers interested in having a tune to plug, but they offered little to record buyers.

To create a more musically satisfying album, Mancini deviated from standard industry practice by rerecording his scores. This not only improved on the original soundtrack's recording quality; it also enabled the composer to "impose a real form on the music."[14] Freed from the confines of the film, Mancini could shape each cue into a separate track with its own distinct identity. According to Mancini, he wanted to create albums from his scores in which "a disk jockey could lay the needle down anyplace and get a tune."[15] This desire to satisfy consumers had important consequences for Mancini's overall approach to scoring. To keep his albums from seeming like a collection of bits and pieces, Mancini found it necessary to furnish his scores with a relatively large number of fully developed themes. These themes were then excerpted and expanded to supply the ten to twelve discrete tracks that made up the typical pop album. With its thematic diversity and its orientation toward tunes, Mancini's dramatic scores might be said to aspire to the condition of the motion-picture musical.[16] Like the songs of a musical, Mancini's themes display a mastery of song forms, a plethora of musical hooks, and an abundance of memorable melodies. A closer look at Mancini's early 1960s scores reveals that many of them are structured according to this multithematic principle. *The Pink Panther* (1964), for example, features some eleven distinct, readily identifiable themes. *Breakfast at Tiffany's* (1961) and *Hatari* (1962) employ nine and eight different themes respectively.

Although I am emphasizing thematic diversity as a distinctive trait of Mancini's scores, I do not wish to suggest that they are haphazardly organized. Rather, one of the reasons that Mancini's scores retain their dramatic power is that his cues are very carefully arranged and spotted. (*Spotting* is the process by which the composer, director, producer, and music editor determine the placement of music in the film.) To assure a certain formal unity in his scores, the composer usually compartmentalized his themes in terms of their function. Generally speaking, Mancini used only two or three themes as the basis of a film's nondiegetic underscore; thus a comparatively small number of themes are repeated and varied to perform the score's various narrational functions, which include establishing setting and characters, signifying emotion and point of view, and building a sense of structural continuity. In *The Pink Panther,* for example, two themes serve most of these functions: the title theme, which serves as a signature for the film's suave jewel thief, the Phantom; and "It Had Better Be Tonight," which serves as a love theme for each of the film's various romantic couplings. *Hatari* is, if anything, even more striking in its compartmentalization of cues. The film's tracking and capture scenes are invariably underscored with either the title theme or "Sounds of Hatari" while the scenes within the compound are consistently scored with source music.[17]

With two or three themes providing the bulk of the film's music, the remainder typically appear only once and are largely included to flesh the score into a satisfying album. In order to make room for these "extra" tunes, Mancini often utilized source music as an opportunity to introduce new musical material. Mancini's strategy was effective insofar as the conventions of realism allowed the music to be more independent in terms of its form and function. Music issuing from a radio, stereo, or dance band could adhere to more conventional musical forms and thus could develop its own formal patterns without regard to the rhythms and shifts of the narrative and visual track. In this respect, diegetic cues offer the composer the opportunity for comparatively more direct musical expression and the viewer the opportunity for a more fulfilling experience of the score in purely musical terms. Typically, Mancini's source cues are shaped according to the conventions of big band or jazz combo performances. An initial riff or melodic hook is developed as a 32- or 12-bar tune, which is then followed by a series of improvised instrumental solos. After the solos, the "head" returns, is repeated, and then extended to accommodate a cadence that rounds off and closes the music's melodic and harmonic structures.

The catch, however, is that this direct expression and apprehension of musical form is not so evident in the film as it is on the accompanying soundtrack album. In most cases, source music functions as background to a dialogue scene and is mixed in a manner that subordinates it to narrative concerns. Moreover, each diegetic cue may be presented as a relatively brief snatch of a larger musical work, a melodic bit motivated only to the extent that it adds variety and commercial value to the soundtrack. In these latter cases, the form is not so much fragmented as truncated; the tune still has structure, but that structure has not been allowed to develop.

Because they issue from a primarily commercial impetus, such cues often lay bare the conventions of such spotting. With so little dramatic function, spotting for source music adheres much more closely to the practices of product placement, and, like other tie-ins, the absence of the music at such moments would have little effect on the film. However, the presence of music at such moments seems to "naturalize" their presence on the album; the inclusion of brief snatches of tunes in these films seems to authorize their usage and make their function appear less nakedly commercial. After all, this is the music to which the characters of the film listen; to that end, the music either gives the characters dramatic nuance or it suggests something about their milieu.

In many of Mancini's scores, a single scene could provide the opportunity to introduce several bits of new material. Consider, for example, the sequence from *The Pink Panther* where Sir Charles Litton (David Niven) attempts to get Princess Dala (Claudia Cardinale) drunk so that he can obtain more information about the Pink Panther. The sequence begins with the tune "Champagne and Quail," an evocative title that suitably captures the social milieu of the two characters in the scene. The music plays faintly in the background as Dala discusses her father, her upbringing, and her virginity. A brief ellipsis leads us into the next part of the sequence in which Dala, now clearly drunk, facetiously explains her love of animals and disdain for people. "Piano and Strings" accompanies this part of the scene, its tinkling piano and lyrical strings coyly suggesting the possibility of romance in this unlikely couple. This is followed by the next tune in the sequence, "The Lonely Princess," which plays as Dala mockingly comments on Litton's efforts to seduce her. The melancholy melody plays slightly against the scene, subtly suggesting the weight of solitude that lurks just beneath Dala's laughter. The music changes yet again as Litton kisses Dala, once again returning us to the romantic mood established earlier. "Royal Blue" continues after

Dala passes out, providing a light backdrop for Litton's comical attempts to move her sleeping figure.

A similarly complex use of source music occurs in *Breakfast at Tiffany's* during the film's most famous sequence, the twenty-minute party scene. According to Mancini, the sequence was one of his biggest challenges as it only involved a half-page of description in the script, but ended up being a full-blown comic set piece. For this sequence, Mancini composed four different pieces of music. The first of these, "Moon River Cha Cha," is a jazzy reworking of the film's signature tune as a light Latin dance number. The remaining tunes are also arranged as sambas and congas, a stylistic choice that suggests both the contemporary urban setting and the casual cosmopolitan decadence of the film's characters.

More important, though, this source music serves several other narrative functions. First, each change in the music reinforces the scene's structure by underlining the sequence's temporal ellipses. Second, by adding more and more instruments to each tune, the music neatly reflects the party's increasing raucousness. In fact, the last tune, "Loose Caboose," masses all of the instrumental resources of Mancini's jazz ensemble together and even thickens the texture of the orchestration further by doubling the melody in thirds. Finally, as in *The Pink Panther*, the formal autonomy of the music is important to its light touch. Rather than emphasize the gags through mickey-mousing, the source music offers a neutral background for the comic material, and subtly underplays such gags as Holly accidentally setting a woman's hat on fire.

In sum, the music for these sequences is emblematic of Mancini's ability to create commercial music that is also dramatically effective. On the one hand, these source cues beautifully support the comic and/or romantic undertones of each scene. On the other, however, Mancini was also able to get four perfectly good tunes for his soundtrack album.[18] Mancini's observation here actually refines a point commonly found in discussions of the composer's work, namely, the description of Mancini as a brilliant melodist. With the innovation of the multitheme score, it is less important that Mancini wrote so many great melodies than that he stocked his individual scores with so many of them.

Orchestration

Orchestration was especially important to Mancini, who once claimed in an interview that he would "kill an orchestrator if he touched my voicings. . . . Even if he touched an interval."[19] To understand Mancini's approach to orchestration, however, it is useful to consider the specific stylistic background for his scores. During the classical Hollywood studio era, film scores generally adhered to Western classical traditions of rhythm and orchestration, and adopted many of the stylistic parameters of the late nineteenth-century Romantic idiom. Certainly individual composers offered different talents and skills to producers—Victor Young, for example, was noted for his melodic gifts, Miklós Rózsa for his skill in scoring period films—but they operated within a range of paradigmatic norms. The combination of these stylistic parameters yielded a fairly uniform group style among Hollywood composers that emphasized leitmotifs, thematic writing, and symphonic orchestrations.[20]

The romantic idiom continued as an option throughout the 1950s, but it no longer wielded so strong an influence as Hollywood composers began to broaden the classical score's range of styles. At one end of the spectrum, polyphonic textures, modal writing, and atonality surfaced more regularly in the works of Rózsa, Alex North, Bernard Herrmann, and Leonard Rosenman. At the other end of the spectrum, various jazz and pop elements appeared in the scores of David Raksin, Elmer Bernstein, and Johnny Mandel.

Along with this broadening of styles, composers also began to subtly move away from the string-dominated orchestrations associated with Hollywood's "Golden Age" of film scoring. In 1952, for example, press releases touted Dimitri Tiomkin's score for *High Noon* as the first composed without the use of a single violin.[21] Similarly, *Forbidden Planet* (1956) features an early electronic score by Louis and Bebe Barron. And Herrmann has been justly celebrated for his unusual instrument combinations, such as his use of string orchestra in *Psycho* (1960) and his use of five organs, vibraphone, and timpani rolls to suggest the surging waters of the underground sea in *Journey to the Center of the Earth* (1959).[22]

Like Nelson Riddle, Frank de Vol, and other jazz arrangers who moved into film scoring, Mancini's style of orchestration largely drew from the big band music of the 1940s and the record studio orchestra charts of the 1950s. This distinctive pop-jazz sound—more Don Costa than Korngold, more Billy May than Miklós Rózsa—took shape in the scores for *Charade* and *Breakfast at Tiffany's,* and usually involved the combination of strings with a twelve- to sixteen-member jazz ensemble. Although the specific arrangement of instruments varied greatly, Mancini's signature sound indicates a tendency to group winds and brass in "four-way close" voicings for upbeat, swing numbers, and to use more open "drop-2" and "drop-4" voicings for slower, more lyrical tunes.[23] Moreover, Mancini's arrangements also belie a tendency to use solo instruments or groups in unison to highlight the melodies of his scores. Mancini's "Main Title" for *Breakfast at*

Tiffany's displays both of these tendencies. The melody of "Moon River" is stated in succession by a solo harmonica, a choir, and the violins. The melody is supported here by a combination of vibraphone, harp, and strings, all of which are arranged in "drop-2" and "drop-4" voicings.

While Mancini's development of this signature sound was largely motivated by a desire for marketable film scores, the composer's smaller canvas during the early 1960s was consistent with a more general emphasis on sparseness and economy in the deployment of orchestral forces.[24] As a result, Mancini's movie jazz sounded quite different from the so-called dramatic jazz of Leonard Bernstein, Elmer Bernstein, and Alex North. Unlike those composers, who simply incorporated certain idiomatic figures and jazz sonorities into a more classical Hollywood approach to orchestration and harmony, Mancini adhered more closely to his roots in big-band arranging. As such, Mancini displayed a lightness of touch that proved capable of great understatement and even irony. This cool style became a perfect complement to romantic comedy, where his lyrical themes added a burnished glow to love scenes and his light touch proved a genteel foil for slapstick stumbles and vulgar visual gags.

Where Mancini differed from some of his contemporaries, however, was in his ability to translate unusual sonorities into brilliant song hooks. As Gary Burns points out, almost any element of a recording can be used as a hook, its only requirement is that it be memorable and ear-catching. According to Burns's typology of hooks, these elements can include unusual harmonic shifts, studio production tricks, or distinctive tone colors.[25] Insofar as orchestration served as a specific resource for song hooks, it thus became another site of industrial pressures on film scoring. For Mancini and other pop composers, the immediacy and materiality of tone color made it an especially effective tool in this regard, as it fits both the exigencies of popular musical forms and the need for music that was dramatically motivated.

In order to satisfy these constraints, Mancini frequently developed the concept for his scores around the sound of a particular instrument. This is especially evident in *Breakfast at Tiffany's*, where the harmonica provides a symbolic and emotional key to the score. The harmonica is first heard under the film's opening credits, accompanying shots of Holly Golightly's early morning pilgrimage to the famous Tiffany's store on New York's Fifth Avenue. Although the sound of the harmonica at first seems incongruous in this context, its association with Holly is motivated by the character's rural past. As in *Hatari*, Mancini's choice of instruments neatly summarizes several of *Breakfast's* thematic oppositions between city and country, wealth and poverty, past and present.

Taking this technique further, Mancini not only developed the concepts for his scores in terms of specific instruments, but also with particular players in mind.[26] Describing the opening of *The Days of Wine and Roses* (1962), Mancini said, "I heard not a French horn, but a specific guy—Vince De Rosa—playing it."[27] Similarly, in developing the "Pink Panther Theme," Mancini conceived the tune with tenor saxophonist Plas Johnson in mind. In fact, many of the traits we associate with the animated Panther—its slinky walk, its cool demeanor, and its playful hipness—are qualities partly attributable to the style and sound of Johnson's performance.

If Mancini were merely a clever jazz arranger with an ear for hooks, then there would be little reason to explore this issue much further. But as he showed with his television work for *Peter Gunn* and *Mr. Lucky,* Mancini was able to get an enormous number of textures and tone colors from a small group of instruments. In his film work, such timbral variations were often accomplished by adding one or two instruments to Mancini's basic studio orchestra sound. For example, when a more idiomatic flavor was desired, Mancini would typically embroider his sound with the appropriate dash of instrumental color. Thus, the occasional electric guitar might be added for rock tunes; congas, timbales, cow bells, and other percussion instruments were added for a more Latin sound; and an accordion might be added to create a more European ambiance.

Moreover, like many other composers, Mancini was also quite capable of using instruments to provide a requisite sense of historical or ethnomusicological detail. In the title theme of *Hatari,* for example, Mancini incorporated several indigenous African instruments, among them the lujon, shell gourds, tree bells, and even giant pea pods. These instruments were then combined with traditional Western instruments. In a somewhat unusual gambit, however, Mancini substituted mandolin, guitar, and finger piano for the more traditional string section of violins, violas, and celli. The result was a sound that reflected and reinforced a number of the film's thematic oppositions between man and animal, Europe and Africa, nature and culture.

In his most audacious scores, however, Mancini also manipulated the tunings of instruments to achieve particular coloristic effects. *Wait Until Dark* (1967), for example, uses two detuned pianos to both establish and sustain the film's menacing tone. To produce this effect, Mancini took two matched Baldwins and tuned one of them down a quarter tone. He then had his two pianists, Jimmy Rowles and Pearl Kaufman, play passages of the score in sequence. The first piano would play one chord and then the second piano would play the same chord right after the first. Ironically, the detuning effect not only captured the heroine's psychological sense of dislocation;

it also produced a rather strong physiological response in the performers. While playing the score, both pianists began to experience dizziness, and Kaufman even had to stop the recording session at one point because the detuning effect was making her nauseous.[28]

As a composer attuned more to sonic rather than purely musical parameters, Mancini was extremely adept at manipulating his signature sound within specific dramatic contexts. While his orchestrations may lack the bold strokes of Herrmann or Morricone, Mancini's sometimes unusual combinations of instruments place him within a more general movement away from the string-dominated sound of the classical Hollywood period. More important, given the industry's need for commercially exploitable music, Mancini displayed an uncanny knack for translating his choice of instruments into sonorial novelties that could function as pop hooks, a skill especially evident in his conception of scores in terms of particular solo instruments. Through his jazzy reworking of the classical Hollywood score, Mancini created a sound that was distinctively his, at once both popular and dramatically appropriate.

Experiment in Terror

Up until this point, I have offered a broad overview of two particularly salient characteristics of Mancini's style: his thematic organization—especially his compartmentalization of themes for source music and underscoring—and his orchestration. In this section, I shall focus on a particular score to illustrate how these two elements interact to both reinforce and complement one another. For this purpose, I have chosen *Experiment in Terror*, which is not only one of Mancini's best scores, but also one that is unfortunately overshadowed by his more popular work on *Breakfast at Tiffany's* and *The Pink Panther*. The score for *Experiment in Terror* is both typical and atypical of Mancini's work during this period. It is typical in the sense that it embodies several of the traits I have already identified. It is somewhat atypical, however, in that it is a score for an urban crime drama rather than the romantic comedies for which Mancini is more celebrated.

The story for *Experiment in Terror* involves a young bank teller, Kelly Sherwood (Lee Remick), who is blackmailed by a mysterious, heavy-breathing, asthmatic killer named Red Lynch (Ross Martin). Lynch threatens to kill Kelly if she does not steal $100,000 from the bank at which she works. Kelly appeals for help to John Ripley (Glenn Ford), an FBI agent working in the San Francisco area. Ripley learns that Lynch has plotted similar schemes in other cities and that three women are now dead as a result. When Lynch's extortion plot is thwarted by the FBI, he kidnaps

Kelly's teenage sister Toby (Stefanie Powers), and threatens to kill her if he does not get the money he expected Kelly to steal. A manhunt leads the FBI to Candlestick Park where Lynch attempts to collect the ransom during a baseball game between the Giants and the Dodgers. Lynch successfully collects the money from Kelly, but is shot and killed near the pitcher's mound before he can make his getaway.

Like many of his other scores during this period, *Experiment in Terror* contains several distinct themes, including many that function as part of the film's source music. In an attempt to cash in on Chubby Checker's successful revival of "The Twist," *Experiment in Terror* features not one, not two, but three such dance tunes, including one that reworks the film's title theme. While each of these tunes was inserted to enhance the soundtrack's marketability, Mancini did not appear to take them very seriously. In Mancini's spotting notes, each song was given a rather nondescript title ("Twist No. 1," "Twist No. 2") and the short score for each features a rather simple sketch of the tune's melody, instrumentation, and a brief accompaniment figure. The songs, however, are nonetheless carefully motivated in terms of their dramatic function. Each is associated in one way or another with Toby, and thus each tune is located within a typical teenage milieu, such as a swimming pool or a malt shop.[29]

Setting also provides the motivation of numerous other source cues. A movie theater, for example, occasions the appearance of two ragtime cues. As Ripley questions Popcorn, an informant with a penchant for old movies, music plays in the background to accompany a "Keystone Kops" film being shown. The first of these two source cues, "The Good Old Days," is scored for bass, drums, soprano sax, and "one tin pan piano" arranged for four hands.[30] The tune is played rather fast and features a syncopated rhythmic pattern characteristic of the genre. The second cue (example 1), "A Bucket of Tears," is a much slower, "old-timey" ballad. It is scored for solo piano, its melody played in octave tremolos. The tune itself is reminiscent of the famous pianola theme Mancini composed for *Touch of Evil.*

Similarly, a stakeout of a nightclub called "The Roaring Twenties" provides the motivation for several other source cues. Unlike the previous instances, however, in this sequence Mancini uses a number of very

Example 1. Henry Mancini, *Experiment in Terror,* "Bucket of Tears." Used by permission of Warner/Chappell Music, Inc.

well-known tunes, such as "Camptown Races," "When the Saints Come Marching In," and "Bill Bailey." These songs are performed Dixieland-style by a band consisting of bass, drums, banjo, trombone, trumpet, and chorus. Interestingly, none of the three tunes used in this sequence appear on the accompanying soundtrack album, perhaps because of their obvious familiarity.[31] Their absence reflects the emphasis RCA Victor placed on original source cues, especially the "big band swingers" for which Mancini was famous.[32]

Instead, the album is fleshed out by a handful of other source cues that are spread out across the film. "Fluters' Ball," the album's opening track, is a loping swing tune heard briefly coming from Kelly's car radio. "White on White" is a tinkling, cocktail piano ballad played briefly as Agents Ripley and Bradley question a waiter in a Chinese restaurant. "Down by the Wharf" is a lilting waltz heard very faintly during the sequence in which Kelly arrives at Fisherman's Wharf and awaits Lynch's instructions for the ransom. Lastly, the album even includes one track that was planned for the film but did not actually appear in the final cut. "Kelly's Tune," a swinging big-band tune, was spotted as a source cue that would immediately follow the opening credits and cover the last part of Kelly's drive home.

As is typical of Mancini's approach to thematic organization, these source cues appear only once and largely function to add a sense of verisimilitude to a particular setting. More important, however, these source cues also enhance the commercial appeal of the score in its circulation as an album. By broadening these brief snatches of music into fully realized album tracks, tunes such as "Fluters' Ball" and "Kelly's Tune" furnish the kind of light jazz for which Mancini was noted, while tracks such as "The Good Old Days" and "Down by the Wharf" afford the album greater variety in terms of themes, meters, tempi, and tone colors. That the *Experiment in Terror* album achieved only moderate sales is perhaps more attributable to the faddishness of the music than to the effectiveness of Mancini's formula. By featuring three "twist" numbers, the film unfortunately tries to hop aboard a bandwagon that had already passed it by.

Yet if Mancini's source cues make for an attractive album, then his underscore provides the "glue" that holds it all together. *Experiment in Terror* relies on two themes for much of its underscore: the title theme, which is consistently used to suggest the presence of the film's asthmatic killer; and "Nancy," which is named after one of the film's early victims and comes to be associated with the mortal danger the killer represents. As example 2 demonstrates, "Nancy" is a chamber piece featuring Mancini's favorite pianist, Jimmy Rowles. The austere melody, initially played as a piano solo, is organized around several open, dissonant chords. The melody is initially

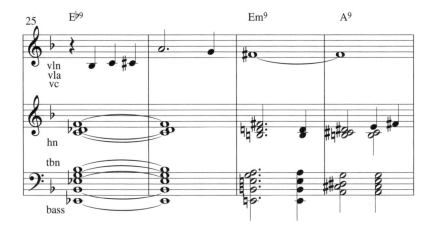

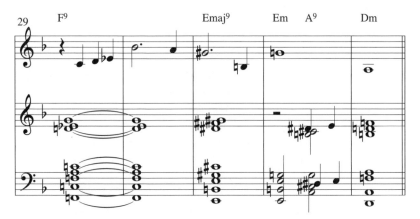

Example 2. Henry Mancini, *Experiment in Terror*, "Nancy." Used by permission of Warner/Chappell Music, Inc.

structured by leaps of a fifth or a ninth, but soon adds several major and minor sevenths to further weaken any feeling of tonality. The theme is given its most complete statement in the sequence where Lynch is revealed to be hiding among the mannequins in Nancy's apartment. Fragments of it appear, however, in several later scenes to suggest Lynch's treacherousness. When Ripley reminds Lisa Sung she is protecting a killer, a little fragment of "Nancy" is incorporated in the cue to remind us that Lynch has already murdered three previous victims. Similarly, when Lynch approaches Toby just after he has ordered her to undress, a brief snippet of "Nancy" underlines not only the mortal danger Toby is in but also the dark sexual charge that Lynch derives from committing these murders. The title tune, however, is by far the most important musical theme of *Experiment in Terror*. Although it has no lyrics, the song nonetheless adheres to classic 32-bar form. It begins quietly, menacingly with a triplet pattern played on the cymbal and a sustained low D played on the organ. The choice of organ here may seem a bit unusual, but it is dramatically motivated by the theme's consistent link to the film's villain. The low, reedy sound of the organ here serves as a musical correlative to Red Lynch's low, wheezing voice.

Building on this ominous opening tone, Mancini gradually adds other instruments throughout the eight-measure introduction. In measure 3, two string basses enter; one of them doubles the low D of the organ while the other plucks out the tonic and dominant to add a slight rhythmic pulse to the piece. In measure 5, Mancini adds a solo electric guitar that has been tuned down to D. Using a "trick vibrato" à la Duane Eddy, the guitarist plucks out an accompaniment figure that essentially outlines a D minor triad. Finally, in measure 7, Mancini adds an autoharp, which strums a D minor chord on the downbeat.

The decision to use the autoharp is perhaps Mancini's most inspired stroke. In his autobiography, the composer notes he was attracted to the instrument's tone quality, especially its great natural decay. Although he acknowledges that the autoharp has traditionally been associated with folk music and the hootenanny, Mancini confesses that he had always found its sound somewhat chilling.[33] Perhaps more important, though, the rather thin, brittle sound of the autoharp offers a brilliant contrast to the sustained, plangent tone of the organ. The juxtaposition of these instruments, and the resulting tension between their timbres, helps to give the score its rather dark, creepy quality. Put simply, the brilliance of Mancini's music for *Experiment in Terror* is that its orchestration provides an effective aural analog to the film's murky mise-en-scène and the narrative's strong undertones of sexual violence.

After the eight-measure introduction, the tune proper begins in measure 9. Here the melody is plucked out on a second autoharp as the first continues to strum chords on each downbeat. This second autoharp states the A section of the tune, which encompasses measures 9 through 16 (see example 3). The elements of mystery and suspense are further reinforced here by the theme's rather modal character. Although the theme initially implies the key of D minor, the C♯s in measures 12 and 15 situate it quite clearly in the Aeolian mode.

Mancini restates the section of the theme from measures 17 to 24, but gradually adds more instruments to thicken its texture. The cellos enter in measure 16 playing a rising countermelody that is picked up by the violas in measure 21 (example 4). This rising string line is a favored device of the composer that is often used for moments of marked dramatic tension. It is repeated shortly after in the cue "Anyone for Anahist," which begins just after Lynch has laid out his blackmail scheme and has instructed Kelly to get in the car and face forward. Often, this rising string line is combined with a second one to allow Mancini to work through a complex series of harmonic suspensions and resolutions. This technique is evident in a number of later cues, such as the one that expresses Toby's horror at having been kidnapped by Lynch.

Example 3. Henry Mancini, *Experiment in Terror,* title song, mm. 9–16. Used by permission of Warner/Chappell Music, Inc.

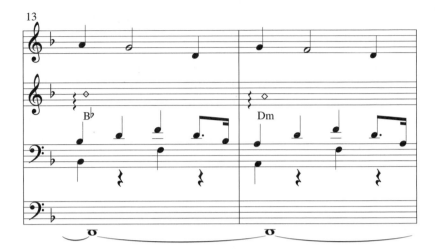

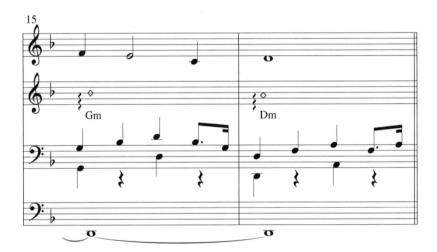

Example 3 (*continued*)

The melody is taken over by the strings in measure 25, which begins the bridge section of the tune. The trombones and horns enter at this point playing a tightly voiced series of ninth chords. The brass thus supports a series of chromatic modulations that move from D minor to its relative major and back again. The melody in this section also displays a higher degree of chromaticism providing a nice contrast to the rather stark diatonicism of the A sections.

The last twelve measures of the piece return us to the A theme, which is now played by four bass flutes. The use of the bass flute is also an important

Example 4. Henry Mancini, *Experiment in Terror,* title song, cello countermelody. Used by permission of Warner/Chappell Music, Inc.

element of Mancini's signature sound, one especially useful in suspense cues for its rather dark, shimmering tone color.[34] In measure 33, Mancini also adds a slightly more complex variation of the rising countermelody that originally appeared in the violas and cellos (see example 5). The piece concludes with a four-measure coda that returns us to the somewhat Spartan sound of the introduction.

As I noted earlier, this title theme is associated throughout the film with Red, the asthmatic villain. It is used for several key moments of the narrative, such as Red's phone call to the FBI, his abduction of Toby, and, in one of the film's more flamboyant moments, his terrorization of Kelly in a women's bathroom while he is dressed as a little old lady. In these scenes, the first five notes of the piece will often serve as a kind of leitmotif, but the mere appearance of the autoharp or organ is enough to signal his presence just offscreen. At the same time as it functions as a leitmotif for Red, the theme also serves as an emotional signifier of the horror he evokes in his victims. In this respect, Mancini's orchestration serves a kind of double function in the film. The chilling sound of the autoharp and the dark, murky tone of the organ suggest the menacing aura of the villain while reflecting the point of view of the characters he terrorizes. Moreover, by signifying the emotions of his victims, Mancini's music can evoke a similarly unsettling response in spectators.[35]

Not every version of this theme, however, uses this particular pattern of orchestration. The one significant exception occurs after Kelly mistakes another man for Red in the "Roaring Twenties" sequence. Kelly follows this man as he leaves the club, an act he mistakes for aggressive, sexual interest. As they drive off from the club, Ripley and the other FBI agents tail them. Mancini underscores their pursuit with a temporally distended variation of

Example 5. Henry Mancini, *Experiment in Terror,* title song, end (countermelody). Used by permission of Warner/Chappell Music, Inc.

the title theme, but here he substitutes alto flutes and alto saxes (an instrumental combination more commonly associated with the FBI) for the autoharp and organ more frequently heard. Mancini varies the cue further by adding an ostinato bass pattern on a low E that marks under the rising countermelody of the cellos. The tenor and tone of the cue marks the FBI's point of view by suggesting its anticipation of Lynch's capture; at the same time, however, Mancini's change in orchestration signals it as a false suspense; the man with Kelly is not the real suspect.

Experiment in Terror provides an excellent illustration of Mancini's contributions to the contemporary development of the film score. By using source music to introduce new musical material, Mancini was able to furnish his score with several new tunes. Some of these were source cues, which were then excerpted and rerecorded to supply the twelve tracks found on the film's accompanying soundtrack album. At the same time, *Experiment in Terror* displays Mancini's interest in exploring unusual and inventive combinations of instruments. This is especially evident in the film's title theme, which combines electric guitar, organ, bass flutes, and autoharps with more conventional arrangements of strings and brass. The dark timbre of the organ, the brittle sound of the autoharps, and the modal character of the melody all contribute to the theme's eerie mood. As the centerpiece of the film's underscore, the theme perfectly captures the sense of unease and controlled rage associated with the film's villain.

Conclusion

In the liner notes for *The Pink Panther* soundtrack, Peter Sellers drolly suggested that the great advantage to Mancini's album is that one can sit and listen to the score without having to sit through the film. "As yet," writes Sellers, "you cannot see the film without having to sit through the music. However, I understand that scientists are perfecting a device that may make this possible."[36] Although Sellers's comments here are facetious, they nonetheless hint at a key characteristic of Mancini's scores: their ability to function effectively both within the film and in several important ancillary markets for film music. In fact, this dual impetus is also summarized by several ads for Mancini's albums, including one for *Dear Heart and Other Songs About Love* that reads, "A new album with more of that money-making 'Moon River' Sound."[37]

The tension in Mancini's work between dramatic and commercial imperatives, however, was partly motivated by a particular historical configuration of industrial pressures and economic interests. As film companies developed their own record subsidiaries in the 1950s, the soundtrack album emerged as the primary site of various kinds of film and music cross-promotions. In order to satisfy both filmgoers and album buyers, Mancini developed an approach to orchestration and thematic organization that both replicated and resolved this tension. On the one hand, he exploited diegetic music as an opportunity to introduce fully fleshed-out tunes, songs that could be excerpted and included in the film's accompanying soundtrack album. On the other hand, Mancini's nondiegetic music was typically organized around a small number of themes, each of which could be varied and developed to serve the specific narrative functions of classical Hollywood underscore. Similarly, timbre and instrumentation could be used to satisfy both of these agendas insofar as they could not only be dramatically motivated, but also could provide sonorial novelties in the form of pop song hooks. Mancini's orchestrations thus participate in a more general shift away from the string-dominated sound of the classical Hollywood score while retaining a certain ear-grabbing appeal for potential record buyers.

As the result of these economic and industrial pressures, Mancini's approach to film scoring serves as a precursor to film music's place within more contemporary constellations of corporate conglomeration. In several recent film scores, such as *Forrest Gump* (1994) and *Batman and Robin* (1997), we see a division of labor that mirrors Mancini's division between source music and nondiegetic underscore. In these films, popular artists, like The Doors, R. Kelly, and Smashing Pumpkins, give the music its commercial sheen while the carefully crafted underscoring of composers like Alan Silvestri and Elliot Goldenthal respectively supply the scores' more traditional narrative functions, such as reinforcing aspects of character psychology and playing the overall mood of scenes. Whereas Mancini introduced new themes through his use of source music, contemporary filmmakers now simply license recordings that can be excerpted and included on the film's accompanying soundtrack album.

Moreover, Mancini's interest in using tone color as a source for pop hooks is reflected in more recent attempts to incorporate new styles of pop music into film scoring. Consider, for example, the influence of rock instrumentation evident in the increased use of various kinds of percussion for action films and the integration of the electric guitar into the composer's palette of orchestral colors.[38] The latter is especially evident in the scores of Ry Cooder, such as *Paris, Texas* (1984) and *Trespass* (1992), and in Michael Kamen's collaboration with Eric Clapton and David Sanborn for the *Lethal Weapon* series. To these we might also add scores resulting from a rock musician's occasional foray into film composition, such as Paul Westerberg's alternative rock score for *Singles* (1992) or Dave Pirnier's guitar noodlings for *Chasing Amy* (1997).

Not surprisingly, the fads of the music marketplace have also placed special weight on particular genres of popular music at certain historical moments. Rap, for instance, became the style du jour of several urban crime dramas and youthpics, such as *Colors* (1988), *Boyz 'N' the Hood* (1991), *Deep Cover* (1992), *Above the Rim* (1994), and *Set it Off* (1996). More recently, interest in British dance music has led some filmmakers to compile scores from the work of techno and trip-hop artists. As representative scenes from *Trainspotting* (1996) and *The Saint* (1997) show, the stylistic combination of rhythmic propulsion, harmonic stasis, and electronic coloring makes this new dance music an especially appropriate fit for chases and action scenes. Such attempts to update the sound of contemporary film scores mirror the attempts by Mancini and other studio arrangers of the early 1960s to incorporate various tone colors associated with jazz and pop.

Mancini's death in 1994 has occasioned the time for a thorough reappraisal of his work. In this essay, I have instigated that reassessment by situating certain aspects of Mancini's music within their proper historical context. We must first understand the larger industrial and economic pressures on film composers of the early 1960s before we can begin to understand the different facets of Mancini's "money-making 'Moon River' sound." As director Allison Anders points out, pop music—and popular culture more generally—has become our culture's common reference point: "popular music is the only reference point we hold in common anymore. We are not all the same religion, we don't hold the same views on whether we eat meat or we don't eat meat, whether we are monogamous or we're not. There's no common ground except for popular culture, so in a way it's what's holding it all together."[39]

Like it or not, Mancini is now a part of that repository of popular culture we all share. Through our understanding of his specific contribution to that culture, we can also begin to understand an important and often neglected part of film-music history.

Notes

1. Timothy Scheurer, "Henry Mancini: An Appreciation and Appraisal," *Journal of Popular Film and Video* 24, no. 1 (1996):34.

2. Mathias Büdinger, "A Conversation with Henry Mancini," *Soundtrack!* 7, no. 26 (1988): 5.

3. William Darby and Jack Du Bois, *American Film Music: Major Composers, Techniques, Trends, 1915–1990* (Jefferson, N.C. : McFarland, 1990), 483.

4. Donald Fagen, "Movie Music: Mancini's Anomie Deluxe," *Premiere* (October 1987): 97–99.

5. Bill McCutcheon, "1961's Best Filmusic," *Films in Review* 13, no. 3 (1962): 179.

6. Page Cook, "The Sound Track," *Films in Review* 16, no. 2 (1965): 105.

7. For more on the history of both cocktail music and cocktail culture, see Joseph Lanza, *Elevator Music: A Surreal History of Muzak, Easy-Listening, and Other Moodsong* (New York: St. Martin's Press, 1994); and *The Cocktail: The Influence of Spirits on the American Psyche* (New York: St. Martin's, 1995). For more specific discussions of the so-called Cocktail Nation, see Karen Schoemer, "Sounds of Schmaltz," *Newsweek* (22 August 1994): 58–59; J. Glenn, "Cocktail Nation," *Utne Reader* (September–October 1994): 83–89; and Randall Rothenberg, "The Swank Life," *Esquire* (April 1997): 70–79. There are also several fanzines devoted to the subject.

8. Joseph Lanza, liner notes for *Shots in the Dark: Del-Fi Does Mancini* (Donna Records, 1996).

9. Janet Staiger, Introduction to *The Studio System*, ed. Janet Staiger (New Brunswick: Rutgers University Press, 1995), 6.

10. Russell Sanjak, rev. David Sanjak, *Pennies from Heaven: The American Popular Music Business in the Twentieth Century* (New York: Da Capo, 1996), 333–66.

11. For more on the development of these recording subsidiaries, see my book, *The Sounds of Commerce: Marketing Popular Film Music* (New York: Columbia University Press, 1998).

12. *Variety*, January 1958, 215.

13. See, for example, "Soundtracks: Single or LP," *Variety*, 22 November 1961, pp. 41 and 43; "Mancini, H'Wood's Hottest Pic Track Artist, Grooving 1-Mil. LP Sales Yearly," *Variety*, 4 March 1964, p. 55.

14. It should be noted, however, that Mancini's conception of an album as a collection of nine or ten distinct tunes adheres much more closely to the conventions of pop album packaging than it does to any classical notion of musical unity or organicity. What strikes one most about Mancini's soundtrack albums when compared with those of his contemporaries is that there is a remarkable and refreshing lack of repetition from track to track. This is not so novel in the cases of *Peter Gunn* or *Mr. Lucky* where Mancini could select cues from many hours of screen time. But it is very unusual for film soundtracks, which by and large rely on a relatively small number of musical materials. Undoubtedly, this variety was a key to the success of his soundtrack albums, which interestingly do not sound much different from his nonsoundtrack albums (such as *Uniquely Mancini* and *The Blues and the Beat*).

15. Interview with the author, 24 May 1993, Beverly Hills, California.

16. Of course, Mancini wrote one of the preeminent musicals of the 1980s, *Victor/Victoria* (1982). He joins a handful of film composers, such as Michel Legrand and Randy Newman, who have written successful scores in the genre.

17. The two exceptions to this are "Your Father's Feathers" and "Baby Elephant Walk," both of which were written to accompany scenes of comic interaction between humans and animals. In fact, Mancini himself claims that the music for the "Baby Elephant Walk" sequence kept the scene in the film; *Sounds and Scores: A Practical Guide to Professional Orchestration* (Northridge, Calif.: Northridge Music, Inc., 1973; repr. 1986), 108–9.

18. Interview with author, 1993.

19. Harvey Siders, "The Jazz Composers in Hollywood," *Downbeat* (2 March 1972): 15.

20. For more on Romanticism's influence on Hollywood film music, see Caryl Flinn, *Strains of Utopia: Gender, Nostalgia, and Hollywood Film Music* (Princeton: Princeton University Press, 1992); and Kathryn Kalinak, *Settling the Score: Music in the Classical Hollywood Film* (Madison: University of Wisconsin Press, 1992).

21. Undated press release, Stanley Kramer Productions, Inc., box 4, *High Noon* file, United Artists Collection Addition, Wisconsin Center for Film and Theater Research, State Historical Society Library, Madison, Wisconsin.

22. For more on Herrmann's approach to orchestral color, see Graham Bruce, *Bernard Herrmann: Film Music and Narrative* (Ann Arbor: UMI Research Press, 1985), 75–116.

23. See Mancini, *Sounds and Scores,* 24–31. In stage band arranging, "four-way close voicing" refers to a means of harmonizing a melody with three other voices grouped as closely as the chord structure allows. "Drop-2" is a slight variant of this approach, where the voice immediately beneath the melody is lowered, or "dropped" an octave. "Drop-4" works similarly.

24. Darby and Du Bois, *American Film Music,* 465.

25. Gary Burns, "A Typology of 'Hooks' in Popular Records," *Popular Music* 6, no. 1 (1987): 1–20.

26. In his autobiography, Mancini writes: "I nearly always precast my players and write for them and around them"; (Mancini, with Gene Lees, *Did They Mention the Music?* (Chicago: Contemporary Books, 1989), 141.

27. *Dialogue on Film 3* (Los Angeles: American Film Institute, 1974), 11.

28. Ibid., 9.

29. The short scores for *Experiment in Terror* are housed in the UCLA Music Library as part of the Henry Mancini Collection. All references to cue sheets, music notes, and timing sheets from the film are references to this collection.

30. This cue was first scored for clarinet rather than the soprano saxophone, but this original sketch was thrown out and replaced by the present one.

31. The archival resources I consulted showed that Mancini had sketched out arrangements for two additional songs that were ultimately not used.

32. See the liner notes for the RCA Victor album, *Experiment in Terror: Music from the Motion Picture Score,* which suggest that the typical Mancini source cue contributes to "the modern style and freshness of the music and picture." Mancini makes a similar point in his autobiography. Describing the rerecording of his scores, he writes, "For the albums, I used the source music that was the common denominator for my record-buying audience. And there was pressure from the record company: they didn't want to know about dramatic music." See Mancini, *Did They Mention the Music?* 101.

33. Ibid., 118.

34. Mancini discusses the bass flute in his manual on orchestration, describing it as one of "the most pleasing sounds in the orchestra" (*Sounds and Scores,* 57–60). The instrument itself is rather large for the flute family and, according to the composer, "a tremendous amount of breath is needed to make a decent sound." Mancini began using the instrument in the late fifties on albums like *The Blues and the Beat* and *Mr. Lucky* and its sound became something of a trademark.

35. The situation is not unlike what Noël Carroll describes as a kind of relay effect in the horror film. When characters encounter a monster in horror fictions, they exemplify for us the way that we as spectators ought to regard those same creatures. According to Carroll, "Our responses are supposed to converge (but not exactly duplicate) those of the characters"; *The Philosophy of Horror* (New York: Routledge, 1990), 17–24. Of course, in cinema, music is often used to reinforce this mirroring effect. For more on music's function as an emotional signifier, see my "Movie Music as Moving Music: Cognition and Emotion in Film Music," in *Passionate Views,* ed. Carl Plantinga and Greg Smith (Baltimore: Johns Hopkins University Press, 1999).

36. Sellers's comments here were somewhat prescient insofar as they anticipated one of the most common features of laserdiscs: many are programmed in such a way that one can listen to the separate components of the soundtrack apart from one another. By separating the sound into discrete analog and digital channels, one can listen to just the music *or* just the dialogue and sound effects.

37. Advertisement for Henry Mancini's *Dear Heart and Other Songs About Love,* in *Billboard,* 9 January 1965, p. 2.

38. For a more complete assessment of electronics's influence on contemporary film scoring, see Lukas Kendall, "The Fifth Element: The Final Frontier?" *Film Score Monthly* 2, no. 4 (1997): 31.

39. Jonathan Romney and Adrian Wootton, eds., *The Celluloid Jukebox: Popular Music and the Movies Since the 50s* (London: British Film Institute, 1995), 119.

PART FOUR

✳

GENDER, ETHNICITY, IDENTITY

✳

MICHELLE LEKAS

Ultrasound

The Feminine in the
Age of Mechanical Reproduction

✳

Technology is lust removed from nature. —Don DeLillo[1]

Music that itself makes so much noise is the silence of all other noises—because when it lifts
its voice, it affirms its solitude [and] asserts that it alone occupies vibrant space.
—Vladimir Jankélevitch[2]

If one really desired a succinct history of film theory, DeLillo's quotation
would certainly suffice. Film incites a lust for itself: its apparatus catalyzes
our memories and emotions even if only to keep us watching. This unsettling property constitutes the grounds for film's popularity as well as its
study. We watch it because it works (*technē*) and then construct competing
frameworks to account for this: a fantasy machinery from which no viewer
is immune and with which every viewer, even the theorist, is complicit.

My concern in this essay involves precisely the above problematic: now
that the academy accepts Cinema Studies as a discipline, how best to *think*
film theory's hermeneutics, both of Ricouerian possibility and suspicion,[3]
to best understand and *teach* the problems inherent in cinema's cultivation
of desire. This simple question lodges directly within a current crack in the
definition of film studies' character that is roughly represented by two competing schools of thought. One program, articulated by a growing number
of scholars (including the editors of this volume) and popularized through
cultural studies theorists along with proponents of psychoanalytic inquiry
such as Slavoj Žižek and Julia Kristeva, celebrates the widening of film studies through radically interdisciplinary tactics. This program is opposed by a
second contingent, fostered primarily by David Bordwell, Kristin Thompson, Dudley Andrew, and Noël Carroll, that identifies such approaches as
overdiffuse and liable to "weaken the logical structure of [film] theory."[4]

While, as Andrew argues, Cinema Studies is not exactly a battlefield, it nevertheless demarcates a contested ground: as university funding shifts directions to the tune of a late-capitalist economy (which seems to be losing patience daily with academia), neophyte programs cannot really be blamed for their attempts at sovereignty over an area of study.[5] But these stabs at legitimacy come at a high price. Any efforts to transform a relatively new discipline into an august and accepted classical field—a field suggestive of, say, musicology—risks instantiation that effectively depoliticizes, and thus erases, both our hope for and our suspicion of *the object* of study itself.[6] And not incidentally, what better way to deflate the desire, or the lust, that drew our attention to the technology in the first place?

This brief introduction is necessary to preface my perhaps unusual methodology here. In countering the centripetal politics of institutions such as the Society for Cinema Studies that attempt to "keep film in film studies," I shall discuss how clearly film depends on associative strategies and alternate art forms (in this case, opera) to make itself *work*. One might be tempted to imagine that such a strategy is de facto unnecessary, particularly considering the influence and popularity of such recent innovators as Robert Ray, who practices surrealistic film theory; Pascal Bonitzer, who experiments with spatiality and film; Michel Chion, Kaja Silverman, Mary Ann Doane, and others who pursue the psychical body of film sound; Caryl Flinn, whose feminist-historical studies resurrect the cinema soundtrack as key to reception; John Mowitt, who investigates the political linguistics of film; and Gilles Deleuze, who has restructured film movement thematically via Bergson.[7] Unfortunately, it is crucial to resist such temptation: in the bulk of the aforementioned enterprises, the absence of linear historiography, developmental ethnofilmography, cognitive study, empiricism, or strict formalism continues to provoke a distinctive uneasiness in film-studies circles.

Although this uneasiness is difficult to document, it is nonetheless there, and as with a virtual particle, one can feel its effects however ephemeral its evidence. Yet I argue that the study of how cinema *works* in correlation with elements outside its singularity as a discipline creates an effect as well: a knowledge effect that is less about maintenance of a field than it is about that field's sustenance.[8] To that end I look specifically at film's use of opera (defined as "work") in terms of cinema's production of desire. Of course, such an investigation is centrifugal in that I am not concerned here with film versions of opera, or of opera's integration in film soundtracks, but with the moments in which cinema truly *needs* opera, and how this dependence alters the filmic apparatus.

This project puts film in an unfamiliar relation with an affiliated art form: here cinema neither vampirizes opera nor stands as its exemplar. Instead, I claim that film employs the operatic to produce a hyperreality that extends its own effects.[9] According to theorists such as Jean-Louis Baudry and Daniel Dayan, film's interpellatory apparatus hails its viewers and sets up the fantasy screen for a play of desire that continually proffers and retracts a lure (a lost object, or *objet petit a*) that never materializes.[10] Naturally this intermittent reinforcement, defined as "suture," is predicated upon a perpetual motion that relies on the very *threat* of the object's presence: if the raw projected image is stripped of fantasy (of love, say, or redemption, or what-have-you), we are left with a specter, or the lure revealed as a thing-toward-death.[11] In this case the split between knowledge (that we will die; that we are watching a concocted image) and belief of the same wavers just as all resolve is weakened by intermittent reinforcement: that resolve wanes just as surely as our desire is compelled.[12]

At the juncture where its object qua object begins to protrude and damage our suspension of disbelief, film's narrative apparatus necessarily opens spaces that invite excess. The cinematic work, in other words, must produce discomfort in order to conjure emotional affect—in order, again, to domesticate that same affect. To this end, film may be "punched up" through a form such as opera (though the operatic, as we will see, endangers cinema's essential reality principle).[13] As touched on previously, Freud's reality (or pleasure) principle with its suspension of disbelief and avoidance of discomfort is central to the way narrative film works, but its paucity in comparison to *jouissant* operatic moments must be managed.[14]

I chose opera as the ideal medium that proves critical to a fuller understanding of Hollywood cinema's politics; opera is, paradoxically, both antithetical to film form and correlate to the excess, or Real, that film calls up and expunges. If, as Baudry claims, film's narrative apparatus envelops all the production, distribution, and reception fragments of its product by collapsing its labor into a seamless presentation that accords the eye (or "I") ultimate authority, opera could easily pose as its Other.[15] Because if cinema's success is contingent upon a delicate alternation of metaphor with metonymy (or repetition with difference),[16] opera throws its fortunes on metaphor alone. Opera's spectacular essence, one could argue, requires the creation of a metaphoric *substitute* world, rather than a representation formed out of details from a contiguous world, in order to hold its audience. This metaphoric world is expressed aptly through Catherine Clément's quotation from Fontanella in *Opera, or The Undoing of Women*: "I always imagine that nature is a great spectacle like that of opera," to which Clément responds, "what owes what to what is thus reversed."[17]

Furthermore, as a complete aesthetic edifice or an often unwieldy *Gesamtkunstwerk* that clomps through the details or metonyms that ballast its production rather than subsuming them, opera increases its capital by *showing* its labor. And it is no accident that the weight of this edifice falls upon the woman: the reproductive figure whose incongruity in opera's parthenogenic world demands that she energetically submit her labor in service of art. Much excellent theoretical scholarship has been done on the enjoyment culled from the opera diva's vocal "grain" or vulnerability and how this enjoyment is paralleled in librettos that regularly resolve in the death of the female lead.[18] Clément's book was one of the vanguard texts in this area, while Ethan Mordden's *Demented: The World of the Opera Diva,* Michel Poizat's *The Angel's Cry,* and Wayne Koestenbaum's *The Queen's Throat* come to grips with the fetishistic relationship between the opera fan and his singer.[19]

As Freud makes clear, the fetish recalls the last scene the child takes in before confronting his mother's genitals and the realization that his "all," or his world, is incomplete.[20] No matter what the object—fur, hair, shoe, garter, foot, arm, mouth—it is transferable to anything that offers completion and becomes, in Stephen Heath's words, "something lit up and heightened that depicts, as under an arc light, a point of theatrical representation for which the subject is installed."[21] For the opera fan, the Diva occupies this impossible position as she must be lit up and is yet ultimately extinguished: to lock into a fetish is to become psychotic. One must always eventually dismiss the voice's echo from the past and return to a more believable present even while the material vocal cords thin and tremble.

It is important to remember that cinema similarly manages female "difference" through a nexus of fetishism and sadism; it attempts, however, to implant these moves firmly into the plot, or into a representation of the fantasy "real" that avoids the physical reality of the star.[22] The labor involved in film production, as well as any suffering endured by its actors, is carefully enfolded within narrative so as not to disturb the reality principle. Ascertaining the materiality in the acting of, say, Judy Garland, Marilyn Monroe, or Vivian Leigh, demands the kind of careful watching that film's technology discourages.[23]

So in contrast to film, opera's symbolic (or phallic) history and presentation boldly dares the spectator to disbelieve its structural premises. In a ploy that Slavoj Žižek has termed "pornographic," opera shows all and reduces its audience to gaping objects, as opposed to narrative cinema's subjectification process, which urges viewers to "react" and show themselves to an impassive, objective screen.[24] In this sense, despite its relatively recent high-art status, opera is more akin to vaudeville, the circus, or a pornographic film than it is to standard Hollywood cinema. Opera does not rely on what Octave Mannoni calls "the other scene," in which the doubling and mirroring of film must allow for the imagination to conceive of two possible scenes simultaneously: the one that it sees and the one that it experiences.[25] As if at the circus, the opera spectator must pull in her breath, look neither to the left nor the right and silently plead for the performers' lives: only then is audience comfort possible.

The significance of these differences hinges on how both film and opera manage excess, and how they formally alter each other. As the feminine is of course the narrative's metonymic catalyst in both media, she is also the dangerous element who threatens at any time to grow excessive and eschew resolution. But why is excess feminine? And why is the opera-cinema relationship problematic in this regard? For the latter question, I argue at the onset that here is where a distinctly materialist psychoanalytic paradigm emerges as useful to organize the antagonism inherent in such an encounter. When two aesthetic forms, particularly those whose principles are rooted in bourgeois Enlightenment philosophy, come into contact there is always a struggle. True opera fans (and to enjoy opera one must be a true fan) have never warmed to filmed versions of their favorite works (say, Losey's *Don Giovanni* or Zefferelli's *La Bohème*), just as novels rarely satisfy when translated to film or theater: the current play *Art* nicely makes this point in terms of theater and painting.[26]

The reasons for this distaste, beyond mere parochialism, point to historical and class frictions among variant media that ostensibly hark back to arguments concerning a mass culture/high culture divide. But this inevitable premise is misleading if one considers that not only did virtually all of these competing expressions rise from a similar principle—that of the newly liberated bourgeoisie representing its "reality" to itself—but that the conflict between mass and high culture derives from the means by which this reality is produced.[27] In other words, as Geoffrey Nowell-Smith observes in a discussion that contrasts performances from Judy Garland and Kiri Te Kanawa: "There is a place for the opposition high/popular culture within this set, but it is not a determining one. If a single factor could be isolated as determining, it would have to be the technology—though not the technology in a pure state, but as applied within the overall apparatus."[28]

Thus the apparatus that translates experience into idea, or being into meaning, develops from a political interchange (as not *everything* is political, but everything aesthetic *is*), in which decisions must be made that determine exactly what the apparatus must risk and to what degree.[29] One can assume that the former resolution is overdetermined, as representation must always gamble on how tightly it builds its fantasy: if the aforementioned "reality" evokes a fantasy image of the bourgeois subject for the same, the more coherent the apparatus renders this fantasy, the less the risk. This risky element, or the materiality of the subject that renders it excessive, irrational, and somehow different from itself could be characterized as an eruption of the Lacanian Real within a symbolic system that, as Bataille envisions it, "is as ugly and dirty as hairy sexual organs, or lower parts: sooner or later they threaten a scandalous eruption in the course of which the asexual noble heads of the bourgeois will be chopped off."[30]

The author, as our noble asexual head, is merely a concept that encompasses all that imbues the apparatus with meaning, and while he needs excess to provide his work with that frisson of danger, he must never lose his head! So he cuts off the body of the figure who also creates, yet in a nonsymbolic fashion alien to him, and negates the *being* of his product.[31] Susan McClary puts this operation to work clearly in her theorization of the gender politics of chromaticism's engagement with "Absolute Music": "it is the sultry, slippery, seductive female who taunts and entraps, and who needs to be brought back under tonal domination and absorbed."[32]

To short-circuit simple binarism here, it is important to note that the metonymic feminine position as *jouissant* or excessive is exactly that: a position. To challenge aesthetic practices that erect themselves by insisting on a feminized position, the feminist critic must perform a twofold task: while never losing sight of the ways in which these practices affect actual women, we must also explore these practices as structures whose intermedial moments are considered just as seriously as their intrastructural elements (plots, characters, dialogue, and so forth).[33] Consequently, although this gendered equation appears to be one of part to whole (metonym/metaphor, syntagm/paradigm, signifier/signified, displacement/condensation, Real/symbolic, and so forth), the crucial query here is how these elements interact to become sexed. And to echo Clément's earlier observation—"what owes what to whom is reversed"—how did *being* ever become a part of, or subservient to, *meaning*?

The initial step in this inquiry involves a return to the respective hierarchical positions of opera and film. It is clear at this point that opera easily occupies (at least in our historical moment) a safe place in the high-cultural pantheon: opera certainly risks a higher degree of incredulity than does cinema. Classical opera's status is such that it need not even maintain a semblance of the "fantasy-real world" that cinema's apparatus summons, and its allegiance to respective works is such that it may foreswear the vernacular and thus defy a key rule (language) that delimits standard cinema. Most decisive, however, is opera's aforementioned phenomenon of the voice.

Whether or not one understands the language of a particular opera, the voice holds sway as a fungible object, and a number of theorists, including McClary, Silverman, Chion, Flinn, and Doane, have drawn out this concept of the voice's materiality. What it has taken advanced technologies like Dolby and Surround-sound to "pick up" selectively on film soundtracks ("Breaths, squeaks, clinks, hums . . . the minor denizens of sound")[34] erupt unbidden from sopranos and tenors forced to contort and magnify their voices. And the uncanny grain in these voices can shock the listener as too Real: too reminiscent of the maternal voice, the lost object inhabiting the overlap between being and meaning that is at once both and neither. This space marks what Lyotard terms "l'inhuman": it is unrepresentable and impossible yet replete with potential as it knows that the latter situation depends upon the former (after all, once one begins to sing, one's vocal potential disappears: possibility is the enemy of potential).[35] Furthermore, the way we receive sounds defies rational logic: like our knowledge that we will die, sound is at once everywhere and nowhere.[36]

According to Chion: "Sound suppresses the notion of a point of view that can be localized. Where do we hear from? . . . Sound does not indicate the outlines of the object from which it emanates [as it is itself an object]. Nor does sound know Euclidian perspective, however hard we try to make it do so."[37] This extra-logical material threatens to shatter the subjective fantasy and erupt, like Bataille's lower parts, as an agent of the death drive, just as opera, with its *jouissant* voices, is obsessed both formally and thematically with disease, madness, and death.[38] And death holds the key to opera's fascination: in Poizat's formulation, "human beings can suffer from their status as speaking subjects, and they can find ecstatic pleasure in seeking to forget or deny their fundamental attachment to language."[39] In conclusion, opera's authenticity as a privileged cultural object rests not only on its willingness to risk excess but its eagerness to do whatever it takes finally to silence the voice's materiality and reintrench the paternal metaphor. Clément has clearly mapped out this program as one of scapegoating the feminine in a particularly violent fashion that assures the triumphant return of metaphoric logic, language, and sanity.[40] And what transpires when opera is implanted—rather than integrated—into cinema's apparatus appears consanguineous to this schema.

First, it is important to repeat that cinema, as opera's feminized, mass-cultural other, needs to call upon opera to amplify its emotional power: the excessive moments available through cinema's own machinery prove too brief and pallid to conjure the subjective destitution that a particular scenario may demand.[41] But there is a second, more quotidian, explanation for film's recourse to high-cultural forms. Deriving from the lowest rungs of technology ("scientific" carnival attractions and urban peep shows), the Hollywood film industry has been trying to raise its cultural stakes since the vogue for "filmed plays" in the late 1910s and early 1920s.

The formation of Adolph Zukor's Famous Players (1912), the inception of the Motion Picture Arts and Sciences "Academy" (1927), the optioning of literary classics (see Griffith's *Enoch Arden* [1911], Zukor's *La Reine Elisabeth* [with Sarah Bernhardt, 1912]) and the emergence of the "artist-director" (Griffith, DeMille, Chaplin) — all represent an oft-pathetic Hollywood tendency: grasping for "quality." Yet Hollywood has always been self-conscious, and even bitter, in the face of its cultural betters: the industry has generally and appropriately expressed this ambivalence through the comedy genre with films such as *Sullivan's Travels, Singin' in the Rain,* and *The Bandwagon.* By deriding the high culture that it both envies and desires, Hollywood and its apparatus have attempted to flip Andreas Huyssen's conflation of mass culture with the feminine position on its ear: as we shall see in film's use of opera, the glimpse of the Real that the film apparatus marshals from its high-culture counterpart is feminized and thrown back upon opera as a whole. Thus the expulsion of the feminine plays out on multiple levels: both opera and film punish "woman" for her materiality: opera views film as a weaker, feminine art, and in return film casts opera as an embarrassing scene of feminine excess that the reality principle must master. If the above argument appears perhaps paranoid, so be it: even Freud, as he examines paranoid interpretations, states, "there is in fact some truth in them."[42] There may be some truth, then, to an insistence that the agon between cultural forms is in fact a battle between men fought on the body of woman.

While the foregrounding of opera in cinema has composed a cultural lampooning strategy familiar to audiences from Bugs Bunny's cross-dressing turn in Warner Brothers' "Looney" *Die Walküre* to the Marx Brothers' pastiche of Verdi in *A Night at the Opera* (1935), the effect of this move is often far more complex than the above examples suggest. Although my knowledge of opera is quite limited, I first became fascinated with this practice's intrusion in the apparatus's reality principle after re-viewing the 1945 drama *The Lost Weekend.* An entrant in the trajectory of Hollywood "alcoholism" exposés (including *What Price Hollywood?* [1932]; *A Star Is Born* [1937 and 1954]; *Come Fill the Cup* [1951]; *The Voice in the Mirror* [1958]; *I'll Cry Tomorrow* [1956]; *From The Terrace* [1960]; *Smash-Up: The Story of a Woman* [1947]; *The Days of Wine and Roses* [1962]; *The Country Girl* [1954]; *The Joker Is Wild* [1957], and on to *Clean and Sober* [1988] and *Leaving Las Vegas* [1995]), *The Lost Weekend* sat squarely within a "serious" genre wherein the protagonist is forced to confront weakness, accept addiction, and either assume a place within the symbolic order of work or refuse to capitulate and embrace death.[43] Vital to this narrative structure is the exposure of the subject as an alcoholic insofar as this constitutes the moment of suspense and frisson of excitement that speeds the plot toward closure and relief. The interesting correspondence between the films listed above, however, is the relative unimportance of this decisive moment in terms of the protagonist's diegetic position. In virtually every feature film from this genre, all of the supporting characters *know* that the protagonist is an alcoholic (especially if she is a woman who, in Hollywood logic, cannot hide her excesses): either the drinker does not bother to hide his addiction at all (*Come Fill the Cup, The Joker Is Wild, What Price Hollywood? A Star Is Born*), or he only imagines (*Days of Wine and Roses, From the Terrace, The Voice in the Mirror, The Country Girl, I'll Cry Tomorrow, Smash Up*) that (s)he's fooling those around him.

The Lost Weekend, however, presents a slightly different scenario. Its hero Don Birnam, played by Ray Milland, attends a matinee of *La Traviata* at which the toasting scene taunts him and drives him to the checkroom to recover his coat and the bottle hidden within it. His claim ticket is confused with an attractive young woman's (Jane Wyman) and as they switch coats after the performance he feels that he can "pull off" a dignified and manly stance with her: he even successfully clinches a future date. Unfortunately, just as she walks off, he swings his coat in a manner suggestive of *Traviata*'s drinkers' gowns and the bottle falls to the ground and breaks. This alarms his new friend and effectively turns their incipient courtship dance into a radical scene of humiliation. From this point, Wyman pities and mothers him: his ritual subjective destitution becomes operatic, or excessive, as his phallic status reduces to a bodily materiality. He now needs not only Wyman's help, but the aid of the apparatus as well, to resuscitate his subjective coherence and close the narrative.

The Lost Weekend is strikingly characteristic of opera's use in film: the uniform tactic of employing opera to reveal a buried weakness or unspoken material excess in a character varies little in structure from film to film. *Tosca, Madame Butterfly,* and *La Bohème* propel the folie à deux in *Heavenly Creatures* (1994); *Madame Butterfly* narrates Alex Forrest's manic quest for the paternal metaphor in *Fatal Attraction* (1987); in *Philadelphia* (1993), the cringe-inducing attempt at summoning the internal otherness of AIDS is played out through Spontini's *Vestale,* Cilea's *Adriana Lecouvreur,* and Giordano's *Andrea Chénier;* and through Massenet's *Thaïs,* Angie (Geena Davis) is forced to confront her mother's schizophrenia in *Angie* (1994).

It is notable that in each of these filmic examples opera protrudes through the soundtrack (often as performance) before its domestication as something kitschy, extravagant, and "unreal" in terms of mass-culture representation. Even in a movie as light as the successfully kitschy *Pretty Woman* (1990), a performance of *La Traviata* is borrowed to strip unfeeling businessman Richard Gere of his businesslike facade as he melts when his unlikely prostitute Julia Roberts weeps at her first opera. At the film's finale, of course, Gere risks his weakness (a fear of heights) while Verdi booms through a truck-mounted megaphone, allowing him to propose, in self-conscious abjection, to Roberts. One could also expound on the homophobic politics that subtend the seduction scene in Tony Scott's *The Hunger* (1983), in which Susan Sarandon literally relinquishes her subjectivity to Catherine Deneuve to *Lakmé;* the gleeful rampage in which Isabelle Huppert and Sandrine Bonnaire slaughter a bourgeois family relaxed before a televised performance of *Don Giovanni* in Chabrol's *La Cérèmonie* (1996), or Mike Hammer (Ralph Meeker) disgustedly breaking a homosexual tenor's record as the man sings along to Flotow's *Martha* in Aldrich's *Kiss Me Deadly* (1955): one must be humiliated, it would seem, for expressing the Real of one's sexuality.[44]

In fact the political crudity of the equation weakened man = homosexual = woman = materiality = excess is structurally comparable to the arbitrariness of the matching of specific operas to particular film narratives. In some cases, the opera choices for soundtrack inclusion do confer an attention to metonym expressed through kitsch: *The Lost Weekend*'s Don Birnam could be our Violetta for whom, as studio system Hollywood would have it, things work out in the end—and who metaphorically substitutes the literal woman for a symbolic symptom.[45] And it is not difficult to comprehend why a film like *There's Something About Mary* (1998) would employ *Così fan Tutte* to pump up a pack of deceptive and manic male figures, or to see the link between *Tristan und Isolde's* "lovedeath" and Joan Crawford's suicide in *Humoresque* (1946). But the narrative logic linking *The Barber of Seville* to its formal use in *Copycat* (1995); or *La Bohème* to *Moonstruck* (1987); or *The Marriage of Figaro* to *Shock Corridor* (1963) (or *Martha* to *Rear Window* [1954] for that matter) is less clear. One could, no doubt, apply tortuous readings to patch a literal segue between libretto and script—*Lorenzo's Oil* (1992) includes *L'Elisir d'Amore,* for instance, because the titular oil is a metaphoric elixir of love—yet the argument that it is opera's *effect,* its excess, that fuels film's apparatus provides the only explanation for its fate by that very same machinery.

To focus on the most striking case of this technological management of excess, I now touch upon a Hollywood classic, *Citizen Kane,* to illustrate the cinema apparatus's use of the operatic to produce a hyperreality that kitschifies the feminine into an accessible commodity. *Citizen Kane* has a place in popular discourse as Classical Hollywood's greatest film and repeatedly appears on international movie critics' lists as the best film ever produced. Released in 1941, the film was received with controversy as the brainchild of twenty-five-year-old "boy genius" Orson Welles. Welles previously earned industry respect with the Mercury Theatre radio dramas that he wrote, directed, and generally oversaw, but it was his "War of the Worlds" broadcast that brought national notoriety. This attention culminated in a three-film offer from RKO—an unheard-of proposition at the time. Welles, it seemed, was different: he demanded latitude from studio management that successful and experienced directors didn't dare request.

But what Welles wanted *wasn't* different: a fact that even the Hollywood establishment recognized. He was the ultimate modernist, the "idea man" who exuded the kind of control his studio counterparts desired. Welles also managed to fully occupy the mythical position of author-director. To an industry that yearned for (high) culture while simultaneously effacing its own production machine, Welles was the answer: the "artiste" who single-handedly created his "work." That Welles's status came at the cost of a credit battle with Herman J. Mankiewicz (*Citizen Kane*'s co-screenwriter) and the deflection of well-deserved praise from cameraman Gregg Toland actually helped matters. The sole creator must fight for his offspring and obscure the means by which movies are produced. Of course, the real *Kane* controversy arose from its source: Charles Foster Kane's life story was based closely enough on that of newspaper magnate William Randolph Hearst to cause something of a scandal. But Welles and Mankiewicz took great pains to separate events in Hearst's personal life and career from actual libelous material, and in this way they garnered a colorful story without suffering legal consequences.

One important detail of this colorful story involved Hearst's long relationship with rising actress Marion Davies. Davies was attractive, an adept light comedienne, and could have progressed well in Hollywood on her own, but Hearst's patronage spelled disaster for her acting ambitions. He threatened her directors, launched bloated advertising campaigns for her films, and tried to force her into heavy dramatic roles not suited to her talents. As a result Davies, while popular in Hollywood, became an object of ridicule and aborted her career while suffering through (not surprisingly) an escalating drinking problem: a condition that servants and friends helped her to just barely camouflage from Hearst. The Hearst-Davies relationship was certainly dramatic and painful enough to serve as a perfect prototype for news-magnate Charles Foster Kane's (Welles) romance with shopgirl turned "opera star" Susan Alexander (Dorothy Comingore).

The parallels between Marion and Susan emerge as painfully obvious in *Citizen Kane*. When Susan meets Kane and hints of her wish to become a singer, we hear her voice as pleasant, light, and passable for popular (mass-culture) tunes. She simply lacks the ability to reach the high notes, maintain the pitch, or assume the volume of an opera soprano. After losing a mayoral race, however, Kane feels compelled to exhibit Susan as a high-culture diva: a substitute to deny his own lack and to complete his subjective fantasy of the well-rounded "man of the world." He desperately acquires ancient Greek and Roman artifacts in an extension of this anxiety, and, like Susan, the high art is stored away in his mansion.

To illustrate Susan's unsuitability for high culture, Welles and Bernard Herrmann, *Citizen Kane*'s composer, asked San Francisco soprano Jean Forward to sing thinly and slightly off-pitch to dub Susan's opera performances. They eschewed hiring a bad singer; they wanted Susan, like Davies, merely in over her head. Occupying her position of Kane's "art collection," Susan demonstrates the resistance of the object: she is incapable of a Galatean transformation into high art. She cannot sing and does not wish to be played for a fool.

And like Marion, Susan lacks a desire to take on the mantle of high culture and serve as a public validation of her husband's pretensions. Kane, through his symbiotic relation to Susan as extension of his phallic stature, continually insists upon her opera career. This insistence thrusts her into the symbolic arena: while Kane imagines that her entry into high culture will inflate his symbolic currency, she is instead made excessive and then naturalized through language (by critics and audiences) into a figure of fun that inflates the *film*. Operating in the imaginary register, Kane transposes Susan's reception onto his own image: when she begs to retire from opera, he offers "I don't propose to have myself made ridiculous" as a reason to continue "fighting" her audiences who represent the voters blocking his entry into politics.[46]

While it is understandable to read *Citizen Kane* as a critique of Kane/Hearst as the would-be modernist author, one must consider Welles/RKO's desire for high-culture status, which drew on its kitschification of the feminine. Though the Kane figure stands as a Benjaminic disavowal of the "aura" and a warning against the hubris of self-created myth in an age that no longer recognizes tragedy, the film's apparatus suggests otherwise. Kane does not fall because of his pretensions to high culture and originality; he is instead punished for his failure to live up to those same pretensions. His pretense, though pumped up with surplus cash and ambition, loses out to a notion of reality (or the reality principle), whereas the film, inflated through its use of the operatic, maintains its status as a "classic." In this sense, Kane "loses" his stature while remaining a "great man," just as the film risks authenticity (through the operatic and its high-art aspirations) while remaining a mass-culture masterpiece.

Susan as opera star, then, performs as the linchpin in the system of her own kitschification. She plays as the stand-in for both the film's and Kane's inauthenticity. Put simply, Susan's "ridiculous" stint as an opera diva provides a stage for the use of the operatic: the amplification of emotion that is judged as threatening and scapegoated for the apparatus's failure to produce reality and Kane's inefficacy of self-origination (production). She becomes kitsch: the accessible commodity that the film denies in itself.

We see this kitschification process at work in two glimpses of Susan's singing career. The first flashback is seen through the eyes of Jeb Leland (Joseph Cotten), Kane's former best friend; the second is Susan's own hindsight account, drunkenly related years later in a shabby roadhouse, "El Rancho," where Susan works as a torch singer. Not incidentally, Susan's is the only flashback in a film "told" retrospectively that overlaps with another (Jeb's): as Maureen Turim explains it, "Only Leland and Susan narrate the same incident, the opening night of *Salaambo*. The film marks this repetition by exactly duplicating the opening shot of the sequence [but Jeb's version] gives us a perspective from behind Susan of her vulnerability in the glare of the lights directed at her."[47]

This repetition, or the metaphoric action of the signified, cements Susan's vision as indistinct and merely reproductive of Leland's. She is further denied authority, or a signifying voice, within her own account. As Turim points out, "the overall continuity of style . . . minimizes the subjectivity of each flashback segment. This is particularly evident in the case of Susan Alexander. The shrill shrew we see raging over her opera reviews or nagging at Xanadu is hardly an image a woman would present of her former self. The misogynist caricature is part of a larger authorial purpose."[48] It would be safe here to assume Susan's desubjectification, or her "aphanisis," in the service of a larger authorial purpose, as the primary operation of kitschification. Yet the operative word remains "shrill," a term that implicates the operatic in a process that posits Susan as the shill for high art: the caricature of reproduction.

For this caricature Welles and Bernard Herrmann concocted a parody of an opera: *Salaambo*, of course, derived from the Ernest Reyes work based on Flaubert's novel of the same name. Even in his heyday, Flaubert's critics found this dramatic account of ancient Carthage kitschy: Sainte-Beuve firmly criticized its "inauthenticity," calling it an instance of "dilettantism which, finding nothing but a few rare debris to fasten upon, is forced to exaggerate hopelessly."[49] Herrmann analogized that description to Susan's voice, constructing an aria "in a very high tessitura, so that a girl with a modest voice would be completely hopeless in it . . . to give the effect that she was struggling in quicksand."[50] The effect, however, accomplished much more: it allowed the viewer to understand and dismiss this feminine hopelessness (Jeb Leland states in his opera review that Susan was "a hopelessly incompetent amateur") with his certainty of mastery intact.

Poor Susan's narrative is completely played out throughout her singing sequences. Although she begins singing privately for the married Kane who enjoys her "simplicity" (he calls her "a cross-section of the American public"), her voice is made public after her and Kane's affair is discovered and ruins his political chances. The exposé of their illicit romance is headlined "Kane in love nest with 'singer,'" and, as Leland comments, "That whole thing [the opera career] about Susie was to prove something; he [Kane] wanted to take those quotes off of 'singer.'" Thus Susan stands in as the material bearer of meaning: she sings to establish Kane's authority, but only at the expense of her own performing body.

At her flashback's opening, Susan acknowledges her position as scapegoat by admitting that "maybe I shouldn't have sang for Charlie [Kane] that first time I met him, but I did an awful lot of singing after that." This awareness emphasizes the pain of her humiliation, her failure to produce in front of "audiences who don't want you, night after night." This humiliation also leads us back to the film's audience: the viewer for whom her failed performances are meant.

For it is the cinema spectator who benefits from her exposure rather than suffering through her faulty arias. She is delivered to the spectator to bolster Kane's tragedy (and reinforce the film's theme) through emotion that minimizes the risk of revealing the reality principle's suturing machinery. She is framed on stage by flashbulbs that analogize the apparatus, which is given the freedom to pan up to the lighting cables that resemble puppet strings and swing out to the operagoers who titter and comment at Susan's vocal stretching.

This freedom offers the spectator knowledge while effacing its own means, thus presenting Susan's humiliation without endangering the film as a "work." Central to this movement is the cross-cutting between Susan and Kane: we see her pain as his tragedy. In short, the viewer may enjoy the cathartic emotion of knowing Susan's pain in terms of Kane's authentic downfall. This operatic heightening of emotion is achieved through two 180-degree cuts between Susan and Kane during her *Salaambo* performance. Her face is held in two lengthy close-ups, during which her heavy makeup and massive head-ornament constitute what Baudrillard termed "the panoply of accessories that code the fetish object."[51] As sacrificial fetish,

Susan's mouth remains forced open as if to allow a view of her inner trauma: a view available through ultrasound. She is externalized in what Silverman calls "the strip-tease" that renders the subject fully knowable.[52] And, as opposed to Kane who quietly suffers as Susan sings, the loudly and fully knowable is kitschy and excessive. Susan's mouth is only allowed to close after she swallows an overdose of sleeping pills in a suicide attempt, and after this narrative clamp-down she "reopens" only to tell Kane's story.

This brief outline of the nexus of modernist "authenticity" (film's reality principle, the operatic, kitschification, and the feminine) is not intended to suggest that every aria recorded on film is tantamount to human sacrifice. Nor is it meant to imply that kitschification of the feminine is exclusive to the operatic. My project here is an emotional reading of emotion: an investigation of the operatic's role among excess, film's narrative apparatus, and the feminine. This reading was spurred by a desire to explore opera's movement of film's effects: an intuitive encounter that establishes film itself beyond the parameters of formalism. Finally, I insist that exploration into film's intertextual (and often anachronistic) encounters with both art and the subjectivity that informs it may lead to "Barthes's "third meaning," to knowledge beyond the signifieds (or mental concepts) of formalism, empiricism, or a fealty to the discipline. As Barthes elucidates this "beyond":

The characteristic of the third meaning is indeed . . . to blur the limit separating expression from disguise, but also to allow that oscillation succinct demonstration. . . . [This] artifice is at once a falsification of itself—pastiche—and derisory fetish, since it shows its fissure and suture. I believe that the obtuse meaning carries a certain emotion . . . we enter into complicity, into an understanding [with the third meaning's sites/figures]. No more, however, is it to be located in language use . . . [it] is a signifier without a signified.[53]

Notes

1. Don DeLillo, *White Noise* (New York: Viking-Penguin, 1985), 285.

2. Vladimir Jankélevitch, *La Musique et l'ineffable* (Paris: Seuil, 1983), 32.

3. Paul Ricouer, "Structure, Word, Event," in *The Philosophy of Paul Ricouer*, ed. T. Reagan and David Stuart (Boston: Beacon, 1978), 109–19.

4. David Bordwell, "Lowering the Stakes: Prospects for a Historical Poetics of Cinema," *Iris* 1, no.1 (1983): 6–7. Also see David Bordwell, Janet Staiger, and Kristin Thompson's *The Classical Hollywood Cinema: Film Style and Mode of Production to 1960* (New York: Columbia University Press, 1985), the bible of formalist "one discipline" film studies that invites in-depth analyses of film production *within its own* context as *the* authoritative means for the medium's scholarship and teaching. Also influential in its insistence on protecting the discipline from renegade agents of psychoanalysis, Marxism, and all Continental philosophy is Noël Carroll's *Mystifying Movies* (New York: Columbia University Press, 1988).

5. Dudley Andrew, "The Limits of Delight: Robert Ray's Postmodern Film Studies," *Strategies* 2 (1989): 157–58. In this article, Andrew responds to Robert Ray's "The Bordwell Regime and the Stakes of Knowledge," which offers a critique of David Bordwell's formalist dominance over the film-studies field and suggests postmodern alternatives to the discipline, including surrealist and baroque tactics as new ways of looking at film to *generate*, rather than simply reflect, knowledge.

6. As I am neither a musicologist nor an examiner of musicology departments, it is perhaps unfair of me to make such a blanket assessment of musicology's conservative tendencies. But I am relying on good evidence from conversations with Susan McClary and from her afterword, "The Politics of Silence and Sound," in Jacques Attali's *Noise: The Political Economy of Music*, trans. Brian Massumi (Minneapolis: University of Minnesota Press, 1987), 149–58.

7. For purposes of brevity (as many authors and texts have, because of space constraints, necessarily been omitted here), see Slavoj Žižek, *Enjoy Your Symptom: Jacques Lacan in Hollywood and Out* (New York: Routledge, 1992); Žižek, ed., *Everything You Wanted to Know about Lacan but Were Afraid to Ask of Hitchcock* (London: Verso, 1992); Michel Chion, *Audio-Vision: Sound on Screen*, trans. and ed. Claudia Gorbman (New York: Columbia University Press, 1994); John Mowitt, "*Xala:* Postcoloniality and Foreign Film Language," *Camera Obscura* 31 (1993): 72–95; Mary Ann Doane, "The Voice in the Cinema: The Articulation of Body and Space," in *Film Sound: Theory and Practice*, ed. John Belton and Elisabeth Weis (New York: Columbia University Press, 1985), 162–76; Pascal Bonitzer, *Le champ aveugle: Essais sur le cinéma* (Paris: Gallimard, 1982); Kaja Silverman, *The Acoustic Mirror* (Bloomington: Indiana University Press, 1988); Caryl Flinn, *Strains of Utopia: Gender, Nostalgia and Hollywood Film Music* (Princeton: Princeton University Press, 1992); Gilles Deleuze, *Cinema 1: The Movement-Image*, ed. Barbara Habberjam and Hugh Tomlinson (Minneapolis: University of Minnesota Press, 1986); Gilles Deleuze, *Cinema 2: The Time-Image*, ed. Hugh Tomlinson and Robert Galeta (Minneapolis: University of Minnesota Press, 1989).

8. I have found, through my own teaching and from observing others, that it is precisely those radical connections and meanings one creates about and between films—meanings that elicit exasperated (and often deserved) protests from undergraduates—which draw students into an engagement with cinema that pushes far beyond plot summary and shot analysis and leads to critical thinking. That said, I concede that such engagement is invaluably enriched by a real knowledge of film history; but limiting film studies to the acquisition of such knowledge does a disservice to the possibilities of discipline.

9. The "hyperreal" refers to the Lacanian Real as discussed in Lacan, *Séminaire XX: Encore*, 40–51. This representational surplus turns on "things as they *really are*," the horrifying bodily substance of the everyday that admits the reality of death. For an interesting nonpsychoanalytic take on the hyperreal, see Jean Baudrillard's *In the Shadow of the Silent Majorities; or, The End of the Social*, trans. Paul Foss, John Johnston and Paul Patton (New York: Semiotexte, 1983), 83–86. Baudrillard's understanding of the hyperreal as "the indefinite scenario of crisis" is relevant to an understanding of the excess that subtends an economy while continually posing as a threat to the same.

10. For the classic text on interpellation in the social economy, a text now indispensable to the understanding of the filmic apparatus, see Louis Althusser, "Ideology and the Ideological State Apparatuses," in *Lenin and Philosophy*, trans. Ben Brewster (London: Monthly Review Press, 1971), 174–76. For an in-depth theorization of the extimate object, or *objet petit a*, that acts as a placeholder for the missing objects (the materiality of that [gaze, voice, breast, feces] which was pulled from the infant upon entry into language, or subjectivity) and remains in the subject as a

leftover piece of substance while it simultaneously stands before the subject as a promise of coherence, see the final chapter in Jacques Lacan, *Le séminaire de Jacques Lacan, Livre XI: Les quatre concepts fondamentaux de la psychanalyse* (Paris: Seuil, 1973).

11. For the definitive article concerning suture as that which "names the relation of the subject to its discourse" (in this case, film), see Jacques-Alain Miller, "Suture (elements of the logic of the signifier)," *Screen* 18, no. 4 (1977–78): 24–34 (the citation above is from p. 25). Also see Kaja Silverman, "Suture" [excerpts] in *Narrative, Apparatus, Ideology: A Film Theory Reader,* ed. Philip Rosen (New York: Columbia University Press, 1986), 219–35. Silverman's work on suture applies this mechanism directly to the politics of film spectatorship. For a useful commentary on the Lacanian Real as a lost object—or *objet a*—stripped of fantasy, see Slavoj Žižek, "Grimaces of the Real, or When the Phallus Appears," *October* 58 (1991): 45–68.

12. This technical practice in which film's machinery produces anxiety only to always unexpectedly "sew things up" for us is not unlike the mechanisms of control practiced by a cruel parent or lover. The unpredictability with which comfort is proffered and denied is more unnerving, according to now familiar behaviorist experiments, than consistent discomfort.

13. The reality principle here is merely the Freudian pleasure principle as described in Freud's *Introductory Lectures on Psychoanalysis,* trans. James Strachey (New York: Norton, 1966), 314–17. Throughout his work, Freud uses the terms "pleasure principle" and "reality principle" interchangeably. For an explanation of narrative film's reliance on the reality principle, see Jean-Louis Baudry, "Ideological Effects of the Basic Cinematographic Apparatus," trans. Alan Williams, *Film Quarterly* 28, no. 2 (1974–75): 39–47.

14. The Lacanian concept of *jouissance* (as separate from its denotative meaning of "enjoyment") is explained as a bliss that at least temporarily shatters subjectivity and is thus in league with the death drive and in constant tension with the reality principle. This surplus of the Symbolic system of language and rationality is explained in Jacques Lacan's *Le séminaire, livre XX: Encore* (Paris: Seuil, 1975).

15. Baudry, "Ideological Effects," 40–44.

16. Film's oscillation between metaphor and metonymy correlates to the notion of suture as a process that continually substitutes satisfaction with anxiety to both capture the spectator's attention and assure his continued viewing. The work of Ferdinand de Saussure and Roman Jakobson is key to this formulation, as is Janet Bergstrom's "Enunciation and Sexual Difference," in *Feminism and Film Theory,* ed. Constance Penley (New York: Routledge, 1988), 159–85, where she articulates Raymond Bellour's textual analysis in terms of gender difference as managed within narrative structure.

17. Catherine Clément, *Opera, or The Undoing of Women,* trans. Betsey Wing (Minneapolis: University of Minnesota Press, 1988), 20.

18. For an explanation of vocal vulnerability and the grain or materiality of the voice that calls forth the maternal voice as a lost object from the presubjective past, see Roland Barthes, "The Grain of the Voice," in *Image-Music-Text,* trans. Stephen Heath (New York: Hill and Wang, 1977), 179–89.

19. Wayne Koestenbaum, *The Queen's Throat* (New York: Poseidon, 1993); Ethan Mordden, *Demented: The World of the Opera Diva* (New York: Franklin Watts, 1984); Michel Poizat, *The Angel's Cry: Beyond the Pleasure Principle in Opera,* trans. Arthur Denner (Ithaca: Cornell University Press, 1992).

20. Sigmund Freud, "Fetishism," in *Sexuality and the Psychology of Love,* ed. Philip Rieff (New York: Collier Books, 1963), 219–24.

21. Stephen Heath, "Lessons from Brecht," *Screen* 15, no. 4 (1970): 107.

22. For a now familiar discussion of the means by which "women" are subsumed and displaced in film narrative, see Laura Mulvey, "Visual Pleasure and the Narrative Cinema." *Screen* 16, no. 3 (1975), repr., *Narrative, Apparatus, Ideology,* ed. Rosen, 198–209.

23. It is fascinating is this regard to watch screen tests and outtakes. Recently, American Movie Classics, the cable channel that claims the rights to a large portion of Twentieth Century–Fox's library, aired a special on the studio's history that featured outtakes from the shelved Dean Martin–Marilyn Monroe comedy *Something's Got to Give.* The perspective that this affords to Monroe's last work and Martin's bemused but rather chivalrous reaction to her obviously disturbed state (reading one simple line, for instance, rendered her helpless) cements the importance of collaborative machinelike cohesion to both producing, and erasing (even to the point of censorship), standard Hollywood films.

24. Slavoj Žižek, "Looking Awry," *October* 5 (1989): 49–62.

25. Octave Mannoni, *Clefs pour l'imaginaire ou l'autre scène* (Paris: Seuil, 1969).

26. In the Broadway play *Art,* a painting that would seem perfectly understandable hanging in MOMA or the Whitney creates consternation and demands much defensive explanation when transferred to a patron's home (or when it becomes the subject of a play).

27. Peter J. McCormick, "Dilthey and Aesthetic Experience," in *Modernity, Aesthetics and the Bounds of Art* (Ithaca: Cornell University Press, 1990), 174–84.

28. Geoffrey Nowell-Smith, "On Kiri Te Kanawa, Judy Garland, and the Culture Industry," in *Modernity and Mass Culture,* ed. James Naremore and Patrick Brantlinger (Bloomington: Indiana University Press, 1991), 71.

29. For a thesis on the reified relation between bourgeois art and politics, see Walter Benjamin, "The Work of Art in the Age of Mechanical Reproduction," in *Illuminations,* ed. Hannah Arent, trans. Harry Zohn (New York: Schocken Books, 1969), 217–51.

30. Georges Bataille, "The Solar Anus," in *Visions of Excess: Selected Writings, 1927–1939,* trans. Allan Stoekel, Carl R. Lovitt, and Donald M. Leslie Jr. (Minneapolis: University of Minnesota Press, 1985), 8.

31. For a discussion regarding being and meaning and the overlap or impossible (Real) space that is neither, see Jacques Lacan, *Séminaire XI,* 141–52.

32. Susan McClary, "The Undoing of Opera: Toward a Feminist Criticism of Music," in Clément, *Opera, or the Undoing of Women,* xiii.

33. For a clear definition of the terms, "element" and "moment"—elements make up the differences with and between objects while moments speak to global conceptual schisms (say, between consciousness and the world)—see Ernesto Laclau and Chantal Mouffe, "Beyond the Positivity of the Social: Antagonisms and Hegemony," in *Hegemony and Socialist Strategy: Towards a Radical Democratic Politics* (New York: Verso, 1985), 93–148.

34. Michel Chion, "Quiet Revolution . . . and Rigid Stagnation," trans. Ben Brewster, *October* 58 (1991): 72.

35. For Lyotard's discussion of the object without value or unrepresentable gap in representation, see Jean-François Lyotard, "Acinema," trans. Paisley Livingston, in *Narrative, Apparatus, Ideology,* ed. Rosen, 350–59.

36. Freud offers a detailed explanation of the split between knowledge and belief that marks our relation to our imminent death[s], that, as in the case of any traumatic element, can only be at once everywhere and nowhere, and that actualizes itself in a wish to return to homeostasis (or to die); see Sigmund Freud, *Beyond the Pleasure Principle,* trans. James Strachey (New York: Norton, 1961), 27–35.

37. Chion, "Quiet Revolution," 73.

38. For an in-depth study of the ways in which disease and death obsessively recur in opera, see Linda Hutcheon and Michael Hutcheon, *Opera: Desire, Disease, Death* (Lincoln: University of Nebraska Press, 1996).

39. Poizat, *The Angel's Cry*, ix.

40. For a description of the tension between language and music in opera that correlates to the masculine and feminine aesthetic properties described here, see also Poizat, "Woman's Cry/ Man's Word," in *The Angel's Cry*, 137–41; Herbert Lindenberger, "Opera as Representation II: Words Against Music, Music Against Words," in *Opera: The Extravagant Art* (Ithaca: Cornell University Press, 1984), 111–15.

41. Andreas Huyssen argues that mass culture has resulted from a consistent modernist process of feminization that privileged males as originary authors (who profess the godlike ability even to deny their own subjectivity: the postmodern project), at the expense of mass culture's value. This thesis is somewhat narrow as it lumps together all mass culture and all masses, thus effacing some fairly radical differences.

In addition, one could maintain very easily that it is a serious mistake to assume homogeneity within cultural forms. There is a wide expanse between Buñuel and Hackford, for example, or between *Battleship Potemkin* and *White Cargo*. Similarly, as Susan McClary and Caryl Flinn have pointed out, it is neither fair nor efficacious to equate, for example, Wagner with Strauss. Still, his argument holds its own if one considers that the more "feminine" elements with a single media may be—following Huyssen's line of logic—classified as kitsch.

Kitsch's meaning, in fact, derives precisely from such judgment calls as it roughly translates from the German as "bad copy." Kitsch acquires its critical currency through commentary on Romanticism: because the Romantics both "copied" and embellished Classicism, and because they attempted to locate classical notions of beauty in finite works, they played with the notion of the masculine transcendental ideal and were thus derided by critics as "feminine."

Andreas Huyssen, "Mass Culture as Woman: Modernism's Other," in *Studies in Entertainment*, ed. Tania Modleski (Bloomington: Indiana University Press, 1986), 189–207; Matei Calinescu, *Five Faces of Modernity: Modernism, Avant-Garde, Decadence, Kitsch, Postmodernism* (Raleigh: Duke University Press, 1987), 225–64; Hermann Broch, "Notes on the Problem of Kitsch," in *Kitsch: The World of Bad Taste*, ed. Gillo Dorfles (New York: Pantheon Books, 1969), 58–67.

42. Sigmund Freud, *The Psychopathology of Everyday Life*, ed. James Strachey, trans. Alan Tyson (New York: Norton, 1960), 256.

43. *Clean and Sober* presents a mixed variation on this theme. Films that focus on a drug user as the protagonist vie with the alcoholic genre for my purposes because the drug abuser is summarily presented as a "lost" social transgressor and therefore as a more interesting figure than the more helpless alcoholic who functions out of weakness. There are rare exceptions to this rule (as in *The Man With the Golden Arm* [1955]) that veer noticeably from this formula, but they are few.

44. For further examples of the cinema's association of the operatic with aberrance and excess (in demeanor, sexuality, situation, and so forth) that it subsequently feminizes with the apparatus, see *Apocalypse Now* (Wagner: *Die Walküre*); *Fitzcarraldo* (Verdi: *Ernani* and Bellini: *I Puritani*); *Welcome to the Dollhouse* and *Days of Heaven* (Saint-Saëns: *The Carnival of the Animals*); *Rear Window* (Flotow: *Martha*); *Man of Flowers* (Donizetti: *Lucia di Lammermoor*); *Copycat, A Clockwork Orange,* and *Unfaithfully Yours* (Rossini: *The Barber of Seville*); *Lorenzo's Oil* and *Prizzi's Honor* (Donizetti: *Elisir d'Amore*); *Kamikaze Hearts, Girl 6, Trainspotting, The Bad News Bears,* and *The Hudsucker Proxy*

(Bizet: *Carmen*); *Humoresque, Reversal of Fortune,* and *Species* (Wagner: *Tristan und Isolde*); *The Mirror Has Two Faces, Five Corners, Carlito's Way, I've Heard the Mermaids Singing,* and *Someone to Watch Over Me* (Delibes: *Lakmé*); and *The Shawshank Redemption* and *Trading Places* (Mozart: *The Marriage of Figaro*).

45. Again, this is predicated upon the Lacanian concept that "woman does not exist, except as symptom of man," from Lacan, *Le Séminaire, livre XX: Encore* (Paris: Éditions du Seuil, 1975), 75–86.

46. For an explanation of the function of the Imaginary Register (in tandem with the Symbolic and the Real), see Jacques Lacan, *The Seminar of Jacques Lacan: Book II. The Ego in Freud's Theory and in the Technique of Psychoanalysis, 1954–1955,* ed. Jacques-Alain Miller, trans. Sylvana Tomaselli (New York: Norton, 1988), 232–60.

47. Maureen Turim, *Flashbacks in Film: Memory and History* (New York: Routledge, 1989), 115.

48. Ibid., 114.

49. Gustave Flaubert, *Salaambo,* trans. J. C. Chartes (New York: Dutton, 1969), 306.

50. Robert Carringer, *The Making of Citizen Kane* (Urbana: University of Illinois Press, 1985), 66.

51. Jean Baudrillard, *For a Critique of the Political Economy of the Sign,* trans. Charles Levin (St. Louis, Mo.: Telos, 1981), 95.

52. Silverman, *Acoustic Mirror,* 68.

53. Roland Barthes, "The Third Meaning," in *Image-Music-Text,* 54.

LUCY FISCHER

Designing Women
Art Deco, the Musical, and the Female Body

✳

Stealing Beauty

We annihilate beauty when we link the artistic creation with practical interests and transform
the spectator into a selfishly interested bystander. The scenic background of the play is not
presented in order that we decide whether we want to spend our next vacation there. The
interior decoration of the rooms is not exhibited as a display for a department store. A good
photoplay must be isolated and complete in itself like a beautiful melody. It is not an
advertisement for the newest fashions. —Hugo Munsterberg[1]

In the quotation above, early film theorist Hugo Munsterberg draws upon
classic aesthetic notions of the separation between the ordinary object and
the artwork. To the extent that the two intermix, the latter is diminished—
reduced and contaminated by the functional and quotidian. Given this view,
we may assume that Munsterberg would not have been delighted by the fate
of the cinema in the 1920s and 1930s. During this era, there was an unprecedented correspondence between the movies and modern design, including
fashion, interior decoration, and architecture. As Donald Albrecht notes:

The adoption of . . . modernism by the popular arts had two notable effects. First, it
successfully promoted the modern style to the general public, making it both more
accessible and more palatable. Even more significantly, it helped create a potent new
iconography. . . . No vehicle provided as effective and widespread an exposure of
[such] imagery as the medium of the movies.[2]

Privileged among the film genres to borrow modernist modes was the
musical, a form that, with its emphasis on spectacle, performance, and
glamour, was well suited to such intertextual flourishes. In particular, the
musical favored one strain of modern design: Art Deco.

One reason for Deco's great influence upon the genre was that, like the
musical, it favored the female form. As Mark Winokur notes, "Hollywood

Deco style . . . allowed a conflation of otherwise aesthetically incompatible . . . elements and motifs in the body of the Art Deco woman."[3] Nowhere is the Art Deco woman more apparent than in the Hollywood musical—a genre known for its female chorus line. While Munsterberg envisioned a cinema that would "be isolated and complete in itself like a beautiful melody," the "Broadway Melodies" that cinema brought us in the 1920s and 1930s were tied to Art Deco and to the commercial world. Primary in this figuration was the Art Deco female—who, in the musical, took the form of a modernist showgirl. If, for Munsterberg, pure art was "like a melody," for the Hollywood musical, a melody was (more crassly) like "a pretty girl."

The Art Deco Aesthetic

> Of all the decorative arts styles, art deco was perhaps the most eclectic, drawing as it did on a wide variety of historical and contemporary sources. —Eva Weber[4]

Before we can examine the role of Art Deco in the Hollywood musical, it is necessary to have a broad understanding of the movement. Art Deco was a popular international trend that flourished between 1910 and 1935 and stressed "classical, symmetrical, [and] rectilinear style."[5] In its ubiquity, Art Deco affected all aspects of design: fashion, crafts, pottery, glassware, jewelry, furniture, statuary, textiles, and architecture. The term itself was not coined until the 1960s (as an abbreviation of the name of the hallmark Exposition Internationale des Arts Decoratifs et Industriels Modernes staged in Paris in 1925): during the 1920s and 1930s, the movement was known as Modernism or the *style moderne*.

In truth, Art Deco was not monolithic, but had many branches and influences. In its insistent modernity, it embraced the imagery of the machine age, both in its use of technological forms (like the gear) and in its overall graphics. As Katherine Morrison McClinton notes, "the backward diagonal lines of the racing car following the direction of its movement" was one of the icons of Art Deco.[6] Not only did Deco adopt mechanical symbols; it utilized new modes of production. Weber remarks: "As an embodiment of the machine age, art deco reflected the recent decades of rapid technological advance and an aesthetic appreciation of mechanical production. Art deco fostered collaboration between the arts and industry, and relied as well on the mass production of its designs" (11). Streamlined and geometric patterns, traits associated with the industrial age, were complemented by such synthetic materials as chrome, stainless steel, aluminum, and glass. The broad aesthetic goal of this style, then, was an attempt to combine elegance and fine craftsmanship with technology, merging artisanship with mass production.

In its emphasis on the industrial, Art Deco firmly reacted against its major artistic predecessor, Art Nouveau, which was known for Romanticism, sentimentality, fantasy, asymmetry, and biomorphism. For critics such as Albrecht, Deco's simplified form was also a new generation's response to other aspects of Victorian culture, in particular the "clutter and fussiness of their parents' interiors."[7] Like Modernism itself, Art Deco was tied to the city; hence it was often deemed the "skyscraper style." Deco's links to urban sophistication derived from its popular use for office towers, nightclubs, hotels, restaurants, and apartment buildings, as well as for prestigious architectural sites such as Radio City Music Hall and the Chrysler Building in New York City. In its bonds to modernity, Art Deco echoed various avant-garde movements. From constructivism and futurism, it inherited its love of the machine; from cubism, its passion for simplified geometric forms; from German Expressionism, its penchant for distortion; and from Sergei Diaghilev's Ballets Russes (which opened in Paris in 1909), its theatrics. A lingering debt to Art Nouveau is clear in sinuous lines, whiplash curves, botanical forms, and Deco's fondness for the image of woman. According to McClinton, modernist pioneers Charles Rennie Mackintosh, Josef Hoffmann, Louis Sullivan, and Frank Lloyd Wright all drew on the "austere side of Art Nouveau" for their development of an early Deco aesthetic.[8]

Other influences venture outside the modern or the technological. Despite its resolute modernity, Art Deco drew on traditional, even ancient, forms. Specifically, it was known for a fascination with the "Primitive," which it rendered through borrowing tropes from Africa, Egypt, Mexico, and the American Southwest. From Egypt (where King Tutankhamen's tomb had been discovered in 1922), Deco embraced Pharaonic imagery (such as sphinx heads, scarabs, and cats). From the broader Middle East, it recycled the Assyrian/Babylonian ziggurat form: a pyramidal, terraced temple tower, with each successive story smaller than the one before. From pre-Columbian Mexico, it drew upon the sunray image, and from Africa the stylized mask and wild-animal imagery.[9] From native America, it embraced geometric patterns used in traditional pottery, jewelry, and basketry. Beyond its attachment to the Primitive, Art Deco invoked the contemporary "Exotic." Thus, certain works belied an attraction to modern African-American forms, especially to jazz. Other Deco works revealed an interest in things Oriental, be they Chinese, Japanese, or Arab. For Winokur, Deco's focus on the Exotic/Primitive "styliz[ed] the accoutrement of ethnicity," while "maintain[ing] a safe distance" from them. It "aestheticized colonialism" and it brought "a tourist's view of the world back to this country."[10]

Finally, Art Deco was also palatable to the general public. As Winokur observes: "Deco was accessible . . . in a way the various other modernisms were not. In fact, the value of Art Deco for its consumers resided in its ability to be avant-garde while circumventing completely the difficult-to-watch wrenchings of reality that were intrinsic to expressionism, surrealism, or cubism" (199). Its consumer orientation, precisely the kind that Munsterberg decried, allowed the Art Deco style to impose itself on all aspects of American culture: clothes, jewelry, interior decoration, architecture, graphics, housewares, and appliances (irons, toasters, radios, lamps, tableware, clocks, and so forth). As Winokur observes, "Art Deco romanticized and then sold soap, tires, and train tickets" (198). Artifacts at the high end were available at Tiffany's but knockoffs at the low end were readily accessible at Woolworth's.

Significantly, among the consumer goods sold to Americans in the Art Deco style were some associated with music. A 1929 advertisement for Steinway and Sons (in *House & Garden* magazine) depicts a modern piano behind which is hung an abstract painting by Sergei Soudeikine entitited "Le Sacre du Printemps."[11] The ad mentions the controversy around Igor Stravinsky's famous ballet of the same name, noting that "its influence upon contemporary music has been widespread and profound." Clearly, the ad wishes to associate the Steinway piano with modern art. On another page of the same issue, a black lacquer Baldwin piano is depicted.[12] The ad copy (rendered in Deco type font) boasts that it is "used in over 200 Radio Stations in the U.S." Here, the phrasing implies that this traditional instrument is also the height of modernity.

The Art Deco Woman

Th[e] Deco shape—a compression and elongation of the Victorian woman's body—would remain a representational norm for at least the next three decades. —Mark Winokur[13]

According to McClinton, Art Deco can be divided into two broad trends, tendencies that we might imagine in terms of traditional notions of gender. On the one hand, there was the "masculine" geometric pole in which "curves gave way to angularity and motifs of design tended to be more dynamic."[14] On the other hand, there was the "feminine" curvilinear mode that favored such sentimental imagery as "rose[s], . . . garlands and baskets of flowers, fountains and jets of water, doves, female deer and nudes" (10). It is from the latter vein that Art Deco's formulation of the female derives. Her representation has its roots in the ethereal woman of Art Nouveau, but in Deco she became more emphatically modern. As

Weber observes, here "even the idealized human figures were often abstracted to such a degree that they resembled human machines or robots."[15] As an instance of this tension between romantic and automaton women, one recalls Fritz Lang's Deco extravaganza *Metropolis* (1926), with its dichotomy between the real and replicant Maria.

The female figure appears in countless Deco objects, from the translucent glass works by French designer René Lalique—with their sculpted maidens or etched nymphs—to the bronze or glass bases for Deco lamps, candy dishes, and candlesticks, which were often shaped to the female form. The tops of glass powder boxes often sported knobs contoured like female bodies or heads. But it was decorative sculpture, items typically sold at jewelry stores, that was most associated with the female figure: "Small sculpture figures were in demand as a decorative accessory in the house of the 1890s and they continued to be used into the twentieth century. They were set on mantelpieces, on library shelves, on marble-topped girandoles or wall brackets."[16] Especially interesting were those made with chryselephantine. Such objects (produced largely in Paris and Berlin)[17] were fashioned from ivory (generally obtained from the Belgian Congo), in combination with materials like bronze, onyx, marble, or wood.[18] They came into vogue as early as 1900 when they were exhibited at the International Exhibition in Paris and at the Royal Academy in London. In their fabrication, they unified techniques of hand carving and mass production.[19]

According to Arwas, chryselephantine sculptures fell into four categories: hieratic, naturalistic, erotic, and stylized (7). "Hieratic" creations were "often mysterious queens of the night, dancers wrapped in the metallic folds of rare and costly fabrics and encrusted with jewels at wrist and ankle, their movements frozen into strange theatrical attitudes." In these works, the primary influence was Diaghilev's Ballets Russes, which was stranded in Paris as a result of World War I and the Russian Revolution. As Arwas notes: "Organised by Diaghilev to show off the most original Russian dancers, choreographers, composers and designers, their impact on art and decoration was enormous." The second major source for Art Deco sculptures was the silent cinema: its costumes, dress, hairstyles, and theatrical mannerisms (7). The "naturalistic" statuettes portrayed female athletes, classical or modern nudes, and dancers. The "erotic" category was characterized by a sinister sense of perversity. Arwas speaks of: "kinky, highly sophisticated women dressed in leather trouser suits, insolently smoking cigarettes; swirling-skirted girls fighting the wine; girls in slips or gartered stockings holding whips; dancers doing a high kick; and haughty girls naked beneath their parted fur coats. They are the dream mistresses of sado-masochistic Berlin between the wars" (9). The "stylized" strain of sculpture was more abstract in form, reflecting the influence of Cubism, Bauhaus, and the Arts and Crafts movement. As Arwas comments, "features are simplified . . . and the treatment of clothing is increasingly geometric and decorative, without any attempt at realism" (9).

Clearly, it was not only the statuettes that had a modern feel (with their polished onyx or marbles bases done in ziggurat style) but also the look of the women represented in them. As Arwas remarks, these works generally depicted "the new woman, slender and boyish in shape, hair bobbed . . . , dressed in fashionably floppy pyjamas or as an Amazon" (8). McClinton, who provides more detail about these sculptures, catalogues:

cocottes [*sic*] with bobbed hair, dressed in trousers, long fitted jackets, cloche hats or hair in banderole and wearing exotic jewelry. An amusing bronze and ivory gamine, with high heels and clinging trousers, shirt neckerchief and peaked cap, poses with her hands in her pockets and smokes a cigarette. Dancing girls in tunic or bikini and turbans balance on one leg with outstretched arms. Others wear long-waisted dresses with bateau or V neckline, full circular skirts longer in the back and trimmed with several rows of ruffles, bowknots or ostrich feathers. All these figures stand on marble bases, circular, square, triangular or stepped.[20]

Winokur sees the modernity of the Art Deco female body as tied to earlier changes in corset and dress fashion spearheaded by the Parisian couturier, Paul Poiret. Poiret converted the corset "from the S-shaping vehicle it had been to one that flattened the hips and buttocks, liberating the waist. Then he redesigned dresses in empire style, further constraining women within a tubular construction" (197). The effect was to "shear" the figure of woman "away from previously accreted meanings—mother, womanhood, domestic angel, and so on" (198). On the one hand, the New Woman signified liberation; on the other, her slim, androgynous contour bore traces of radical constraint. As Winokur comments, Art Deco's female figure was a vision of woman "as apparently free but literally hobbled to prevent any menace" (196).

The abstracted female body was also one well suited to consumerist manipulation. As Winokur notes:

the Poiret-inspired woman's body was compressed—"streamlined"—in order to sell things, reduced to zero in order to allow it to mean only what it sold. Breasts, for example, were reined in so that the feminine would not also mean the maternal. Streamlining the body, reducing its complexity, the absolute numbers of planes it contains, provided an analogy to the things sold: cars, trains, planes, etcetera. (199)

While the Art Deco Woman sold products, her sculpture was a product in and of itself. While, in the fin de siècle period, such artifacts constituted expensive acquisitions, by the 1920s they were manufactured for the middle class, who purchased them as tasteful home furnishings or coveted gifts.[21]

Art Deco And The Musical

Some [chryselephantine statuettes] are right out of the Ballets Russes,
others from a smoky Parisian nightclub. —Victor Arwas[22]

In fundamental ways, Art Deco was a design movement tied to the cinema. First, some of the primary architectural sites for its application were those of movie theaters: picture palaces such as the Pantages in Los Angeles, the Paramount in Oakland, California, and Radio City Music Hall in New York City. Second, the logos of certain studios (Twentieth Century–Fox, Universal, RKO)[23] were realized in Deco print fonts, and myriad movie posters, advertisements, and lobby cards were rendered in modernist graphic style. Third, the film screen itself became a "display window" for Art Deco products: furniture, sculpture, lamps, glassware, and clothing. One need only examine the sets and costumes for such dramatic films as *The Single Standard* (1929) or *The Kiss* (1929)—both attributed to Cedric Gibbons (1893–1960)—to see how Deco permeated cinematic mise-en-scène.

But perhaps the most intriguing genre to examine here is the film musical, whose centrality to Art Deco springs from many factors. First, the musical (with its chorus line) had always depended upon the female figure, a fixation of Art Deco iconography. Second, many of the fashions of the Deco era, were first inspired by dance, a crucial element of the musical genre. Primary here was the impact of Leon Bakst's costumes for the Ballets Russes. Third, as we have seen, one of the favored subjects for decorative sculpture was that of the female dancer. Consider the titles of the following works: "The High Kick," "Genre Dancer," "Egyptian Dancer," "Russian Dancer," "Pirouette," "Dancer" (all by Demetre Chiparus).[24] The fact that so many of Chiparus's sculptures focused on choreography is no surprise, given that, according to Alberto Shayo: "Paris in the 1920s was inebriated with dance, in any and every form."[26] Beyond the Ballets Russes, there was a plethora of music hall venues, including the Folies Bergères, the Cigale, the Moulin Rouge, the Olympia, the Alcazar, and the Alhambra (30). Some chryselephantine sculpture even represented particular dancers of the period. Chiparus's "Russian Dancers" depicts Nijinsky in Diaghilev's "Scheherazade" (148); "The Dolly Sisters" portrays a vaudeville team by that name (167). Fourth, musical imagery (independent of dance) was a common motif in Art Deco design. One mural of the period sports a banjo, wood pipe, and saxophone.[26] A chryselephantine figure called "The Snake Charmer" shows a woman playing a horn.[27] A French glass sculpture depicts Pierrot strumming a banjo.[28] Finally, the abstract, spectacular sets of the musical film (often liberated from the constraints of realistic decor) presented a mise-en-scène with maximum potential for the extravagant Art Deco aesthetic.

Designer Deco

Almost every set and costume [in *Swing Time*] fairly shouts "Art Deco." —Ellen Spiegel[29]

While Art Deco dominated the musical in many ways, its most obvious influence was on set and costume design. Privileged in this regard were a film's production numbers—those moments when the conventional drama ceased and the narrative erupted into music and dance. Of all the Hollywood Deco designers of the 1930s, one of the most renowned was Van Nest Polglase (1898–1968), who worked at RKO from 1932 to 1942 and supervised the famous cycle of Fred Astaire/Ginger Rogers musicals. While all of Polglase's sets were inspired by Art Deco rhetoric, his mise-en-scène for the dance scenes is most spectacular. Typical of these is the number in *Swing Time* (1936) when Astaire sings "Never Gonna Dance," then seduces Rogers into an extended ballroom routine (see figure 1). As in most of their movies, the number is "integrated" into the film's narrative. Rather than occur on a formal stage, it takes place in a "diegetic" locale— here, a nightclub where the couple is spending an evening.

Many aspects of the sequence are striking in relation to Deco themes. First of all, its cabaret site is one of luxury, glamour, and romance. Clearly, this reflects notions of Deco as "cutting edge" modern, a style associated with the upper classes. As Woolworth's stocked inexpensive versions of precious Art Deco lamps, jewelry, and sculpture, so the movies sold elite style to the general public. Furthermore, the look of the nightclub reflects Art Deco simplicity. The space is geometrically organized and composed primarily of stark black and white. The prominent meandering flight of stairs not only provides an engaging space for dance, but echoes Deco's interest in ziggurat and curvilinear structures. As Spiegel notes, in *Swing Time:* "Round tables meet long vertical wall panels, curving double staircases have sharp-cornered steps, sinuous moldings end in angular corners, and straight lines, whether on walls, dresses, or furniture, clash with unexpected semicircles."[30] While columnlike supports give the set an exotic or primitive feel, the high-tech materials used in its construction (glass or Bakelite floors, chrome accents) stress modernity. Polglase's "Big White Set" became a "fixed architectural institution" that "appear[ed] in one form or another in nearly every Astaire-Rogers film."[31] Finally, the costumes in the number are streamlined and elegant. While Astaire is dressed in a trim,

Figure 1. Fred Astaire and Ginger Rogers in *Swing Time* (1936). Photo courtesy The Museum of Modern Art/ Film Stills Archive.

black tuxedo, Rogers wears a soft, white form-fitting gown—like one in a chryselephantine sculpture by Philippe entitled "The Swirling Dress."[32] Clearly, the actors' attire serves not only to render them chic, but to display their dynamic, choreographed bodies.

While such production numbers (based on the couple) propose an equality of male and female dancers, they reveal a hierarchal relation that is consonant with Art Deco's sexual politics. As Sally Peters notes: "In this landscape, the female body is a prize actively sought by the male, who uses his power, his finesse, and especially his body as lure."[33]

Also important is the music that accompanies the Astaire/Rogers number; it belies a modernist sensibility. The song "Never Gonna Dance" is backed by a syncopated beat and draws upon the discourses of jazz and blues. These musical roots are echoed in the song's lyrics: "Have I a heart, that acts like a heart, or is it a crazy drum—beating the weird tattoos, of the St. Louis Blues?" When Astaire and Rogers begin to dance, the music recaps "The Way You Look Tonight," a romantic ballad with an entirely different feel. Finally, the couple perform a waltz to the strains of a Strauss-like composition. Clearly, the score for this number evinces a sense of pastiche—like a Braque or Picasso collage.

Deco "Primitive"

> He remembered the African fetishes he had seen at Halliday's so often. There came
> back to him one, a statuette about two feet high, a tall, slim, elegant figure, from West
> Africa, in dark wood, glossy and suave. It was a woman, with hair dressed high, like a
> melon-shaped dome. He remembered her vividly; she was one of his soul's intimates.
> Her body was long and elegant, her face was crushed tiny like a beetle's, she had rows
> of round heavy collars, like a column of quoits, on her neck.
> He remembered her: her astonishing cultured elegance, her diminished, beetle face,
> the astounding long elegant body, on short, ugly legs, with such protuberant
> buttocks, so weighty and unexpected below her slim long loins. She knew what he
> himself did not know. She had thousands of years of purely sensual, purely unspiritual
> knowledge behind her. —D. H. Lawrence, *Women in Love*

In the quotation above, D. H. Lawrence recounts the thoughts of a character in *Women in Love,* one of the great modernist literary texts of the 1920s. Clearly, in Rupert Birkin's fascination with an African sculpture, we see the modern era's attraction to allegedly "Primitive" motifs—a trend apparent in Art Deco. On the one hand, Birkin's thoughts belie a racist/colonialist sense of the African as "primitive" (as nearer to beetle than human). But, on the other, his musings bespeak an essentialist awe for the African as closer to nature—a force (Lawrence felt) Western, industrialized society had lost or perverted.

In the art of the Deco era, African sources were numerous. This is not surprising given that important exhibitions of African art (such as the Paris Exposition Coloniale of 1931) were launched in Europe during the 1920s and 1930s.[34] In cataloguing such African influences, one thinks of the work of black, San Francisco artist, Sargent Johnson, who fashioned ceramic and metal sculpture as well as mural bas-relief. Among his terra-cotta busts is one from 1933 entitled "Negro Woman" which shows the traces of African masks. As Weber notes:

With these heads, which he also made in copper, Sargent Johnson drew on African primitive art as an appropriate antecedent to express the growing pride of Afro-Americans in their ethnic origins. Such primitivist models also became an important source of inspiration for other painters and sculptors of the Harlem Renaissance, among them Aaron Douglas, Charles Alston, Archibald Motley, Richmond Barthe and Augusta Savage. Johnson's heads were elegantly idealized; they depicted not individuals but noble types representative of the dignity and rich heritage of the black race.[35]

Also central to Deco discourse was the celebration of African American tropes. As McClinton notes, "In the 1920s everything Negro came into fashion—jazz music and dances including the black bottom, the charleston and the turkey trot."[36] For this reason, many works of chryselephantine sculpture "reflect the interest in . . . nightclubs and dance crazes of the new Jazz Age."[37] Similarly, certain porcelain figures of the period depicted jazz musicians engaged in playing their instruments.[38] In the film musical, this attachment to an African American aesthetic was expressed in the genre's employment of black performers and appropriation of jazz music. Here, one thinks of the tap routines of Bill Robinson (in such films as *Dixiana* [1930], *Harlem Is Heaven* [1932], *The Little Colonel* [1935], *The Littlest Rebel* [1935]), but also of Astaire's blackface minstrel homage to "Bojangles" in a number from *Swing Time.*

But it is no accident that, in the passage from *Women in Love,* Birkin recalls a statuette of an African *woman* (or that Sargent privileges the female face for his mask). As was typical of Modernism, woman's body is a highly charged site. Within the canon of the musical, the actress who most captured society's passion for things "African" was the American performer Josephine Baker (1906–75). Raised in Missouri and initiating her theatrical career in Harlem, she rose to fame in Paris as a dancer in the French music hall. As Sylvie Raulet notes: "In 1925, Josephine Baker, in the Revue Nègre drew fashionable Paris to the Théâtre des Champs-Elysées, where she fascinated the audience with her jerky rhythms and revived the success of the Ballets Russes."[39] Baker later starred in several French films, among them *Princess Tam Tam* (1935), directed by Victor Greville. In this movie, she plays Alwina, an African woman who is discovered in Tunisia by a French aristocrat. He polishes her charm and brings her back to Paris, where he introduces her to high society as a princess. In one scene, Tam Tam goes to a nightclub, where a stage show is in progress.

The first part of the performance features a host of showgirls who dance to conventional popular music. At first, they revolve around a stage, displaying their costumes, in a manner reminiscent of the routines of Florenz Ziegfeld. Then the women (now in quasi-cubistic outfits, with spiral-framed arms that resemble "slinkies") execute a soft shoe. Following this sequence (which also features Busby Berkeley–esque overhead shots), we move to a scene of Chinese acrobats balancing swirling plates on poles, accompanied by imitation Chinese music. Finally a bare-chested black man loudly beats upon a drum with his hands.

As Tam Tam sits in the audience, sipping a drink, she listens to the percussive sounds. Soon, the alcohol and music affect her and she begins to move, succumbing to the number's tempo. A woman in the audience dares and taunts her, asking: "How can you resist that music? . . . Dance, come on, dance!" Tam Tam then leaps on stage and begins to gyrate—tossing off her shoes and stripping down her clothes until she is almost in "native" dress. While the music, costume, and decor of the routine have a Latin feel (and we see gauchos and close-ups of the band playing maracas), the camera privileges the black drummer, lending the sequence an African aura. To make the segment's polymorphous nationality more chaotic, a turbaned Indian man watches from the sidelines and another periodically chimes a gong on stage. While the number's ethnicity is wildly diverse, it is unified by Oriental and Primitive themes. The routine comes to a crescendo with Tam Tam dancing at a feverish pace—shimmying frantically, rubbing her belly, and jumping up and down with legs spread apart. The sequence's assertive montage and use of extreme (almost blurred) close-ups of her face also afford it an almost experimental style. Throughout the performance, we cut to reaction shots of the white (primarily male) European audience, simultaneously horrified and intrigued by Tam Tam's primal, erotic dance (alternately staring at the stage and, protectively, shading their eyes).[40]

Deco Decadence

> The importance of the cinema in art was it gave designers and decorators a chance to let themselves go, untrammeled by the limitations imposed by bourgeois purses and bourgeois domestic tasks. In them we see Art Deco in its fully-realized form.
> —Bevis Hiller[41]

Both *Swing Time* and *Princess Tam Tam* follow the form of the "integrated" musical, with dance numbers realistically sutured into the narrative, but the musicals associated with Busby Berkeley propose a different model. The dramas in which they transpire would lead us to believe that the routines we witness are performed on a conventional stage, and yet the numbers themselves create such an "impossible geography" that they can only exist within the cinematic universe. Hence, Berkeley's numbers resonate with extreme abstraction and mark a complete break with the dramatic line. It is precisely this quality that lends them such interest. Liberated from narrative logic, Berkeley's production numbers become autonomous designs, which can be interpreted not only for their symbolic discourse on the figure of woman (one that encapsulates myriad cultural clichés of femininity),[42] but also for their articulation of the codes of Art Deco—a major factor in Berkeley's work. The unearthly space in which Berkeley's numbers evolve allows him to "let go" his Art Deco imagination, "untrammeled" by the restrictions of narrative coherence.

Curiously, however, the music that accompanies his numbers is highly traditional and at odds with the modernist look of his costuming and set design. "The Shadow Waltz" (from *Gold Diggers of 1933*, with songs by Al Dubin and Harry Warren) proceeds in conventional three-quarter time and is sung by a choir of angelic female voices. A similar waltz rhythm and vocalization informs "The Words Are in My Heart" from *Gold Diggers of 1935* (also written by Dubin and Warren). Finally, "By a Waterfall" (from *Footlight Parade* [1933]) reminds one of a Jeanette MacDonald/Nelson Eddy operatic piece, with its refrain: "By a waterfall, I'm calling you-oo-oo-oo."[43] Likewise, the sensibility of the "framing stories" with which Berkeley's musical routines begin is often quasi-Victorian.

But the production numbers are something else and bear the stamp of an Art Deco aesthetic. First, one must consider the mise-en-scène, often an abstract version of the Big White Set. In "The Shadow Waltz" (designed by Anton Grot), showgirls appear on a white, curvilinear structure, which is placed upon a jet black floor (probably of glass or Bakelite). Similarly, in "The Words Are in My Heart" (another Grot extravagaza), women play streamlined white pianos that stand upon an onyx floor. Tiered steps (that spread out like fan blades) lead to a huge, geometrically decorated window in the background. In "Dames" (from the 1934 movie of the same title, designed by Robert Haas and Willy Pogany), showgirls sit at Deco-style vanities or soak in tubs adorned with neon-trimmed mirrors. In "By a Waterfall," bathers swim in a pool that is located within an ornate Deco architectural space, again conceived by Grot. At the end of the number, they form a pyramid—a shape that draws upon the "frozen fountain motif" so popular in Deco ornamentation. This iconography was found in several sites at the 1925 Paris exposition: atop the Porte d'Honneur and in Lalique's crystal fountain.[44] For this reason, Richard Striner deems it "a worldwide symbol" of the *style moderne*.[45] It was then reproduced in numerous consumer items or objets d'art of the period (including a diamond tiara by Mauboussin).[46]

Other moments of "By a Waterfall" invoke Art Deco graphics. In one shot, two bathers are shown in mirror-image profile, posed in close-up in the foreground, at opposite ends of a black and white arch. The composition is insistently pictorial and reminiscent of Art Deco layouts. Contributing to its graphic force is Berkeley's use of a void black background that throws the foreground into sharp relief. At another moment, when the camera reveals bathers swimming underwater, the imagery sparks associations to Deco female figures sculpted or etched in glass. Here one thinks of works such as Lalique's "Suzanne" (1932), an opalescent molded figurine,[47] or of Vicke Lindstrand's vase for Orrefors (1937), etched with a nude female torso.[48]

Beyond their look, Berkeley's sets function as elaborate stage machines, evoking Deco's industrial imperative. At the end of "By a Waterfall," the bathers are posed on a complex four-tiered rotating fountain (see figure 2). In "The Words Are in My Heart," pianos turn on a rack of tiered steps. And, in "Dames," the dancers are transported on a moving set that resembles a Möbius strip. Berkeley also emphasizes the camera as high-tech tool. In "The Words Are in My Heart," it travels under the floor; in "By a Waterfall," it goes below the water; in "Dames" it twirls through a mirrored chamber.

Costumes also extend Berkeley's Deco vision. "The Shadow Waltz" begins with a framing story in which Ruby Keeler appears wearing a flouncy, form-fitting white dress decorated with an abstract sequined motif. When the production number begins, myriad women appear wearing geometric, modern-day versions of the "hoop skirt" that create complex spirals as they move (see figure 3). Significantly, Phillipe Devriez's bronze figure "Dancer" depicts a woman with almost the same attire.[49]

One of the major tropes for which Berkeley is known is the high-angle shot (from the studio ceiling) of chorus girls below, arranged so that their bodies create a design. Such moments occur in "By a Waterfall" when the bathers form concentric rotating circles or join shoulders to create a snake-like line. A similar sequence takes place in "The Shadow Waltz" when a high-angle shot of individual dancers holding illuminated violins reveals a larger, overall violin pattern. Perhaps Berkeley's signature compositions are those that transpire in "Dames" or "By a Waterfall." Here, an aerial shot displays a starlike or circular pattern of women below whose choreographed movements shift to create a kaleidoscopic effect. Clearly, these images might be read to dehumanize women, to make of them "biotic tile[s] in an abstract mosaic."[50] But it is also true that the geometric forms they assume relate to the lexicon of Art Deco. Significantly, when (in "Dames") the bodies of showgirls "morph" into a black and white animated pattern, the arrangement they form mimics the border of their towels.

But there are other issues at play in Berkeley's numbers that relate to Art Deco iconography. First, there is simply the obsessive presence of women in his numbers, far beyond the requirements of the musical chorus line.

Figure 2. "By a Waterfall" from *Footlight Parade* (1933). Photo courtesy The Museum of Modern Art/ Film Stills Archive.

Rarely, in fact do we see men, except during the framing stories (for example, Dick Powell in the introductions to "Dames," "The Words Are in My Heart," "The Shadow Waltz," or "By a Waterfall") or during a topical piece like "My Forgotten Man" (from *Gold Diggers of 1933*), which concerns World War I veterans. More typical are numbers like "The Words Are In My Heart," in which hordes of women play pianos, or "By a Waterfall," in which bevies of bathers frolic in a pool. On one level, Berkeley's feminine fixation can be read in terms of the director's penchant for voyeurism and

Figure 3. "Shadow Waltz" from *Gold Diggers of 1933*. Photo courtesy The Museum of Modern Art/ Film Stills Archive.

fetishism; on another level, it reflects the hyperbolic visibility of the female in Art Deco rhetoric.

Most particularly, it is in the Berkeley production numbers that we feel the incarnation of Deco sculpture (which, as we recall, focused on the figure of the female dancer). There is a bronze piece by Chiparus entitled "The Girls" in which the women look precisely like a musical chorus line.[51] Yet another of his works portrays a woman with top hat and cane.[52] By the time of the Berkeley production numbers, however, the lines of influence are somewhat reversed. While initially it was the stage and screen that inspired the sculpture, by now it is the sculpture that inspires the screen. Thus, when, in "The Words are in My Heart," the showgirls grab the edges of their dresses and spread their accordion folds, we are reminded of the prevalence of outstretched fabric in such pieces as Chiparus's "The Sunburst Dress," "The High Kick," "Egyptian Dancer," "Pirouette," or "The Long Skirt."[53]

Alternately, the semi-nude swimmers of "By a Waterfall" are reminiscent of the "naturalistic" strain of Deco statuary that often portrayed female athletes. For example, I own a small bronze Deco ashtray that incorporates the figure of a woman in a diving pose (precisely like some shots from the Berkeley number). Furthermore, the metallic look of the bathers' caps and hair in "By a Waterfall," invokes a sense of sculptural material. In the moments when the swimmers appear in a nymphlike mode, they also resemble the mythic strain of Deco statuary, which favored maritime characters, such as the Lorelei. Here one thinks of Waylande Gregory's white glazed figurine "Persephone,"[54] of Lalique's "Sirène," or of Armand Martial's bronze statue "Leda and the Swan." Finally, when in the production number "We're in the Money" (from *Gold Diggers of 1933*) a row of showgirls who line up behind Ginger Rogers makes her appear to have multiple arms, we are reminded of the exotic theme in Deco as apparent in such sculptures as "Odeon Dancer," "Dancer with Fan Headdress," "Dancer with Turban," or "Fan Dancer."[55]

Aside from statuary, lamps were important Deco objects that employed the female form. Most noteworthy were the Frankart boudoir pieces produced in the late 1920s: "small table fixture[s] created by Arthur von Frankenberg, [which] used nudes to hold up illuminated cylinders or globes."[56] As Richard Striner notes: "Through such fixtures the spirit of the 1925 Paris exposition was diffused to the point of pervasiveness in the years between the world wars. Here was exotica—or perhaps just a dose of escapist whimsy—for everyman and everywoman."[57] Similar to these lamps were those in which a metal figure was placed before a sheet of glass, behind which was concealed a bulb. When the lamp was lit, the female figure was illuminated in silhouette, emphasizing her corporeal outline. Finally, as McClinton observes: "One of the most interesting lighting developments of the Art Deco period was the illuminated plaque or figure. These popular decorative lighting pieces may have first been introduced by Lalique to display his glass to the best effect. Whatever prompted their making, the idea caught on, and illuminated plaques and glass figures with concealed light globes were made by all manufacturers of decorative glass."[58]

Various types of Deco lamps are echoed in Berkeley production numbers. In "The Shadow Waltz" (whose very title suggests illumination), dancers carry neon-lighted violins (with trailing cords) that make the women seem virtually "plugged in." When, in "By a Waterfall," the set lights are dimmed and the pool water lighted, the bathers alternately appear in dramatic black silhouette against a background of white or seem illuminated themselves. Finally, in the "Pettin' in the Park" routine from *Gold Diggers of 1933*, women undress behind backlit screens and their suggestive contours are projected on the surface. As Weber notes, Deco style was profoundly influenced by theatrical lighting, a source evident "in the exterior night illumination of skyscrapers and other art deco buildings, as well as in the innovative and spectacular use of neon and fluorescent light at the Chicago and New York's world's fairs of the 1930s."[59]

Yet another important Art Deco icon is recycled in Berkeley's production numbers. Frequently, popular Deco objects of the period contained the image of women holding or throwing balls or, perhaps, tossing giant bubbles. This image appears on a set of Anchor Hocking glassware of the era, as well as in such sculptures as Godard's "The Bubble Dancer" or F. Preiss's "Balancing" and "The Beach Ball."[60] Sometimes the globe the female figure carries is designated as the moon, as in "Aurore Onu" a French bronze and alabaster piece from 1925.[61] This kitsch imagery appears in several Berkeley production numbers. In "Pettin' in the Park," we find a group of women outdoors in wintertime. As snow falls, they are seen with giant white globes (presumably huge snowballs) that they proceed to hold above their heads. In a high-angle shot, Berkeley transforms the group into an abstract pattern of black and white. In "Dames," the showgirls carry large black balls as they "fly" up to the ceiling-mounted camera.

What is interesting about Berkeley's contribution to the Art Deco musical is his use of instrumental iconography within the decor of the number itself. Such imagery was prevalent in Deco movie theater design. In the Oakland (California) Paramount, for example (built in 1931), there are images of accordions, tambourines, banjos, and clarinets etched into the glass panels of entry doors. And on the walls of the Women's Smoking Room is a mural of a female Muse holding a lyre. Elsewhere in the theater corridors are bas-reliefs of Artemis blowing a horn. Clearly, in Berkeley's use of neon violins in "The Shadow Waltz" and rotating pianos in "The Words Are in My Heart," we find the impulse to take traditional musical iconography and update it with a high-tech modernist flourish.

Conclusion: "A Tableau of Jewels"

Film fashions were . . . inextricably tied to the bodies of women and to the representation of the female form. —Jeanne Thomas Allen[62]

In recent years, it has become a commonplace to discuss the relation between fashion and film. Thus, scholars like Charles Eckert, Jane Gaines, and Charlotte Herzog have written essays about the history of couture as realized through the movies.[63] For obvious reasons, this discourse has focused on the figure of woman. When it comes to the 1930s musical, however, the connections between style and cinema become more radical and intriguing. Most films may stimulate scholars to examine the clothing or accessories worn by screen actresses (as barometers of contemporary vogue), but in the case of the 1930s film musical, it is a style of woman herself that is at issue. Specifically, the genre's figuration of the female bespeaks an Art Deco rhetoric: it is from there that her vision derives. In truth, however, the dynamic is multivalent: the iconography of Art Deco itself incorporated elements of theater, ballet, and film. Thus, the trajectory of influence moves in two directions simultaneously. By the time of the 1930s musical, the screen world was saturated with artifacts of the *style moderne.* Within this context, the live bodies of women became substances of another order—ones reminiscent of Art Deco sculpture and objets d'art. In a sense, the directors of 1930s musicals were cinematic Pygmalions, animating Deco's frozen visions of the female form rather like the ancient Greek king of Cyprus who fell in love with a female statue, then begged Aphrodite to bring her to life.

Beyond the examples already cited, one other warrants consideration: a number from *The Hollywood Review of 1929,* an early musical based upon the vaudeville format. Devoid of any narrative, the film presents a pastiche of variety acts introduced by Jack Benny; these routines range from comic skits to songs, and from dramatic readings to dance numbers. Among them is the "Tableau of Jewels," a musical piece with sets attributed to Cedric Gibbons and Richard Day and costumes credited to Erté. As the curtain opens, we see a two-tiered structure composed of white sinuous lines that recall wrought-iron, a popular Deco material. As the set rotates against a black background, we view women in diverse white costumes, statically posed, each contained in a kind of niche (a popular Deco architectural detail). All look like delicate chryselephantine sculptures, especially those of the exotic genre. One woman, for example, sports Turkish harem pants and an Arab headdress. Unlike Berkeley's chorines, they do not move. Neither do they parade down stairs like the famous Ziegfeld Girls. Instead, they are displayed, like stationary figurines upon a shelf.

With a similar gesture, the silent film *Our Dancing Daughters* (1929) opens with the image of a decorative bronze statue of a woman doing the Charleston. It then cuts to a pair of evening slippers on the floor that (through a dissolve) become "filled" by a woman's feet. It next shifts to an image of a woman's legs dancing in front of a three-paneled mirror, then dissolves to a full shot of the same subject. The next image presents an extreme long shot of the woman (played by Joan Crawford) in her bedroom, which is a lush Deco interior. A few shots later, the woman stands before glass shelves built into a window; these are replete with Art Deco bric-a-brac and statuary. On the top tier, in a prominent position, is one of a female figure in a dance pose. This opening sequence (of a movie that proved to be an anthem of the New Woman in the Jazz Age) traces the precise progression we have delineated in this essay: from Deco decor to film set, from sculptured statuary to screen star, from modernist mode to movie musical.

While Hugo Munsterberg decried the kind of photoplay that would function as "an advertisement for the newest fashion," he did not anticipate the rise of a new fashion that would serve as a prototype for the screen world.

Notes

My thanks to Jessica Nassau for research assistance on this project.

1. Hugo Munsterberg, "From The Film: A Psychological Study," in *Film Theory and Criticism: Introductory Readings,* 4th ed., ed. Gerald Mast, Marshall Cohen, and Leo Braudy (New York: Oxford University Press, 1992), 355–361. The citation is from p. 361.
2. Donald Albrecht, *Designing Dreams: Modern Architecture in the Movies* (New York: Harper and Row, 1986), xii.
3. Mark Winokur, *American Laughter: Immigrants, Ethnicity, and the 1930s Hollywood Film Comedy* (New York: St. Martin's, 1996), 196.
4. Eva Weber, *Art Deco in America* (New York: Exeter Books, 1985), 11.
5. Katharine Morrison McClinton, *Art Deco: A Guide for Collectors* (New York: Potter, 1986), 6.
6. Ibid., 8.
7. Allbrecht, *Designing Dreams,* xi.
8. McClinton, *Art Deco,* 6.
9. Weber, *Art Deco in America,* 14 and 19.
10. Winokur, *American Laughter,* 202.
11. [Steinway and Sons advertisement], *House & Garden* (February 1929), 185.
12. [Baldwin Piano advertisement], *House & Garden* (February 1929), 144.
13. Winokur, *American Laughter,* 197–98.
14. McClinton, *Art Deco,* 11.
15. Weber, *Art Deco in America,* 11.
16. McClinton, *Art Deco,* 185.
17. Alastair Duncan, *Art Deco* (London: Thames and Hudson, 1988), 121.
18. Victor Arwas, *Art Deco Sculpture: Chryselephantine Statuettes of the Twenties and Thirties* (London and New York: Academy Editions and St. Martin's, 1975), 5.
19. Ibid., 7.
20. McClinton, *Art Deco,* 193.
21. Arwas, *Art Deco Sculpture,* 11.
22. Ibid., 8.
23. Howard Mandelbaum and Eric Myers, *Screen Deco: A Celebration of High Style in Hollywood* (New York: St. Martin's, 1985), 18–19.
24. Arwas, *Art Deco Sculpture,* 17–23.
25. Alberto Shayo, *Chiparus: Master of Art Deco* (New York: Abbeville, 1993), 28.
26. Bevis Hiller, Art Deco catalogue for an exhibit at the Minneapolis Institute of Arts (8 July–5 September 1971), 55.
27. Arwas, *Art Deco Sculpture,* 66.
28. McClinton, *Art Deco,* 135.
29. Ellen Spiegel, "Fred and Ginger Meet Van Nest Polglase," *Velvet Light Trap* 10 (1973): 17–22; citation is from p. 22.
30. Spiegel, "Fred and Ginger Meet Van Nest Polglase," 19.
31. Arlene Croce, *The Fred Astaire and Ginger Rogers Book* (New York: Outerbridge and Lazard, 1972), 25.

32. Arwas, *Art Deco Sculpture,* 49.

33. Sally Peters,"From Eroticism To Transcendence: Ballroom Dance And The Female Body," in *The Female Body: Figures, Style, Speculations,* ed. Laurence Goldstein (Ann Arbor: University of Michigan Press, 1991), 145–58; citation is from p. 151.

34. McClinton, *Art Deco,* 9; Sylvie Raulet, *Art Deco Jewelry* (New York: Rizzoli, 1985), 41.

35. Weber, *Art Deco in America,* 113.

36. McClinton, *Art Deco,* 9.

37. Duncan, *Art Deco,* 122.

38. Ibid., 112.

39. Raulet, *Art Deco Jewelry,* 41.

40. For another, more extended discussion of *Princess Tam Tam,* see Kalinak, "Disciplining Josephine Baker," in this volume.

41. Hiller, Art Deco catalogue, 47 (my emphasis).

42. Lucy Fischer, *Shot/Countershot: Film Tradition and Women's Cinema* (Princeton: Princeton University Press, 1989).

43. Although the score to *Footlight Parade* is credited to Dubin and Warren, "By a Waterfall" is by Irving Kahal and Sammy Fair.

44. Raulet, *Art Deco Jewelry,* 52.

45. Richard Striner, *Art Deco* (New York: Abbeville, 1994), 23.

46. Raulet, *Art Deco Jewelry,* 128.

47. Alastair Duncan, *Encyclopedia of Art Deco* (New York: Dutton, 1988), 106.

48. Ibid., 111.

49. Hiller, Art Deco catalogue, 88.

50. Fischer, *Shot/Countershot,* 138.

51. Duncan, *Encyclopedia of Art Deco,* 28.

52. Ibid., 122.

53. Arwas, *Art Deco Sculpture,* 17, 20, 21, 22, and 27.

54. Respectively, Alastair Duncan, *American Art Deco* (New York: Abrams, 1986), 110; McClinton, *Art Deco,* 134; Duncan, *Encyclopedia of Art Deco,* 122.

55. Arwas, *Art Deco Sculpture,* 25, 33, 44, and 46.

56. Shriner, *Art Deco,* 65.

57. Ibid., 65.

58. McClinton, *Art Deco,* 96.

59. Weber, *Art Deco in America,* 19–20.

60. Arwas, *Art Deco Sculpture,* 50 and 90–91.

61. Duncan, *Encyclopedia of Art Deco,* 32.

62. Jeanne Thomas Allen, in *Fabrications: Costume and the Female Body,* ed. Jane Gaines and Charlotte Herzog (New York and London: Routledge, 1990), 124.

63. See essays in *Fabrications,* ed. Jane Gaines and Charlotte Herzog.

KATHRYN KALINAK

Disciplining Josephine Baker
Gender, Race, and the Limits of Disciplinarity

✳

I begin with a description of a production number from a film made in the
1930s. Dozens of chorus girls appear in a chic nightclub in precision drill
formation executing intricate geometric patterns to repeated variations of
the music's identifying theme. The music changes and suddenly a woman
leaps onto the stage from a nearby vantage point to become part of the
spectacle. As she descends the set's central prop, a winding staircase, she removes first her shoes and then her evening dress to reveal a less constricting
costume. She begins to dance to a conga drum.

This scenario might seem to describe a typical (if not a literal) moment
from any number of Warners' musicals of the period. But the chorines are
white and the woman is black. She is played by Josephine Baker, an African
American entertainer, dancer, and chanteuse, the sensation of Paris in the
1920s. The combination of her gender and her race makes it impossible for
Princess Tam Tam, one of two films in which Baker starred, to have been
produced in the Hollywood studio system.

This production sequence encodes and relays culturally empowered definitions of gender and race in a number of fascinating ways: the structure
of the narrative itself, which posits Baker's character as powerless to resist
the rhythms of the conga drum; the gaze of the spectators, diegetic and
otherwise, who construct Baker as spectacle; the montage, which literalizes
Baker's fetishization; the chorines' visual representation and their conventional Busby Berkeley–style choreography set in opposition to Baker's
strikingly modern dance based upon West African traditions;[1] the juxtaposition of musical styles between the idiom of the French music hall in the
chorines' introduction and the exotic conga rhythms for Baker's appearance; the convergence of Baker's offscreen and onscreen character through

her dance; and the historical context of the French fascination with black women. In fact, this production number foregrounds and links Baker's gender and race to such an extent that I would call it a flashpoint in the representation of gender and race in film.

The question that concerns me here is how gender and race become encoded in film, and, in a larger sense, how representations of race and gender circulate through culture. Literary theory (particularly narratology), film theory, feminist theory, historical inquiry, ethnographic study, art history, the history of dance, and critical musicology—all provide tracings of these forces. Traditional academic disciplines constitute fields of inquiry for investigating Baker; they are bounded, however, not only by the nature of the questions that are posed within them but by the cultural, political, and practical demands that circumscribe the questions. Indeed, the multitudinous ways in which the conga number from *Princess Tam Tam* constructs its meaning cast into sharp relief the limits of disciplinarity and prompt an investigation of its usefulness for a critical understanding of Baker as a cultural product.

The field of cultural studies has led the attack on disciplinarity, arguing that, in its insularity, it works to maintain the status quo: "Rationalized as the protection of the integrity of specific disciplines, the departmentalization of inquiry has contributed to the reproduction of the dominant culture by isolating its critics from each other."[2] Interdisciplinarity, which amalgamates a limited number of traditional disciplines in a highly disciplinary way, perpetuates the problems. Combining elements, however imaginatively, from various disciplines does not necessarily confront the lines drawn between them, posing something of a dead-end in terms of escaping the limitations disciplinarity entails. What cultural studies called for was a new paradigm: nondisciplinarity.[3]

Contemporary postcolonial studies take up the cudgel, arguing that disciplinarity itself has been one of the forces perpetuating the dominance of white, Eurocentric culture and its motivating engine, racism. In its place, postcolonial studies has adopted nondisciplinarity as a defining strategy. I am thinking of the issue of *Screen* entitled "The Last Special Issue on Race," edited by Isaac Julien and Kobena Mercer. In their provocatively titled introduction, "De Margin and De Centre," Julien and Mercer argue that current conceptualizations of disciplinarity and interdisciplinarity cannot address the issues of race and ethnicity adequately. They call for a discourse for race that refuses both the agendas of individual disciplines and the orthodoxies that lurk in the concept of interdisciplinarity. What they seek to do is no less than de-center the terms and constitution of any discussion of race.[4]

A key feature of the seminal *Unthinking Eurocentrism: Multicultural-ism and the Media* is the breakdown of disciplinary borders that Julian and Mercer solicit.[5] Here authors Robert Stam and Ella Shohat commandeer the "freedom to wander among diverse disciplines, texts, and discourses, ancient and contemporary, high and low. As a disciplinary hybrid, the book develops a syncretic, even cannibalistic methodology" (8). For Stam and Shohat, a dissolution of the disciplines is prerequisite to their project: a cri-tique of the media in the postcolonial era.

I turn now to an analysis of *Princess Tam Tam,* offered in this spirit, as an example of the ways crossing borders and disregarding disciplinary mar-gins can force us to ask new and different questions. In the case of *Princess Tam Tam,* such an inquiry leads us to study the film in terms of its narrative construction; its use of the cinematic apparatus to position Baker as fetish and spectacle; its historical roots in the Western world's construction of race; its exploitation of Baker's star persona; its relationship to ethno-graphic spectacle; its connection to Modernism; its musical accompani-ment; its choreography; and above all, its underlying mechanisms of gen-der and race, which empower each of these discourses.[6]

On the surface *Princess Tam Tam* radiates a kind of racial utopia, the so-cial milieu of 1920s France, where society is color-blind, and a black woman can move freely from Africa to Paris, from the streets to a swank nightclub, and from a black lover to a white one. Yet there is a complex contradiction between the surface of the film and its underlying framework, a troubling tension between the film's liberal intentions in terms of racial and sexual equality and their execution in the ideological terrain of the twentieth cen-tury. The film and Baker are caught somewhere between the two, inheri-tors and carriers of the intersection of gender and race in the Western world.

The structure of the narrative itself is propelled by this dialogue, a com-plex interplay between the film's attraction toward and ultimate disavowal of race. Baker troubles this exchange with the lure of the racial Other, com-plicating the film's ideological message as well as its narrative trajectory. The film tells the Pygmalion-like story of a Tunisian shepherdess, Alwina (played by Baker), and her transformation into the fictitious Princess Tam Tam through the agency of a rather professorial novelist named Max de Miracourt and his colleague, Coton. The film opens in the Paris apartment of Max, who has lost his poetic muse and cannot write. Lucie, the selfish wife who literally kicks him out of bed, is posited as the cause of his crea-tive angst. Female sexuality as the wellspring of male creativity is a familiar stereotype that plays upon the patriarchal equation of female sexuality with fertility, both physically and intellectually. That Lucie is the cause of Max's creative sterility is explicitly stated in the dialogue: "My talent's gone because of the life you make me lead." The root of the problem is Lucie's preoccupation with Parisian café society and her subsequent refusal to maintain intimate relations with Max. As a result he announces that he might as well "sleep in the other room." When Coton tells him, "In this atmosphere you'll never write your novel," they agree to seek inspiration in Africa, specifically in Tunisia, "among the savages, the real savages," where they meet Alwina, played by Baker. Despite the fact that the film was conceived as a vehicle for Baker, *Princess Tam Tam*'s narrative will transpire around Max's quest to find his muse and reclaim his masculinity by substituting one woman for another.

Max's muse is situated in and through female sexuality; and it is a mark of the film's liberal intentions toward race that it goes unmentioned that Alwina's color is different from Lucie's. Yet the matter of race does make a difference, a difference revealed in the deep-seated cultural stereotypes about race that are part of the film's ideological terrain. One such stereotype lies behind the film's narrative propulsion, that Max must find a muse to write, a definition of creativity in which females become interchangeable commodities (it really matters little which woman supplies the creative spark). But, to be absolutely precise, the women in *Princess Tam Tam* are not quite interchangeable, for Alwina's color sets her apart. In order to cure Max of the writer's block imposed by the failure of his white, Western wife to provide him with a sexual, and thus creative, outlet, the film ups the sexual ante, so to speak, by offering him the more powerful sexuality of black, African Alwina (see figure 1).

Despite the casualness with which the narrative appears to treat it, Baker's race is a central and defining trope in the film. In fact, *Princess Tam Tam* taps into a virulent discourse on race and sexuality circulating through Western culture that has historically equated persons of color with savagery, indolence, and hypersexuality. The particular French twist on this tradition has been to focus on black female sexuality, the "Black Venus," a preoccupation that extends from the Middle Ages through the nineteenth century and beyond.[7] (One need only think of the film *Diva* to recognize the continued strength of this legacy.)

As early as the twelfth century, the monastic Peter Abelard was writing to Héloïse of the seductive sexuality of black women, noting that "the skin of black women, less agreeable to the gaze, is softer to touch, and that the hidden pleasures that one tastes within their love are more delicious and delightful."[8] In the seventeenth century, the black woman emerged in French travelogues where she was frequently described in terms of her

Figure 1. *La Princesse Tam-Tam.* Photo courtesy The Museum of Modern Art/ Film Stills Archive.

unbridled sexuality, insatiable lust, and lax (or nonexistent) morals.[9] Discourses of French colonialism and the development of the slave trade helped to reinforce the ideological positioning of the black female as seductive and hypersexual. As Tracy Sharpley argues,

Under slavery, the black female became a commodity to be bought and sold as well as sexually exploited at the whim of the French. This sexual vulnerability translated into the creation of a fantasmatic, masculinist colonial discourse—a function of the gaze—that writes and integrates the black woman into a pre-existing system of knowledge and representation, that defines black women as hypersexual.[10]

This stereotype helped to empower the sexual exploitation of black women by their white owners and thus became a crucial component of colonialism itself.

With the advent of theories of evolution in the nineteenth century, race again came to the forefront of cultural consciousness, as did the persistent stereotypes that attended it. As Cameron Bailey writes:

Anthropological and medical authorities at the turn of the century invented an evolutionary scale that placed Africans at the bottom of humanity's ladder and Oxbridge-educated men at the top. One of the most important criteria was sex. To the nineteenth-century "man of science," treading water between Darwin and Freud, sex was an important, but as yet fully untapped, well-spring of theory. With the unconscious still untheorised, he could go about measuring genitalia and quantifying "sex drives," with the conviction that the results would provide an indicator to one's position in the order of things.[11]

By connecting the size of sexual organs to sexual drive, nineteenth-century science linked skin color to heightened and potentially dangerous sexuality. The black woman held special interest for the nineteenth-century man of science, who reduced and equated her to her sexual organs, which were examined, dissected, and theorized in an attempt to explain her. Black women, because of their gender and race, became the sight of a double alterity, the primitive and the hypersexualized. It is the trail of this discourse that finds its way into *Princess Tam Tam* and becomes attached to Baker and the character she plays, Alwina.

It is not the only discourse that trails Baker. Equally important in framing Alwina is the tradition of ethnographic cinema. Here the work of Fatimah Tobing Rony, especially *The Third Eve: Race, Cinema, and Ethnographic Spectacle,* is extremely useful. Ethnographic film, as a category, has always been defined by race, by the attempt to understand the Other through visual scrutiny. Of course, the camera's lens only finds what it expects to see there and Rony explicates how "natives" have always been represented in ethnographic film: "exotic, as people who until only too recently were categorized by science as Savage and Primitive, of an earlier evolutionary stage in the overall history of humankind."[12] This ethnographic discourse seeps into the representation of Baker herself and of the various characters she portrays on film. Rony reminds us that when Baker arrived on the Parisian art scene she was described in terms consistent with the "natives" of ethnographic film:

Woman or man? Her lips are painted black, her skin is the color of bananas, her cropped hair sticks to her head like caviar, her voice squeaks. She is in constant motion, her body writhing like a snake or more precisely like a dipping saxophone. Music seems to pour from her body. She grimaces, crosses her eyes, puffs out her cheeks, wiggles disjointedly, does a split and finally crawls off the stage stiff-legged, her rump higher than her head, like a young giraffe. . . . This is no woman, no dancer. It's something exotic and elusive as music, the embodiment of all the sounds we know. . . . And now the finale, a wildly indecent dance which takes us back to primeval times.[13]

Ultimately Baker was constructed by the media as "ethnographic spectacle, a monster, neither man nor woman, neither human nor animal."[14] Baker's appearance as Alwina in *Princess Tam Tam* reflects this discourse, which can be glimpsed in Alwina's cinematic introduction into the film (more on this later), her narrative function, her costumes, her choreography, and her musical performances.

The specter of race haunts Baker and her various filmic appearances but that specter is complex and multifaceted; it carries with it the lure of race as well as its disavowal. French colonialism, along with its racist underpinnings, has always incorporated a certain fascination with the exoticism of the Other. In the twentieth century, that fascination was circulated as a cultural commodity, most notably through the work of the Modernists. In fact, Baker, in whom colonialism and Modernism seemed to converge, provided inspiration for a veritable Who's Who of Modernist artists: Picasso, Calder, Cocteau, Colin, Le Corbusier, and Léger. The Modernists' fascination with Baker hinges not only on the exotic attraction of the racial Other but on a distinctive lack in the white, Western world, a lack that the energies of the racial Other (and *only* those of the racial Other), fulfill. Modernists had found in Africa a source of inspiration, a well of creativity. Karen C. Dalton and Henry Louis Gates Jr. in their recent article on Baker and dance describe the Eurocentric myths about Africa that circulated freely in Paris of the 1920s: "African creative expression was spontaneous, collective, instinctive, uncensored either internally or externally, free of rules, and in touch with potent, mysterious, nonrational, and subliminal forces."[15] Modernists were searching for a new vocabulary as well as new definitions of creativity itself. They found both in Baker. For the Modernists, Baker provided both the link to this uncontaminated African tradition and the creative inspiration for a culture drained of its ability to provide meaning.

We can see this process mirrored in the ideological work of *Princess Tam Tam:* novelist Max de Miracourt's fascination with Alwina is driven by her position in the film as racial Other. The initial description of Tunisia connects Alwina's homeland to a mythical Africa: Max describes it as the place of "savages, the real savages." And because of that savagery it is here and only here that Max can create his new novel. Alwina provides the spark: the exotic and unharnessed sexual energy that Max's white, Western wife cannot offer him. Max seems an altogether typical Parisian of the 1920s in appropriating Alwina as the solution to his creative sterility.

Yet the racist legacy of the French colonial past was never entirely erased and the use to which writers, artists, and intellectuals put Baker often replicates not only the fascination but the threat of her race. Michele Wallace's concept of "the negative scene of instruction" can be very helpful here in understanding the complexities of the relationship between Baker and Modernism (and, by extension, between Alwina and Max in the film). Wallace uses the concept of the negative scene of instruction in reference to the situation of Euro-American artists who "borrow" from African American art: "the exchange is disavowed and disallowed—no one admits to having learned anything from anyone else."[16] For Wallace the reluctance of Eurocentric art to acknowledge the contribution of the Other betrays cultural anxiety, an anxiety that manifests itself in the stereotype of the Primitive as a mute and inferior counterpoint to the artist. Inspiration has its limits, especially when that inspiration emanates from the racial Other. Certainly something of this process is enacted through Modernism, manifesting itself through representations of Baker that distill and inscribe her into an archetypal "Sauvage." Baker herself acknowledged that her privileged position in Parisian society was largely dependent upon her ability to conform to existing racial stereotypes about the primitive and the unspoiled. France in the 1920s and 1930s provides an interesting pressure cooker where the French rage for all things exotic (and a genuine openness toward African American artists and intellectuals) clashes with the racist colonial legacy. It is this confrontation that can be read in *Princess Tam Tam*, a confrontation that yields a film genuinely fascinated with and sympathetic to Baker on the surface, and one whose underlying structure marks her as a signifier of her race. *Princess Tam Tam* is above all a cultural product and as such embodies the historically complicated, deeply ambivalent, and contradictory French attitudes on race.

One level on which these tensions are worked out is that of costume. In the opening credits, Baker is presented as Cleopatra, her hair concealed in an Egyptian-style headdress. The iconographic power of this image resonates with the star persona of Baker. Yet in the mise-en-scène Baker is captured in close-up framed by large, prickly cacti, as Elizabeth Coffman observes, a "threatening geography, a virtual *vagina dentata*."[17] As Alwina, Baker is introduced to us in the film wearing some rather nondescript "native" clothing. But again, Baker's star persona resonates in the remarkable jewelry around her neck and arms. Such tensions and contradictions created by costume are less evident on the level of the narrative, whose trajectory exploits costume to help explain Alwina's ultimate unfitness for Parisian society. Alwina/Baker must relinquish her "native" clothing in order to be transformed into the refined lady of Max's fantasy. But throughout the film, the Western dress Max expects her to wear both annoys and restricts her; she is frequently seen, as she is in the conga production number, slipping out of her shoes and sometimes even her clothes. (There is a wonderful irony here: Baker loved expensive shoes.) The suggestion that no clothes can contain her plays upon deep-seated racial stereotypes that construct the black female body as a sexual force that cannot be restrained.

Alwina's sexuality and its connection to animality can also be traced to the nineteenth-century discourse on race where it became commonplace to associate persons of color races with the animal kingdom and particularly to connect their sexuality to wildness and bestiality. I would argue that there is also some spillover from the contemporaneous French fascination with race that posited a connection between persons of color and primitivism. In *Princess Tam Tam* Alwina is a shepherdess by trade, and in the opening sequence she snuggles a lamb before hoisting it over her shoulder. She will later play with a monkey, actually climbing a tree to go after it. That she becomes identified with animals in the film is directly alluded to on the level of narrative. In one particularly uncomfortable scene, a European tourist complains of the odor of musk when Alwina approaches. (Musk is defined in the film as the smell of wild animals.) Max himself describes her as a tiger and a wild animal. Here Baker's onscreen character becomes entangled with her offscreen image as Baker's star persona heightens and reinforces discourses on race that are subtly being drawn with regard to Alwina. Baker's well-known and frequent public appearances with her pet leopard, Chiquita, her "native" dance numbers and costumes, and her own personal style (described in a recent biography as "jungle elegance")[18] seep into Alwina's characterization, binding offscreen to onscreen and reinforcing a representation of the black woman as an essentially animal force outside the purview of civilization.

For Max, Alwina is the embodiment of his muse. They meet initially in a Tunisian street where she steals oranges and he pays for them. Later, he agrees to let her be his guide to the ancient Roman ruins at Dougga. Here an Orientalist fantasy is unleashed to intersect with and strengthen the film's racial politics. Alwina is not only presented as the racial Other but as a North African and as such she is inscribed by the markers of Orientalism as well:[19] primitiveness and savagery (hence the connection to animals), spontaneity, inhibition, erotic sensuality, sexuality, mysticism, and paganism. Max spies her dancing with abandon on the Roman ruins he has come to view, like a priestess in harmony with the mysteries of some pagan cult, intimately connected to ancient civilization. Max invites her to his villa to transform her into a lady. It could almost be Shaw's Henry Higgins talking: "First, polish and educate her, then study her reactions." Her test will be to "pass" as Princess Tam Tam among elite Parisian café society. Unlike Higgins, however, Max has an ulterior motive: Alwina inspires him. He will pretend to be in love with her and tell her story, "an interracial story, a contemporary novel." And, in fact, Max's colleague and accomplice, Coton, transcribes Alwina's responses from behind a screen conveniently placed in Max's rooms. The film's engagement with the discourse of ethnographic film is a powerful undercurrent in the film, surfacing in several scenes such as this one. Here Max and Coton view Alwina as a subject to be spied upon and analyzed. Earlier, a group of European tourists soaking up a bit of local color do much the same, secretly watching Alwina dance in blissful ignorance of their presence.

It is in this sequence, which transpires on the steps of a Roman amphitheater in Dougga, that the music becomes directly engaged in the film's ideological project. That music has an explicitly ideological function and is neither innocent of nor unaffected by the values of the culture in which it exists has been forcefully argued by theorists of the Frankfurt School.[20] Current scholarship in the growing field of critical musicology has placed music distinctly in the realm of the social. A recent target has been the representation of gender and race in music. Susan McClary's work on *Carmen*[21] and Jonathan Bellman's anthology, *The Exotic in Western Music*, exemplify this avenue of exploration.[21] Defining the "exotic" in Western music, for example, Bellman argues that the "suggestion of strangeness is the overriding factor; not only does the music *sound* different from 'our' music, but it also suggests a specifically alien culture or ethos. Aural signifiers of difference always carry with them evaluation and judgments. One of the most salient of these connections is the one between the exotic and "forbidden and desirable sexualities."[22] The score for *Princess Tam Tam* provides a case study of the ways in which such culturally received notions become encoded through music. The film's score thus becomes part of the nexus of meaning that constructs definitions of race and gender and positions Baker within it.

Baker had been a major star of Paris café life for years when her business manager/husband Pepito Abatino engineered a film career for her, first *Zou Zou*, starring Jean Gabin, and second, *Princess Tam Tam*, in which Baker herself was unquestionably to be the star. *Zou Zou* gave Baker the chance to prove herself as a marketable property on celluloid, but it gave her only limited opportunity to show what she was famous for: the exotic and risqué dancing she performed at the Folies (see figure 2). In one scene in *Zou Zou*, Baker cavorts behind a curtain at an audition, unaware that her shadow can be seen by the producers. Although she becomes a star of the French music hall in the film, Baker is allowed only brief moments to capitalize on her trademarks as a performer. *Princess Tam Tam* was meant to change that. Her initial production number, if you will, the one that takes place on the steps of the Roman ruins, repeats many of the choreographic movements first glimpsed in *Zou Zou*. In the chicken walk, Baker walks like a chicken, head thrust forward and back, shoulders hunched forward and hips pushed back, reinforcing the animality associated with Alwina and exaggerating her sexual presence.[23]

The music that accompanies Baker during her dance at the Roman ruins is the same conga that she will dance to later in Paris, one of the film's many narrative improbabilities. It is also one of the interventions of race. The conga, of course, has absolutely nothing at all to do with Tunisia, as Baker

Figure 2. *Zou Zou.* Photo courtesy The Museum of Modern Art/ Film Stills Archive.

herself was quick to point out.[24] In fact it is a Latin American dance form, specifically Brazilian, which borrows its name from the long cylindrical conga drum and its characteristic rhythm from slave dances traditionally performed to celebrate the end of the workday. That a Tunisian shepherdess should be dancing to a Latin American dance craze not only exceeds the bounds of narrative probability, it points to the soundtrack's infiltration by racial politics as well as the narrative's. The conga is hardly authentic. It is a construction, or more accurately a reconstruction, of indigenous rhythms into a form more accessible to Western listeners. Bellman's argument with regard to the function of exoticism in Western music could well be applied here. "The exotic equation is a balance of familiar and unfamiliar: just enough 'there' to spice the 'here' but remain comprehensible in making the point."[25]

Interestingly, the use of exotic rhythms to accompany Alwina taps into a tradition circulating through Hollywood films of the same period (and beyond) that exploits non-Western rhythms as signifiers of the primitive and the uncivilized. From Indian music in the classic Hollywood western to African polyrhythms in films set in colonial Africa, non-Western rhythms connote savagery. They function as what Robert Stam and Louise Spence call "a kind of synecdochic acoustic shorthand for the atmosphere of menace in the phrase, 'the natives are restless.'"[26] Even something as simple as rhythm can powerfully (and largely subconsciously) position the spectator according to the logic of white ethnocentrism.

In *Princess Tam Tam,* music not defined as mainstream is marginalized and becomes Other. What happens to this Other-ness in the film mirrors a process at work in Western culture at large: musical styles and forms transpiring outside the purview of the dominant culture are either excluded from the canon of musicalness, if you will, or eventually co-opted by the culture and redefined or conventionalized to fit and reinforce familiar stereotypes. Thus music becomes yet another mark of ideological intervention, mirroring the film's underlying politics of gender and race.

Music's ideological subtext can also be heard in the leitmotif associated with Alwina, first in her appearances in Tunisia and later in Paris. Like the conga motif, it is built upon Western musical conventions for the exotic, specifically drawing upon Orientalist musical conventions to construct a primitive and uncivilized existence for Alwina outside Western civilization.

Orientalism in music has a long lineage, so long in fact that one might be tempted to call it a pedigree. Composers in the West as early as the fifteenth century evoked the Orient through a series of exotic musical practices that yoked difference to inferiority. As recent critics have pointed out, Western musical practices were perfect for such a move. In her work on the exotic, the erotic, and the feminine, Linda Phyllis Austern puts it this way: "The strident dualities and inherent hierarchies of pitch and harmony associated with tonality loaned themselves particularly well to stock Western intellectual conceptions of dominant versus submissive, masculine versus feminine, and familiar versus strange, from the very beginning."[27] The musical impulse toward the East initially gelled in the *alla turca* style of the eighteenth and early nineteenth centuries in a set of melodic, rhythmic, and harmonic markers for "Turkishness." Actual Turkish music was never on offer. In its place was what Mary Hunter has called "a deficient or messy version of European music."[28] Thus Turkish music, and by extension all things Turkish, became connected to lack, inferiority, and even irrationality.

Orientalism in music exploded in the nineteenth century and (this may come as no surprise) especially in France. Not coincidentally, I think, the French began their colonization of Africa in 1830. The function of the Orient for western Europe in the nineteenth century contained many of the same contradictions that Africa held for Modernists in the twentieth: it was a source of spontaneity and uncorrupted natural beauty, and thus of inspiration, as well as a place of barbarousness and savagery. The Orient was a place to be defined and controlled by the West. Above all, the Orient was a cultural fantasy, a projection of everything that was lacking in the West, especially eroticism.

It was in the nineteenth century that the Orient became associated with femaleness,[29] when patriarchal discourses (women as unknown and unknowable, intuitive, irrational, sensual, sexual, and foreign) were harnessed to colonialist rhetoric to represent the Orient as a female racial Other, in need of masculine, Western control. Music played an increasingly important role in the process, which connected the Orient, the Other, and femaleness, and nowhere more observably than in opera (and to a lesser extent, ballet), where such ideological operations took a more visible form through dramatization on the stage. Here Orientalism flourished. I think Ralph P. Locke has it right when he argues that such operas "served to distract attention from the realities of Western exploitation of, and geopolitical scramble over, the Middle East."[30]

What French Orientalist operas offered instead was a fantasy of exoticism and eroticism projected onto the female racial Other (*Thaïs, Aida, Samson et Dalila, L'africaine, Cléopatre*, and, of course, *Carmen*, to name a few.) The rather variable markers of "Turkishness" from the previous century coalesced into a more recognizable set of musical signifiers: simple melodies, unusual rhythmic patterns, modal digressions, and a tendency toward chromaticism, among others. Here the "simplicity" of the alien culture, its lack of musical sophistication, and its "deviance" from the norm centered on the female who came to represent the Orient and who brought with her the lure and the danger of alien sexuality.

Orientalism did not disappear with the nineteenth century. As Locke argues:

Well into the twentieth century, France was to remain the center of Middle Eastern evocation (e.g., Saint-Saëns, Ravel) and perhaps of musical exoticism generally (e.g., Olivier Messiaen, Pierre Boulez), no doubt in large part because of the country's unique position as both a major musical center . . . and a major colonial power (121).

Popular music continues to circulate Orientalist stereotypes from the "Hootchy Kootchy Dance" that accompanied Little Egypt at the Columbia Exposition of 1893 to the song that provides the main title of Disney's 1992 feature film *Aladdin*, "Arabian Nights" (as well as the theme song for the Disney television show of the same name).[31] It is worth pointing out in this connection that Josephine Baker in 1936 recorded the song "Nuit d'Alger."[32]

It is this musical heritage the film enters into with Alwina's leitmotif. The Orient of Orientalism is, of course, a social construct where the cultural imaginary and physical geography intersect. For western Europe, the Orient has always meant the Near and Middle East, and the way *Princess Tam Tam* conflates the two, through music, demonstrates what Hunter has described as "a classically Orientalizing blurring of boundaries among different sorts of Others."[33] Alwina is Tunisian, but her leitmotif is inflected by Arabia, particularly through its connection to one of the most famous musical expressions of Orientalism: Tschaikovsky's "Danse Arabe" for the character Coffee in *The Nutcracker*.[34] There are some striking similarities between the two pieces in the way they exploit musical conventions for the Orient. The first is an arresting rhythmic pattern they share that adds an accent to a conventional rhythmic configuration, specifically, $\frac{6}{8}$ meter with accents not only on the expected first and fourth beats but on the fifth beat as well. Adding an extra accent marks the rhythm as exotic and attaches to it the undercurrent of savagery. It is this rhythm that serves as a *basso ostinato,* that is, a repeated and sustained line of accompaniment in the bass. The second similarity is a highly chromatic melody based on a variation of the traditional minor scale, which raises the fourth degree of the scale and lowers the seventh. In using musical conventions so clearly coded for the Orient, the score for *Princess Tam Tam* taps into a powerful fantasy about race and gender that, as I have been arguing, is reinforced by multiple levels of the text.

The two pieces of music most associated with Baker in the film are the conga and her "Arabian" leitmotif. On the surface these musical portraits designate different geographic spaces. But in the system of representation the West has constructed for them, they are interchangeable. The West tends to conflate all difference outside of itself, reducing the wide variety of music produced outside of western Europe and the United States to a generic Other. Having Josephine Baker, an African American, play a Tunisian accompanied by an "Arabian" leitmotif and dance a Latin American dance suggests that the only difference worth noticing is the one that distinguishes Western from non-Western. The score's disregard for national, ethnic, and historical difference speaks of an essentialism with regard to race where any musical practices other than those of the dominant culture are interchangeable. Such politics of exclusion reinforce the position that other levels of the text have created for Baker. Music is a crucial part of the apparatus that sustains her representation as racial Other.

These kinds of slippages between non-Western musical discourses proved characteristic of Baker's stage performances as well. In her autobiography, Baker describes one of her production numbers:

Again and again we rehearsed a flamboyant number about the French colonies, which included Algerian drums, Indian bells, tom-toms from Madagascar, coconuts from the Congo, cha-chas from Guadeloupe, a number laid in Martinique during which I distributed sugar cane to the audience, Indochinese gongs, Arab dances, camels and finally my appearance as the Empress of Jazz.[35]

Baker, stripped of any ethnic, racial, historical, or geographic particularity, is reduced to the archetypal savage. Her image is now available to be read as what Rony has called "the stereotype of the ethnographic primitive": immutably and transhistorically exotic and savage, a spectacle of race.

The film's big production number (discussed at the beginning of this essay) showcases the conga and reinforces the connection between race and sexuality that inhabits the film. Baker's performance is extremely sensual and sexual. A revealing costume (she wanted to dance in a gauze dress; the producer insisted it be lined with silver lamé) displays her legs and her breasts; the choreography not only accents these body parts (the shimmy, for instance) but attaches aggression and even threat to this sexuality (the aggressive leap with which she leaves the staircase or the threatening posture she includes in the routine). The creation of Baker as spectacle culminates in the rapid-fire montage of her ecstasy that ends the number. In fact, this display is so powerful and frightening that Max and Coton, seated in the audience, cannot bear to watch it. On the narrative level, what they are troubled by is Alwina's inability to resist the call of the wild (and the wild, here, is, of course, her racial heritage) and the apparent ease with which she can shed the manners and attitudes of upper-class Parisian society they have taught her. But their discomfort is also triggered by an aggressive and uncontrollable sexuality, the result not only of Alwina's gender but especially of her race, so apparently on display. That many in the audience do not share Max and Coton's concerns (in fact, some spectators seem genuinely appreciative of Baker's display) seems to me to be one of those moments that mark the film as genuinely French.

I have held off discussing the function of the cinematic apparatus per se in the representation of Baker until this moment when her performance as Alwina and her presence as a French stage star converge, where the line between Baker as Alwina and Baker as star of the Folies Bergère is erased. Here, more than at any other moment in the film, Alwina/Baker is inscribed through the cinematic apparatus with the marks of ideologically encoded definitions of gender and race and constructed both as a lure and a threat because of them.

In fact, the entire dance sequence, including the chorine's lengthy introduction to Alwina/Baker's appearance, is a racial and sexual fantasy designed to allow the white, male spectator the forbidden pleasure of miscegenation. In the introductory chorine section, this takes the form of nonwhite male mastery over white female sexuality. (In the Alwina/Baker section, it is, of course, reversed.) In the chorine introduction, women are created as spectacle. Designed to be looked at through relayed point-of-view shots from various spectator positions within the film, the chorines are, moreover, complicit in their objectification, exposing their bodies with looks of ecstasy directed at the camera. The threat of sexual difference that this spectacle unleashes, however, must be contained, and here it is covered over through the fetishization of the chorines, ultimately reduced to body parts through a persistent pattern of close-ups and rendered interchangeable and unrecognizable by the bird's-eye and other aerial shots.

Into this fantasy of sexuality is injected race, initially a sexual fantasy of white female oppression at the hands of the male of color. This takes its most virulent form in the figure of the swarthy sultan who commands the chorines' movements and who is mirrored in the Asian plate jugglers who spin the dancers on plates (complete with conventionalized Chinese musical accompaniment). Males in this sequence become stand-ins for our own presence as spectators, literal relay points for the construction of women as spectacle. They also function to embody the dominant ideology of race, which defines nonwhite sexual power as dangerous, bestial, and malevolent. Something of this danger is diffused when the symbol of race is a woman (as with Baker), but the representation of race as ultimately Other, alluring, yet terrifying, aggressively sexual and sexually threatening, remains.

It is interesting to note the change in camera work when Baker appears on the dance floor. Clearly, the power of her star persona affects her representation. The chorines are fetishized by the camera, fragmented into faceless, nameless, and interchangeable body parts. But Baker was an international star with an audience paying to see her, and at least initially she is captured by the camera in long shot with her full body visible to the audience. But the camera's escalation of the power of her performance exacts a price. Max and Coton repeatedly turn away from her, unable to look at the sight of her sexuality unleashed, a cue to us as audience to do the same, if not literally (who can stop watching her?) then figuratively. Yet, the more frenzied her dance becomes the more the camera begins to subject her to techniques of objectification: close-ups on body parts, a distancing montage structure, and quick, almost subliminal shots of Alwina/Baker, the musicians, and their instruments. That race is specifically a factor here can be seen through the narrative (Alwina is powerless to resist the call of the exotic conga rhythm as she is goaded onto the dance floor by a white woman whose motive is to see Alwina humiliated). But it is the camera that reveals the ideology of race the most insidiously in structuring her dance in a different way from the white chorines.

Alwina/Baker's sexual ecstasy is not only more heightened than the chorines', it is more clearly articulated in facial and bodily gesture. In fact, because her sexuality is more heightened, Alwina/Baker is more rigidly inscribed by the camera through techniques of objectification and containment such as quicker cuts, tighter close-ups, and a montage that disorients and distances us both spatially and temporally. Even her choreography defines Baker as different. Elizabeth Coffman in her work on Baker and dance points out: "Her movements are less restrained and less frontally oriented [than the chorines]. Baker defies most conventions of Western ballet dancing; she turns in circles, with her back to the audience; she moves her head up and down; she shakes her breasts."[36]

I return now return to my earlier claim that culturally empowered definitions of gender and race affect the very trajectory of the narrative. One of the narrative's biggest surprises comes at the end when the camera pans from an intimate moment between a maharajah and Alwina to a smoking pot. As the camera dollies in on the smoke, the image suddenly becomes obscured by it and a dissolve covers the match cut to smoke emanating from a similar pot back in Max's study in Tunisia. Alwina's trip to France and her conquest of Parisian society is now represented as the fictive imaginings of Max who has produced these events in his head as part of the creative process for his latest novel. As Baker's presence does in the spectacle of her dance number, Alwina's function as creative spark to the white male novelist troubles the film. The cost of admitting the necessity of the racial Other, of putting the energies of the racial Other on display, is disavowal. The lure of race proves too threatening and Alwina's integration into Western society is shown to be a piece of fiction, a fantasy constructed by the white male writer.

This narrative turn, if you will, provides an example not only of the kind of distantiation that race imposes, but of the cost of its inclusion in the narrative. Max's fantasy of black female sexuality occasions narrative confusion, even deception. At precisely the moment when the narrative is seeking resolution, it is catapulted into turmoil: although there is a powerful framing device at the end of Max's narrative-within-a-narrative, there is no clear enactment of the frame anywhere in the film. It is almost as if the frame is added as an afterthought, an ineffectual and costly cover-up for the troubling twin presence of gender and race, affording us a rare glimpse into the repressed unconscious of both the text and the culture to which it belongs. Race disturbs the very coherence of the narrative itself.

Alwina herself has been no illusion. But, in *Princess Tam Tam*, Alwina eventually loses Max. With the novel (appropriately entitled *Civilisation*) complete, Max returns to Paris. Alwina settles down with Dar, Max's Tunisian servant, and has a child. Baker herself thought that she should at least end up with the maharajah. But the film places her precisely where it is the most comfortable with her: married to one of her "own kind," enveloped in marriage and motherhood. At a book signing for Max's novel, Coton remarks: "Too bad Alwina isn't here." Max speaks for the film when he says: "She's better off where she is."

Academic inquiry, by its very nature, is compartmentalized, a reflection of the departmentalization of the academy itself. Transcending the boundaries set up by such a framework is a difficult but necessary strategy: only by stepping outside of boundaries can we come to see them. Richard Johnson has used the metaphor of cartography to illustrate this point. Disciplines provide useful maps, but "the danger is that such cartography foregrounds a tiny bit of the social process, especially the activities of the specialist intellectuals. We may become entranced by the lines and squiggles on the maps and never reach a more direct investigation of broader social and cultural processes."[39]

In the case of Josephine Baker and *Princess Tam Tam*, it is these social and cultural processes that ultimately help us to understand her meaning. To discipline Josephine Baker, to focus inquiry on the "lines and squiggles," is to risk missing the defining contours of the map itself, the determining force of gender and race.

Notes

I would like to thank the editors for insightful commentary on earlier drafts of this essay. Special thanks to Sandy Flitterman-Lewis for her inspiration.

1. For a detailed examination of the influence of modern dance on film, and particularly the impact of modern dance on Josephine Baker's performances, see Elizabeth Coffman, "Women in Motion: Dance, Gesture, and Spectacle in Film" (Ph.D. diss., University of Florida, 1995).

2. Henry Giroux, David Shumway, Paul Smith, and James Sosnoski, "The Need for Cultural Studies: Resisting Intellectuals and Oppositional Public Spheres," *Dalhousie Review* 64, no. 1 (1984): 472. Giroux et al. draw attention to the work of Michel Foucault in this context and apply his work on the nature of discipline in the modern world to academia. "What is characteristic of disciplinary technologies is their capacity simultaneously to normalize and hierarchize, to homogenize and differentiate" (474). It is this very concept of discipline, installed and validated in Western culture since the classical period, that facilitates the disciplinarity of academic disciplines (and marginalizes discourses that exceed them). See also Michel Foucault, *Discipline and Punish: The Birth of the Prison*, trans. Alan Sheridan (New York: Vintage, 1979).

3. See, for instance, the work of Stuart Hall, especially "The Emergence of Cultural Studies," *October* 53 (1990): 11–23. Hall argues for a different kind of interdisciplinarity, one that does not center around the "question of which disciplines would contribute . . . , but of how one could decenter or destablize a series of interdisciplinary fields" (16). Richard Johnson's work is also particularly germane; "Cultural Studies and Educational Practice," *Screen Education* 34 (1980); repr., *The Screen Education Reader: Cinema, Television, Culture*, ed. Manuel Alvarado, Edward Buscombe, and Richard Collins (New York: Columbia University Press,

1993), 247–62. He argues that "conventional 'disciplinary' boundar[ies]" not only limit the scope and nature of intellectual inquiry but also foster a kind of "theoretical partisanship" that blocks critical understanding (249). He posits a new concept to escape the "narrowing" of disciplinarity: "a more open interdisciplinary or non-disciplinary way" (248).

4. Isaac Julien and Kobena Mercer, "Introduction: De Margin and De Centre," *Screen* 29, no. 4 (1988): 2–9.

5. Robert Stam and Ella Shohat, *Unthinking Eurocentrism: Multiculturalism and the Media* (New York: Routledge, 1994).

6. For a discussion of how *Princess Tam Tam* fits within the aesthetic of Art Deco, see Fischer, "Designing Women," in this volume.

7. Tracy Sharpley's work on the history of black women in French intellectual history has informed my own thinking on this topic: Tracy Sharpley, "Through the White Male Gaze — Black Venus" (Ph.D. diss., Brown University, 1994).

8. Quoted in Sharpley, "Through the White Male Gaze," 16.

9. See Sharpley, "Through the White Male Gaze," 22–27.

10. Ibid., 38.

11. Cameron Bailey, "Nigger/Lover: The Thin Sheen of Race in *Something Wild*," *Screen* 29, no. 4 (1988): 29. For a more detailed analysis of the discourse of race in the nineteenth century, see Sander L. Gilman, "Black Bodies, White Bodies: Toward an Iconography of Female Sexuality in Late Nineteenth Century Art, Medicine, and Literature," in *Race: Writing and Difference,* ed. Henry Louis Gates Jr. (Chicago: University of Chicago Press, 1986), and "The Hottentot and the Prostitute: Towards an Iconography of Female Sexuality," in *Difference and Pathology: Stereotypes of Sexuality, Race and Madness* (Ithaca: Cornell University Press, 1991).

12. Fatimah Tobing Rony, *The Third Eye: Race, Cinema, and Ethnographic Spectacle* (Durham: Duke University Press, 1996), 7.

13. Josephine Baker, quoted in Rony, *The Third Eve,* 199.

14. Rony, *The Third Eye,* 199.

15. Karen C. C. Dalton and Henry Louis Gates Jr., "Josephine Baker and Paul Colin: Dance Seen Through Parisian Eyes," *Critical Inquiry* 24 (1998): 903–34; citation is from p. 906.

16. Michele Wallace, "Modernism, Postmodernism and the Problem of the Visual in Afro-American Culture," in *Out There: Marginalization and Contemporary Cultures,* ed. Russell Ferguson, Martha Gever, Trinh T. Minh-ha, and Cornel West (New York and Cambridge, Mass.: New Museum of Contemporary Art and Massachusetts Institute of Technology, 1990), 45.

17. Elizabeth Coffman, "Uncanny Performances in Colonial Narratives: Josephine Baker in *Princess Tam Tam,*" *Paradoxa* 3, nos. 3–4 (1997): 379.

18. Phyllis Rose, *Jazz Cleopatra* (New York: Doubleday, 1989), 143.

19. Is it possible to write on Orientalism in any one of its many guises and not recognize a debt to Edward Said? I acknowledge my debt here, particularly to *Orientalism* (New York: Vintage Books, 1979).

20. See particularly Theodor W. Adorno, "On the Fetish-Character in Music and the Regression of Listening," and "The Sociology of Knowledge and Its Consciousness," in *The Essential Frankfurt Reader,* ed. and trans. Andrew Arato and Eike Gebhardt (New York: Continuum, 1982), 270–99 and 452–65; and Hanns Eisler and Adorno (uncredited), *Composing for the Films* (New York: Oxford University Press, 1947). For a more contemporary articulation of this position see Jacques Attali, *Noise: The Political Economy of Music,* trans. Brian Massumi (Minneapolis: University of Minnesota Press, 1985); Christopher Ballantine, *Music and Its Social Meanings* (New York: Gordon and Breach, 1984); Claudia Gorbman, *Unheard Melodies: Narrative Film Music* (Bloomington: Indiana University Press,

1987); Richard Leppert and Susan McClary, eds., *Music and Society: The Politics of Composition. Performance and Reception* (Cambridge: Cambridge University Press, 1989); and Caryl Flinn, *Strains of Utopia: Gender, Nostalgia, and Hollywood Film Music* (Princeton: Princeton University Press, 1992).

21. See especially Susan McClary's groundbreaking essay on Carmen, "Sexual Politics in Classical Music," in *Feminine Endings: Music, Gender and Sexuality* (Minneapolis: University of Minnesota Press, 1991), 53–79.

22. Jonathan Bellman, Introduction to *The Exotic in Western Music*, ed. Jonathan Bellman (Boston: Northeastern University Press, 1998), xii.

23. Interestingly, Elizabeth Coffman ("Women in Motion"), analyzing the influence of modern dance on film, demonstrates how Baker's characteristic pose has circulated throughout art history, pointing to the ways that art has been infiltrated by and perpetuates racial stereotypes as well.

24. Josephine Baker and Jo Bouillon, *Josephine*, trans. Mariana Fitzpatrick (New York: Harper and Row, 1977), 101.

25. Bellman, Introduction, xii.

26. Robert Stam and Louise Spence, "Colonialism, Racism and Representation: An Introduction," *Screen* 24, no. 2 (1983): 18.

27. Linda Phyllis Austern "'Forreine Conceits and Wandring Devises': The Exotic, the Erotic, and the Feminine," in *The Exotic in Western Music*, ed. Bellman, 27.

28. Mary Hunter, "The *Alla Turca* Style in the Late Eighteenth Century: Race and Gender in the Symphony and the Seraglio," in *The Exotic in Western Music*, ed. Bellman, 51.

29. This represents a distinctive change from the *alla turca* conventions, which embodied the deviance of "Turkishness" in male Islamic figures. See Hunter, "The *Alla Turca* Style," and Ralph P. Locke, "Cutthroats and Casbah Dancers, Muezzins and Timeless Sands: Musical Images of the Middle East," in *The Exotic in Western Music*, ed. Bellman, 104–36.

30. Locke, "Cutthroats and Casbah Dancers," 119.

31. Henry Giroux has examined the lyrics for "Arabian Nights" and the ways in which they contribute to the stereotyping of Arabs. See "Animating Youth: The Disneyfication of Children's Culture," *Socialist Review* 24, no. 3 (1995): 40–41.

32. Pointed out by Ralph Locke in "Cutthroats and Casbah Dancers."

33. Hunter, "The *Alla Turca* Style," 53.

34. Is it a coincidence that the most erotic choreography in the ballet is usually reserved for Coffee? I wonder, too, if race isn't subtly part of her very name.

35. Josephine Baker, quoted in Rony, *The Third Eye*, 199–200.

36. Coffman, "Uncanny Performances," 392.

37. Johnson, "Cultural Studies and Educational Practice," 247–48.

PART FIVE

✳

METHODOLOGICAL

POSSIBILITIES

✳

RICK ALTMAN
WITH McGRAW JONES AND SONIA TATROE

Inventing the Cinema Soundtrack
Hollywood's Multiplane Sound System

✳

By far the majority of writing on film sound has concentrated on a single soundtrack component at a time. Numerous books treat the history, theory, and aesthetics of film music. Increasingly, studies have been devoted to filmic uses of language: dialogue, dubbing, intertitles, subtitles, the voice, voice-over. Even sound effects have received separate attention, particularly since digitally massaged tracks created by a new generation of sound designers began to complement traditional studio work. To these separate studies we owe our current understanding of film sound. Even though this focused approach may be logical and useful, it begs several questions about film sound. As a counterbalance to generations of single-component studies, this essay will instead concentrate on interactions among music, dialogue, and sound effects; it will in turn make new theoretical, methodological, and historical proposals.

The Soundtrack in Crisis

What is our object of study? One answer requires examining the kinds of notation that are used to concretize sounds. The most obvious case is that of language, typically represented by clear transcription of all foregrounded dialogue and narration. This traditional representational system privileges sounds that make linguistic meaning while ignoring sublinguistic sounds (grunts, coughs, throat clearing) and all nonlinguistic sound variations (such as differences in volume, tone, or reverberation level). In spite of differences in sound quality, audibility, and audience, the same typeface and print size are commonly used to represent every filmic use of language: in filmscripts as well as studies of screenplays, voice-over narration, and gendered voices. Not only do filmscripts reduce film dialogue to the same linguistic common denominator—whether shouted over the din of factory noises or masked by traffic to the point of inaudibility—but many apparent quotations are in fact borrowed from a screenplay or shooting script eventually modified during shooting, dubbing, or mixing.[1] For those who analyze film dialogue and voices, the object of study is in fact not the film soundtrack, nor even a specific identifiable portion of the film's sound, but a linguistic construct substituted for the film's actual sound.

A similar situation holds with music. Just as dialogue analysts prefer to concentrate on a printed text often closer to a linguistic recipe for production than to a film's actual sound, music critics often base their analyses not on the music as heard in the film but on the music as composed. "The recording stage is the composer's golden moment," says Irwin Bazelon, quoting Laurence Rosenthal; "after that everything is downhill."[2] Immediately after recording, the composer loses control over the music. As Bazelon points out, echoing many another musician, the music "may be cut to pieces, edited and reedited, with different segments spliced together, cues used out of context from their original conception, volumes lowered indiscriminately, balances destroyed or severely altered, entrances and exits changed—everything, in truth, to make a composer hearing the music in conjunction with the film for the first time wonder what happened to the notes he wrote" (53). In compensation for such insensitive treatment, Bazelon offers a series of examples from autograph film scores as originally recorded on the recording stage, thus exemplifying the standard critical reaction to Hollywood bowdlerization. Instead of analyzing music *in* films (as produced by the film industry), Bazelon prefers to discuss music *for* films (as written by the composer). Just as the original scores quoted by Bazelon (and many others) ironically divert interest from the film's actual soundtrack, so the recently popular "soundtrack" albums, typically reproducing the pre-mix recording stage version, offer anything but the soundtrack itself.

Nowhere in these dialogue- or music-specific approaches is the interaction among sounds recognized. Is the dialogue masked by an explosion? Is the line deferred until after the explosion? Does the music peak just before or simultaneously with the explosion? Is the explosion tuned to match the music? Is a single continuous dialogue carried over the reaction shots to the explosion, or are there multiple fragmented bits of language? Does the music dip under all or some of these dialogue events, or does it dominate the dialogue throughout? Are the variations in any given sound component (music, dialogue, effects) attributable to causes internal to that component, or are they the result of sharing the soundtrack with the other sound components?

Michel Chion has repeatedly asserted that there is no such thing as a soundtrack in film, by which he means that film sounds are defined more through their relationship to image events than through internal sound-to-sound coherence. Unlike the frame for the image, Chion specifies, "there is no auditory container for film sounds . . . and therefore, properly speaking, *there is no soundtrack*."[3] Like most critics of film music and dialogue, Chion sees sound-to-sound connections as at best secondary.

This essay argues, to the contrary, that film sound—taken as a single complex unit rather than as three or more separate components—cannot be understood without analyzing relationships among soundtrack components. Nor can we understand the history of film sound without recognizing the growing importance assumed by these intercomponent, intrasoundtrack relationships. Just as image analysis benefited from introduction of the comparative and relational notion of mise-en-scène, or "putting onto the stage," so understanding of the soundtrack requires the concept of mise-en-bande, or "putting onto the sound track." Mise-en-scène analysis foregrounds relationships among image components; mise-en-bande analysis concentrates on the interaction among the various components making up the soundtrack.

This essay presents the results of an initial set of mise-en-bande analyses. Concentrating on early sound film, this inquiry reveals important modifications in the pattern of interaction among sound components. Of particular importance is a move from the late 1920s clash between separate sound elements to the mid-1930s construction of a fully coordinated, "multiplane" soundtrack capable of carrying and communicating several different messages simultaneously. This reading offers a historical rather than theoretical response to Chion's provocative claim that there is no soundtrack. What we mean today by the term "soundtrack" was not in fact automatically created by Hollywood's conversion to sound; on the contrary, the history of early Hollywood mise-en-bande is precisely the history of the soundtrack's creation. Only through a clash among separate sound elements, and the resulting negotiations among rival claimants, was the soundtrack established as an independent concept and space.

This analysis rests on three basic hypotheses, consistent with the "crisis historiography" that has been developing over the past few years.[4] First, every soundtrack results from social and cultural work, as well as technical labor, and thus from conflicting contemporary commitments to differing sound types and uses. When multiple individuals are responsible for producing and assembling a soundtrack, their interaction reflects their differing allegiances regarding sound quality and use. Even when a single individual produces and mixes the entire track, that individual constitutes a site where conflicting positions and desires intersect. Second, whenever recorded sound reaches the limits of sound-system dynamic capacity, or human attention capability, access to the soundtrack is increasingly disputed by separate sound interests (creative personnel and sound technicians; the sound subsystems of music, dialogue, effects). Third, none of our notation systems offers an appropriate language or method for analyzing the conflict or coordination of soundtrack components. We need a new notation system that respects the coherence of the film soundtrack while charting differences in individual components, in order to facilitate delineation of the relationships among components and the implicit rules that govern establishment and maintenance of those relationships.

A New Notation System

Most attempts to represent film sound employ conventions developed for transcribing language and music. Ironically, the very power of these notation systems restricts them to the domain for which they were developed. While the use of writing to present dialogue and voice-over clearly facilitates the analysis of linguistic content, its very specificity walls it off from nonlinguistic sounds. Similarly, the specialized nature of musical notation precludes representation of connections between music and other sounds, thus hiding relationships among sound components. For example, even though musical notation provides absolute dynamic indications (from pianissimo to fortissimo), it cannot represent the relative dynamics on which film sound depends so heavily (for example, is the music louder or softer than dialogue or effects?). A musical score may provide exact information on instrumentation and pitch, but only a comparative frequency analysis will explain why one voice is enhanced and another masked by the same violin passage. Without a sense of relative reverberation levels we would be unable to distinguish background from foreground sounds, yet our repertoire offers no technique to represent such information (in part because decisions about volume or relative reverberation levels are made not by musicians but by the mixers who fold a musical composition into a soundtrack).

The figures accompanying this article offer a preliminary attempt to rectify this situation. Developed in collaboration among the authors, this method involves plotting in the upper half of each figure relative volumes for the various sound components present in a given film sequence; the bottom half provides a shot-by-shot breakdown, plot description, and important dialogue. Providing just as much information as traditional shot-by-shot description, this configuration encourages a new kind of analysis by subordinating image data to the representation of sound and therefore foregrounding the relationship among sound components.

A few words about our procedure are in order. The figures reproduced here plot only volume, but the same notation could easily be applied to other variables, such as frequency or reverberation. Times are measured from the start of the opening credits. Volume levels are based solely on careful listening; because individual sound components are not presented on isolated channels, they cannot be analyzed with oscilloscopes or computer software. Such automatization would be possible only with single-component tracks like the dialogue of films destined for international distribution. For similar reasons, the volume scale is neither exact nor calibrated in precisely the same manner for all films. For each film the scale attributes a value of ten to the loudest individual sound (typically found in the opening credits or the film's conclusion), with other sounds plotted accordingly.

The scene represented in figure 1 takes place near the middle of Warners' 1928 part-talkie *Noah's Ark*. During World War I, German refugee Marie (Dolores Costello) passes as French in order to gain employment at the Théâtre des Alliés, where, while working as a member of the chorus line, she encounters Russian officer Nickoloff (Noah Beery), who is convinced that he recognizes her. A cursory glance at the 145-second conversation represented here reveals a characteristic trait of early sound film. With all sounds located in the medium-loud range, this sequence obeys a simple on/off logic. Each sound component is either fully on or totally off, and the scene, therefore, is all foreground and no background. The only variations in music volume are attributable to musical conventions inherited from silent-film practice. The increase in volume as we cut to shot i underscores Marie's recognition of Nickoloff, while the swell during shot p reflects the intense battle of nerves resulting from Nickoloff's attempt to blackmail Marie. Coming and going according to the film's narrative needs, the dialogue maintains the same volume whenever it is present.

As one can easily imagine from figure 1, this scene's dialogue is not easy to follow, even though both speakers remain close to the camera. Because music volume is always near that of the dialogue (and even at one point louder), music and dialogue regularly interfere with each other. Each sound component obeys its own logic, independently of all other sound, and is produced as if it were the only sound present. The orchestra leader obeys the printed dynamics, as if accompanying a silent film (where music would have no competition from other sounds); the actors speak and are recorded at levels appropriate for a theater (where dialogue would have no competition from other sounds). The soundtrack, thus, is a site of a conflict; the

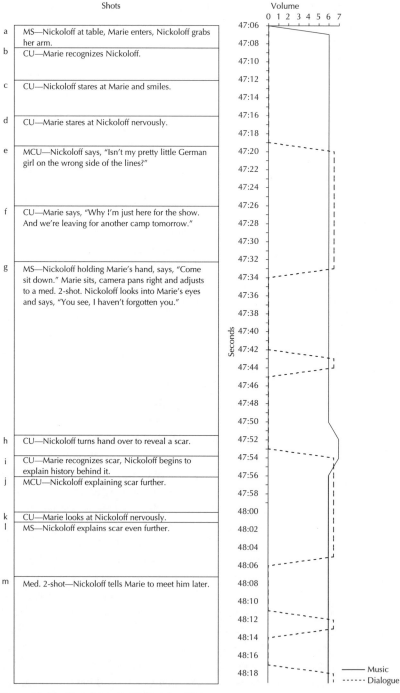

Figure 1. *Noah's Ark* (1928): Théâtre des Alliés.

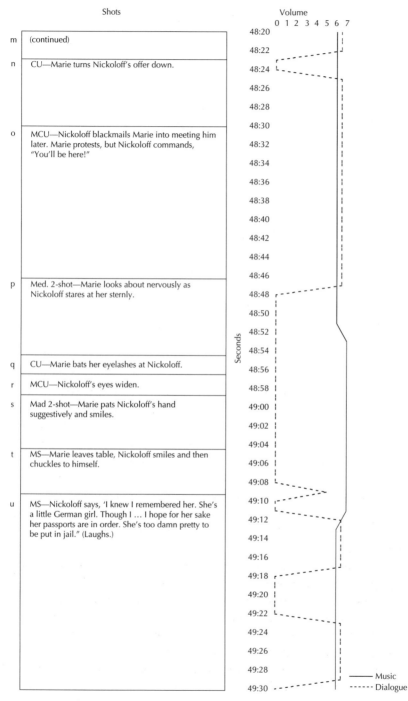

	Shots		Volume 0 1 2 3 4 5 6 7
m	(continued)	48:20 – 48:22	
n	CU—Marie turns Nickoloff's offer down.	48:24 – 48:30	
o	MCU—Nickoloff blackmails Marie into meeting him later. Marie protests, but Nickoloff commands, "You'll be here!"	48:32 – 48:46	
p	Med. 2-shot—Marie looks about nervously as Nickoloff stares at her sternly.	48:48 – 48:54	
q	CU—Marie bats her eyelashes at Nickoloff.	48:56	
r	MCU—Nickoloff's eyes widen.	48:58	
s	Mad 2-shot—Marie pats Nickoloff's hand suggestively and smiles.	49:00 – 49:04	
t	MS—Marie leaves table, Nickoloff smiles and then chuckles to himself.	49:06 – 49:08	
u	MS—Nickoloff says, 'I knew I remembered her. She's a little German girl. Though I … I hope for her sake her passports are in order. She's too damn pretty to be put in jail." (Laughs.)	49:10 – 49:30	

Seconds

———— Music
- - - - - Dialogue

Figure 1. *(continued)*

scene's location may be called the Theater of the Allies, but it is also a theater of war between dialogue and music.

Figure 2 represents another two-component sequence, Mayor Stebbins's disastrous automobile ride from Warners' 1927 ode to the automobile, *The First Auto*. Once again, we note the music's uniform level. "This is my domain," the music seems to say; like the bully on the block, the music confidently declares sole ownership, daring others to take up the challenge. This is precisely what the sound effects do. After a period of relative eclipse, where the effects take a back seat to the music (shots b–h), the sound-effects track suddenly comes out swinging, landing eight separate blows in the space of a minute (shots i–t). The music may dominate the scene through continuity, but the effects achieve greater saliency through their discontinuous, punctuating, high-volume strategy.

We can easily recognize here traces of the historical practices that relegated sound effects to a rather limited role in the mature silent-film accompaniment scheme. Whereas some nickelodeon-era practitioners had experimented with nonstop atmospheric sound effects, the post-1910 rise of musical accompaniment carefully matched to a film's narrative thrust had excluded all effects but (discontinuous, punctual, high-volume) sounds tailored to the narrative or to intermittent comic episodes.[5] Just as the music in early sound films is marked by the conventions of silent-film musical accompaniment, so sound effects in films of the late twenties often merely continue the sound-effect strategies that dominated the previous period. Though films of this period sometimes offer short stretches of what might be called realistic or atmospheric effects (such as the automobile and crowd noise in shots c through h), the potential of these background effects to serve as a guarantor of reality is quickly undermined by a switch to discontinuous sound events. Seven times in a space of forty seconds, from shot i to shot q, the automobile effects suddenly and inexplicably go silent, thus privileging comedy and revealing an auctorial hand, rather than stressing coherent diegetic space and the independent existence of the diegesis.

The primary benefit of this graphic representation strategy derives from the opportunity it affords to analyze a film's mise-en-bande, the relationship between and among various sounds. Additionally, this system foregrounds important image/sound correspondences—or their absence. A glance at the scale of each shot quickly reveals that soundtrack volume is not coupled to the scale of the image, either for the music or the sound effects (whether generalized crowd and automobile sounds or synchronized effects like gunshots and horses neighing). Even a distant look at the second part of figure 2 shows each sound-effect spike taking place according to a similar strategy wholly within a unit composed of one, two, or three whole shots. At the start of each of the eight units (consisting of shots i, j, k, l–m, n, o–p, q, and r–s–t) we hear no sound effects; as the unit proceeds, timed effects are introduced; then, just before the end of the unit, the sound-effects track once again goes silent. While the music assures continuity, the sound effects create an episodic feel—a relationship reversed in Hollywood's mature mise-en-bande, where nearly continuous background effects guarantee continuity (both textual and diegetic), while episodic music intermittently reinforces atmosphere or mood.

It is tempting to assume that the neat correspondence between sound units and image units in this sequence derives from the limitations of early sound technology. To be sure, mixing and rerecording were not standard techniques for mid-1927 sound-on-disc productions. It would be a mistake, however, to conclude that technological limitations dictate this sequence's mise-en-bande. On the contrary, this scene could easily have been shot silent, with the synchronized soundtrack subsequently recorded on a sound stage featuring an orchestra, an automobile, enough extras to sound like a crowd, and a sound-effects specialist. Indeed, this is precisely how the sequence would have been recorded a decade later. There would, however, have been one major difference. Instead of using the sound to punctuate the dividing line between shots, the sound would have been systematically carried over the cuts, thus unifying space and time rather than reinforcing the film's image segmentation.

If cinema had continued to use sound as it is employed in the second half of this sequence from *The First Auto,* then Chion would perhaps be right about the nonexistence of the soundtrack as a separate entity, for in this case sound mixing clearly remains entirely subservient to image editing; meanwhile, the music drones on as if from an unattended phonograph in the next room. The all-or-nothing strategy employed for music and effects alike suggests that this sequence is inhabited by two separate and wholly uncoordinated "tracks," one devoted to music and the other to sound effects. Wholly dependent on earlier sound practices, this solution failed to last out the decade.

Figure 3 represents a short scene from the middle of Warners' first all-talking film, the 1928 *Lights of New York.* Unlike *The First Auto* and *Noah's Ark,* which were overseen by directors inexperienced with sound (Roy Del Ruth and Michael Curtiz), *Lights of New York* was directed by Bryan Foy, who had cut his teeth on a long line of Vitaphone shorts. Only fifty-seven minutes long, with each of the seven reels governed by a unity of time and place that French neoclassical playwrights might envy (but that can easily appear plodding and uninventive from today's vantage point), this film

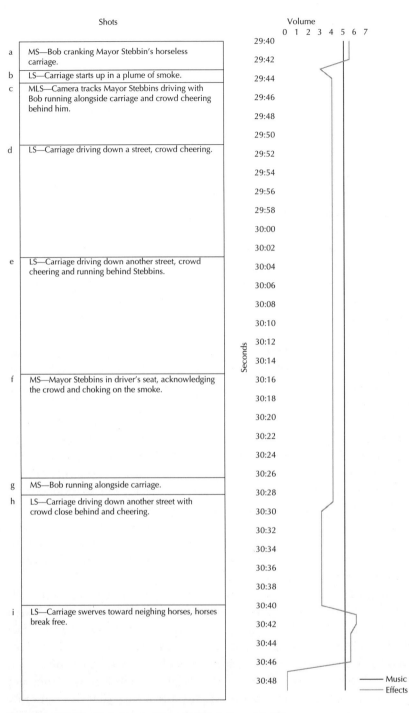

Figure 2. *The First Auto* (1927): Mayor Stebbin's first auto ride.

	Shots		Volume 0 1 2 3 4 5 6 7	Seconds
j	MLS—Carriage driving through street and scaring horses.			30:50 30:52 30:54
k	LS—Carriage drives through fence and yard of man who fires his rifle at them twice.			30:56 30:58 31:00 31:02
l	MLS—Carriage moving down another road.			31:04 31:06
m	LS—Carriage driving down a road, swerves right through a fence.			31:08
n	MLS—Carriage bursting through trees and over a young man lying on the ground.			31:10 31:12
o	MLS—Carriage driving down another road.			31:14
p	LS—Carriage drives through a group of chickens.			31:16 31:18
q	LS—Carriage drives through open horse stable and horses scatter.			31:20 31:22 31:24 31:26 31:28
r	LS—Carriage driving down another road.			31:30
s	LS—Carriage driving over grassy plain.			31:32
t	Extreme LS—Carriage driving over a cliff and into a lake.			31:34 31:36 31:38 31:40
u	LS—Carriage passengers swimming to shore.			31:42 31:44 31:46

——— Music
········· Effects

Figure 2. *(continued)*

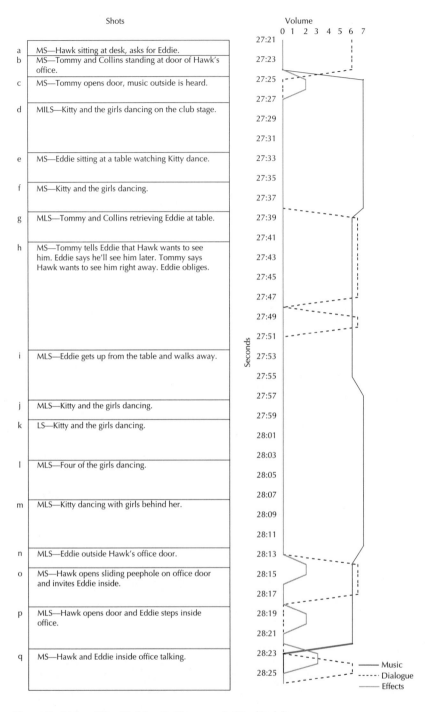

Figure 3. *Lights of New York* (1928): First scene in Hawk's club.

deserves much of the criticism that it has received. When actors in long shot huddle under a barber shop's hanging lamp, one is easily reminded of the scenes in *Singin' in the Rain* that lampoon actors speaking to potted plants and other microphone hideaways.

The awkwardness of early sound handling is well exemplified in figure 3. Shots 1 and 2 depict the office of bootlegger Hawk. Even though the office is located right next to the nightclub stage we hear only dialogue during these shots. As soon as henchman Tommy opens the office door, however, a tidal wave of music floods the soundtrack. At the end of the scene, when good guy Eddie finally enters, the process is simply reversed: with the closing of the door the music is once again instantaneously stripped from the soundtrack. Like the music and dialogue of *Noah's Ark* and the music and effects of *The First Auto,* the music in *Lights of New York* is generally treated in a simple all-or-nothing manner. A more gradational approach to sound would have bridged onscreen and offscreen space—a standard device of later Hollywood sound—but in 1928 each circuit's on/off switch remained more important than the potentiometer (volume control) that would shortly begin to dominate Hollywood mise-en-bande.

However simplistic the film's basic either/or approach to offscreen sound, figure 3 does reveal a few more sophisticated techniques. Fueled by decades of silent-film accompaniment, early sound films seem to take music for granted, spreading it in a uniform layer across every frame of the image. Variations in volume, when they occur at all, are almost always musically motivated. Dialogue must therefore compete for the listener's attention with high-volume music. As figure 3 shows, however, the four dialogue passages in this scene manage to sneak in when the music is not at the fortissimo level that it occupies fully half the time. In shots a–b, the music is not brought up until the dialogue is out of the way; in shot q the music is removed before dialogue begins.

This either/or strategy is not the sole device, however. When Hawk's lieutenants approach Eddie to convoke him to a meeting with Hawk, their dialogue takes place just a few feet away from the orchestra and a line of dancing girls. The cut from a medium long shot (g) to a medium shot (h) clearly signals the conversation's importance, which is recognized on the soundtrack by dipping the music beneath the dialogue. The volume reduction may be minimal, but it is precisely the ability to make such gradational sound-level adjustments that heralds a compromise solution to early sound-cinema's characteristic jurisdictional conflict. Shortly after conclusion of this conversation, the music level is restored to its former peak, only to dip again in expectation of the next dialogue passage (shots n–o), which is once more marked by an attention-concentrating cut from medium long shot to medium shot. The reduction from fortissimo to forte may be insufficient to bring out every word fully, but it does keep the dialogue from being totally stepped on. Executed here in a rudimentary manner, this innovation will enjoy a long and glorious history.

The logic underlying this technique was much debated during Hollywood's conversion to sound. Several sound technicians (led by Bell engineer and Western Electric executive Joseph P. Maxfield) insisted that sound scale should slavishly emulate image scale.[6] Recognizing the limitations of a strict engineering strategy as a model for sound quality, others (including Harry F. Olson, creator of RCA's innovative directional microphone) suggested that sound should reflect the level of the spectator's psychoacoustic interest.[7] Indeed, the repeated cuts from medium long shot to medium shot just as the music is dipping under the dialogue suggest that this new mise-en-bande approach is psychoacoustically inspired. Not only do image and sound work in tandem to reinforce and satisfy viewer needs, but each sound component is carefully adjusted in response to changes in other sound components.

Hardly audible in *Lights of New York*—or in any other film of the 1920s—the new psychoacoustic approach to mise-en-bande was consecrated early in the 1930s as a standard convention of Hollywood sound treatment. Figure 4 offers a particularly clear view of this process. In the opening scene of Universal's 1932 *Back Street* (directed by John Stahl), an enterprising traveling salesman pitches his line to Ray Schmidt, the "toniest girl in Cincinnati" (Irene Dunne), while couples dance and families dine. As compared to the preceding figures, figure 4 reveals several particularities of Hollywood's new approach to sound. Most striking is the virtual omnipresence of low-level atmospheric sound effects. Earlier sound effects had been intermittent, sharp, salient, and carefully synchronized to visual activities; *Back Street* offers sound effects that are continuous, muffled, and unconnected to any specific onscreen activity. The semi-sync nature of these effects has an entirely new effect on the auditor. Whereas synchronized effects (such as the shotgun blasts or the neighing horses in *The First Auto*) separate performance space from audience space, atmospheric effects like those in *Back Street* envelop the audience in a generalized sound ambience, with the sound seemingly coming from all around, thus sonically "enrolling" spectators in the film's space.[8]

These sound effects are thus used in a manner exactly opposed to the scene's dialogue. Always foregrounded, this scene's four sustained dialogues (shots a–b, j–k, o, and p–s) remain constantly audible above the music and effects. Furthermore, the dialogue is always synchronized with the image. However much the effects create a generalized three-dimensional space, the dialogue locates the auditor/viewer squarely opposite the onscreen speakers. In this system effects and dialogue perform complementary and coordinated roles. While atmospheric effects anchor the diegesis, creating a sense of continuous reality, the dialogue furthers the narrative, inviting auditors to attend to specific characters foregrounded by their speech. Sharing the soundtrack as two entirely separate regimes (unlike the earlier system where most sound effects were simply a form of dialogue—the "voice" of objects), effects and dialogue serve as vehicles for two radically separate modes of auditor identification.

Music is essential in facilitating this dual identification structure. Instead of the earlier on/off approach, music is here allowed to range over the entire volume spectrum. Like atmospheric effects, the music thus remains continuously present, even when its volume is reduced to assure maximum dialogue comprehension. In this particular scene, the music derives from a diegetic source (the beer garden band), but it is not treated in the manner traditionally associated with diegetic sound sources. Instead of basing volume levels on apparent spectator distance from the sound source, this scene at every point simply subordinates music volume to the dialogue. Before the dialogue begins, the music volume is diminished just enough to assure comprehension. When the dialogue ends, the music returns to full volume—even when the arrival of a new dialogue passage will force another reduction in just a few seconds (see, for example, shot p, where full-volume music lasts only three seconds).[9]

This system has two functions: to guarantee comprehensible dialogue and to confect a soundtrack with virtually constant total volume. Were we to plot the combined volume of dialogue and effects from virtually any classical Hollywood scene with music, we would find a graph of peaks and valleys, of narrative and atmosphere, of adventure and repose. Adding in the music volume, however, we would find nearly level total volume. Compensating for differences in the other sound components, the music sees to it that overall attention remains high, even in the absence of specific events. In its high-volume mode (when there is no dialogue to compete with), music thus serves a pseudo-narrative function, providing a relay between specific narrative events. In its low-volume mode (when it plays under dialogue or narratively important effects), music joins atmospheric effects in assuring continuity and a generalized sense of space.

This scene from *Back Street* exemplifies an innovative method of combining sound components that would become Hollywood's mixing standard. Whereas early sound films simply transported to the soundtrack diverse and contradictory conventions derived from various preexisting sound traditions (silent films, public address, legitimate theater, vaudeville,

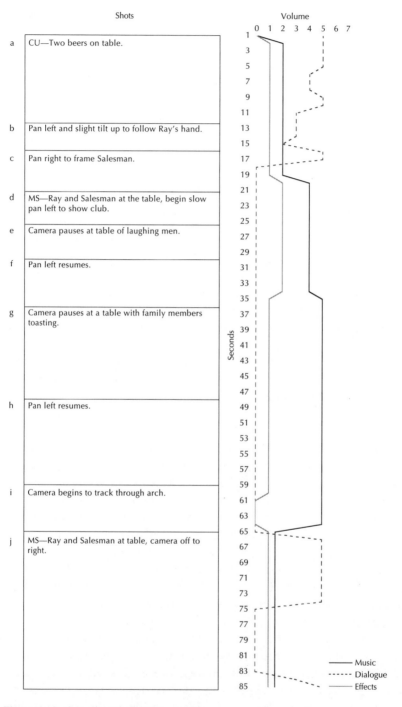

Figure 4. *Backstreet* (1932): Opening sequence.

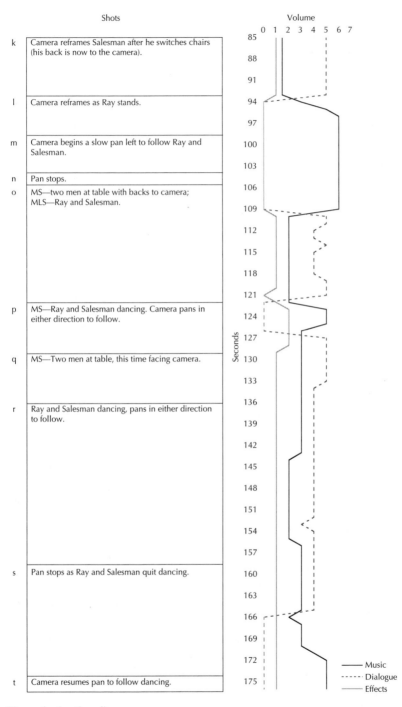

Figure 4. *(continued)*

phonography), *Back Street* offers an integrated soundtrack dependent on a series of new principles. Earlier effects had been discontinuous; classical Hollywood sound effects can be continuous because they are embedded in a multiplane sound environment facilitating simultaneous presentation of foreground and background sounds. Dialogue and music can now share the same soundtrack without getting in each other's way thanks to systematic deployment of an intermittent strategy. Instead of conflicting, all three can be integrated into a single soundtrack through the serial or simultaneous application of realist or psychoacoustic principles.

Chion rightly asserts that the existence of sound does not alone make the "soundtrack" an acceptable analytical category. For a soundtrack to exist as an independent entity, individual sounds have to be constructed in relation to each other as well as to the image. This is precisely what took place in Hollywood's treatment of sound between 1925 and 1932. Separate components were increasingly combined according to a new set of conventions designed to facilitate simultaneous coexistence of multiple sound types in a single sound space. As these conventions were solidified, the soundtrack itself became an independent reality.

Multiplexing as Systemic Negotiation

How should we construct the creation of the soundtrack as a separate but multiple entity? Before Hollywood's conversion to synchronized sound, the elaboration of sound accompaniment had been simplified by two important factors. First, silent-film accompaniment is typically univocal in nature, involving either live music, or a lecturer, or live dialogue, or mechanically reproduced sound, but rarely more than one of these sound sources at a time. The question of how to combine various different sounds was thus infrequently broached in the silent-film trade press. Second, the one instance where two types of sound were regularly combined—live music and sound effects—was regulated by long-established traditions governing musical ensembles. Because silent-film sound-effect producers (usually drummers) were also members of the orchestra, they remained under the baton of the conductor. As such they were bound by prevailing traditions; like other musicians, they respected existing conventions regarding the integration of multiple lines into a single coherent musical performance. The dominance of an already negotiated standard for sonic cohabitation made it easy for mature silent-film accompaniment to achieve this coherence.

Hollywood's conversion to synchronized sound led to a more complex situation. While the earliest sound treatments simply replicated the standards of a familiar sound performance—silent-film accompaniment (Warners'

Don Juan [1926]), amplified public address (Will Hays's speech introducing the inaugural Vitaphone shorts program), or a phonograph record (most of the other items from that program)—the introduction of conversational dialogue and the realistic use of effects complicated affairs, with early sound films regularly combining existing sound practices, without regard for the diminished effect of each separate component. As we have seen in the case of *Noah's Ark,* for example, music and dialogue often contested the right to the audience's attention, with each undermining the effect of the other. Bounded by the sound system's dynamic limits on the one hand and the limits of human attention on the other, the soundtrack became an arena that multiple sound conventions sought to dominate. Not only did music, dialogue, and effects clash, but also differing traditions regarding the "proper" way to present sound: live versus recorded music, ex cathedra lectures versus situated dialogue, narrative sound effects versus vaudevillesque comic effects.

To each of these countervening approaches correspond a group of workers, a set of economic commitments, and a body of beliefs regarding the value of a particular sound strategy. This is why the trade press of the period is filled with pointed arguments for and against diverse approaches to sound. Some disagreements are familiar, like the technical spats opposing sound-on-disc to sound-on-film. More important for the evolution of mise-en-bande are quarrels opposing intelligibility to realism or close-up sound to sound/image scale-matching and economic clashes between owners out to make a buck and workers out to save their jobs. New mise-en-bande conventions affected groups of all sorts. Researchers, manufacturers, technicians, exhibitors, and unions all had an interest in what at first seems no more than a technical affair: the establishment of standards for selecting, combining, and reproducing sounds on the film soundtrack.

In other words, because changes in technology and technique affect material interests as well as philosophical investments, the new recorded soundtrack triggered open competition that took several forms. Separate components (and implicitly the sound traditions from which they are derived) made countervening and mutually exclusive claims to soundtrack space. The same rivalry also invaded the set and the theater, where technicians vied for jobs and power.[10] Even the distant domain of technology was heavily marked by competition between corporations (ATT versus RCA), general strategies (telephone versus radio approaches), and specific hardware (omnidirectional versus directional microphones). Thus was the cinema soundtrack thrust into a jurisdictional struggle.

Eventually, competition gave way to a process of negotiation. Instead of confronting (and thus undermining) each other, sounds were fitted together in novel ways, so as to allow simultaneous communication of multiple information channels. Thanks to interstitial and multiplanar logic, multiple sound components eventually succeeded in sharing space limited by dynamic range and human attention. Guaranteeing reality and fidelity through a nearly continuous but backgrounded effects track, the new mise-en-bande assured intelligibility through a foregrounded but intermittent dialogue track (which no longer had to assure scale-matching fidelity because the effects had taken up the cause of realism). Similarly, variations in volume helped music provide continuous commentary, while making way for narratively important dialogue. Benefiting multiple users, the new overdetermined, multiplexed mise-en-bande simultaneously satisfied the needs of narrative, realism, and identification. Whereas silent cinema subordinated all sounds to the music and its conductor, sound cinema negotiated soundtrack policy with all interested parties. What today we call the soundtrack is thus the multiplane product of a historical crisis characterized by conflict and negotiation, eventually resulting in rule-governed cohabitation.

Notes

1. For several examples, see Rick Altman, "Filmscripts: A Manifesto," *Quarterly Review of Film Studies* 2 (1977): 88–95.

2. Irwin Bazelon, *Knowing the Score: Notes on Film Music* (New York: Arco, 1975), 52.

3. Michel Chion, trans. and ed. Claudia Gorbman, *Audio-vision* (New York: Columbia University Press, 1994), 68 (emphasis in original). See also *La Voix au cinéma* (Paris: Editions de l'Etoile, 1982), 13–14.

4. See "Sound Space" and "Introduction: Sound/History" in *Sound Theory/ Sound Practice,* ed. Rick Altman (New York: Routledge/AFI, 1992), 46–64 and 113–25; "Deep-Focus Sound: Citizen Kane and the Radio Aesthetic," *Quarterly Review of Film and Video* 15, no. 3 (1994): 1–33; and "Penser l'histoire (du cinéma) autrement: un modèle de crise," *Vingtième siècle* 46 (1995): 65–74.

5. See Rick Altman, "Reading Positions, the Cow Bell Effect, and the Sounds of Silent Cinema," *Cinema(s)* 3 (1992): 19–31, and "Naissance de la réception classique: la campagne pour standardiser le son," *Cinémathèque* 6 (1994): 98–111.

6. On this topic, see Rick Altman, "Sound Space."

7. See especially Harry F. Olson and Frank Massa, "On the Realistic Reproduction of Sound with Particular Reference to Sound Motion Pictures," *JSMPE* [Journal of the Society of Motion Picture Engineers] 23, no. 2 (August 1934): 63–81; and Rick Altman, "The Technology of the Voice," part 1, *Iris* 3, no. 1 (1985): 3–20; part 2, *Iris* 4, no. 1 (1986): 107–19.

8. The "surround sound" impact is further strengthened by the film's failure to provide sound matches for obvious image cues (the children clinking beer glasses) or to amplify foregrounded effects (Ray slapping the salesman). Later Hollywood practice requires sound matches for all clearly visible sound cues. In addition, all narratively important sounds are afforded the same status as dialogue; that is, they are "sweetened" (amplified) so as to stand out from other (atmospheric) effects. The use of room tone in later Hollywood practice guarantees that even moments of "silence" will bear (just) audible witness to diegetic reality.

9. In 1934, with general distribution of Warners' apparatus known as the "up-and-downer," Hollywood studios began automatic reduction of music levels when dialogue begins. This device simply measured changes in volume on the separate dialogue input, and automatically adjusted music volume accordingly. See W. A. Mueller, "A Device for Automatically Controlling Balance Between Recorded Sounds," *JSMPE* [Journal of the Society of Motion Picture Engineers] 25, no. 1 (July 1935): 79–86.

10. On this topic see Rick Altman, "Le son contre l'image ou la bataille des techniciens," in *Hollywood, 1927–41,* ed. Alain Masson (Paris: Editions Autrement, 1991), 74–86.

ANNABEL J. COHEN

Film Music
Perspectives from Cognitive Psychology

✳

In the language of cognitive psychology, cinema is a multisensory stimulus that, millisecond by millisecond, impinges on sensory receptors and excites networks of neuronal activity in the mind of every film spectator. Writing in 1936, long before the emergence of a rigorous cognitive psychology, literary critic Walter Benjamin (1969) described the daunting perceptual-cognitive challenge that cinema presents to each member of the audience:

Let us compare the screen on which a film unfolds with the canvas of a painting. The painting invites the spectator to contemplation; before it the spectator can abandon himself to his associations. Before the movie frame he cannot do so. No sooner has his eye grasped a scene than it is already changed. It cannot be arrested. . . . The spectator's process of association in view of these images is indeed interrupted by their constant, sudden change. (240)

With its reference to the visual domain, Benjamin's comparison of the vicissitudes of the cinema screen to the painter's static canvas is apt as far as it goes. But no account of cinematic experience is complete without consideration of the auditory domain, that of music, speech, and sound effects. For example, Michel Chion emphasizes that what we see is always altered by what we hear. He refers to the "added value" of sound that "engages the very structuring of visions . . . by rigorously framing it" (Chion 1990, 7). Cognitive psychology enables us to examine in an experimentally controlled way how joint stimulation from the auditory and visual domains operate in our cognition of the cinema.

To illustrate the use of, and perhaps need for, a cognitive approach to

In keeping with the standards of psychology literature, social-sciences citation style is used in this chapter. *Eds.*

film music, consider a brief sequence from *Parenthood*. While depicting an ordinary Little League baseball game, the camera tracks the trajectory of a baseball and focuses finally on a young player. This is his moment. Will he catch the ball or not? First he fumbles and then miraculously recovers the ball. On the surface, the excerpt depicts an everyday childhood baseball game, but Randy Newman's music tells us that this is not an ordinary event. Rousing triplets in the full orchestra, along with unresolved harmonies, accompany the ball's flight. As the boy catches the ball, the music ceases; the umpire yells, "He's outa there," immediately followed by a jubilant brass fanfare in $\frac{4}{4}$ time. Can there be disagreement that these contrasting music selections produce associations that add meaning to the film? Surely not. The rousing triplets and unresolved harmonies heighten the audience's understanding of the emotional significance, but also anxiety and uncertainty, of the young boy and his father. The fanfare celebrates the boy's success, and so too then does the audience. In this example, film music clearly adds meaning for the audience.

Suppose we now play back only the musictrack from the excerpt. The music might conjure up images (past visual associations) of the ball, the boy, the fumble, or the catch. Thus, a second role of music is to aid the audience in remembering parts of the film, reinforcing the connection among film events and eliciting associations.

Without music, the images seem prosaic, mundane, even lifeless; with music, however, the world of film comes alive. Through music however, film spectators become part of the crowd watching the game, forgetting the theater seat and the screen. It is ironic that music is such a powerful vehicle in this regard. For most of the excerpt under discussion, diegetic sound effects are absent: only music is heard behind a "silent" crowd. In the real-life situation, the opposite would obtain: ambient crowd noise and no music in the background. In the film, as soon as the boy catches the ball, diegetic sound effects return. A psychological sense of reality continues in spite of the discontinuity in the audio background. Does the film audience miss the diegetic sound? Does the audience even notice the absence? Does the music make the event more compelling?

This examination of one fairly representative excerpt from a Hollywood film points to three functions of film music: (1) music interprets and adds meaning; (2) it aids memory; (3) it suspends disbelief. But it is one thing to postulate these functions of film music speculatively and another to subject the postulates to convincing empirical tests. Here is where the methods of cognitive psychology prove useful. With its reliance on controlled experiments, cognitive psychology can place a provocative but speculative theory on solid psychological foundations. Empirical evidence from psychology experiments helps complete our understanding of how music aids the audience's comprehension of a film.

Meaning

It is generally assumed that musical soundtracks influence the interpretation of images they accompany. For example, Royal Brown (1994) describes music's tendency to narrativize film images. He makes the general assumption that "musical scores very often tell our emotions how to read a given filmic sequence" (54). Similarly, George Burt (1994) writes of music's power to "open the frame of reference to a story and to reveal its inner life in a way that could not have been as fully articulated in any other way" (4). Showing how a particular passage of music influences an interpretation of a film clarifies the statement that "film music influences interpretation." Possible contributions of cognitive psychology to this issue are reviewed below.

For instance, one of my experiments investigated a single dimension of emotional meaning (happy/sad) as a product of the interaction between a monophonic melody and one moving object. The musical examples used repeating broken major triads that differed in only two respects: tempo and pitch. These musical examples were presented at a slow, moderate, or fast tempo and were low, medium, or high in pitch. Previous work in the auditory dimension alone had revealed that tempo and pitch height controlled listeners' judgments on a five-point happiness/sadness rating scale (Trehub, Cohen, and Guerriero 1985). In other words, low pitch on average led to a rating below three and high pitch led to a rating above three. Slow and fast tempo led to low and high numerical judgments, respectively. The visual stimulus in the audiovisual experiment was a computer-generated ball that bounced at one of three heights and at one of three speeds. Again, perhaps surprisingly, previous work had suggested that these dimensions led to systematic judgments on the happy-sad dimension. Low, slow bounces were judged as sad, and high, fast bounces were judged as happy (Cohen 1993).

As might be expected, the experiments show that when the auditory and visual dimensions are congruent (low bounce/low pitch, or high bounce/high pitch), the judgment is consistent with the presentations of either audio or visual modality alone. When the audio and visual dimensions diverge, however, the judgment tended to fall between the rating for either the audio or visual dimension alone. A slow melody in a low register, for instance, produced judgments of the high-fast ball that were lower (less happy) than they were in the absence of the music, even when subjects were asked to judge only the ball. They seemed unable to resist the systematic influence of music in determining their interpretation of the image. This suggests that, in the simplest case, the cognition of film music is additive: it sums up associations or meanings mentally generated by the different film and music components.

Using slightly more complex video and audio materials, another study measured multiple scales of affective meaning employing the semantic differential technique (Marshall and Cohen 1988).[1] Here, the video material was an animation involving three geometric objects, a small circle and a small and a large triangle. In general, viewers tended to interpret the action of the inanimate objects in a stereotypic and anthropomorphic way; for example, typically viewers see a large bully persecuting a loving, innocent couple. The experiment was designed to test whether and to what extent music alters this basic meaning of the animation. Two contrasting musical scores, A and B, were judged, using rating scales, by different groups of listeners, and a third group judged the film.[2] Then, with either music A or music B in the background, two other groups judged the film overall and each of the three geometric characters. The ratings of the film overall differed with respect to the soundtrack, as might be expected; of special interest, however, was that the apparent effect of music extended to judgments of the geometric objects. The small triangle, for example, seemed more active with one of the musical scores. It is likely that congruence between the temporal patterns of the latter music and the motion of the geometric figures drew attention to the small triangle, which permitted musical meanings to become linked with the small triangle. If this hypothesis, which forms the basis of the "Congruence-Associationist framework" discussed below, is correct, then different music could elicit a different visual focus of attention.

Studies using live-action films suggest that the Congruence-Associationist hypothesis extends to a more typical filmgoing experience. In one experiment (Cohen 1993), two video excerpts—in one, a woman runs from a man, in the other, two men fight—were selected from a film by an amateur director, and two contrasting music selections were used. Once again the film and two music selections were evaluated by independent groups of viewers. Here, the results were mixed: although music strongly affected the interpretation of the male-female chase, the music for the fight scene did not have a strong effect on viewer interpretation. In retrospect, it is clear that the extent of musical influence depends to a large extent on the degree of visual ambiguity. The fight scene was more highly determined than the male-female interaction, which could be interpreted as representing either an aggressive interaction or amorous play. Here ambiguity was probably created by the cultural understanding of gender roles; presumably, music resolves some of the ambiguity of the situation. A final experiment in this series confirmed that music helps determine meaning in an ambiguous situation (Bolivar, Cohen, and Fentress 1994). Here, the visual examples consisted of wolf interactions in which it is unclear whether the wolves are playing or fighting. In this case, too, music was found to have a direct impact on judgments concerning the character of the interaction.

Thus, all four studies reviewed above (the bouncing ball, geometric animation, human interactions, and wolf interactions) found that music helps define the meaning of a scene and that the effect of music is most pronounced when the situation depicted is ambiguous. At the same time, statistical analysis suggests that associations of image are processed independently of musical associations, and that the final meaning we receive from a film is additive, the result of the total associations generated, a finding consistent with a modular theory of mind, which will be discussed below. Not only do these empirical findings of cognitive psychology assure us that film music influences film interpretation, but they also tell us something about what the various components of the music contribute, how much they contribute, and under what circumstances, such as visual or narrative ambiguity, this contribution is maximized.

Memory

A second common assumption of film-music scholarship that can be given empirical support using the method of cognitive psychology concerns effects of musical memory for film. For example, Claudia Gorbman (1987) states that, in just one presentation, a musical leitmotif comes to represent the protagonist Mildred Pierce, in the film of the same name (1945). Here, Gorbman makes an assumption about how musical memory works. Similarly, in Woody Allen's *Oedipus Wrecks* from the *New York Stories* trilogy, the famous ballad "All the Things You Are" is presented during two interactions between a middle-aged wimpy lawyer (played by Allen) and a loony psychic (Julie Kavner) who has taken more than a professional interest in the male protagonist. Does a third presentation of the song while Allen is alone (fondling a roasted chicken leg which Kavner had given him) elicit the audience's memories of Kavner? What evidence is there that music transfers its meaning to another similar situation, that music and film become integrated in the mind, or that the music brings back images of the film and acts as a retrieval cue for the film? Such results, which seem quite intuitive, are in fact somewhat difficult to test empirically.

Nevertheless, aspects of these claims can be empirically tested. One study (Cohen 1995) concludes that music does little to aid in the memory of visual cues because visual recognition is sufficiently high that supplementation is unnecessary. At the same time, the study also demonstrates that subjects are quite capable of remembering pairings of music and images. What then is the function of these music and image pairings? Boltz, Schulkind, and Kantra (1991) found that music aids in directing visual attention; music, in short, marks images for conscious attention, but the extent to which it does so depends on timing and congruence in meaning. In this study, the music either accompanied a scene's outcome and thereby accentuated its affective meaning, or foreshadowed the same scene and thereby created expectations about the future course of events. The background music was either congruent or incongruent with the episode's outcome. In a subsequent recall task, violations of expectation facilitated memory in the foreshadowing condition, while mood-congruent relations led to better performance in the accompanying condition. Results from a recognition task further revealed that music helped subjects recall scenes they did not otherwise remember. The findings were discussed in terms of the ability of background music to manipulate visual attention depending on whether the music either precedes or accompanies the visual image, and whether it is congruent or incongruent with the image. Such evidence, together with the positive results from explicit questioning (Cohen 1995), supports the conclusion that music may be linked with image information in a single presentation, a conclusion that the intuitive model of the cognition of leitmotifs presupposes.

Furthermore, the effects of music on memory for images may extend beyond those discussed above. For example, Thompson, Russo, and Sinclair (1994) show that music influences judgments about perceived closure in a film narrative. They note that in nonmusical contexts, closure has been found to influence memory, and they suggest that future studies of music on closure in film could be directed also to memory issues.

Suspension of Disbelief

Gorbman has stated that "music removes barriers to belief; it bonds spectator to spectacle, it envelops spectator and spectacle in a harmonious space" (1987, 55). From a cognitive standpoint, Gorbman's statement raise an interesting question: how could music produce this profound effect of suspending disbelief? If recall of visual material is neither worse nor better when accompanied by music; and if music is equally well retained whether or not it is accompanied by images, then it appears that musical information does not significantly compete with visual information for mental-processing resources. Likewise, it has also been shown that music does not interfere with the cognitive ability to process dialogue or vice versa (Cohen, unpublished). It is possible therefore that music is processed independently of both film and speech at the early stages of perception, and only at later stages of cognition is the information integrated. If this is so, music requires mental resources beyond those needed to process either image or dialogue. One explanation for the presence of music in film might be that, to some extent, this increased activation heightens our sense of the diegetic film world as real. The real world typically stimulates auditory and visual senses simultaneously. Thus, mentally processing music and film creates a situation mentally more similar to that of real life than processing film alone. But music does not typically accompany real-life events as it does in film. So it may also be that the affective associations of music contribute something lacking in the reality constructed by the film.

As shown in behavioral research of Bolivar et al. (1994), subjects can process music and visual material simultaneously when asked to do so and they can also direct their attention to one or the other modality. Anecdotally, filmgoers are typically unconscious of most film music. Using a survey, Archie Levy (personal communication 1990, 1993) showed the extent to which music escapes notice in films. He asked people leaving a theater what they thought of the music. Most people thought it was fine. Not a very surprising comment, until it is noted that the film had no musical cues except under the opening credits.[3] While music in film serves as a vehicle used to transport emotional meaning, it is a vehicle that is often "inaudible" (Gorbman 1987), much as the font of this page is transparent until I draw attention to it. We can discriminate between `Courier` and *Galliard*, but when reading, we don't really much care whether it is one or the other, as long as it is legible. Similarly, the viewer-listener accepts the musical meaning, but acoustical properties of the music itself seem to function transparently as a kind of "acoustical font."[4]

The situation may be analogous to cognitive psychologist Anne Treisman's concept of illusory conjunction in visual information processing (Treisman and Schmidt 1982). Treisman rapidly presented visual elements on a computer screen, for instance, short lines or simple forms in various orientations and in various colors. Forms and colors were presented only in some colors or orientations. For example, a line tilted at sixty degrees might appear as blue but never as red while a line tilted at ninety degrees would be red but never blue. Subsequently, subjects were presented with visual objects and asked how sure they were that various combinations of features had been previously presented. Subjects often claimed they had seen objects that in fact had not been presented. It is true that the parts of the objects may have been seen, for example, blue color, square shape, sixty-degree orientation, but the parts had never been presented together. That the parts were previously seen together, however, is an illusion.

Something similar may happen with music and images. In this analogy, we can consider music to have two components: an affective component and an acoustical, structural component. When these two components of music are presented simultaneously with a visual image, the conjunction of the affective element and the visual image makes a new meaningful whole, a whole much closer to our sense of reality than the visual image alone, or than the visual image conjoined with both affective and acoustical components. Through the illusory conjunction process, the affect, originally carried via the acoustic properties of music, attaches to the visual stimulus. One or both of two hypothetical processes may account for this disjunction of acoustical and affective information. First, a reality test may exist that must be passed in order for information to achieve conscious attention. The visual information plus the affect from music can pass this test because in real life visual information is often associated with such feelings. For example, when children are playing Little League baseball, spectators feel sad when the child fumbles the ball. (For unknown reasons, a visual depiction of such a scene does not generate this emotional response on its own.) Thus, the visual scene plus the feeling of sadness passes the reality test. However, visual information plus the acoustic aspect of music would not pass the reality test, because the combination of musical sounds and Little League baseball does not match reality. The match to reality is important because it may relate to psychological attentional processes. Many things vie for our attention, and Grossberg (1995) argues that only those that match typical expectations receive attention. He has proposed an Adaptive Resonance Theory (ART) of attention that entails such a mechanism whereby information in short-term memory proceeds to consciousness only if matched by predictions based on "realities" of long-term memory. Such predictions can be based on the schemas we have developed through experience and hold in long-term memory in order to interpret moment-to-moment experiences. The same idea, however, applies to arbitrarily constructed experimental stimuli (like geometric objects of different colors and orientations).

A second but not mutually exclusive mechanism for how music might aid film in constructing its reality arises through overloading the mental processes responsible for the separate visual and auditory senses. The flood of stimulation provided by music and film may somehow reduce the criteria for reality—anything creating this much mental activity must be taken seriously though perhaps in the same way as a dream suspends disbelief

(Mitroff and Bennis 1993, 56–58). An extension of this is the notion that the less realistic the images, the more music must contribute to a suspension of disbelief; for example, music is more likely to need to "suspend disbelief" in a cartoon than a documentary. These ideas are speculative, but admit to further testing.

Cognitive psychological studies of memory and attention can thus begin to account for the mind's ability in the cinematic context to exploit the semantic, affective dimension of music while ignoring the acoustical aspect not anchored in the image. Subjects in experiments can seem oblivious to the acoustical dimension of music (although they will focus on it and remember it when asked to do so, in the same way that we see the font when asked about it). A cognitive theory such as ART can account for the failure of the acoustical dimension of music to reach consciousness.

Modularity, Domain Specificity, Music, and Cinema

Film music encourages us to consider the extent to which certain domains of experience are addressed distinctively by the brain. As a clear example, it has long been known that a part of the temporal cortex called Wernicke's area, in the left hemisphere in right-handed individuals, specializes in the cognition of speech (reviewed in Patel and Peretz 1997; Peretz 1993). There is a class of sounds that, if interpreted as speech, are processed in the left hemisphere but, if interpreted as nonspeech music, are processed elsewhere. Sounds are apparently sent to Wernicke's area to be processed as speech and to somewhere else to be processed as music. Evidently, the brain treats certain information on the basis of its function (Dingwall 1993). Whereas this suggests separable and independent modes of mental processing, there is also evidence that information from these different sensory inputs can be integrated at higher levels of cognition. Several studies have shown that song lyrics, for example, provide memory retrieval cues for the music associated with them, and vice versa (Crowder 1993; Crowder, Serafine, and Repp 1990). Something similar likely occurs with film music, as it has been demonstrated that music can alter the interpretation of visually presented action (Cohen 1993) and even influence the extent to which a filmed action appears completed (Thompson et al. 1994).

The relative cognitive independence of music and image seems consistent with Fodor (1983), who argues that the sensory input systems must be modular. Modularity of the mind starts with a fairly obvious fact of physiology: the peripheral visual system encodes activities that take place at the retina, not at the cochlea. Modularity has a number of important consequences, one of which is that not all the information obtained from the perceptual and cognitive activity of peripheral modular processes can be recovered through conscious reflection. The outputs of the modular input systems likely connect in order to make a holistic experience. This means that the holistic experience is synthetic, that is, an illusion. Our perception of reality is a construct to the extent that it appears integrated. In the fifteen years since Fodor's celebrated treatise on modularity, a number of neurophysiological and psychological studies have provided additional evidence on the extent of separable mental processes. Some of these are reviewed below as being relevant to our concern about how the complexity of music can be handled amid the simultaneous processing of other complex media.

Historically, the first evidence of a special brain area for music was revealed by Milner (1962) in patients who had only one cerebral hemisphere intact. An undamaged right hemisphere, as compared to left, was associated with better performance on a Seashore task of musical memory. Similar results were obtained using a more extensive music test battery from Gordon (Kester et al. 1991). Studies of patients with unilateral temporal lobectomy have also revealed enhanced learning and retention of melodic material when the right hemisphere is preserved (Samson and Zatorre 1991). Other studies with patient populations have shown that melodic imagery and perception (Zatorre and Halpern 1993) and timbre sensitivity (Samson and Zatorre 1994) are lateralized to the right hemisphere. In normal listeners, lateralization of musical and verbal functions has been shown through dichotic listening tasks (different sounds to two ears). A left-ear (right hemisphere) advantage for musical information and a right-ear (left hemisphere) advantage for verbal information is typically reported (Kimura 1964, 1967). Although information from each ear goes to both hemispheres, the ear advantage implies privileged processing by the contralateral hemisphere. PET (Positron Emission Tomography) scan studies conducted by Zatorre and his colleagues further support the notion of special brain loci for music.

Results have revealed that the brain activity is systematically related to the type of musical task (Zatorre, Evans, and Meyer 1994). In other words, different parts of the brain "light up" when certain kinds of listening occur. The part of the brain involved in rhythmic activities is a more primitive part of the brain, the cerebellum, which is associated with movement and balance (Jourdain 1997). It is an area that would also be involved in dance and motor responses to the music. When a song is presented with lyrics, part of the right hemisphere is stimulated by the music and part of the left hemisphere is stimulated by the words. This result is fully consistent with the work of Milner and Kimura. Zatorre, Halpern, Perry, Meyer, and Evans (1996), which also showed that musical perceptual and imaging tasks activate almost identical areas in the temporal cortex and supplementary motor area. In other words, musical (that is, auditory) images (in the absence of external stimulation) and music perception (auditory representations accompanying stimulation) entail the same brain activity.

The brain-imaging tasks confirm that several aspects of musical processing occupy different areas of the brain than does speech processing. This is consistent with the idea that processes considered to represent distinct media, such as speech and music, do not compete for the same brain space. Separate, independent systems for verbal and musical information are also implied in psychological studies of short-term memory by Deutsch (1970). In these studies, subjects on each trial heard one tone followed by a comparison tone and were asked whether the second tone was the same as the first tone. This task was not difficult, but, if a sequence of different tones was interpolated between the first and last tones, then the task became more difficult. The interpolated tones interfered with the memory for the first tone. However, when a series of spoken numbers replaced the interpolated tones, memory comparison of the first and last tones once again became easy. This demonstrates that tones were processed by the brain independently of verbal information, like spoken numbers.

The psychological evidence that different media, in this case speech and music, may excite independent brain activities is consistent with the views on intelligence of Gardner (1983/1993), who has argued for eight types of intelligence, music being one of these.[5] Other intelligences relevant to the present discussion are linguistic and spatial. Modularity and the notion of separate intelligences are consistent with the view that music activates separate parts of the mind distinct from visual-spatial and verbal information, the chief aspects of the cinematic experience.

The neurophysiological and psychological studies taken together support the view of domain-specific mental structures for storage and processing of visual, verbal, and musical information. This provides a foundation for understanding how music can function in a variety of ways in cinema.

Congruence-Associationist Framework for Understanding Film-Music Communication

A preliminary framework representing some aspects of the processing of cinema is presented in figure 1. The framework is essentially a flow diagram that highlights certain aspects of the independent and interactive processing of the three primary media in cinema. It also illustrates that, through structural congruence, music directs specific visual attention and conveys meaning or associations (Cohen 1990, 1993). Hence the framework is referred to as Congruence-Associationist.[6] It emphasizes that music is a vehicle transporting a variety of information, only some of which is relevant to a particular cinematic goal. The brain seems to be able to select what is useful for the goal at hand. A prime example is the role that affective meanings or associations from music provide to a visual narrative; in this case, the sounds themselves are almost of no concern whereas the affective meaning conveyed by the music is often of critical importance.

The diagram represents six levels of information flow, from A to F. Level A represents the surface structure—of speech, video, and music. At level B, each of these is analyzed into components by domain-specific systems. For music, this means decomposition into temporal structures and emotional meaning (affect). (There are, of course, other kinds of feature analysis that would take place, but the diagram emphasizes these two.) Level B affords the possibility for cross-modal congruencies to take control and automatically lead preliminary attention only to a portion of the visual information, shown here as the material within the oval.

To explain further: cognitive psychologists typically have applied Gestalt principles to visual pattern and lately to auditory information (for example, Bregman 1990, 1993; Narmour 1991). Rarely are the principles applied to the two domains at once. But film music provides an opportunity for this application. It is my view that music accompanying a film automatically elicits bottom-up principles that entail grouping across auditory and visual domains. When the auditory information and visual information are structurally congruent, the visually congruent information becomes the figure, the visual focus of attention. What I am suggesting is that Gestalt theoretic ideas (I have avoided the word "principles" here because it implies more precision than is actually the case), which are typically applied to visual or auditory domains independently, can be applied equally productively to conjoint visual and auditory dynamic information. It follows that, through innate Gestalt grouping processes, music can define the visual figure against the audiovisual background; music can sometimes determine what is the visual focus of attention.

These ideas relate to those in the film-music literature on sensitivity to, and effectiveness of, congruent musical and film structures. An example is Prokofiev's score for the famous "Battle on the Ice" sequence in *Alexander Nevsky,* where the temporal contour of the melody mimics the static visual contour of the scene. "Mickey-mousing" supplies countless other examples. In these instances, the composer or director has intuitions that similar formal or structural congruence between music and video patterns promote an appreciation for the content of the film. The present framework enables research on the following questions: To what extent is the cross-dimensional structural congruence encoded? How accurate must the congruence be for

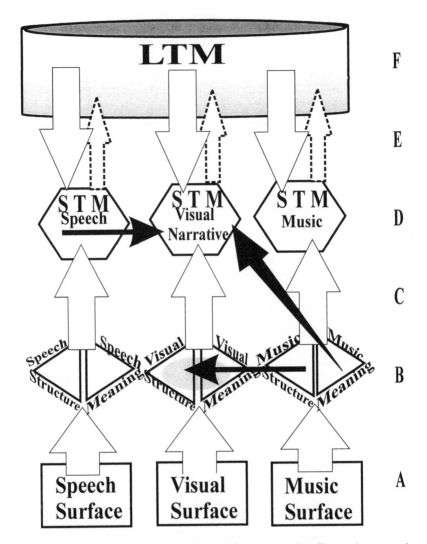

Figure 1. *Congruence-Associationist Framework* for understanding film-music communication. Information-flow diagram of mental activity underlying the joint processing of continuous media of speech, video, and music. At A, the physical surface features of each domain are represented. At B, the surface is analyzed into structural and meaning components. Musical structural information combines with similar visual structural information such that corresponding visual patterns receive priority in traveling (via C) to short-term memory (STM) at D. Level D represents modular STM systems for speech, visual narrative, and music. Note that information from music meaning (at B) travels both to the visual narrative STM at D and to the music STM at D. Information in STM is attended if matched by information sent from long-term memory (LTM) at F. Hypotheses to make sense of the emotional, speech, and visual information are generated at F to match the visual narrative STM at D. Some of this information at D may travel back to LTM (via E) to form new long-term memories at F. Attention to the music is also supported by the analysis through synthesis and a matching approach represented by levels D, E, and F. A similar process is envisioned for speech.

it to be effective? What dimensions in the auditory and visual domains can be manipulated to establish congruence? To what extent does audiovisual congruence focus visual attention?

Returning to the remainder of the framework of figure 1, information is transferred by level C to short-term memory (STM) at D. Certain visual information has priority of transfer, specifically, that in the gray oval. In other words, not all of the visual information that is potentially available reaches short-term memory. In addition, information on musical meaning is transferred not only to a music STM station but also to the visual STM station. The visual STM station is referred to as the STM Visual Narrative. The term *narrative* indicates the goal of the STM process to make sense of the visual information using whatever information is at hand. Thus, the affective quality of music is directed here because it is useful in determining the meaning of the visual scene.

To explain how we become conscious of this material in STM, we turn to Grossberg's (1995) model of conscious attention. This model asserts that material in STM must be matched by material in long-term memory (LTM). Assuming that experiences in LTM include affective tone, it is conceivable that a matching process would take place for visual and affective information from a film, whereas the acoustical properties of the musical accompaniment that gave rise to the musical affect would not be matched. In other words, material in STM would be matched by material generated by hypotheses from LTM at F. This would explain why the acoustical aspects of the music would not generally be attended to: the acoustical aspects of the music do not make sense to LTM (where is that background music coming from?), and no hypotheses would be generated easily to include it (unless, of course, music were part of the diegesis, for example, attending a concert or taking a music lesson). Thus, the main phenomenal experience (E) is one of a narrative with visual and emotional components. Running in parallel, all aspects of the music can be processed at a conscious level (see levels D, E, and F in the music column), as it is known that simultaneous tasks can co-occur (Neisser and Becklin 1975), and there is evidence that background music is remembered (Boltz et al. 1991; Cohen unpublished). (A similar process is envisioned for speech as well, but this is not the focus of the present essay).

This framework explains the puzzling and paradoxical role of background music in film. Music adds information that is both consistent and inconsistent with the narrative. The affective quality is consistent; the acoustical aspects of the music are not. Although the affective associations produced by the music seem to belong to the corresponding images, the sounds that produced those associations do not. Somehow, the brain attends to this affective meaning, while ignoring or attenuating its acoustical source (see Cohen 1994). Fodor (1983) and many others have commented that only some of the information that is encoded reaches consciousness. In the case of background music, it seems that the affective meaning of the music reaches consciousness but the acoustical musical surface does not, at least in the stream focusing on the visual interpretation. Of course, there may be exceptions to this general notion. Some individuals may in fact be particularly sensitive to film music and actually attend films because of it, just as a minority of individuals have absolute pitch and are aware of the actual note name and frequency of musical tones they hear.

Conclusion

I have attempted to show here how the effects of film music on meaning, memory, and the construction of a reality within a film can be addressed from a cognitive perspective. A Congruence-Associationist framework has been proposed as a basis for new research. In particular, I have hypothesized that conjunctions of musically generated affective associations and film meanings account for a sense of reality or suspension of disbelief created by films. I have also suggested that music draws upon a pool of resources, that, at some level, is independent of resources needed for processing and remembering narrative, speech, and visual aspects of the film.

The proposed framework accommodates formal (structural) and associationist (meaning) aspects. The framework enables systematic exploration of effects of music on visual meaning, memory, and belief. It takes into account bottom-up and top-down processing, typically used in accounts of cognitive processing within a single domain (such as Narmour 1991), here extending that theory to several domains simultaneously. The framework also incorporates constraints of memory. This framework will perhaps facilitate cognitive research on the role of music in cinema and assist in building bridges among cognitive researchers and film-music scholars in the humanities. It may elucidate the awesome cognitive capability of film spectators who make sense of an artful barrage of auditory and visual information—a barrage that in only limited ways matches the patterns of stimulation to which we are accustomed in the real world.

Notes

This work was supported by research grants from the Social Science and Humanities Council of Canada (SSHRC) as well as a SSHRC Canada Research Fellowship. Appreciation is expressed to the editors of this volume and to Charlene Morton for suggestions on an earlier version of this essay.

1. This procedure was invented by Osgood, Suci, and Tannenbaum (1957). It uses many bimodal adjective pairs (like happy-sad, hot-cold, nice-awful) in order to obtain affective meaning on three basic independent dimensions, Evaluation, Potency, and Activity. Osgood's first studies of meaning concerned auditory stimuli, and he was very interested in synaesthetic experience. Tannenbaum (1956) also published a study on the role of background music in live drama and television performance.

2. Using separate groups for each excerpt of interest avoids the problem of bias from prior exposure.

3. Such inattention to music extends to other media involving image-music relationships. In another study (Cohen 1987), students watched a slide presentation about their university campus. The presentation had one of four backgrounds: jazz, appropriate, inappropriate, or none. All subjects were asked to rate the appropriateness of the musical soundtrack. Only one of twenty-four subjects in the condition that had no soundtrack commented on its absence. All others indicated their appreciation of this nonexistent background music; their average fell between that for appropriate and inappropriate music.

4. As David Raskin has written of film music, "its great usefulness is the way in which it performs its role without an intervening conscious act of perception" (in Burt 1994, 5). John Huston credits Alex North with being able to "convey an emotion to the audience with its hardly being aware of the existence of a score" (in Karlin 1994, 204). Inaudibility is of course a major claim of Gorbman's (1987).

5. Gardner's evidence for the intelligences is based on specialized neural centers for these intelligences, a unique developmental course, examples of precociousness as well as isolated presence in savants, cross-cultural universals in the display of these abilities, and distinct notation systems that have emerged for each.

6. The framework extends the Congruence-Associationist framework introduced by Marshall and Cohen (1988) and clarified by Bolivar et al. (1994). A model of attentional focus that considers the interaction of accent structure and association has also been proposed by Lipscomb and Kendall (1994).

References

Benjamin, W. (1969). "The Work of Art in the Age of Mechanical Reproduction." In *Illuminations,* ed. H. Arendt, trans. M. Zohn (219–53). New York: Schocken.

Bolivar, V. J., A. J. Cohen, and J. C. Fentress. (1994). "Semantic and Formal Congruency in Music and Motion Pictures: Effects on the Interpretation of Visual Action." *Psychomusicology* 13:28–59.

Boltz, M., M. Schulkind, and S. Kantra. (1991). "Effects of Background Music on Remembering of Filmed Events." *Memory and Cognition* 19:595–606.

Bregman, A. (1990). *Auditory Scene Analysis.* Cambridge, Mass.: MIT Press.

Bregman, A. S. (1993). "Auditory Scene Analysis: Hearing in Complex Environments." In *Thinking in Sound: The Cognitive Psychology of Human Audition,* ed. S. McAdams and E. Bigand, 10–36. New York: Oxford University Press.

Brown, R. (1994). *Overtones and Undertones: Reading Film Music.* Berkeley and Los Angeles: University of California Press.

Burt, G. (1994). *The Art of Film Music.* Boston: Northeastern University Press.

Chion, M. (1990). *Audio-Vision: Sound on Screen.* Ed. and trans. C. Gorbman. (1994). New York: Columbia University Press.

Cohen, A. J. (1987). "Effects of Musical Soundtracks on Attitudes toward and Memory for Information in a Slide Presentation." Joint meeting of Canadian

Society for Brain, Behavior and Cognitive Science and the British Experimental Psychological Society, Oxford, England.

———. (1990). "Understanding Musical Soundtracks." *Empirical Studies of the Arts* 8:111–24.

———. (1993). "Associationism and Musical Soundtrack Phenomena." *Contemporary Music Review* 9:163–78.

———.(1994). "Introduction to the Special Volume on the Psychology of Film Music." *Psychomusicology* 13:2–8.

———. (1995). "One-Trial Memory Integration of Music and Film: A Direct Test." Paper presented at the annual Meeting of the Canadian Acoustical Association, Quebec.

———(Unpublished). "Processing of Music and Film: Independence and Integration. Manuscript in progress.

Crowder, R. G. (1993). "Auditory Memory." In *Thinking in Sound: The Cognitive Psychology of Human Audition,* ed. S. McAdams and E. Bigand. 113–45. New York: Oxford University Press.

Crowder, R. G., M. L. Serafine, and B. Repp. (1990). "Physical Integration and Association by Contiguity in Memory for Words and Melodies of Songs." *Memory and Cognition* 18:469–76.

Deutsch, D. (1970). "Tones and Numbers: Specificity of Interference in Short-Term Memory." *Science* 168:1604–5.

Dingwall, W. O. (1993). "The Biological Basis of Human Communicative Behavior." In *Psycholinguistics,* ed. J. B. Gleason and N. B. Ratner, 40–48. New York: Harcourt, Brace, Jovanovich.

Fodor, J. (1983). *Modularity of Mind.* Cambridge, Mass.: MIT Press.

Gardner, H. (1983/1993). *Frames of Mind: The Theory of Multiple Intelligences.* New York: Basic Books.

Gorbman, C. (1987). *Unheard Melodies: Narrative Film Music.* Bloomington: Indiana University Press.

Grossberg, S. (1995). "The Attentive Brain." *American Scientist* 83:438–49.

Jourdain, R. (1997). *Music, the Brain and Ecstasy: How Music Captures Our Imagination.* New York: Morrow.

Karlin, F. (1994). *Listening to the Movies.* New York: Schirmer.

Kester, D. B., A. J. Saykin, M. R. Sperling, M. J. O'Connor, L. J. Robinson, and R. C. Gur. (1991). "Acute Effect of Anterior Temporal Lobectomy on Musical Processing." *Neuropsychologia* 29:703–8.

Kimura, D. (1964). "Left-Right Differences in the Perception of Melodies." *Quarterly Journal of Experimental Psychology* 16:355–58.

———. (1967). "Functional Asymmetry of the Brain in Dichotic Listening." *Cortex* 3:163–78.

Lipscomb, S., and R. Kendall. (1994). "Perceptual Judgment of the Relationship Between Musical and Visual Components in Film." *Psychomusicology* 13:60–98.

Marshall, S., and A. J. Cohen. (1988). "Effects of Musical Soundtracks on Attitudes to Geometric Figures." *Music Perception* 6:95–112.

Milner, B. (1962). "Laterality Effects in Audition." In *Interhemispheric Relations and Cerebral Dominance,* ed. V. B. Mountcastle, 177–95. Baltimore: Johns Hopkins University Press.

Mitroff, I., and W. Bennis. (1993). *The Unreality Industry.* New York: Oxford University Press.

Narmour, E. (1991). "The Top-Down and Bottom-Up Systems of Musical Implication: Building on Meyer's Theory of Emotional Syntax." *Music Perception* 9:1–26.

Neisser, U., and R. Becklen. (1975). "Selective Looking: Attending To Visually Significant Events." *Cognitive Psychology* 7:480–94.

Osgood, C. E., G. J. Suci, and P. H. Tannenbaum. (1957). *The Measurement of Meaning.* Urbana: University of Illinois Press.

Patel, A. D., and I. Peretz. (1997). "Is Music Autonomous from Language? A Neuropsychological Appraisal." In *Perception and Cognition of Music,* ed. I. Deliege and J. Sloboda, 191–215. Hove, U.K.: Psychology Press.

Peretz, I. (1993). "Auditory Agnosia: A Functional Analysis." In *Thinking in Sound: The Cognitive Psychology of Human Audition,* ed. S. McAdams, and E. Bigand, 199–230. New York: Oxford University Press.

Samson, S., and R. Zatorre. (1991). "Recognition Memory for Text and Melody of Songs after Unilateral Temporal Lobe Lesions: Evidence for Dual Encoding." *Journal of Experimental Psychology: Learning, Memory and Cognition* 17:793–804.

———. (1994). "Contribution of the Right Temporal Lobe to Musical Timbre Discrimination." *Neuropsychologia* 32:231–40.

Stein, B. S., and J. D. Bransford. (1979). "Constraints on Effective Elaboration: Effects of Precision and Subject Generation." *Journal of Verbal Learning and Verbal Behavior* 18:769–77.

Tannenbaum, P. (1956). "Music Background in the Judgment of Stage and Television Drama." *Audio-visual Communication Review* 4:92–101.

Thompson, W. F., F. A. Russo, and D. Sinclair. (1994). "Effects of Underscoring on the Perception of Closure in Filmed Events." *Psychomusicology* 13:9–27.

Trehub, S. E., A. J. Cohen, and L. Guerriero. (1985). "Development of Emotional Sensitivity To Music." *Proceedings of the 12th International Congress on Acoustics,* Toronto, 3:K5–4.

Treisman, A., and H. Schmidt. (1982). "Illusory Conjunctions in the Perception of Objects." *Cognitive Psychology* 14:107–41.

Zatorre, R. J., A. C. Evans, and E. Meyer (1994). "Neural Mechanisms Underlying Melodic Perception and Memory For Pitch." *Journal of Neuroscience* 14:1908–19.

Zatorre, R. J., and A. R. Halpern (1993). "Effect of Unilateral Temporal-Lobe Excision on Perception and Imagery of Songs." *Neuropsychologia* 31:221–32.

Zatorre, R. J., A. R. Halpern, D. W. Perry, E. Meyer, and A. C. Evans. (1996). "Hearing in the Mind's Ear: A PET Investigation of Musical Imagery and Perception." *Journal of Cognitive Neuroscience* 8:29–46.

About the Contributors

✳

RICK ALTMAN teaches film at the University of Iowa. He is author of *The American Film Musical* (Indiana University Press, 1987) and editor of *Sound Theory/Sound Practice* (Routledge, 1992). His most recent book is *Film/Genre* (British Film Institute, 1999).

JAMES BUHLER is assistant professor of music theory in the School of Music, The University of Texas at Austin. He is the author (with David Neumeyer) of several articles on analyzing film music and is currently working on a book on mass culture and the dialectic of Enlightenment.

ANNABEL COHEN is professor of psychology at the University of Prince Edward Island. She edited a special issue of the psychology of film music for *Psychomusicology* and serves on the Editorial Board of *Psychology of Music*.

WENDY EVERETT is professor of film at the University of Bath. She is editor of *European Identity in Cinema* (Intellect, 1996) and a contributing editor of *Literature Film Quarterly*.

LUCY FISCHER is director of the Film Studies Program at the University of Pittsburgh. She is author of *Sunrise* (British Film Institute, 1998), *Cinematernity: Film, Motherhood, Genre* (Princeton University Press, 1996), *Shot/Countershot: Film Tradition and Women's Cinema* (Princeton University Press, 1989), and editor of *Imitation of Life/Douglas Sirk, Director* (Rutgers University Press, 1991).

CARYL FLINN is the author of *Strains of Utopia: Gender, Nostalgia, and Hollywood Film Music* (Princeton University Press, 1992).

KRIN GABBARD teaches in the Department of Comparative Literature at

the State University of New York at Stony Brook. He is author of *Jammin'*
at the Margins: Jazz and the American Cinema (University of Chicago
Press, 1996) and editor of *Jazz among the Discourses* (Duke University
Press, 1995), *Representing Jazz* (Duke University Press, 1995), and (with
Glen O. Gabbard) *Psychiatry and the Cinema* (University of Chicago
Press, 1987).

KATHRYN KALINAK is author of *Settling the Score: Music and the Classical Hollywood Film* (University of Wisconsin Press, 1992).

MICHELLE LEKAS is an instructor in the Department of Cultural Studies
and Comparative Literature at the University of Minnesota.

JUSTIN LONDON is associate professor of music at Carleton College. He
is author of several articles in the forthcoming revision of the *New Grove
Dictionary of Music* and at present is completing a monograph on metric
complexity.

MARTIN MARKS teaches music at MIT. He is the author of *Music and the
Silent Film: Contexts and Case Studies, 1895–1924* (Oxford University
Press, 1997).

DAVID NEUMEYER is professor of music theory in the School of Music
and Leslie Waggener Professor in the College of Fine Arts, The University
of Texas at Austin. He formerly taught at Indiana University.

SCOTT PAULIN is a Ph.D. candidate in musicology at Princeton University. He has published articles on queer theory and film music in *Spectator*
and on the film *Single White Female* in *Camera Oscura*.

MURRAY POMERANCE is professor and chair of the Department of So-
ciology at Ryerson Polytechnic University. He is the author of *Magia
D'Amore* (Sun and Moon, 1999) and (with John Sakeris) editor of *Bang
Bang, Shoot Shoot! Essays on Guns and Popular Culture* (Simon and
Schuster, 1999; Pearson Educational, 2000).

RONALD RODMAN is associate professor and chair of the Department of
Music at Carleton College. He is currently working on a book on music for
television.

JEFF SMITH is assistant professor of film and media studies at Washington University. He is the author of *The Sounds of Cinema: Marketing Popular Film Music* (Columbia University Press, 1998).

Index

✳

Blanchard, 111
Bland, James, 191
Blanton, Jimmy, 144
Bleiche Mutter. See *Deutschland, bleiche Mutter*
Blitzstein, Marc, 187
Bloom, Ken, 185 n. 15
"Blue Danube," 129
Blue Kitten (Stothart), 189
Blues and the Beat, The (recording), 269 n. 14, 270 n. 34
Bobrinskoy, Alexei, 246 n. 24
Bogart, Humphrey, 164, 184 n. 6
Bogdanovich, Peter, 207, 244 n. 1
Bohème, La (1965) (Zeffirelli), 279
Bohème, La (Puccini), 283, 284
"Bojangles," 305
Bolivar, V. J., 364, 366, 375 n. 6, 375ref.
Boltz, M., 365, 373, 375ref.
Bondy, A., 141 n. 38
Bonitzer, Pascal, 208, 244 n. 5, 276, 290 n. 7
Bonnaire, Sandrine, 284
Boorman, John, 108
Bordwell, David, 17, 23 n. 3, 24 n. 12, 26 n. 41, 58, 64–65, 79 n. 1, 80 nn. 19 and 23, 116 n. 10, 275, 289 n. 4, 290 n. 5
Bouillon, Jo, 335 n. 24
Boulez, Pierre, 328
Bourne, Michael, 144, 154 n. 1, 156 nn. 13, 15, and 17
Boyz N the Hood (1991), 268
Brakhage, Stan, 154
Bransford, J. D., 377ref.
Brantlinger, Patrick, 292 n. 28
Braque, Georges, 304
Bratton, J., 139 n. 4, 140 n. 21
Braudy, Leo, 314 n. 1
Brav, Ludwig, 24 n. 5
Breakfast at Tiffany's (1961), 248, 252, 254, 256, 258
Brecht, Bertholt, 137
Bregman, A. S., 371, 375ref.
Brewster, Ben, 290 n. 10, 292 n. 34
Broadway Melody, The (1929), 205 n. 19
Broch, Hermann, 293 n. 41
Brown, Royal S., 17–18, 27 n. 45, 27 n. 47, 28 n. 61, 83 n. 58, 95 n. 11, 116 n. 5, 204 n. 6, 244 n. 3, 246 n. 33, 362, 375ref.
Browne, Nick, 29 n. 63
Bruce, Graham, 270 n. 22
Brutalität in Stein (1960), 121, 129

Buchanan, Charles L., 65, 80 n. 24
Büdinger, Mathias, 247, 268 n. 2
Buelow, George J., 25 n. 23
Buffalo Bill and the Indians (1976), 149, 150–51
Buhler, James, 3–4, 23 n. 1, 25 n. 21, 26 n. 37, 27 n. 45, 83 n. 53, 182, 183 n. 4, 186 n. 25
Buhrman, T. Scott, 84 n. 60
Bumstead, Henry, 217
Buñuel, Luis, 293 n. 41
Burlingame, Jon, 29 n. 61
Burnes, Albert J., 150
Burns, Gary, 256, 270 n. 25
Burt, George, 11, 24 nn. 13–14, 204 n. 6, 362, 375 n. 4, 375ref.
Buscombe, Edward, 333 n. 3
Bush, W. Stephen, 58, 79 n. 1
"By a Waterfall," 307–11
Byrd, Craig L., 55 n. 2, 56 n. 22, 57 n. 35

Calder, Alexander, 322
California Split (1974), 142
Calinescu, Matei, 293 n. 41
Cameron, Ken, 245 n. 13
"Camptown Races," 259
Capitol (recording company), 248
Captain Blood (1935), 91, 184 n. 9
Cardinale, Claudia, 253
Carlito's Way (1993), 294 n. 44
Carmen (Bizet), 17, 84 n. 70, 177, 294 n. 44, 325, 328, 335 n. 21
Carmen Fantasy (Waxman), 20
Carnival of the Animals, The (Saint-Saëns), 293 n. 44
Carpenter, Elliot, 174
Carringer, Robert, 294 n. 50
Carroll, Noël, 11–12, 13, 24 nn. 12, 15, and 19, 116 n. 10, 270 n. 35, 275, 289 n. 4
"Carry Me Back to Old Virginny," 191, 192, 194, 194 fig., 196, 199, 199 fig., 200, 201, 201 fig.
Carter, James, 148
Carter, Ron, 144
Carver, Raymond, 143, 155 n. 5
Casablanca (1943), 6, 18–19, 21, 161–78, 179–80, 184 nn. 6, 7, 9, and 12, 185 n. 15
Cassavetes, John, 154
Ceremonie, La (1996), 284
Chabrol, Claude, 284
"Champagne and Quail," 253
Channel Four (company), 107

Index / 385

Ratner, N. B., 376ref.
Raulet, Sylvie, 305, 315 nn. 34, 39, 44, and 46
Ravel, Maurice, 328
Ray, Robert B., 156 n. 23, 276, 290 n. 5
RCA (company), 357
RCA Victor (recording company), 260
Reagan, T., 289 n. 3
Rear Window (1954), 18, 245 n. 23, 284, 293 n. 44
Rebecca (1940), 12
Reddig, William M., 154–55 n. 2
Redman, Joshua, 144, 151
Redupers (1978), 128
"Regiment de Sambre-et-Meuse, Le," 194 fig., 199, 199 fig., 205 n. 18
Reifenstahl, Leni, 52
Reine Elisabeth, La (1912), 282
Reise ins Licht, Eine—Despair (1978), 119
Reitz, 128
Remick, Lee, 258
Repp, B., 368, 376ref.
Reprise (recording company), 250
Republic Pictures (studio), 27 n. 50
Resurrezione, La (Handel), 13
Return of the Jedi (1983). See *Star Wars*
"Reverie," 205 n. 15
Reversal of Fortune (1990), 294 n. 44
Reyes, Ernest, 287
Rheingold, Das (Wagner), 68
Rhino (recording company), 248
Richardson, Miranda, 142, 145, 147
Ricoeur, Paul, 113, 117 n. 27, 275, 289 n. 3
Riddle, Nelson, 248, 255
Rieff, Philip, 291 n. 20
Riesenfeld, Hugo, 74
Ring of the Nibelungen, The (Wagner), 50–51, 61, 79, 124
River, The (1936), 10, 24 n. 6
Rivera, Benito V., 25 n. 23
RKO (studio), 19, 164, 189, 285, 286, 301, 302
Robe, The (1953), 109
Roberts, Julia, 284
Robertson, Pamela, 244 n. 4
Robin Hood: Prince of Thieves (1991), 149
Robinson, Bill, 305
Robinson, J. Bradford, 55 n. 8
Robinson, L. J., 376ref.
Rodman, Ronald, 3, 6, 19, 20, 24 n. 17
Rogers, Buck, 34
Rogers, Ginger, 189, 302–4, 314 n. 31
Rogue Song, The (1929), 189

Romberg, Sigmund, 188, 189, 191, 205 n. 15
Romney, Jonathan, 271 n. 39
Rony, Fatimah Tobing, 321, 330, 334 nn. 12–14, 335 n. 35
Roosevelt, Franklin, 155 n. 3
Rope (1948), 245 n. 23
Rosa, Vince de, 257
Rosand, Ellen, 25 n. 23
Rosar, William H., 28 n. 55
Rose Marie (Friml/Stothart), 189
Rose Marie (1936), 204 n. 8
Rose, Phyllis, 334 n. 18
Roseaux sauvages, Les (The Wild Reeds, 1994), 101, 107
Rosen, Philip, 80 n. 16, 291 n. 11, 292 nn. 22 and 35
Rosenman, Leonard, 11, 255
Rosenstone, Robert, 22, 29 n. 71
Rosenthal, Laurence, 340
Rosolato, Guy, 110, 117 nn. 18 and 20
Ross, Annie, 143
Rossini, Gioacchino, 196, 205 n. 19, 293 n. 44
Rothapfel, Samuel L., 81 n. 31
Rothenberg, Randall, 269 n. 7
Round Midnight (1986), 155 n. 4
Rowles, Jimmy, 257, 260
"Royal Blue," 253
Rózsa, Miklós, 19, 248, 255
Ruppert, Peter, 132, 141 n. 30
Rushing, Jimmy, 144
Russell, Bertrand, 86, 87
Russell, Ken, 133
Russell, Ross, 154–55 n. 2
Russo, F. A., 365, 377ref.
Rutherford, Margaret, 110
Rye, Renny, 113

Sabaneev, Leonid, 84 n. 61, 187, 204 n. 5
Saegebrech, Marianne, 131
Said, Edward, 334 n. 19
Saint, The (1997), 268
Saint-Beuve, Charles Augustin, 287
Saint-Säens, Camille, 19, 287, 293 n. 44, 328
"Salaambo," 7, 287–88
Salerno-Sonnenberg, Nadja, 20–21, 29 n. 62
Salinger, Conrad, 21
Samson et Dalila (Saint-Säens), 328
Samson, S., 369, 377ref.
Sanborn, David, 267
Sand, George, 29 n. 70

Sperling, M. R., 376ref.
Spiegel, Ellen, 302, 314 nn. 29–30
Spontini, Gasparo, 283
"St. Louis Blues," 304
Stacey, Jackie, 27 n. 41
Stahl, John, 352
Staiger, Janet, 26 n. 41, 79 n. 1, 249,
    269 n. 9, 289 n. 4
Stam, Robert, 318, 326, 334 n. 5, 335 n. 26
Star Is Born, A (1937 & 1954), 282, 283
Star Wars (1977), 4, 25 n. 21, 33–54, 55–
    57 nn. passim
Star Wars Trilogy: A New Hope, The (re-
    cording), 55 n. 6
"Stardust," 108, 109, 110, 112
Stargazers, The , 113
Starobinski, Jean, 229, 246 n. 36
Stein, B. S., 377ref.
Steiner, Fred, 23 n. 3, 24 n. 7, 25 n. 34,
    28 n. 61, 183 n. 1, 187, 204 nn. 1–2
Steiner, Max, 5–6, 15, 19, 21, 25 nn. 33–34,
    69, 70, 82 n. 44, 90–92, 95, 116 n. 8,
    161–78, 179, 183 nn. 2–4, 184 nn. 7, 8,
    and 12, 185 nn. 13, 17, 19, and 20
Steinway & Sons (company), 298,
    314 n. 11
Stevens, George, 105
Stewart, Rex, 156 n. 18
Stilwell, Robynn, 24 n. 14, 29 n. 64
Sting, The (1973), 245 n. 21
Stoekel, Allan, 292 n. 30
Stokowski, Leopold, 212
"Storm Clouds" (Benjamin), 207–44,
    244–46 nn. passim
Stothart, Herbert, 6, 187–204, 204–
    6 nn. passim
Stothart, Jr., Herbert, 189, 204 nn. 7 and 9
Strachey, James, 291 n. 13, 292 n. 36,
    293 n. 42
Straub, Jean-Marie, 119, 120, 140 n. 20
Strauss, Jr., Johann, 107, 304
Strauss, Richard, 14, 43, 62, 206 n. 25,
    293 n. 41
Stravinsky, Igor, 19, 22, 182, 298
Streamers (1983), 149
Striner, Richard, 307, 311, 315 nn. 45 and
    56
Strohm, Reinhard, 205 n. 13
Stuart, David, 289 n. 3
Stuart, Rex, 148
"Student Drinking Song, The," 193, 194
    fig., 200, 205 n. 15
Studlar, Gaylyn, 27 n. 41, 184 n. 5

Suci, G. J., 375 n. 1, 377ref.
"Sugarbaby," 131
Sullivan's Travels (1941), 282
Sunset Boulevard (1950), 21
Suspicion (1941), 228
Sweethearts (1938), 204 n. 8
Swing Time (1936), 302, 305, 306
Syberberg, Hans-Jürgen, 119, 120, 122,
    125–26, 140 n. 17
Symphonie Fantastique (Berlioz), 91
Symphony no. 2 (Mahler), 125
Symphony no. 5 (Beethoven), 89, 177
Symphony no. 5 (Tchaikovsky), 205 n. 16
Symphony no. 6 ("Pastoral") (Beetho-
    ven), 14
Symphony no. 8 (Mahler), 133
Symphony no. 9 (Beethoven), 5, 122, 123,
    125, 126, 128, 129, 130, 140 n. 13

"Tableau of Jewels," 313
"Tabor and the Pipe, The," 194 fig.
Tambling, Jeremy, 25 n. 31, 79 n. 2
"Tango della Rose," 165 fig., 174
Tannenbaum, P. H., 375 n. 1, 377ref.
Tanner 88 (1988), 150
Tannhäuser (Wagner), 124
Tarkovskii, Sergei, 117 n. 15
Tati, Jacques, 130
Tatroe, Sonia, 8, 55 n. 5
Tchaikovsky, Peter I., 205 n. 16, 329
Téchiné, André, 101, 107
Tempest, The (Shakespeare), 222
Thaïs (Massenet), 283, 328
"That's What Noah Done," 185 n. 15
Thelonious Monk: American Composer
    (1991), 152
Thelonious Monk: Straight No Chaser
    (1988), 152
There's Something About Mary (1998),
    284
Thieves Like Us (1974), 149
Thirty-Nine Steps, The (1935), 208
Thomas,Tony, 28 n. 57, 29 n. 61, 116 n. 7,
    183 n. 3, 184 nn. 8–9
Thompson, Kristin, 23 n. 3, 26 n. 41,
    79 n. 1, 275, 289 n. 4
Thompson, W. F., 365, 368, 377ref.
Thomson, Virgil, 10, 24 n. 7, 24 n. 8,
    28 n. 58, 187
Tibbett, Lawrence, 189
Tiomkin, Dmitri, 184 n. 9, 208, 255
Titanic (1997), 20
Toch, Ernst, 19

Index / 395

"When the Saints Come Marching In," 259
White Cargo (1942), 293 n. 41
"White Negro, The," 154, 157 n. 29
"White on White," 260
Widgery, Claudia, 24 n. 6
Wilder, Billy, 104
"Will You Remember?" 192, 194 fig., 195, 197–99, 199 fig., 200, 201, 202
Williams, Alan, 62, 64, 80 n. 16, 291 n. 13
Williams, Christopher, 22, 29 n. 69
Williams, John, 25 n. 21, 34–35, 44, 47–48, 52–54, 55 n. 2, 56 nn. 20–22, 57 n. 35, 208
Williams, Mary Lou, 142, 143, 146, 147, 156 nn. 11 and 17
Williams, Raymond, 29 n. 73
Willner, Hal, 143, 144, 147
Wilson, Dooley, 173–74
Wing, Betsey, 291 n. 17
Winkler, Max, 66, 81 n. 29
Winokur, Mark, 295, 297–98, 300, 314 nn. 3, 10, and 13
Wolzogen, Hans von, 81 n. 37
Wootton, Adrian, 271 n. 39
"Words Are in My Heart, The," 307–12
Wright, Frank Lloyd, 297
Wright, Rayburn, 188, 204 n. 3

Wright, Robert, 205 n. 21
Wright, Stephen H., 27 n. 49
Wyman, Jane, 283
Wyndham-Lewis, Dominic Bevan, 209
Wynn, Keenan, 149

"Yesterday," 129
"You Must Have Been a Beautiful Baby," 166 fig.
Young, Lester, 142, 144, 147, 150, 152, 155 nn. 2 and 11, 156 n. 17
Young Mr. Lincoln (1939), 27 n. 43
Young, Victor, 255
"Your Father's Feathers," 269 n. 17

Zatorre, R. J., 369, 377ref.
Zeffirelli, Franco, 279
Ziegesar, Peter von, 156 n. 15
Ziegfeld, Florenz, 305
Zielinski, Siegfried, 22–23, 29 n. 74
Žižek, Slavoj, 83 n. 53, 207, 244 n. 5, 275, 278, 290 n. 7, 291 n. 11, 292 n. 24
Zohn, Harry, 292 n. 29, 375ref.
Zou Zou (1934), 325–26
Zuckerbaby (1985), 131
Zukor, Adolph, 282
Zwerin, Charlotte, 152, 156 n. 25

DATE DUE

HIGHSMITH #45115